GATEWAY TO TERRORISM

Mohammad Amir Rana

A NEW MILLENNIUM PUBLICATION

GATEWAY TO TERRORISM
Copyright © New Millennium 2003

ISBN 0 75411 875 4

Published by
NEW MILLENNIUM
332 Kennington Road
London SE11 4LD

Printed & bound in UK
for New Millennium Publication

GATEWAY TO TERRORISM

PUBLISHER'S NOTE

The rugged terrain of the Hindukush (Pakistan, Afghanistan and Occupied Kashmir) has been the stage of a heinous plot – a plot between Islamic jihadis, Pakistani Intelligence and limitless American interests. The consequence was the creation of a Frankenstein monster in the form of Taliban, who was out to create a cultural faultline between Islam and 'others'.

This story has been a favourite theme in many acclaimed works, especially after the black morning of 9/11. However, this book presents this complex story in a unique way.

The author, Mr Mohammad Amir Rana has engaged himself in a great deal of research, both documentary and in the field, that would have been impossible, or at least highly dangerous, for any other writer who was neither a Muslim nor a Pakistani citizen. He managed to gain access to government sources as well as jihadi leaders and foot-soldiers involved in these groups operating from inside Pakistan and was, therefore, able to analyse and provide insight into the way these groups recruit, train and find funds. Some of his revelations about the origins, the organisations, the funding and the operational practices of these groups is revelatory and disturbing and would surely be of interest to political leaders and media organs as well as a general readership of the western world, bearing in mind the events of 11 September 2001, subsequent wars and the rhetoric of western political leaders about international terrorism since that time.

What differentiates this book from others is the way different sources have been made use of, as well as the way this story is unfolded in the complex topography of that area.

Existing literature on the origin, development and growth of terrorist organisations relies on secondary sources and few government records. But the author made access to 'real' terrorists to gain insight into the 'making of a terrorist'. The book also makes a significant advancement on the onslaught of terrorist organisations and their networks.

The book is originally written in Urdu. Hence it is studded with many Urdu terms. We have tried to make a faithful translation of the book, and to deal honestly with the beautiful connotations of the Urdu language for the benefit of the English readers in the West.

We have tried to get relevant photographs and maps to include in this book. But due to time-lock, it will appear in the second edition.

FOREWORD

How many religious, sectarian and jihadi organisations are there in Pakistan? Which are the areas they are working in and what is their style of functioning? What are their organisational strength and what are the sources of their sustenance? These are the issues that the current book addresses. Possibly, this is the first book of its kind that treats all these issues. It was a difficult task, rendered more difficult after the sequence of events following 11 September 2001. During the course of research, acquiring information became more and more difficult.

At last, when I managed to get access to a madrasa or organisation, I myself had to go under an examination first. Some unpleasant incidents also took place. For five months I travelled through forty-seven towns of Pakistan and Azad Kashmir visiting 125 well-known madrasas and offices (of organisations). I managed to have 160 interviews with jihadi organisations and their members. During this process, I had an access to a considerable amount of written documents. All this was not easy, but timely help from friends made the tasks relatively easier to accomplish.

All efforts have been made to keep the format of the book informative and referential, with minimum of analysis. If some analytical reasoning has crept in the first part, it is due to the nature of the interviews and reports (references to which have been given at the end), and not because of any personal predilection. In Part Two, the organisations have been classified according to their agenda, their network and organisational strength. The budgets of organisations given in the book take account of those that came into existence between February 2002 to 15 May 2002. Several organisations that were later dissolved but whose offices and units were functioning during the period have also been studied. It is quite possible that some changes have taken effect later; particularly in the case of some jihadi organisations that have since been dissolved or disbanded. They have interchanged their offices in Azad Kashmir and Frontier Province.

Among the friends who helped me during my research, foremost was Mohammad Said Khan, a well-known journalist in Islamabad, who accompanied me to many places in Azad Kashmir and the Frontier Province. Mohammad Akhtar Khan in Karachi, Majid in Quetta, Said Asad in Muzaffarabad, Khwaja Kashan in Hajira, Faisal in Kotli, Nasir Ahmad in Multan, Mohammad Khalid in Shujaabad, Mohammad Asim in Bhalpur, Salim Khan in Mirpur Khas have helped me substantially in gathering information. In Lahore, Masood Alam and Maqbool Arshad extended their sincerest cooperation and helped me get in touch with people. Special thanks are due to those mujahideen and members of religious organisations who helped me at great personal risk. Here I must make it clear that those among them who wanted to remain incognito have been given pseudonyms.

As it is the first book of its kind, it is quite possible

that particular aspects of the issues studied here have not been adequately addressed. Such lack will be redressed in subsequent editions. I solicit readers' help in this endeavour.

Mohammad Amir Rana

Contents

PART ONE

PART TWO

List of Tables

PART ONE

PART ONE

Chapter I
JIHADI CULTURE

During the course of the last two decades, thirty thousand Pakistani youth have died in Afghanistan and Kashmir, two thousand sectarian clashes have taken place and twelve lakh youth have taken part in the activities of jihadi and religious organisations. This jihadi culture was born of the Afghan war, inspired by the Iranian Revolution and nurtured by the American 'Operation Cyclone'. Osama bin Laden's wealth and his extremist thoughts spearheaded its growth and the Taliban gave it practical shape. In consequence, Pakistan got neither Kabul nor Srinagar, but was itself saddled with terrorism.

By the time the Soviet army entered Afghanistan, religious forces in Pakistan had already succeeded in suspending the rule of the People's Party in undemocratic ways and installing a military dictator. They gave him the title 'Mard-e Momin' and shared power with him. During the Afghan War America patronised these forces and invited all godly people of the world to unite against Soviet apostasy. Most of the religious leaders of Pakistan responded enthusiastically to this call, declared the Afghan War as jihad and began to send youths to Afghanistan to participate in it.

America invested huge resources in this war. Brezensky had revealed on 3 July 1979, that Jimmy

Carter had approved a secret fund of 500 million dollars that was kept secret even from the Congress and the people. According to John Palgere, 'The objective of this fund was to found a world terrorist organisation that would encourage Islamic fundamentalism to root out Soviet influence from the Middle East. CIA gave it the name "Operation Cyclone" and earmarked an amount of four billion dollars for this fund. A considerable sum from that fund was to be spent in establishing madrasas in Pakistan.' He further states: 'The zealots of the Islamic groups from Pakistan were also sent to the espionage training camp of CIA in Virginia where they learnt the first lessons in terrorism and thus the future members of Al-Qaida were groomed. Some youths were given training in terrorism in the Brooklyn Islamic School under the aegis of the World Trade Centre. In Pakistan they were led by the officers of the British M16 and ISI.' An article, 'Pakistan's Jihadi Culture' by Jessica Stern was published in the journal of the state department of the USA, where it is said on the authority of Millet Birden, who was director of CIA in Pakistan from 1986 to 1989, that during the war in Afghanistan, Saudi Arabia and the USA had provided Pakistan 3.5 million American dollars. In addition to weaponry and narcotics, Jihad was the prime business in this part of the world.

During the war in Afghanistan ISI was reorganised on the model of 'Operation Cyclone' and the CIA and the ISI controlled the war. However, Pakistan suffered grievously because of this reorientation of ISI. The agency strengthened its grip on the state and tried to control governments duly elected by the people. To topple governments and install new ones became its pastime. At the time of the general elections in 1988, the largest alliance of religious groups 'Islami Jamhoori Ittihad' confronted the People's Party with the slogan 'You lost Dhaka, we've won Kabul'. When the People's Party came to power it could not change state policy, despite its liberal orientation. There was no change in the Afghan and Kashmir policies. The Taliban experiment was carried out during this period. ISI was not ready to compromise on the above issues under any circumstances. During the first phase of her rule, when Benazir Bhutto had visited Muzaffarabad, ISI briefed her about the Hurriyat Movement in Occupied Kashmir and recommended status quo in the Kashmir policy. Benazir Bhutto approved of the policy and the future plan. No one ever thought of changing the character and style of ISI before 11 September 2001.

ISI and the governments working under its influence gave a fillip to the jihadi culture. The 'raw materials' for jihad were collected from two sources:

- Religious madrasas
- Students of government schools and colleges

To collect the human resource from madrasas, the Afghanistan War Fund of America was used to establish an intricate network of madrasas. Religious schools of differing persuasions were used for this end. Students from these madrasas played a seminal role in the Afghan War. It has to be pointed out here that before 1980, the madrasas in Pakistan numbered 700 which increased at the rate of 3 per cent per year. This rate galloped to a whopping 136 per cent in 1986. And now the number of big madrasas (i.e. madrasas that give degrees of MA and PhD) is 7,000. New madrasas were built mainly in Frontier Province, southern Punjab, and Karachi. Later, these places turned out to be the nursery of jihad. The well-known intellectual researcher of Azad Kashmir, Syed Mahmood Azad says, 'If maulvis are given some incentives, they will agree to send their wards to jihad. They started sending to jihad students who were to become teachers and interpreters of Islam. Thousands of students were put in the service of the agencies for terrorist training. The compulsion of the government was that it could not send its army to Afghanistan. America began to pump in money and different agencies were bought over. Then another front was discovered, namely Kashmir, where these madrasa students were put to use. No maulvi had ever been/is interested in the independence of Kashmir. Jihad has become a business, fanned by the print media.'

The students' organisations of different persuasions that had considerable influence in school and college campuses also provided human fodder for jihad. They started sending their members for military training. The list of martyrs from six jihadi organisations indicate that student martyrs from schools and colleges outnumbered those from madrasas by five times. Religious organisations also used their ordinary members and unemployed youths in this task.

The American interest came to an end with the exit of the Soviet army from the area, but the war had far-reaching implications for Pakistan. One obvious manifestation of this was the jihadi culture that had taken roots there. To end it immediately would have meant that 'Afghan Jihad' was not sanctioned by sharia. That is why religious organisations and madrasas kept on propagating this culture with patronage from the government. In the meantime the situation in Occupied Kashmir got conducive for jihadi activities. In 1987, election was rigged there most shamelessly to defeat the 'Muslim Front'. This upset the Kashmiri youths who began to participate in guerrilla activities for the state's liberation. Jammu and Kashmir Liberation Front (JKLF) was already conducting militant training. Youths began to join it in large numbers now. Jamat-e Islami also started militant activities there.

By 1987, it had been decided to organise a militant movement in Occupied Kashmir. In this regard, leaders of Jamat-e Islami and JKLF kept meeting Ziaul Haq and officers of secret services. According to a prominent member of Jamat-e Islami, 'The leaders of Jamat-e Islami and JKLF had a final meeting with Ziaul Haq in 1987. It was decided that the two organisations would speed up militant activities in Occupied Kashmir, and Pakistan would give them comprehensive support.' By 1989 the militant movement intensified, and demonstrations were held in Pakistan and in many other countries in defence of the right of the Kashmiri people. The jihadi organisations in Pakistan took advantage of this and reached Occupied Kashmir to help the people. This changed the complexion of the Hurriyat Movement in the next three years, turning it into a veritable jihadi organisation. Pakistani youths were gradually inducted in this jihad and slowly the leadership of the movement for independence in Occupied Kashmir passed on to the jihadi leaders in Pakistan.

When the Hurriyat Movement was turning itself into a jihadi organisation, its first target was JKLF that was struggling for self-determination for the people of Kashmir. Jamat-e Islami's Hizbul Mujahideen targeted both the Indian army and the JKLF, a fact admitted by some leaders of Hizbul Mujahideen even now. Amanullah Khan, leader of JKLF had said in a press conference in Islamabad in 1991:

> Hizbul Mujahideen is not only liquidating fighters of JKLF, but also informs Indian army about our hideouts. In consequence about 500 important commanders of JKLF have already been killed.

In Muzaffarabad a leader of JKLF who wanted to remain incognito because of his government job said, 'Actually, ISI had given Hizbul Mujahideen the task of liquidating JKLF altogether from Occupied Kashmir. This is because JKLF demanded an autonomous Kashmir and it was the largest organisation. Several leaders of JKLF were bought over; this led to the splitting of the organisation into at least twenty splinter groups, thus eroding its strength. It should be remembered that we had begun the movement at a time when several leaders of religious groups were hobnobbing with Shaikh Abdullah.'

As the JKLF receded to the background, the influence of Pakistan-based jihadi groups increased in Occupied Kashmir and their leadership passed into the hands of religious leaders.

After the war in Afghanistan, the Kashmir front became a source of strength for the jihadi forces in Pakistan, and the jihadi organisations began to operate openly inside the country. Jihadi fund-raising, jihadi gatherings, the frequent visits of jihadi leaders in mosques, and their general acceptance by people fostered the growth of jihadi culture in Pakistan. However, by this time another dangerous manifestation of this culture had become evident in the form of sectarian clashes. There were close linkages among jihadi and sectarian groups. In the words of the leader of a sectarian group, 'The jihadi organisations are fighting against forces of unbelief (kufr) outside the country and we are fighting against apostasy inside the country.' Funds began to pour in from Saudi Arabia and other Arab countries for organisations and madrasas of Deobandi and Ahl-e Hadith persuasions, while Shia organisations enjoyed the patronage of Iran. Thus the battle of faith began to be fought in Pakistan with the help and fund from abroad. A third force that had kept aloof from jihad in Afghanistan and Occupied Kashmir since 1994, also emerged on the scene to assert its identity, giving birth to a number of new organisations such as Dawat-e Islami, Jamat Ahl-e Sunnat, Lashkar-e Islam, and Sunni Tahreek.

These were the circumstances and the background that gave rise to jihadi culture which took religious organisations from strength to strength. The wish to investigate the ostensible and hidden aspects of this culture is the prime pivot that led me to research in this area.

From Muzaffarabad to Hajera

To have a first-hand knowledge and observation of jihadi organisations and jihadi culture, I decided to go first to Azad Kashmir that had become the base camp of all jihadi organisations. After the speech of General Musharraf on 12 January 2002, it was being said that the mujahideen were gathering there. But I had no idea of the difficulties that I had to face later. In Lahore I could gather information without great difficulty, and thus had no clear notion of the challenges I was going to face ahead.

Before starting for Azad Kashmir I had got letters of reference from Masood Alam, Ex-PRO, Kashmir Centre, Lahore, and other friends to important mujahideen leaders and personalities. A friend from Rawalpindi, Mohammad Said Khan, accompanied me. He had worked with a foreign channel during American raids on Afghanistan and was out of job during those days.

After reaching Muzaffarabad, we had to meet a doctor first who was entrusted with the responsibility of arranging for our stay and organising meetings with the jihadi leaders. We were supposed to inform him from Lahore about our arrival, but could not manage to do so, and landed up in his clinic unannounced, gave him the letter and introduced ourselves. He was alarmed and told us about the difficulties in the way. But seeing our determination he became silent. Then, in an effort to discourage us, he said, 'Very few mujahideen have remained in this area. Most of them have been sent to the borders.' Meanwhile some patients arrived and the doctor asked one of his friends to take us to the nearby hotel for tea. This gentleman was a professor of education in Allama Iqbal University and had come home to spend the vacation. He introduced us proudly to a number of shopkeepers in the market in the following way, 'They are journalists from Lahore – my friends.' We met about fifteen persons and each of them welcomed restrictions on the jihadi organisations. We felt that people of this area were happier than the Pakistanis at the steps taken by the government. They said, 'Mujahideen used to fight among themselves in the market, did all kinds of mischief and extorted money from people forcefully.' After meeting these people we reached a hotel in Chahla where we met Naseem Vani, deputy chairman of Zarb-e Islami – a meeting that proved to be profitable. We also met some other members of small mujahideen groups and worked out a schedule of detailed meetings with them. Our host said that if we had arrived a couple of days earlier (we had reached Muzaffarabad on 17 January 2002) we would have seen many mujahideen wielding Kalashnikovs roaming the streets. Now they had gone underground. We spent about two hours in these meetings. When we returned to the clinic, it was closed. This was the first shock.

We asked our host about the address of another contact and the search for him began. The night was advancing, and so was the chill in the air. We decided to make arrangements for our stay first, and then look for other things. We got rooms easily in the state guest house at Muzaffarabad. We had the telephone numbers of several important mujahideen leaders. We phoned Abdul Aziz, leader of Lashkar-e Tayyaba, and sought an interview with him. We were asked to phone again in the morning. Farooq Quraishi of Al-Barq agreed to meet us at noon. The secretary of Hizbul Mujahideen commander, Syed Salahuddin, fixed our meeting with him at 1 p.m. The office of Major Tariq of Tahreek-e Jihad asked us to contact them early next morning. We were happy to contact so many important people in such a short time. After fixing the schedule we contacted Advocate Noorullah Quraishi who was in his chamber. Noorullah Quraishi, originally from Srinagar, had been in Pakistan for the last seven years. He looked disappointed with the jihadi organisations, their sectarian character, and their internecine clashes. We had a long chat with him during which we gathered a lot of information and useful contacts from him.

As we got up next morning, we phoned Major Tariq's office and was told that he had gone out of town last night. Then we called at the office of Lashkar-e Tayyaba. We were told the same thing about Abdul Aziz Alvi. But we had a greater surprise waiting for us when we contacted the office of Syed Salahuddin. We were told that he had just left for 'Bagh'. After five minutes we called up the office of Hizbul Mujahideen giving another name and were told that he was in a meeting and would be free after half an hour. When we called them after half an hour in our own names, we were given the earlier reply. The operator-secretary was finally fed up with our persistence and said, 'Why are you after my life? Pir Sahib (Syed Salahuddin is known by this name) is not allowed to meet anyone.'

We found the circumstances quite despairing. Till yesterday things appeared quite bright. Finally, we met Said Asad Sahib in the department of social welfare. His book, Shaoor-e Farda (Future Intimations) was banned by the government. Shaoor-e Farda was the collection of letters written in jail by the JKLF leader Maqbool Bhat. The government of Azad Kashmir had banned it as it was alleged to oppose the stand of the government. Said Asad had never been close to any jihadi organisations, but he helped us meet his friends who gave us important information. Among these friends was Syed Mahmood Azad who was a known Kashmiri intellectual and researcher who researched the workings of jihadi organisations. But because of the circumstances prevailing at the time, he was not ready to open up. After talking for a few hours about various things, when he came to the main topic he still remained circumspect and did not talk specifically about any particular organisation. However, his occasional remarks were very helpful in understanding the jihadi culture in Kashmir. From the background of the Afghan War he took us to the jihadi front in Occupied Kashmir references to which will come in subsequent chapters. During the course of our conversation an important leader of a jihadi organisation who was a friend of Azad Sahib arrived there. He told Azad Sahib that his 'double cabin' had been stolen and that was why he had come to Muzaffarabad. He also participated in our conversation, but when he left, Azad Sahib remarked, 'The bit about stealing must be humbug. He must have sold it off as the sources of funding have dried up.'

That evening there was a party at Sangam Hotel organised by Jamat-e Islami to honour the leaders from the north and their supporters. There we heard a wide spectrum of views expressed by leaders. Some of the views were quite unusual and could not have been expressed in Pakistan at any stage. Here we met Pakistan Human Rights Commission's representative from Muzaffarabad, Farooq Niazi. He promised to provide us with records of human rights violation on the part of jihadi organisations. After a gruelling day when we reached the guest house we found that we had been expelled from there.

The man in charge of the guest house told us that our rooms had been rented out to others and we must leave, even though the chowkidar had told us earlier that many rooms were vacant. This was a worrying situation. There was an army rest house nearby. We went there and sought rooms, but got the same reply. The rest house of the forest department also refused to take us in. There are only two standard hotels in Muzaffarabad – Sangam and Neelam View. The rent there could have upset our budget, but we took the risk and approached them for booking, but were told that there was no room. These hotels and the rest houses are situated on two opposite sides of the city. We combed the city from end to end seeking a shelter for the night. It was 2 a.m., chilly winds were blowing and Said and I were wandering on the streets lugging our bags. Finally, we got a room in a dingy hotel, but the rent demanded was higher than that in the guest house. Being helpless, we took the room but it was not possible to spend even a few hours there. A stifling stink emanated from the room, even as buffets of smoke from charas cigarettes coming through the window assailed our nostrils. We spent four hours sitting, and came out when the call for the morning prayer was coming out from mosques. Said Khan remarked that we must leave Muzaffarabad immediately, or we might get into a terrible mess. But I said that at least we should try to meet Farooq Niazi. However, the phone number we were given turned out to be wrong and when we reached his chamber at the appointed time, we found it locked.

After this we proceeded towards Rawlakot and managed some wink of sleep on the way. The moment we reached the station two youths thrust themselves on us and badgered us to know our identity. We got suspicious of them but accompanied them to the nearby hotel. There they probed us further and wanted to know why we had come to Azad Kashmir. Which agency had sent us – RAW or ISI? After several hours of interrogation they were reassured about us, said that the situation in Azad Kashmir was not conducive to the kind of research for which we had come, and advised us to leave. We said that at least we should be allowed to spend the night at Hajera, to which 'permission' was granted promptly.

In Hajera, our host was Khwaja Kashan, the president of National Students Federation (student wing of JKLF). We came to know that the mujahideen were brought there in trucks and they were seen to proceed towards the border. Here we also met Kamaluddin Azad, the patron of Harkat-al Jihad al

Islami. We got the opportunity to see his madrasa about which the Indian TV channel 'ZEE News' had said a couple of weeks ago that it was a large terrorist centre. Maulana Kamaluddin Azad was very happy at this, although the total number of students in his madrasa was fourteen, aged between ten and twelve, their instruction limited to reading and memorising the Holy Koran. He was supporting Harkat-al Jihad at the instance of Jamat-e Islami. Several interesting incidents took place in Hajera. When we went out with Khwaja Kashan someone was following us. Khwaja Kashan said that he was an IB inspector. He turned his head and said loudly, 'They are my guests.' But the follower continued to follow us though he slackened his pace. We entered a tea stall. A young man was sitting at a table at one corner. We were told that he was also the agent of some secret organisation. Later, when I travelled through big towns of Azad Kashmir, particularly border towns, I found that these secret agents had become part of everyday life there. People knew who was working for which agency. The agents themselves did not feel constrained to conceal their identity.

The visit to Hajera was fruitful. After spending the night there we started for Muzaffarabad. We decided to change our strategy this time. Rather than trying to meet central leaders we would meet common mujahideen and gather information from other sources, and rather than introducing ourselves as journalists we should appear as sympathisers of these organisations that would make information gathering easier. We returned from Muzaffarabad to Islamabad, and after one week went back to Azad Kashmir. This time we faced no difficulties.

Mujahideen Clout in Azad Kashmir

January 2002 was a peaceful month in Azad Kashmir, particularly for the people of Muzaffarabad, Bagh, and Awla Kot who breathed a sigh of relief. The mujahideen, who made an open display of firearms in markets and highways and created an atmosphere of terror by firing in the air, suddenly disappeared. Jabbar, a shopkeeper in the central market of Muzaffarabad said, 'Muzaffarabad has become calm and quiet. This calm is like that of the jungle where a hunter fires a gunshot that stirs the atmosphere for a while and then everything becomes quiet.' At least six jihadi organisations used to extort monthly contribution from Jabbar forcefully. 'So, you are happy with General Musharraf's decision?' Jabbar replied, 'We shall be really happy when the government is able to confine the jihadi organisations to their camps only. Now we live in fear lest they reappear.'

In Hajera, Faiz Ahmad said that a commander of Harkat-al Jihad, Sajjad, would throw a hook on the telephone wire passing by his office and make national and international calls. The nearby shops began to receive inflated telephone bills. When a departmental inquiry was conducted, Sajjad was caught red-handed, but the administration could not do anything. He became even bolder and began to harass the shopkeepers who had complained. He would wave his Kalashnikov before their shops and glare at them.

Once or twice he came to fisticuffs with them after which the Harkat-al Jihad sent him to some other town.

'Can mujahideen do this?' Khwaja Abdul Hameed Bandey of Rawlakot said, 'They stand by the girls' school when the classes get over and try to impress the girls with their manoeuvres and weapons. Those mujahideen who come from Punjab are more prone to such unruly behaviour.' Bandey who was also a homoeopath said further, 'The Pathan mujahideen are comparatively decent. They try to maintain their influence but do not indulge in cheap tactics. The Punjab youths imagine themselves as "heroes". When they do not get this opportunity in their own place they come here and do mischiefs.'

I felt that because of the irresponsible behaviour of some mujahideen, the local people do not have a good opinion about Punjab (here Punjab means Punjab and Sind). Later I came to know stories about other mujahideen who were not from Punjab. For example, majority of the youth in Al-Umr Mujahideen come from Occupied Kashmir and Azad Kashmir. Keel sector is its nerve centre. There, Noor Mohammad, the owner of a Billiard club, said: 'Often the mujahideen appeared in the club and played with grenade bombs in such a way as though they were balls. This creates terror in people. Sometimes they started playing billiard with grenades that could have detonated. Although no untoward incident happened here we lived in terror. Now there is peace for sometime.' He further said: 'We could only request them not to do such things. In reply they would threaten me saying that they would close this gambling den.' A Pakistani captain said on condition of anonymity, 'The mujahideen were getting out of control. They were spreading terror in many areas in the name of jihad. Even they were challenging the army.' The captain recounted an incident: 'Some mujahideen of a particular organisation had hired a taxi from Muzaffarabad to Keel sector for eight hundred rupees. When they reached their camp in Keel they tried to fob off the driver with five hundred rupees. When the driver demanded the full amount they started beating him right on the road. Meanwhile an army truck arrived there. A havildar got down and asked what was happening. The driver was crying. The mujahideen contemptuously asked the havildar to leave. The havildar got angry. There were six more soldiers on the truck who got down. The mujahideen were five in number. As they aimed their guns, the soldiers also sprang to action. By that time we had got to know about it. We picked up the mujahideen and brought them to the "army area". We offered them good hospitality till they paid the driver the full fare and apologised to the soldiers.'

The complaint that the jihadi organisations extorted money forcefully from people was common in several areas of Azad Kashmir. I came to know in Kotli that the shopkeepers had once resorted to strike on this issue. A news agency reporter, Faisal, told me there, 'The real problem was that the government of Azad Kashmir never came down heavily on the mujahideen for their unlawful activities. Though these mischiefs are normally done by new recruits, their activities have seriously harmed the cause of jihad and the independence movement. The jihadi organisations had even started to interfere with the functioning of the administration.' There was an interesting incident in Quetta last year when an officer of the ministry of health had visited the place in connection with the polio vaccine campaign. The local commander of Lashkar-e Tayyaba, Maulvi Khadim Hussain, followed him along with a group of mujahideen, and threatened him to leave the place immediately. Khadim Husain's stand was that the children were being given drops for family planning in the guise of polio vaccine, so that the productivity of these children comes down drastically. He later announced in a gathering, 'Islam does not allow family planning. So, don't vaccinate the children, and make a total boycott of iodised salt.'

Nasir Ahmad, a schoolteacher in Muzaffarabad said, 'The mujahideen have been coming to our schools for jihadi proselytisation. They had no permission from the government. When we complained to the education department nothing happened.' He reported that the mujahideen of Lashkar-e Tayyaba harassed and manhandled the headmaster of his school for preventing them to preach their ideology to the students without permission. The matter did not end there. The following Friday the local mosque was going to slap the decree of 'kufr' (apostasy) on him. He saved his skin by apologising to them ignominiously.

One hears of many such incidents in Azad Kashmir. However, the unseemly activities of some mujahideen are not limited to Azad Kashmir, but spread to many areas in Pakistan as well. For example, in Shujaabad area of Multan a tea-stall owner, Mohammad Naseer, told me that his son was beaten mercilessly by members of Lashkar-e Tayyaba merely because his ball had struck the motorcycle of two mujahideen who were speeding past. When he went to the police station to report the incident the clerk chided him instead and said, 'Do you know that a paan-wallah with a shop near Jhind railway station was harassed by the mujahideen for playing his tape recorder loudly?'

How do such youths come to be there in jihadi organisations? And why don't the jihadi organisations take action against them? When I asked these questions to the mujahideen they replied, 'These are mere propaganda against us. If such cases did happen we would not have been allowed to stay in Azad Kashmir. However, if such incidents come to our notice we take stringent action.' Their replies and their attitudes indicated that many mujahideen are victims of the delusion of 'heroism'. Abdul Hameed Bandey of Rawlakot had told me that Indian films engender the aspiration of heroism in them and the jihadi organisation provides an opportunity to actualise it. I had already met 'Commander Shah Rukh Khan'.

What I Saw in Jihad?

Following are two incidents published in the April 2000 issue of the monthly, *Sada-e Mujahid* (Voice of Mujahid), mouthpiece of Harkatul Mujahideen, published from Rawalpindi:

ILLUMINATED HANDS AND LEGS

Down the ages, fighters in the arena of jihad have witnessed with their own eyes divine help and kindness descending on them. This is true even today. On 9 December 1999 an incident has been broadcast on the radio that was narrated by Atishbhai from K2 Communication Point. The incident goes like this: Three friends were travelling through the deep forest of Kashmir in the darkness of the night. As they were walking, suddenly the feet of the person walking at the front began to shine and emit light. The friend behind him touched that light and his hand began to shine. When the third one wanted to catch the light his hands also began to shine. Thus the light grew stronger. They picked up grass from the earth which also began to shine. It went on for a while and then the light faded out. The three friends were the *mujahid* brothers Saroor Khalil of Wazirabad, Gujranwala, Shahin Bhai of Hyderabad, and Bhai Abdullah. This writer has himself heard it on radio. Believe me, whoever trusts in Allah, the Almighty offers him special help.

THE STOVE BURNT FOR THIRTEEN DAYS WITHOUT OIL

We were staying in our hideout during the chilly weather. Every night we had to burn the stove for three hours. Our supply of oil had run out and we were worried. I performed an extra prayer and put on the stove and it got ignited. It burnt for three hours and we did our essential chores. My companions were amazed at this divine help. One day they challenged me saying I poured the oil in the stove during daytime and ignited it at night. I entreated them to believe me, but as human beings are weak by nature they did not. The stove has been burning for seventeen (?) days, and I was reminded of the story associated with the

Prophet's companion whose *chakki* (grinding stone) would work without grains and wheat came out of it. Anyway, one of my companions got up and opened the stove. It was totally dry. All of them were stunned and paid obeisance to Allah. This incident was related to me by *mujahid* brother Maqbool who belongs to the Bagh district of Kashmir and battled against the Indian army for three years in Occupied Kashmir.

Many incidents like the above two are published in the journals of jihadi organisations and fuel the emotion and zeal of the youth. Some mujahideen also told me stories like the following: A *mujahid* was seriously wounded in an attack by the Indian army when a fairy appeared and picked him up in her wings. When he got back to senses he found himself in a forest in perfect health, as though nothing happened to him. One *mujahid* told me that one day the Indian army patrol saw them during launching but passed them by as though they had not seen them. Then a tiger appeared and led them to the mujahideen camp. Finally, in Kotli one *mujahid* of Lashkar-e Islam, Hafiz Yaqoob, told me that such incidents are circulated intentionally to ignite the passion and emotion of the youth.

How They Get New Recruits?

Different jihadi organisations adopt different policies to get new recruits. Among them are: jihadi education in mosques, working among the students of madrasas, pamphlets, brochures, books and journals, etc. They open their branches in far-flung areas and establish contact with people, organise jihadi gatherings and programmes. The students' wing of jihadi organisations, also play an active role, indoctrinating students in colleges and schools. Al-Badr Mujahideen is special in this regard in the sense that it has introduced new ways like jihadi demonstrations, jihadi exhibition, jihadi *mushaira*, jihadi march, and so on. Jaish-e Muhammad has introduced a new element – they go to gatherings and classrooms and preach their ideology and at the same time recruit members for indoctrination. The daily *Dawn* of 17 February 2001 published a special report on this. According to the report, the headmaster of a high school in Rawalpindi said that the Jaish-e Muhammad sent him advance information that they were coming. Apart from that they did not seek permission from any authority, and landed up at the time of the morning assembly and began recruiting students for a month's military training in Mansehra. Some boys not only gave in their names for training but were so impressed after listening to their jihadi activities that they contributed money as well. According to the headmaster, the most important cricket player of the school also joined Jaish-e Muhammad. He first went for three months' training, then came to school for a couple of days, after which he permanently shifted to the training camp of Jaish-e Muhammad.

After Jaish-e Muhammad, Harkatul Mujahideen and Lashkar-e Tayyaba also adopted these means which were profitable both for recruitment as well as for procuring jihad funds.

Following are the impressions of a few mujahideen of Jaish-e Muhammad indicating why they joined this organisation. These impressions were published in the fortnightly, *Jaish-e Muhammad*, Karachi, October 2001.

1. My name is Mohammad Sadeeq. I am from Takhla, Frontier Province. I have studied up to matriculation in school and can read the Holy Koran. I was free after appearing in the matriculation examination when one of my friends gave me an audio cassette recording of Maulana Masood Azhar, leader of Jaish-e Muhammad. I went home and listened to the cassette that was about the demolition of the Babri Masjid. I was deeply impressed by it and decided to spend the rest of my life in the way of jihad. Then I went to Madrasa Khalid Zubair where I took my initial training. Recently I took training in Madrasa Ahmad Shaheed, and in a few days I shall proceed to Kashmir.

2. My name is Shah Faisal. I am from the district of Sangla in Sewat Frontier. I have studied up to matriculation in school and can read the Holy Koran. Then I left for Karachi where we have a cloth store. I used to read newspapers and journals which often carried, reports about the oppression in Kashmir. I thought of fighting against that oppression by joining the jihad. Then I took training from Madrasa Ahmad Shaheed, and within a few days I shall leave for Kashmir.

3. My name is Zakaullah. I am from Gujranwala. I studied up to class IX and then began to work as a labourer. I had great fascination for jihad from my boyhood. I read in books that Allah rewards jihadi martyrs with paradise. I was a sinner and this seemed a means of salvation for me. With this thought I left

51

for Madrasa Syed Ahmad Shaheed in Balakot.

4. I am Abdurrahman from the district of Faisalabad. I am illiterate, and cannot read or write anything. I used to work in Sabzimandi (vegetable market), Faisalabad, as a porter. Once during the month of Ramzan a hotel was open in Sabzimandi and people were eating there openly, defying the religious injunction. Suddenly some mujahideen belonging to Harkatul Ansar arrived there. They closed down the hotel for the day and gave an impassioned speech on jihad. This speech left a deep imprint in my mind and I decided to join the jihad. Then I went to Madrasa Khalid bin Walid for the training. So far I have worked in different fronts; now I am going to Kashmir.

5. I am Naim Siddiqui from Mansehra district in the Frontier. I am illiterate. When I was a small boy the responsibility of the family fell on my shoulders. I left my house in search of livelihood. In Islamabad I used to bake roti for students in Masjid Furqan. The imam of the mosque often gave discourses on jihad. After listening to him a number of times I was greatly moved. After that when I listened to the cassette of Maulana Masood Azhar about Babri Masjid I decided to join the jihad. I took leave from Masjid Furqan and began working as a car driver. Once Hazrat Maulana Masood Azhar had come to Rawalpindi when I got the chance to hear him directly and the desire to join the jihad rose again. I often went to the mosque where many mujahideen came to meet our respected Maulana Sadeeq Sahib. Meanwhile the economic condition of my family

improved considerably, and I left for Madrasa Syed
Ahmad Shaheed for training. Now I am going to
Kashmir.

6. I am Mohammad Yar Afghani, from Gardez,
Afghanistan. I used to work as a labourer in
Jalalabad. From there I came to Peshawar. Then I
came to Muzaffarabad with a friend. When I was a
small boy I heard stories of jihad from members of
my family and had decided that when I grew up I
was going to join it. One day when I went to see my
friend Haq Nawaz Bhai, he told me that this world
is mortal, every human being is liable to die some
day. Then why not we join jihad and earn merit for
the afterlife? Then I went to Madrasa Syed Ahmad
Shaheed for training. I completed training from
there, and now I am going to Kashmir. I am leaving
behind a cassette. If I become a martyr, give this
cassette to my friend Haq Nawaz so that he listens
to it and gets associated with jihadi activities.

7. My name is Mawia. I am from Bagh district in Azad
Kashmir. I am seventeen. I studied up to class IV in
school, then I went to Madrasa Ta'limul Quran
Hanfia to memorise the Holy Koran, where I did
fifteen chapters. Then I went to Madrasa Mahmood
Ghaznawi for training. My reason for joining jihad
is the speech by Maulana Masood Azhar Sahib that
he had delivered in our city, Bagh. Now I am going
to Kashmir.

Chapter II
JIHADI ACTIVITIES

Occupied Kashmir

The strong feeling of hatred against the Indian government and the oppressive Indian army in Occupied Kashmir made the situation conducive for the operation of jihadi organisations. There are some militant organisations consisting of only Kashmiri youth, but they also seek help from Pakistani jihadi organisations to intensify their struggle. Moreover, the local mujahideen in Kashmir suffer from lack of weaponry and other resources. According to Nasim Wani, vice chairman of Zarb-e Islami, 'Normally Pakistani jihadi organisations work under the supervision of local mujahideen. But these organisations just allow them to work as guides and keep leadership in their own hands. One problem is that most of the Kashmiri jihadi organisations have their base camp in Azad Kashmir and most of the mujahideen have to go there for training. There, they get in touch with other organisations and sometimes get inducted into sectarian groups.'

These contacts and resources are the primary reason for the presence of non-Kashmiri mujahideen in Kashmir. Apart from Pakistan, mujahideen from Afghanistan, Saudi Arabia, Middle East, and Europe find their way to Kashmir where they come with their own resources. Normally, foreign mujahideen are found in greater numbers in organisations of Deobandi and Ahl-e Hadith persuasions. The list of martyrs belonging to different jihadi organisations help us determine the ratio of foreign mujahideen in Occupied Kashmir. The following list (Table I) is made on the basis of the record of the past ten years.

Table I: *Martyrs Belonging to Different Jihadi Organisations*

Organisation	Arab martyrs	Afghan martyrs	Martyrs from Europe and other countries
Harkatul Mujahideen	18	32	4
Lashkar-e Tayyaba	9	150	13
Hizbul Mujahideen	3	17	–
Jaish-e Muhammad	7	29	5
Al-Badr	12	80	7
Harkat-al Jihad	14	120	10

In June 1999, Lashkar-e Tayyaba sent a group of 200 mujahideen in Occupied Kashmir. This was the first time that such a large group of mujahideen was sent to Kashmir. Commander Abu Shuaib Noorastani was the leader of this group. Before this, the maximum number of mujahideen were sent in Kashmir by Harkat-al Jihad.

Azad Kashmir

All jihadi organisations claim that they are fighting for the independence of Kashmir, and the right of self-determination of the people there. Most of these organisations also have their base camp in Azad Kashmir. However, the tendency among the people of

55

Azad Kashmir to join jihadi organisation is less strong, although the same cannot be said about the people of Punjab and the border areas. One reason for this is said to be the fact that the number of madrasas in Azad Kashmir is very small. There are only eight madrasas up to the *alia* (graduate) stage of which five are of Deobandi, one of Ahl-e Hadith, two of Barelvi and one of Shia persuasions. However, the number of mosques is about five thousand and most of them are of Barelvi persuasion. The jihadi organisations adhering to this school of thought are the largest in number, but these are not very well-knit groups. Moreover, Kashmiri youth do not show any great inclination for joining sectarian groups. Rather, they show preference for pure Kashmiri organisations. One *mujahid* of Bagh (Azad Kashmir), Ikramullah, said that this is because they know the facts about sectarian groups and are not happy about their overall character.

The government of Azad Kashmir patronises all jihadi organisations without making distinctions. Its prime minister and other ministers have been participating in the programmes of jihadi organisations, and go out of the way to show support to these organisations. It is interesting that the youth from several political families of Azad Kashmir can be found among the members of these organisations. Mumtaz Ahmad, the leader of the People's Party and prime minister of Azad Kashmir, had allowed his home to be used as office by Jaish-e Muhammad.

Punjab Province

Punjab Province is the nerve centre of the jihadi organisations. They derive 50 per cent of their human resource from here. According to a survey of ten such big organisations, the martyrs belonging to these organisations run into more than 10,000, out of which 4,000 died in the Afghan War and the rest died in Occupied Kashmir. The number of madrasas here runs into 5,500, of which 3,000 are of Deobandi, 1,500 of Barelvi, 800 of Ahl-e Hadith, and 120 of Shia persuasions. In addition, Jamat-e Islami runs about 100 madrasas. Students in these madrasas come not only from Punjab, but also from Azad Kashmir and other provinces as also from foreign countries. The contribution of the madrasas of Punjab towards the human resources of jihadi organisations is to the tune of 40 per cent of its total population.

The desire to join jihadi organisations is more intense among the youth of Multan, Bahawalpur, and Dera Ghazi Khan districts. One intriguing fact is that the number of youth from schools and colleges in jihadi organisations is larger than those from madrasas. It also came to light here that the youth are victims of the delusion of 'jihadi heroism'. For example, Akbar Khan, a *mujahid* of Jaish-e Muhammad in Sargodha, said, 'Jihad provides honour, money, and adventure.' Most of the mujahideen that we met in Punjab were either unemployed youth or those who had left studies midway. The following is an interview with Mohammad Iqbal of Multan, aged twenty. He has been associated with Harkatul Mujahideen for the last four years, has received militant training, and has been waiting for 'launching':

Q: Since when have you joined the jihad?
A: Four years.
Q: How did you come to join?
A: Initially, I was associated with Tablighi Jamat. One day some members of Harkatul Mujahideen came to our mosque. I got introduced to them and got to know about the importance of jihad from them. I started to go to their offices and developed an affinity with them. I came to Mansehra Maskar in 1999 for the first time and stayed here for six months. Seeing the passion and zest of the mujahideen here, I felt enthused and decided to dedicate my whole life to jihad.
Q: What did you do before joining Harkatul Mujahideen?
A: After the matriculation examination I remained unemployed for quite some time. Then I worked in a tailoring shop, but there was no excitement there.
Q: Why are the people of Multan joining jihadi organisations in such large numbers?
A: Many mujahideen belong to Multan. But still hard work is needed to make the environment conducive for jihad. When I go home, people at my home and *mahalla* tell me, 'You have had enough of jihad. Now do some other job.' It is difficult to make them understand that jihad is not for a month or a year but a lifelong pursuit. I tell them that jihad is as obligatory as the five times prayer in a day, but no one listens to me.

Q: Have you come here with the consent of your family?

A: Not when I came here first. But when I returned from Maskar my people were amazed to see the change in me. When I was leaving home this time, circumstances had deteriorated. Restrictions were being imposed. But Abba and Amma bade me farewell with prayers.

Q: Harkatul Mujahideen owes allegiance to Deobandi school of thought. Are you also given religious instructions?

A: Undoubtedly. We are told whatever is right. There is no place for sectarianism in jihad. Though some organisations are sectarian, for example, Lashkar-e Tayyaba. When new *mujahids* of Lashkar-e Tayyaba come to Maskar they are brainwashed. When during *namaz* the new *mujahids* do not raise their hands, they are nudged to do it, to conform to their ways.

Mohammad Iqbal had been totally indoctrinated to jihad. He did not want to do anything else in life. The question is what he will do if he does not get an opportunity of 'launching', and if total restrictions are imposed on jihadi activities.

Frontier Province

The Frontier Province became the base camp for jihadi activities during the Soviet-Afghan War. An extraordinarily large number of madrasas were opened here and religious groups began to try all kinds of means to get students for those madrasas. The interest shown in the Afghan War by the Pakhtuns in Frontier

Province was also because of their cultural and
linguistic affinity. That is why religious groups faced
no difficulty in taking roots there. During the Afghan
War the number of madrasas here increased by 30 per
cent. Till 1979, there were 350 madrasas here, which
increased to 1,281 in 1999. About twelve lakh youth
from Frontier Province participated in the Afghan War
and 15,000 of them died on the front. As opposed to
this, the number of martyrs from Frontier Province
who died in Occupied Kashmir is 3,000. The reason
for this is said to be: 'Afghanistan was the closest jihad
front and its claim on the jihadis was foremost.'

Of the 15,000 youth who died in Afghanistan, 60 per
cent came from madrasas. The rest 40 per cent was
constituted by students from schools and colleges, and
individuals from the tribal areas. In Occupied Kashmir,
the number of madrasa students who died is 700. This
difference in proportion (between Afghanistan and
Occupied Kashmir) is due to the fact that in Occupied
Kashmir, the main activity of madrasa students is in
the nature of *tabligh* (preaching). The leadership of
jihadi organisations were in the hands of individuals
graduating from madrasas, but as far as the militant
activities were concerned, mujahideen coming from
outside madrasas were preferred. An important leader
of Harkatul Mujahideen in Dera Ghazi Khan made the
following dangerous declaration: 'Mujahideen coming
from madrasas are more valuable to us, because their
instructions and preachings have a far-reaching impact
on the nature of society. That is why we want to save
them.'

Aqeel Yusufzai, a journalist from Peshawar, told me

that the people of Frontier Province are religious by temperament. They participate in jihadi activities in large numbers because, in addition to being religious, they are also very emotional, and their emotions can be inflamed easily. I took interviews with three mujahideen, although I met a total of eighteen. Among the eighteen, two were from the madrasa of Sewat, and the rest were either post-matriculation students who had given up studies or were unemployed.

The following interview is of Mohammad Saleh of Sawabi who had joined Harkatul Mujahideen in April 2002. It was the time when jihadi organisations were finding it difficult to have new recruits. I met Mohammad Saleh in the office at Kotli where he had come a week earlier, and was waiting for militant training. His age should be eighteen:

Q: What is your education?
A: I have studied up to class VII.

Q: Were you studying in a madrasa?
A: No, in a school.

Q: What is your father?
A: He has a grocery shop.

Q: How did you come in touch with Harkatul Mujahideen?
A: They came to our mosque and gave discourses. They told us what was happening to Muslims in Kashmir and our sisters there. They said that to save their honour is our responsibility now. I read similar things in newspapers and wished to join jihad.

Q: Were you associated with any religious groups

earlier?

A: No. I only spent three days with Tablighi Jamat.

Q: Tablighi Jamat does not support any violent jihad, do you know?

A: I know. The mujahideen told me that paradise is in the shadow of swords, whereas Tablighi Jamat confines itself to mosques.

Q: Didn't your family stop you (from joining)?

A: They did. I tried to persuade them for four months but they didn't agree. Finally, when I resorted to hunger strike, they relented.

Q: Who accompanied you from Sawabi to Kotli?

A: Zubair Bhai (secretary of Harkatul Mujahideen in Kotli).

Q: The jihadi camp is closed now. How will you receive training?

A: Nothing to worry. The camp at Manesahar will open. If not, I'll receive training here.

Q: Do you watch films?

A: (laughing) I used to.

Q: Did you have a favourite hero?

A: (after great hesitation) Badr Munir and Amitabh Bachchan.

Q: But Amitabh Bachchan is an Indian.

A: I don't like him now.

Q: What do you intend to do after jihad?

A: I just want to do this till I become a martyr.

From the interview it is evident that Mohammad Saleh is semi-educated, emotional, and romantic in temperament. His circumstances and temperament are not very different from those of the new recruits from other provinces. Mansoor who was a member of Jaish-e Muhammad for one year had the same feelings. He said, 'The honour for Muslims now lies in jihad.' When he was asked whether he was not giving more attention to the 'lesser jihad' ('jihad-e asghar', i.e. military struggle) than to the 'greater jihad' ('jihad-e akbar' i.e. self-purification), his reply was: 'In Pakistan, many organisations are fighting against the government. This is the greater jihad. Our purpose is also the same.' In Frontier Province, large organisations like Harkatul Jihad al-Islami, Hizbul Mujahideen, Lashkar-e Tayyaba, and Al-Badr are conceived and youth in large number join them. However, in some tribal areas, organisations such as Tahreek-e Taliban, and in Malakand Division Sufi Mohammad's Tahreek-e Nifaz Shariat Mohammadi are very active. The last-named not only helped the Taliban in Afghanistan militarily, but also actively cooperated with the organisations named above. In the northern areas of Kohat and Dera Ismail, some Shia organisations are also active. Among them Hizbul Mumineen is important, the rest are small groups without any clout.

The general atmosphere of Frontier Province has always been conducive to jihadi organisations. However, after the American raids on Afghanistan that began in October 2001, and whatever happened to those who had gone to help the Taliban (many of them died or were imprisoned), the atmosphere in Frontier Province and specifically in Malakand Division is now less conducive to them.

Sindh Province

Sindh is known as the land of peace, its earth specially conducive to mysticism. It is said that every Sindhi is steeped in mysticism. But in the last one decade there is a trend visible among the Sindhi youth of joining militant organisations. According to the claims made by different jihadi organisations, the number of martyrs from Sindh has already touched 500. Out of them seventy belonged to Jaish-e Muhammad, 115 to Harkatul Mujahideen, 123 to Lashkar-e Tayyaba, 103 to Hizbul Mujahideen, thirty-eight to Lashkar-e Islam. The rest belonged to smaller groups. The trend of joining jihad among the Sindhi youth has increased in the last five years. In comparison, the linguistic and nationalist organisations have lost some influence in those years.

Javed Mohammad Land is the commander of Jaish-e Muhammad in Khairpur. He joined jihad at the age of seventeen. Now he was twenty-two. He had fought in different fronts in Afghanistan and spent four months in a year in the front. His deputy, Shoaib Jan, was also associated with jihad for five years. Before joining Jaish-e Muhammad, Javed Land was associated with Harkatul Ansar and Harkatul Mujahideen. When Jaish-e Muhammad came into being he joined it. He asserted that in Khairpur alone there were 100 trained militants; of them twenty had received training in the past one year (2000–01). He said that some agencies helped them in crossing the Line of Control. According to him jihadi trend is increasing in the Sindhi youth day by day.

Lashkar-e Tayyaba is the most successful jihadi organisation in Sindh. Masmool Abu Osama of Shahdadpur said that he had received militant training in Afghanistan in 1993. According to Abu Osama, Sindhi youth were enthusiastically participating in jihadi activities. 'We help the families of martyrs. We are helping 200 such families where a male member had died in Occupied Kashmir. From this you can deduce how zestfully they are participating in militant activities.'

Several jihadi organisations have also established their camps inside Sindh. There is the camp of Lashkar-e Tayyaba in Maldasi Shahdadpur where preliminary militant training is imparted. Camps attached to Madrasa Jaish-e Muhammad in Shikarpur and Harkatul Mujahideen's Masjid Manzilgah indicates the growing hold of these organisations in Sindh. But Karachi came on the top as far as providing human resource was concerned. Here, the number of madrasas exceeds 2,000 which supply human resource to all jihadi organisations.

After Karachi, come Sukkur, Khairpur, Jekobabad, Larkana, and Hyderabad. In these five districts the number of madrasas is 400 that belong mainly to Deobandi and Ahl-e Hadith persuasions. However, the point to be noted here is that the majority of youth joining jihadi organisations from this area is not from madrasas.

On 11 March 2001, a survey report about jihadi activities inside Sindh was published in *The News*. According to this report, the ratio of Sindhi youth joining jihad, in comparison with other provinces, is

25 per cent. Twenty per cent of them do not stay at their homes. This report also includes the impressions of Sadullah Jatoi, father of Munir Ahmad, a *mujahid* from Shikarpur. Munir Ahmad had gone to Afghanistan in July 1997 and had not come home since. Sadullah is eighty-two, and a heart patient. He has been told that his son had died in Mazar Sharif but he did not believe this and felt that his son would certainly return some day. Sadullah Jatoi said that those who sent his son to battle should themselves go there to fight. According to the report, Mahmood Shaikh (Thal), Ibrahim Samru (Larkana), and Abdur Rahman Panwar (Shikarpur), and Abdul Aziz Mangi (Dakan) had also gone for jihad and did not return. Their families were still waiting for them.

Baluchistan

In general, there is no visible tendency among people to join jihadi activities in Baluchistan. However, in this area there is considerable influence of Jamiat Ulema Islam (F) and Jamat-e Islami. Moreover, Jamiat Ulema Islam is also the most important political party here. The number of Baluchi mujahideen is less in Afghanistan and Occupied Kashmir than those from other provinces. The lists of martyrs published by different jihadi organisations show that from 1999 to March 2002, there were 112 martyrs from Baluchistan most of whom died in Afghanistan.

As for jihadi activities, Quetta, Dera Bugti, Mengalabad, Bonistan, and Chaman have remained the most prominent. Innumerable youth from

Chaman were employed in Afghanistan during Taliban's rule; they also fought against the Northern Alliance. Chaman is an important border town of Afghanistan from where access to Kandahar and Spain Baldak is very easy. People from both sides travel here without any restrictions. During Taliban's rule, people from here travelled in large numbers to Kandahar to perform the two Eid prayers in a year under Mullah Umar. Chaman had special importance during the war against the Soviet army by Taliban and later against the Northern Alliance when this city was the main centre from where weapons were supplied. Many of the truck drivers here said that the cargo that they carried in their trucks might have included weapons also. One truck driver, Hashim, said, 'I am surprised by one fact – when I drove my truck I was frequently stopped for checking at the border. But when I carried the goods of some particular contractors I was never stopped. It happened several times.' In Baluchistan, Quetta is the biggest centre for jihadi organisations. The offices of Lashkar-e Tayyaba, Al-Badr, Harkatul Mujahideen, Harkat-al Jihad, Hizbul Mujahideen, and Jamiatul Mujahideen Al-Alami operate here. Though Lashkar-e Tayyaba and Harkatul Mujahideen have shifted their offices elsewhere they continue their activities like recruitment and training there.

Even though the jihadi organisations are not too active in Baluchistan, the temperament of people here is similar to that of people across the border, and the jihadi culture that has been spreading in Pakistan has also struck roots here. For example, in December 1998, members of Jamiat Ulema Islam (F) and Harkatul

Mujahideen had raided video shops and cinema halls in Quetta. Similarly, in Chaman, Jamiat Ulema Islam had campaigned against cable network.

The events in Afghanistan always leave their impact on Baluchistan. The political and social developments there influence the people here substantially. The religious and political organisations in Baluchistan have remained in the forefront in helping the Taliban. Maulvi Abdul Sattar, an important member of Jamiat Ulema Islam, said, 'We helped the Taliban in all possible ways. The students from our madrasas went there for jihad.' When I asked why the presence of Baluchi *mujahids* are minimal in Occupied Kashmir, he said, 'Afghanistan is closest to us, and its claim on us is foremost.'

What Happened to the Tribal Mujahideen in Afghanistan?

According to an estimate, about 10,000 volunteers had gone to Afghanistan from the Frontier Province to help the Taliban. The largest group among them was Tahreek-e Nifaz Shariat Mohammadi whose 6,000 volunteers had gone to Afghanistan. Other organisations such as Harkatul Mujahideen, Harkat-al Jihad, Jaish-e Muhammad and Al-Badr had also sent their volunteers there.

The first contingent of Tahreek-e Nifaz Shariat Mohammadi had reached Mazar Sharif in November 2001 when American planes were dropping bombs there. On 8 November, General Dustom occupied Mazar Sharif. The Taliban tried to confront them and sent 115 tribal mujahideen to the front. On 11 November, a local Taliban commander sent for two commanders of Tahreek-e Nifaz Shariat Mohammadi whose names were Mahmood Jan Malik and Gur Khan and took them away. Both these commanders were from Der district. Mohammad Zahir Shah, an inhabitant of Shamsi Khan village of Der, who was present there said, 'Those two commanders were not seen after that. Later we came to know that they had already reached Pakistan. That evening the Taliban commander came to our compound. We were cooking the evening meal. He said that he was shifting from there because of some emergency. At that moment we felt that there was something wrong. We were shifted to a different spot. We were 141. He instructed us not to fire in case of any attack and not to change our position under any circumstances. When he was leaving we asked him to take us along with him, but he replied that he would be coming back soon. At about 11 at night intense firing began. We received instruction from the Taliban through walkie-talkie to give up arms. The same Taliban that had welcomed us in daylight were now robbing us of our arms. "We only want your machine guns and *kaashnikofs*." The Taliban entered our compound and disarmed us. Then they drove us away – "return to Pakistan by the Sarobi pathway". Hardly had we travelled about 40 km when a local mujahideen group stopped us. They robbed us of our light weaponry and pistols. When we advanced from there, another group raided us and robbed us of our watches and other belongings. After four more hours we reached Tamir Bazar. From there we hired a pick-up and reached Sarobi. From there we reached Jalalabad. We were further robbed at Tamir Bazar and Sarobi, so much so that even our shoes were taken off. If we tried to protest we were beaten up. By now we did not have enough money to reach home. Many begged and walked their way home.'

Some volunteers fared much worse than this. About 200 volunteers died in unfavourable conditions. Two hundred volunteers were captured by Zaman Khan, commander of General Dustom, who claimed ransom to the tune of fifty-two thousand to three lakh rupees per prisoner. They were released only after the ransom was paid. Various commanders of the Northern Alliance had captured about 500 volunteers for ransom. After capturing them the commanders sent their agents to the tribal areas for negotiations and to strike deals. The government departments did not interfere with these transactions.

The reaction against such treatment of volunteers was very strong in Der and Sawat. The local people who had always been kind to the Afghan refugees turned against them. They were conducting raids on their camps and villages. The Afghan refugee camp at Chakdara was severely affected by this. The refugees who earlier participated in political and social events were confined to camps only. On the occasion of Eid the refugees used to sell their products in the markets of Der and Malakand. This time the police did not allow them to do so.

Have the people of Der and Malakand turned away from jihad after they were treated by the Taliban so shabbily? When I spoke on this issue with a member of

Jamat-e Islami, Mulk Afkari, in Timargira, he said: 'The feeling of jihad can never be extinguished. All the people of this area are not disappointed with the Taliban. They had already said that volunteers should not be sent. People understand this. Of course, the fate meted out to some volunteers was deplorable. This has harmed Tahreek-e Nifaz Shariat Mohammadi. Even before the volunteers went to Afghanistan our stand was that only material assistance should be provided to the Taliban. Volunteers should go only when there is a call for them. But people got themselves into a frenzy and went there, and began to cry foul when they were in trouble.' Malik Afkari admitted that this has certainly harmed the cause of Islamic movement there: 'Sufi Sahib committed the error of not maintaining any record of the volunteers, and not organising them properly. It was a mob that met its deserved fate.' However, a journalist from this area, Aqeel Yusufzai, told me in Peshawar, 'When members of Tahreek-e Nifaz Shariat Mohammadi were gathering volunteers in Der, Malakand, and Sawat, members of Jamat-e Islami were also with them. But when the volunteers were proceeding to the front, they retreated. One reason for this could be that they wanted to discredit Tahreek-e Nifaz Shariat Mohammadi because it was emerging as their rival in the political arena.'

Chapter III
TRAINING STAGES

The training stages are the same in the training camps of most of the jihadi organisations. To prepare a mujahideen commando through all the relevant stages requires at least eighteen months. In case of contingency, commandos could be launched with six months' military training. This training has many stages:

Foundation

This stage continues for the first thirty days. In this stage recruits are given ideological indoctrination and not physical training. The sectarian groups give recruits their particular religious and ideological orientation. For example, Lashkar-e Tayyaba conducts a twenty-one-day course, to explain to the recruits the merits of Ahl-e Hadith school of thought.

Al-Ra'd (Thunder)

This stage continues for three months when, in addition to military training, recruits continue with their ideological training. Before admitting recruits to this stage some organisations conduct physical and mental tests. Other conditions are: the recruit should be unmarried, should not suffer from any chronic disease, should be literate, and should be ready to dedicate his whole life to jihad.

Guerrilla Training

Guerrilla training normally extends to six months. In this stage the entire concentration is centred on military training. After the completion of this stage, *mujahids* may be sent for launching. Only those who have already dedicated their life to jihad can participate in guerrilla training. Before training they are required to make their will and hand it over to the commander.

Jindla

This is the most difficult stage during which the recruits are taught how to make weapons and ammunitions. Side by side, they are taught how to use heavy weaponry. This stage continues for nine months. All recruits do not join this course. Only those who have already participated in some militant action can join it. Only some organisations like Lashkar-e Tayyaba, Hizbul Mujahideen, and Harkat-al Jihad al-Islami have the resources to conduct this course. Of course, they lend their services to other jihadi organisations as well.

Doshka

This stage consists of training in hand-operated weapons. This is a specialised course for those who have already undergone guerrilla training. It continues for seven to ten days. All mujahideen must undergo this course.

Domella

This course consists of training in operating weapons from the shoulders. This continues for at least one month. All mujahideen need not take this course. Only group commanders are required to do it.

Zakazak

This course specialises in imparting training on how to operate heavy weapons like cannons and tanks. The facilities for this training were available only in the camps in Afghanistan. The Taliban had donated a tank to Harkat-al Jihad for this training.

How is Launching Done?

How did the mujahideen cross the Line of Control? I was very eager to know.

'It is not easy for mujahideen to come to Azad Kashmir from Occupied Kashmir and then go back for launching,' said a *mujahid* of Jaish-e Muhammad to me.

'But there must be some way?' I asked.

'There are several ways.'

'Do the Pakistani army and ISI help?'

'They do not help everyone.'

'This means they do.'

'Not now.'

'Why?'

'I am not allowed to say.'

After investigating for three months and talking to a number of mujahideen I came to know that there are three ways of crossing over to Kashmir for launching:

THROUGH NEPAL

Only mujahideen leaders adopt this route because it is the most expensive. It requires one lakh to one-and-a-half lakh rupees to launch one *mujahid*, in arranging fake passports and in travel expenses. The fake Indian passports are made in Kathmandu; if not, one has to go to Lucknow. The travel from Nepal to Lucknow can be dangerous as it is undertaken with the help of illegal papers. In order to save money, many *mujahids* do not acquire visa that makes them more vulnerable to capture. If all 'papers' are in order, this method of launching is considered the safest.

THROUGH DUBAI OR DHAKA

This method is also expensive, adopted only by leaders and other important mujahideen. They acquire Indian visa from Dubai or Dhaka. Alternatively, they manage fake passport of India or a European country. The same method is undertaken for return.

THROUGH THE LINE OF CONTROL

This is the most risky method. The groups crossing over the Line of Control can hardly reach their destination in entirety. If twenty-five out of a group of thirty can reach the destination, it is considered a successful launching. Various jihadi organisations also look for other safe routes.

Jaish-e Muhammad had started launching through Fort Abbas, Chulistan border. But when the church was attacked in Bahawalpur in October 2001, Jaish's camp in Chulistan was folded up, and their passage through the border was totally prevented.

A *mujahid*, having completed his training, comes to the office at Kotli or Muzaffarabad where his name, addresses, and circumstances are recorded. His personal belongings and will are deposited in the office. From here he is sent to the border. The Occupied Kashmir consists of three provinces: the Valley, Jammu, and Ladakh. It shares its 750 km long border with Pakistan, which is divided in many sectors. Mujahideen are launched through these sectors. Every border camp has its own requirements, difficulties, and its particular circumstances. In the light of this, it is not necessary that all mujahideen who come to the camp are launched immediately. They have to wait for days, even three to four months. Sometimes it might happen that they are launched immediately. The weather plays the most important role in launching – the best season in this regard is October to January. During this period water turns into ice, snow falls periodically, the whole valley remains covered with snow, and there is no snow storm and no landslide. The most difficult period for launching is considered to be the months between February and April.

The assistant of a launching commander told me: 'We divide Kashmir border in two parts: the low border area that touches Jammu and the high border area that touches the Valley and Ladakh. The advantage of the low border is that it is easier to cross than the high mountains. But the difficulty is that because of the easy terrain the Indian army is able to keep a strict vigil on it. In some areas there are fences, barbed wire, and strong lighting. It is difficult to dodge the enemy in these areas, though the routes here are the shortest –

they can be covered in one or two days, even a few hours. The high border is advantageous in the sense that the Indian vigil there is not as strict because of steep mountains and forests. Landmines have been laid along the border, but during snowfall they are buried under snow and explode rarely. However, to cross steep mountains – as high as 12,000 to 18,000 feet – is an extremely strenuous job. Mujahideen have to travel three to ten days in these routes to reach their destination.'

Role of Guide

The guide plays an important role in launching. These guides are the herdsmen who graze their sheep and cattle in those mountains. They are known as *bakrwal*. They are familiar with every nook and cranny of the mountains. They are neither associated with nor have any sympathy for any of the organisations. They simply sell their services for money. A guide charges 25,000–35,000 rupees for one round; a coolie/porter that carries goods charges 10,000–12,000. With a caravan of ten porters travel two half-guides (who do not travel the whole way but guide the caravan to a particular destination) who charge 10,000–15,000 rupees. One *mujahid* told me that they have created such an efficient network that supplies can be sent to any far-flung areas of Occupied Kashmir, directly from the centre to the mujahideen, at two days' notice.

Keeping in mind the seminal role guides play, some jihadi organisations have groomed their own guides. For example, Al-Umar Mujahideen, Hizbul Mujahideen,

Jamiat Al-Mujahid, and al-Jihad are paying attention to this aspect. Some small groups have taken up the task of training guides only, and supplying them to jihadi organisations on payment basis.

Chapter IV

RELIGION, JIHAD, AND JIHADI ORGANISATIONS

The way religion was used in the Afghan War demonstrated its potential, and it facilitated the growth of religious organisations. In 1970 there were only thirty religious organisations in Pakistan and they were not very active. Among them seven were of Deobandi, five of Barelvi, four of Ahl-e Hadith, and three of Shia persuasions. Jamat-e Islami was regarded as a non-sectarian organisation. From 1980, new religious organisations began to appear on the scene, and the old ones were split into parts. Now the total number of religious organisations in Pakistan is 237. One reason for this phenomenal increase is the increasing number of madrasas whose principals started forming their own organisations. The madrasas started getting zakat money and other aids from the government that was spent in streamlining these organisations. Maulana Hasan Mahmood, an important member of Jamiat Ulema Islam, Peshawar, remarked: 'The secret agencies also funded many religious organisations. They encouraged conflict among these organisations so that they do not unite and come to power, and at the same time work for them.'

The organisations that came into being during

1979–90 were mainly of jihadi and sectarian nature. The rate of growth of jihadi organisations was 100 per cent, whereas that of sectarian organisations was 90 per cent. All big jihadi and sectarian organisations were born during this period. Religious sentiments pervaded the atmosphere in the country and religious organisations took full advantage of that. They turned the 'lesser jihad' into 'greater jihad'.

It must be pointed out, however, that there is great disagreement among these organisations about the concept of jihad. Majority of organisations owing allegiance to Ahl-e Hadith school of thought support only 'greater jihad'; they support militant jihad only under certain conditions. (Their views have been treated in detail in the chapter on Ahl-e Hadith.) Some Deobandi organisations also feel that the current situation and circumstances are not ripe for militant jihad. Several important maulanas from Jamiat Ulema Islam think that the so-called jihad in Afghanistan and Kashmir does not pass the test of sharia. They published their statements to this effect (detailed discussions follow in subsequent chapters). And the leaders of Tablighi Jamat feel that jihad is not permissible at all in Afghanistan and Kashmir.

At this point, I do not want to go into a detailed discussion of 'greater jihad' and 'lesser jihad' and the specific conditions they must fulfil. I will simply quote some extracts from the writings of Mufti Rasheed Ahmad who is the greatest ideologue of Deobandi school and is regarded as the patron of many Deobandi organisations. These will help us understand the real character of many organisations. In a chapter titled

'Jihad-e Akbar' (greater jihad) the Mufti says:

'Jihad-e Akbar' means – to struggle against the self and evil environment. On the one side, there is Allah's commands and on the other side, there are physical urges and the temptations of the Devil. To remain steadfast in the way of Allah despite all worldly temptation is called 'Jihad-e Akbar'. It is called so because of the following four reasons:

1. The real meaning of jihad is protection of religion. Protecting the borders of the country is a part of it.
2. Fighting in the front affords greater opportunity to satisfy one's senses, urge for fame, and even money. If the fighter dies then he is awarded titles like 'martyr', medals etc. and money and job to his relatives (sic). As opposed to this, one does not gain anything by remaining steadfast in the way of Allah. One even stands to lose materially by rejecting impermissible sources of income.
3. While fighting in the battlefront, the duration is short and the destination seems close. To remain true to the way of religion requires hard work for the whole life.
4. The jihad of maintaining true religion and moral character is much more difficult than the jihad of fighting in the battlefront. You will encounter many people who can fight heroically in battle, they can even lay down their lives, but they do not leave their sinful ways. This proves that to leave sinful ways is more difficult than laying down one's life.

In another chapter he says:

The great Islamic scholar Ashraf Ali Thanavi was asked why he did not take part along with other political parties in the jihad against the British. He replied 'For jihad an "amir" (leader/commander) is necessary and for electing an amir everyone's consent is necessary.' The people who had approached him said – 'We elect you as our amir.' He replied 'All other leaders will not agree to my leadership. If you are confident then get their signatures. If you are able to do that and I am made an amir, then I will ask everyone to surrender their wealth that will be spent on jihad and not on personal comforts. (After the jihad is over, the wealth will be returned.) I will make much better use of the wealth than them (*sic*). After having that wealth I will not take the name of jihad for ten years. Rather, I will spend it in the physical and psychological well-being of the army and use the wisdom of the ulema in the education of people so that they become true Muslims. And after that I will declare jihad.'

Jihad (pamphlet), Al-Rasheed, Karachi

In the light of the above, when I asked a leader of Jaish-e Muhammad why they did not fight against injustice and oppression in Pakistan, he replied, 'After the Kashmir independence, it will be the turn of Pakistan.' I asked a similar question to Abdul Rasheed Turabi, the amir of Jamat-e Islami in Azad Kashmir, 'After independence (of Kashmir) what will be the character of mujahideen and where will they go?' His reply was, 'We will concentrate on rectifying the system (government) in Pakistan.'

In sum, the religious organisations gave a fillip to jihad both inside and outside the country. They have become so bold that several of them threatened to 'raid'

Islamabad. However, a maulana from Muzaffarabad said, 'These raids are announced by organisations only to hike their prices.'

Disagreement Among Jihadi Organisations

It is no secret that serious disagreements exist between jihadi organisations on ideological and other issues. The disagreement between Harkatul Mujahideen and Jaish-e Muhammad, the conflict between Al-Badr and Hizbul Mujahideen, the mutual allegations hurled against each other by Lashkar-e Tayyaba and Tahreekul Mujahideen, the mutual acrimony between Al-Barq and Sunni Jihad Council have often bagged headlines in newspapers and jihadi journals. The bloody encounter between Hizbul Mujahideen and Pir Panjal regiment (Hizb-e Islami) has been witnessed by people in Kotli Nakyal sector which they still remember.

What are the reasons for this conflict? It will come subsequently in the relevant chapters. However, I must record here the position taken by a leader of Hizbul Mujahideen: 'The seeds of disagreement are sown in jihadi organisations by the secret service agencies so that it becomes easier to "handle" them. The larger the number of organisations, it is easier for the secret agencies to handle them.' Several incidents are recorded below that demonstrate the level of discord between these organisations:

Discord Between Tahreekul Mujahideen and Lashkar-e Tayyaba

In Lahore, an important member of Central Jamiat

Ahl-e Hadith gave me a pamphlet with the title, 'Traitors Disguised as Leaders', which contains detailed descriptions of the violent disagreement between Tahreekul Mujahideen and Lashkar-e Tayyaba. The writer is Mohammad Ashfaq Gondal. Extracts:

> During the days when Tahreek Ahl-e Hadith was at the peak of its popularity in Kashmir, an organisation by the name Lashkar-e Tayyaba was formed in Pakistan to undercut its popularity. They also established their branch here and tried to destroy the unity of Ahl-e Hadith.

FALSEHOOD 1

Without the help of any Kashmiri organisation they (Lashkar-e Tayyaba) could never have reached Occupied Kashmir. The ISI emptied a cantonment area, and the mujahideen gave it the name Al-Badr (the present writer has spent a couple of days there). They spread the rumour that they have conquered the spot from the Indian army that was occupying it, and that it was their battlefront now. It was as though only they were doing jihad and no one else. When people got to know that this was no battlefront at all, that the real jihad was going on in Occupied Kashmir through guerrilla attacks, they sent a couple of their members to the Valley through the help of Al-Barq with the instruction that these members should be made martyrs as soon as possible by sending them in a difficult mission. If that happened, they could publish their photographs in their journal *Al-Dawa* and demonstrate to people that they were also fighting inside Occupied Kashmir. That is exactly what happened. Abdur Rauf, commander of Tahreekul Mujahideen in Kupwara, reported: 'When I came to know that some mujahideen had arrived I went to meet them. When they saw me performing namaz in a specific way they were surprised and asked me: "Are you from Ahl-e Hadith?" I replied: "I am not an ordinary member of Ahl-e Hadith but one of the officers of Tahreekul Mujahideen, the organisation that Ahl-e Hadith patronises." They and their commander Alladitta alias Abu Hafs were extremely surprised, and said that they were told by their leaders that there was not a single member of Ahl-e Hadith in Kashmir. Their leaders had said to them, "We will go there (Kashmir) with the Barelvis, we will convert them to our school of thought and then form an organisation of Ahl-e Hadith." When I told them in detail about Tahreekul Mujahideen, they decided to work with us. However, when Hafiz Said (Sahib) came to know of it, he phoned the commander of Al-Barq, and instructed him to send the newcomers to some difficult mission before they could associate with us. The following day we participated in the funeral prayer of Abu Hafs and his companions. When I came to Pakistan I read such exaggerated stories about them published in *Al-Dawa*. These stories had no connection with actual facts.'

FALSEHOOD 2

On the one hand, they claimed themselves as the prime *thekedars* (leaders) of jihad, on the other, they also claimed to be the protectors of the *muhajirs* and collected contributions from them. They published an advertisement on the title page of *Al-Dawa* in February 1990 that 50,000 refugees from Kashmir had arrived at Muzaffarabad and for them a centre had been opened by Markaz Dawa Al-Irshad where they were being looked after. The advertisement appealed to people to donate liberally for these uprooted people. The fact is that there were not even 500 refugees who had crossed over in February 1990, and the Dawa people have opened no centre for them till date. They were telling lies after lies for accumulating money through contributions. In the September 1990 issue of the journal, Amir Hamza writes: 'An additional 1,000 refugees have reached Azad Kashmir taking the total up to 1,500.' Seven months earlier, the number of refugees was 50,000. Now, after the arrival of 1,000 more we are told that the total number of refugees is 1,500! What duplicity!

Falsehood Upon Falsehood

The journal *Al-Dawa* publishes stories of fighters and martyrs in such exaggerated terms that mujahideen (of other organisations) and people familiar with the ground situation in Kashmir split their sides with laughter. These fighters are sometimes guided by a cat, sometimes by a bear; sometimes a snake keeps guard over them. Sometimes they perform *namaz* on bear's droppings; sometimes their clothing is pierced by showers of bullets but they are not injured. They can injure twenty Indian army men with a single punch; sometimes their swords change the direction of tanks and armoured cars; sometimes enemies take to their heels hearing their names. Sometimes a bear plays host to them, sometimes a monkey. Their dresses are torn to shreds, they lose their senses, but they do not have a single scratch on their body. There have been such martyrs whose valorous exploits were published ad nauseum, and then after a few days they are seen in flesh and blood. How long will Ahl-e Hadith dupe the people? There are hundreds of young men like us who have seen through their duplicity and are repenting now.

Commit a Crime to Conceal a Crime

When they were faced with questions from all sides as to why instead of allowing their members to work with Tahreekul Mujahideen in Kashmir they put them under Al-Barq and thus got them killed, they decided to split Tahreekul Mujahideen into two. They tried their best and invested the fund collected in the name of jihad to buy over some Tahreekul Mujahideen members, and in this they were helped by ISI. Thus a fake Tahreekul Mujahideen was born. Slowly, Ahl-e Hadith's influence faded away. Markaz Dawa was also split into two or three groups. Its commanders like Tamizuddin formed their own groups. Thus, they played a major role and spent considerable resources in getting Tahreekul Mujahideen split into rival groups. The sincere mujahideen and the resources collected for jihad were used in internecine battles, raiding rival offices and killing rival commanders. This is a shameful stain on the record of Ahl-e Hadith that can never be erased.

(This pamphlet bears the year of publication, 1996. Below the report is written: Courtesy, *Siratul Mustaqeem*, Karachi.)

Discord in Jama't Al-Dawa

Jamat Al-Dawa is now the worst victim of discord and division. One group is supporting Professor Hafiz Mohammad Said as amir while another group wants to replace him with Professor Zafar Iqbal. According to Dawa sources, Hafiz Mohammad Said had appointed people of his community (Gujar) in all important positions. Professor Zafar Iqbal who has the support of doctors and engineers is not only opposing this nepotism but he also has serious reservations about the policies pursued by Hafiz Mohammad Said. Jamat Al-Dawa always opposed the democratic government at the centre. Now it has opened a political wing which, according to Professor Zafar Iqbal, is against the fundamental policy of the organisation.

Discord Among Jihadi Organisations of Deobandi School

There are six big jihadi organisations of Deobandi persuasion and they have been rival to one another on different issues. Jamiatul Mujahideen al-Alami which is known as the jihadi wing of Jamiat Ulema Islam (Ajmal Qadri group) does not cooperate with other jihadi organisations. Harkat-al Jihad al-Islami and Harkatul Mujahideen split because of organisational differences. Jaish-e Muhammad came to be born as a result of discord with the central management. A more deplorable thing is that all these organisations are engaged in vilification campaign against one another without regard to decency or social norms. For example, in the April issue of the monthly *Zarb-e Haq*, Karachi, the following report about Maulana Masood Azhar, amir of Jaish-e Muhammad, was published:

> I do not know what we will gain by sending callow youths to Kashmir and getting Kashmiri women raped by Indian army men. When one hears on audio cassette Maulana Masood Azhar's statement that the Prophet said that a jihadi will have just one wish in life and that is martyrdom, one will be restless to join jihad in any part of the world and taste the bliss of martyrdom. Just as a frog breathes through his entire body, when one hears Maulana Masood Azhar's passionate speech he will think that the Maulana is also tasting heavenly bliss through his entire body. Like his heart, his muscles will also shiver in fear of God. A *mujahid*, much senior to Maulana Masood Azhar, whose brother was the first martyr in Kashmir jihad, told me the following: 'Maulana Masood Azhar used to say in his speech: "When the first bullet hits you, you'll be delighted; when the second bullet hits you, you'll find greater pleasure; the more the bullets hit you, your pleasure will go on increasing. You will wish it never to stop." However, Maulana Fazlur Rahman Khalil told me one day to show Maulana Masood Azhar how to counter the enemy. I took him along with some others to the hilly tract and let them sit behind a mountain. Then I started firing in the direction of the enemy. By mistake one bullet hit the earth some distance away from Maulana Masood Azhar and a pebble struck him. He began to howl.

His companions began to run in the direction of the enemy position. I controlled them with great effort, as I had great difficulty in stopping Maulana Masood Azhar's pathetic howling.'

It should be remembered that *Zarb-e Haq* patronises Harkatul Mujahideen. Such unprintable materials are published in jihadi journals and innumerable pamphlets that indicate the level of bitterness that exists among these organisations.

How several organisations like Jamiat Al-Mujahideen, Al-Badr Mujahideen, and Hizb-e Islami were born out of Hizbul Mujahideen will be recounted in the relevant chapters. What is to be noted here is that the United Jihadi Council has never made any serious effort to remove the mutual discord among these organisations.

Jihadi Leaders

Leaders of religious organisations, sectarian organisations, and jihadi organisations are asked the following two questions of which one never got satisfactory answers. The questions are very simple:

1. Why jihadi leaders never go to the battlefront, and why they never send their children?
2. Where does the money come from for glorious mansions and offices, large Pajero jeeps, armed guards, etc.? If you can afford all this, why not the common mujahideen?

These questions exercise the minds of not only the common people, but also a large religious group as well, as will be evident from the following extracts.

The mouthpiece of Jamat Ahl-e Hadith, *Siratul Mustaqeem*, published an article, 'Jihad in Allah's Path' by Anwar Kashmiri, in its December issue of 1994. A few excerpts (unedited) from this article follow:

> One principal objective of the efforts put in by jihadi leaders and ulema in Afghanistan, Kashmir, Bosnia and Palestine is to acquire funding. In their discourses and published literature, they consistently underline the importance and value of jihad. They refer to the jihadi exploits of Prophet's companion, Rizwanullah Alaihi in a very arresting, often sentimental, way to ignite the passion of the listeners/readers who are inspired to take part in jihad according to the best of their abilities. The poignant description of the rape of Muslim women, of the fight between Truth and Falsehood, of the miracles that take place in the battlefront create tumult in the. mind of youths who get restless to participate in jihad to redress the injustice. However, the point of reflection here is – whether the investment of billions of dollars and thousands of youthful lives is not going in vain because of a few opportunist and self-seeking individuals?

> It can be observed that most of the leaders are seen moving around in air-conditioned Pajero cars. They exhibit cell phones in their hands round the clock in such a way as though they were instructing each *mujahid* in the remote battlefront. For travelling from one city to another these leaders are provided with the fastest service of PIA. The question is – when the leaders spend 50 per cent of the resources for their own comforts why they complain about the poverty

of the mujahideen?

It is regrettable that while the mujahideen are not provided with basic minimum provisions and outfits, and they are sent to fight the enemy in unfavourable conditions, their leaders ride posh cars and indulge in drawing room politics in their plush, air-conditioned and carpeted offices. My personal experience is – jihad has provided permanent employment to several unemployed youths for whom it has offered salvation both for this world and the hereafter, and they are resorting to self-indulgence to the hilt. Their reason for joining jihad is simply pursuit of employment and some illusion of success in life, and not any religious sentiment. Their pursuit of self-indulgence actuates them to cash in the rape of Muslim women in Bosnia and Kashmir and exploit the simple-mindedness of ordinary Muslims.

If they had really dedicated them to jihad in Allah's way they would be seen in the first row of mujahideen in the battlefront. Instead of drawing room politics they would be seen spending their time in the camps of mujahideen and muhajirs, helping them. They would have bought wireless sets for mujahideen in place of Pajero for themselves. Instead of eating rich dishes themselves, they would have tried to improve the mujahideen's quality of food and their outfits. In Azad Kashmir, they shoot films of injured mujahideen and helpless muhajirs, get their photos published, organise one or two demonstrations, open one or two training centres, and thus become the greatest champions of jihad. These films and photos are shown to simple-minded Muslims to raise more money that is spent on their own luxurious life style. And the cycle goes on.

Sada-e Jamaia, the mouthpiece of Jamiat Ulema Islam (Samiul Haq) published an interesting rejoinder to the above in its January 2002 issue:

> It was quite appropriate for our leaders like Maulana Fazlur Rahman, Maulana Shah Ahmad Noorani, Qazi Husain Ahmad and Maulana Samiul Haq to stay behind for the practical guidance of people. Some individuals and organisations were hoping that they would proceed for jihad leaving the field open for liberal-secular organisations... They are regretting that their desire has not been fulfilled.

Mohammad Khalid of Harkatul Mujahideen, Multan, said that their leader Maulana Fazlur Rahman Khalil had indeed participated in the battlefront, now he had concentrated on organisational management which was also jihad in another form. Syed Salahuddin, the supreme commander of Hizbul Mujahideen, has been living in Pakistan for a long time. His jihad is said to consist in providing leadership. Hundreds of such explanations are given, but none of them will provide satisfactory answers to the two questions asked.

Chapter V

JIHADI ORGANISATIONS, ISI, AND CIA

I started my work on jihadi and sectarian organisations in January 2002. The national and international configuration of events at that time indicated that jihadi organisations would now cease to exist or would be allowed to operate in very limited spheres. Maulana Masood Azhar and Hafiz Mohammad Said were under house arrest and jihadi leaders had gone underground. ISI is known to have fostered the growth of jihadi organisations and provided them protection. I thought I should know the ISI's position now so that I would also have some idea of the risk I was taking. Appointments with several ISI officers were organised with the help of a journalist friend. My first question was: 'Will the jihadi organisations be crushed?' The reply was unexpected: 'How is it possible? How can we ignore their role in bringing the Kashmir problem to the forefront?' This gave me a clue to the kind of difficulties I was going to face in my research. However, no officer was ready to admit that ISI helps jihadi organisations. The jihadi leaders also refuse to admit this fact, although one jihadi organisation may allege that another organisation is the stooge of ISI.

Is it possible for jihadi organisations to operate

without the consent of the government and the ISI? In this regard, the position of Dr Khalid Mahmood Samru, general secretary of Jamiat Ulema Islam, Sindh, is as follows: 'I think that the jihadi organisations have the support of secret agencies. I am against the character of these organisations in Pakistan. Why the Pakistani army do not fight in Kashmir? Why are our youth being sent to be killed there? The army is using our youth for its own end. Where does the big budget earmarked for the army each year go? One thing is clear: these jihadi groups cannot function without the patronage of the government. Is there any militant training camp in Pakistan that operates without the help of Pakistani army? How do the jihadi leaders come to acquire their cell phones, Land Cruisers, and weapons? Where do they get their funds from? Certainly, all this cannot be acquired simply with the contribution of the people, because we know that such big amounts cannot be raised through public contribution. We have been working in Sindh for so many years; we could never manage this.' Replying to a question, he said, 'There are 50,000 members of Jamiat Ulema Islam in Pakistan who have resolved that none of them will acquire military training. If anyone wants to act as a volunteer he is free to do so. We have no militant wing. No member of Jamiat Ulema Islam is helping the Taliban in Afghanistan. We just provide them moral support.'

A similar statement was given by Maulana Hasan Jan, a central leader of Jamiat Ulema Islam (F) and former member, National Assembly, to the BBC Pushto service in March 2002: 'Jihad and haj cannot be

performed without an amir. Forming jihadi
organisations was against the tenets of Islam.' A week
after this statement was made, Maulana Fazlur
Rahman issued a statement from Qila Saifullah,
Baluchistan, in national papers, to the effect that the
Qadianis are behind the current campaign against the
jihadi organisations. These statements have little to do
with ISI, but they demonstrate difference of opinion
among the leaders of the same Jamat. As far as the
relation between ISI and jihadi organisations is
concerned, Faisal, a journalist, said succinctly: 'The
new jihadi set-up being formed now is the result of ISI
pressure. Because of the irresponsible behaviours of
some jihadi organisations, the ISI is incorporating
them into the organisations operating in Occupied
Kashmir, or changing the leadership of these
organisations. All such decisions are being taken in
Muzaffarabad.' This view was corroborated from the
office of Harkatul Mujahideen, Kotli, where we learnt
that Maulana Fazlur Rahman Khalil was trying for the
greater clout of Harkatul Mujahideen in the new set-
up, and was busy meeting important people in
Rawalpindi. Similar things were heard about Bakht
Zamin, amir of Al-Badr. He was in touch with top ISI
brass seeking greater role for Al-Badr.

Apart from ISI, we got to know about the relation of
jihadi organisations with foreign agencies. A leader of
Hizbul Mujahideen from Kotli claimed that CIA has
been distributing funds among jihadi organisations
through Ghulam Nabi Fani. When Hizbul
Mujahideen came to know of it, it severed all
connections with Fani. It is said about Rabeta Alam-e

Islami that this world organisation was working in American interest. The following is an extract from a religious journal:

> The mujahideen leadership gets full return for sacrificing innocent lives. Recently a Kashmiri woman was captured with 1 lakh American dollars. The politicians of India and Pakistan know very well that Kashmir is bleeding because of American funding. The leader of Harkatul Mujahideen, Maulana Fazlur Rahman reported, 'America had instructed through Rabeta Alam-e Islami that we should initiate jihad in the Chinese province of Sinkiang. I replied that we have grown up now. We won't do jihad at your bidding.' Mufti Nizamuddin Shamzai had revealed that a jihadi organisation was buying over ulema, on behalf of Rabeta Alam-e Islami, Washington, by distributing money in Pakistan. He threatened to expose it, but so far no Maulana has dared to confront Rabeta Alam-e Islami.
>
> *Zarb-e Haq*, Monthly, Karachi, April issue, 2002

Some jihadi leaders believe that America is assisting some jihadi organisations so that (i) Kashmiri people are given the right of self-determination and (ii) America can establish its base here and spread its influence in India, Pakistan, China, and the Middle East. They also believe that ISI is helping America in this endeavour. A section of Ulema also believed that the Taliban was a creation of America. For example, in the same issue of *Zarb-e Haq* referred to above a letter of Sahibzada Atiqur Rahman Gilani was published. An extract from this letter runs as follows:

The Taliban came into existence all of a sudden and within a short time took Afghanistan in its hold. We had expressed our views earlier through the pages of *Zarb-e Haq* the gist of which is being given here: When Taliban was formed, one officer of ISI had said to me openly in a brief meeting in Tank market: 'You always wanted Nizam-e Khilafat. Now your wish is being realised in Afghanistan. Why don't you go there with your companions and work with Taliban?' I replied, 'How is it that you want it (Nizam-e Khilafat) there and not in your own country, although the first claim (to it) is always of your own country?' Hearing this he turned his tail and left the spot immediately as though he had given out a secret. Any sensible person will understand that ISI which is not ready to establish Nizam-e Khilafat in Pakistan can do so in Afghanistan only at the bidding of America. When I talked to Maulana Sher Mohammad Sahib, ex-amir of Jamiat Ulema Islam, Karachi Division, on the phone, he said the same thing – that our wish for Islamic Government was being fulfilled in Afghanistan. I asked him, 'Islamic Government or American Government?' Hearing this he burst out laughing and said, 'How could you know this secret?' After that a delegation of Jamiat Ulema Islam went to Afghanistan under the leadership of Maulana Mohammad Khan Shirani. With reference to this delegation the well-known Maulana from our area, Saleh Shah Sahib, told us that the secret of Taliban movement is known to only eight people. No one can say anything about their objective. That is why Jamiat Ulema Islam cannot rely on them. In the beginning Maulana Fazlur Rahman, leader of Jamiat Ulema Islam, also said that the fight between Taliban and Northern alliance was a fight between Iranian and American companies. Then a time came when Maulana Sher Mohammad travelled to Afghanistan and reported about Taliban that they have been chosen by Allah for special assistance. After the Prophet's companion, if there were any Muslims imbued with Islamic ideals, it were they. It is also a fact (he said) that Islam is a natural religion, and when a people will get the assistance of Nature in protecting their religion their faith will grow and deepen. They will get such peace and contentment, as a child gets after he meets his long-lost mother. But the same Maulana Sher Mohammad Sahib, after sometime, began to say that the Taliban was part of an American conspiracy.

RAW and Jihadi Organisations

From time to time many jihadi organisations claim that they had been infiltrated by agents of Research and Analytical Wing (RAW), and that timely action against them saved their organisations from greater damage. In August 2000 Lashkar-e Tayyaba claimed that it had so far captured thirty such agents that had infiltrated their ranks at the instance of Indian secret services, especially RAW. Among them there were three women too. The Lashkar-e Tayyaba source said, 'The women have been let off, the rest twenty-seven have been surrendered to (Pakistani) secret services and they are still in their custody. They were all Hindus, and disguised themselves as Muslims.' A similar claim was made by Harkatul Mujahideen in January 2000 although its leader Maulana Fazlur Rahman Khalil refused to admit the existence of Al-Faran. (This organisation had kidnapped European tourists in 1995 for the release of Maulana Masood Azhar.) He claims that this organisation was floated by RAW to malign Harkatul Ansar (in 1995 Harkatul Mujahideen was a part of it). And now, several leaders of jihadi organisations claim that the ex-chief commander of Hizbul Mujahideen, Abdul Majid Dar has been bought over by RAW.

It is possible that jihadi organisations are infiltrated by RAW agents. However, a Jaish-e Muhammad recruit from Muzaffarabad says that when a *mujahid* shifts loyalty to another organisation or opposes the decision of the leadership he is promptly accused of being a RAW agent.

Jihadi Organisations and Al-Qaida

Jihadi organisations like Harkat-al Jihad al-Islami, Harkatul Mujahideen, Jaish-e Muhammad, Al-Badr Mujahideen, and Lashkar-e Tayyaba have often admitted to their close association with Osama bin Laden. Not only that Osama bin Laden had a strong hold on these organisations, many of them have received material and technical assistance from him (the details will come in succeeding chapters). Osama bin Laden also played a vital role in resolving differences and discord among different jihadi organisations. Moreover, in the jihadi training camps of Afghanistan, Arab mujahideen and members of Al-Qaida received military training together. One index of the relation between these organisations and Al-Qaida can be seen in Osama bin Laden's global movement IIFAJC (International Islamic Front Against Jews and

Christians). The foundation of this organisation was laid by Osama bin Laden in Khost, Afghanistan, in February 1998. According to a report published in *The Herald*, Karachi, all the jihadi organisations of the world were invited on this occasion. From Pakistan representatives of Harkatul Mujahideen and Harkat-al Jihad al-Islami had gone to attend the function. Later, other organisations had a meeting with Osama bin Laden in 1999 in which many important decisions were taken. One decision among them was about intensifying efforts for an Islamic state in Kashmir. According to the Harkatul Mujahideen sources, it was also decided that Kashmir should be made the base camp of all Islamic movements, and Islamic rule should be imposed there forthwith. After this meeting, jihadi organisations had, on their own, tried to impose sharia laws in different areas. Restrictions were imposed on women's dress and movement outside home. Harkat-al Jihad al-Islami even announced the collection of *jeziya* from the areas under their control.

Islamic State of Kashmir

The sources in Harkatul Mujahideen say that various powers are after Kashmir. America wants an autonomous status for it so that it can establish its base here. India wants to latch on to it by force. About Pakistan one cannot be sure when it will sacrifice Kashmir to American interests. Under the circumstances, it is necessary that the jihadi organisations should advance their agenda of declaring an Islamic state in Kashmir. 'Was any such proposal under discussion in the meeting of the jihadi organisations? Was it discussed in the 1999 meeting with Osama bin Laden?'

'It could have been discussed. Now that Pakistan has gone to the American camp, maybe such a proposal will be under consideration (anew).'

Chapter VI
JIHAD AND SECTARIANISM

The mutual discord among jihadi and sectarian organisations not only produces extremism in religious beliefs but also it is manifested in its worst form in the battlefront. Several Kashmiri mujahideen told me in Azad Kashmir that the jihadi organisations in Occupied Kashmir, instead of fighting the oppression of the Indian army, keep fighting among themselves. It often happened that different organisations sent their mujahideen for the same mission. There, instead of achieving their target, they got fiercely entangled in fisticuffs over questions of faith. In Occupied Kashmir, one often hears about Deobandi and Ahl-e Hadith groups intensifying their sectarian tendencies, 'conquering' many mosques and removing *shirk o bidat* (associationism and accretions/popular culture) from the areas.

Noorullah Qureshi, an advocate, is from Srinagar, Occupied Kashmir. He has been living in Muzaffarabad from 1995 and working as a lawyer. He is close to different jihadi organisations. About this aspect of jihadi organisations in Kashmir he said: 'The real concept of jihad has been maligned by these so-called jihadi organisations. And they have damaged the soul of Kashmir. The entire Kashmir – this side and the other side – was known for its spirituality. People – Hindus and Muslims – are drawn to mysticism. When passing by the shrine of a Muslim Pir, Hindus show utmost reverence; if they have to go to a dargah they take off their shoes from a distance. In other words, people of both the communities revered spiritual figures. The sectarian jihadi organisations have destroyed this atmosphere. Several jihadi organisations have made it their mission to conquer mosques and dargahs.' He reported an incident in Anantnag, 'Several mujahideen of Ahl-e Hadith had hidden themselves in a dargah for some days. While leaving, they put it to flames saying that the centre for *shirk* should be destroyed. This filled the local people with hatred for them. This sectarian sentiment lies at the background of Mazar Sharif mishap also. The jihadis of a particular persuasion put it to fire. I am totally disappointed by the character of the maulanas and these organisations. They continue fighting among themselves – here as well as there. The journey for Kashmiri independence has become longer because of them. For independence there, political processes must be strengthened. I am happy with General Musharraf's steps.'

Similar sentiments were expressed by Naseem Vani who belongs to a non-sectarian jihadi organisation, Zarb-e Islami. He is also from Srinagar. According to him, the sectarian organisations have vitiated the environment of mutual tolerance and harmony in Kashmir. There, they either fight among themselves or kill unarmed Hindus and women; then they return here as champions of jihad. Faruq Rahmani, leader of People's League, an important political group in Occupied Kashmir, also expressed similar views, 'I told Lashkar-e Tayyaba a long time ago that their activities will cause more harm than good. What we feared has happened.'

Beginning of Sectarian Tension in Pakistan

From 1987 to March 2002, a total of 1,016 people died in sectarian clashes. In this period 2,450 were injured in 1,342 incidents. From 1990 to March 2002, 593 people died from the Shia community and 388 from the Sunni community. Forty-four people from the police and other law-enforcing agencies also died in sectarian violence. Important leaders and ulema from rival sides were also among the dead.

How did the harmony among groups of different persuasion come to an end? Why did sectarian violence get a fillip? During research, these questions were uppermost in my mind. As I collected the views from rival sides and read their literatures, I found the answers to be extremely complex. Religious differences combined with personal gain and ambition, social and political reasons to make them more complicated. One can also see the role of foreign powers. Rival groups have emotional and other kinds of links/rapport with different Islamic countries from where they get support. These are the external factors. But to make an in-depth study of this phenomenon will probably require more time.

The sectarian tendencies got a fillip in 1985 when Maulana Haq Nawaz from Jhang founded Sipah Sahaba. However, the seeds of sectarianism were sown much earlier. The position of Sipah Sahaba in this regard is this: 'When the Iranian Revolution took place in 1979 the Shia organisations in Pakistan got a new lease of life. They were encouraged to bring about an Iran-like revolution in Pakistan. With this end in view, Shia youths were trained in Iran, the first practical demonstration of which came in evidence in the opposition against Ziaul Haq's *Zakat O Ashar* ordinance in 1979. This encouraged the Shias and they began to disseminate literatures in Pakistan that openly maligned the Prophet's companions. Shia ulema began to defame the Prophet's companions openly in public gatherings. This needed to be countered as they were denigrating our way of faith. The initiative was taken by Maulana Haq Nawaz and Sipah Sahaba was born.' As opposed to this, Tahreek-e Ja'fariya's stand is as follows: 'Ziaul Haq wanted to impose Hanfi Sharia in Pakistan without caring for the rights of the Shias. Hanfi laws were imposed on us as well. This was against the fundamental principles of our faith. We started the movement which was successful. Some people make allegations against Tahreek-e Ja'fariya saying that Sipah Sahaba came into being as a reaction to it. Actually Tahreek-e Ja'fariya was founded because throughout the country Deobandi and Wahabi organisations were taking roots. The leadership of Nizam-e Mustafa was in their hands and Ziaul Haq was their man. So our stand was that as Jamiat Ulema Islam and Jamiat Ulema Pakistan, while pursuing their own way of faith, were regarded as national political parties, we should also have an organisation on similar lines. No one should have objected to this. Ziaul Haq had an aversion to our organisation because it opposed his dictatorial policies. To suppress us and our point of

view, he employed his agencies to establish Sipah
Sahaba that declared us as "kafir" and cast aspersions
on our loyalty to Islam and Pakistan. We could not put
up with this.'
   These were the positions of two large sectarian
organisations. However, was the actual situation really
as described above?
   In 1977, before the imposition Ziaul Haq's martial
law, the following organisations of Shia school of
thought were there:

1. All Pakistan Shia Conference. Its leader was Nawab
   Muzaffar Ali Khan Qazalbash
2. Idarah Tahaffuz Huqooq Shia (Organisation for
   Protection of the Rights of Shias)
3. Shia Political Party
4. Wafaq Ulema Shia (United Shia Ulema)

Among these, Wafaq Ulema Shia led by Mufti Jafar
Hussain was the most effective. When Ziaul Haq
imposed Zakah & Ashar Ordinance in 1979, this
organisation came out and demonstrated against it.
Imamia Students' Organisation (ISO) planned to
capture parliament and a huge demonstration was
organised in Islamabad. Eventually the government
had to accede to their demands. This was the first
victory of the Shia community.
   This was the first show of strength on the part of
the Shia community. Before this, when the first Shia–
Sunni clash took place in 1963, Shia community was
not so organised. After those clashes, it had started
organising itself.
   This massive show of strength encouraged

Tahreek-e Ja'fariya. It built a network throughout the country. Tahreek-e Ja'fariya's main source of strength was its student wing, Imamia Students' Organisation. Both the organisations had the moral and material support of the revolutionary government in Iran. Here I must refer to a book – *Iran: Afkar o Azaim* (*Iran: Thoughts and Objectives*) by Nazir Ahmad. The book does not contain the place and year of publication. However, about the writer it is written that he was the manager, National Press Trust, Islamabad, from 1981 to 1985. Besides, he was also a member of the cultural attaché office attached to the Pakistan embassy in Tehran. Though the book is of sensational nature, the writer gives references from Irani newspaper clippings, articles, and Tehran Radio. For example, about the relation between Tahreek-e Ja'fariya and Irani government, he refers to the article 'Impact of Iranian Revolution on the Shias of Pakistan' that was published in three instalments on 13, 15, and 16 June 1991 in the Persian newspaper, *Kihaan*. Some excerpts:

> Tahreek-e Nifaz Fiqh Ja'fariya has become a dynamic organisation that is doing effective work for Iran in Pakistan. It has spread its activities to the far-flung areas of Pakistan despite the opposition from Pakistan government and Sipah Sahaba (which is a stooge of the Saudi family). In the background of the commonality that exists between the people of Iran and the Shias of Pakistan, there are great opportunities in Pakistan for facilitating the objectives of the revolution in Pakistan.

Similarly, he refers to the May 1993 issue of an English monthly published from London:

> This was stressed in the meeting of the Irani Cabinet that Iran will use its influence to bring about a government of its choice in Pakistan. As Iran possesses enough spiritual strength to bear on the Pakistani Shias, it is possible for Iran to mould the situation in Pakistan.

It is evident from the above extracts that foreign interests are at work in the growth of sectarian organisations and their violent clashes. This is also no secret anymore that the Iranian government provides financial assistance to the Shia organisations, and there is discord among these organisations about the use of funds. This is not limited to Shia organisations only. The organisations owing allegiance to Ahl-e Hadith and Deobandi school of thought get funds from Arab states. With the help of these funds they not only propagate Deobandi and Wahabi thoughts, but also want to implement their ideology by acquiring power. Foreign interests – religious and political – have often come in the way of resolving sectarian tensions in Pakistan. Most sectarian organisations showed greater loyalty to foreign interests and their own way of faith than to the nation. One cannot criticise or object to this attitude because that is regarded as interference in matters of faith, and thus the situation gets more complicated. In spite of this, there were some efforts to end sectarian tension at the level of government and religious organisations.

Milli Ekjahti Council (National Unity Council)

Sectarian tensions gripped Pakistan in 1986. Ahl-e Hadith scholars, Allama Ehsan Elahi Zaheer and Maulana Habibur Rahman Yezdani were killed in 1986 and 1987 respectively. In 1988, Allama Arif Husaini, president of Tahreek-e Ja'fariya and in February 1990, Maulana Haq Nawaz Amir, Sipah Sahaba, were done away with. On 11 December 1990, the Iranian counsellor, Sadiq Ganji was killed. In 1992, it was heard that both Tahreek-e Ja'fariya and Sipah Sahaba had acquired arms to fight each other as also to fight law-enforcing agencies. That year the members of Sipah Sahaba attacked the police in Jhang with rocket launchers in which five policemen were killed. In 1994 sectarian violence reached its apex that left seventy-three killed and more than 300 wounded in different incidents. For the first time, mosques came under attack and seven Shia and Sunni organisations got involved in it, among whom Sipah Sahaba, Sipah Mohammad, Tahreek-e Ja'fariya, Lashkar-e Jhangvi, Mukhtar Force, Ahl-e Hadith Youth Force, and Tanzeemul Haq were prominent.

Against the background of these violent incidents, Maulana Samiul Haq and different religious organisations began efforts to reduce sectarian violence. They formed Milli Ekjahti Council and most of the big organisations became part of the council. A moral code was agreed upon. In spite of this, there was no let-up in sectarian tension. One reason for this is said to be that though in the beginning the Milli Ekjahti Council was quite active, but with the passage of time its authority got eroded, and rather than using the platform for conflict resolution, some organisations began to use it for gaining political advantage.

Pakistan government has been trying to restore harmony among different groups. Different governments formed the Ulema Commissions. These commissions put in place a code of conduct that was agreed to by all sectarian organisations. But the wave of sectarianism did not stop. Sectarian organisations had consolidated themselves so much that they do not seem to be in a mood to compromise. According to Maulana Azhar Mushtaq of Karachi: 'If harmony is established between different communities and a compromise is reached between them, sectarian organisations will have no role to play. If they have no role, how will their leaders sustain themselves?'

Sunni Tahreek

Before Sunni Tahreek was formed, the tension between Tahreek-e Ja'fariya and Sipah Sahaba was called Shia-Sunni conflict. When Sunni Tahreek was formed, it took the stand that it was Wahabi-Shia conflict and a third force, i.e. Ahl-e Sunnat (Barelvi) was also there. Sunni Tahreek further added to the intensity of sectarian tension. Instead of the Shias, Deobandis and Ahl-e Hadith became the targets of Sunni Tahreek. It was felt that this organisation was formed to undercut the influence of Sipah Sahaba. But that did not happen, and all the three big organisations started conducting internecine battles.

111

Different Sectarian Organisations

Inspired by Sipah Sahaba and Tahreek-e Ja'fariya, many such organisations were formed whose impact was limited to particular areas. Such organisations inflamed passions and totally muddied the sectarian scene. Organisations such as Tahreek Difah Sahaba, Tahreek Ta'ffuz Namoos Sahaba, Mukhtar Force (Shia), Sunni Ekjahti Forum, and Sipah Mustafa were formed.

Business Interests in Sectarian Conflicts

Akhtar Khan, a journalist in Karachi, said: 'Some industrialists/traders are behind several sectarian organisations. They provide them money and use them against their business rivals.' This journalist is associated with a big Urdu newspaper. He said that he personally knew several leaders of Sunni Tahreek and Sipah Sahaba who admitted to this in his presence. For example, some leaders of Sunni Tahreek took lakhs of rupees for campaigning against a shoe manufacturing company from its rival company. It was given a religious and emotional colour by spreading the rumour that Allah's name is written on the sole of the shoe. Sipah Sahaba made an inventory of the factories and manufactures of Shia traders. Similarly Tahreek-e Ja'fariya made allegations against the owners of certain companies saying that they had sinned against the Imam. According to Akhtar Khan, this tendency is more evident in Karachi than in other parts of the country, and the patronage of industrialists, who are interested in settling business and personal scores against rivals, has added to the growth of these organisations. How did the petty functionaries of these organisations suddenly acquire weapons, cars, and cell phones? The agents of industrialists work in and manipulate these organisations. Maybe the leaders are not always aware of it, but this seems hardly likely. Similarly, campaigns are also carried out against Qadiani traders and manufacturers.

This aspect of sectarian organisations has remained hidden from the public gaze so far. Can some investigation be done to unearth the linkages? Akhtar Khan's view was, 'It can be done though it is very risky.'

Relation Between Sectarian Organisations and Jihadi Organisations

The nexus between sectarian and jihadi organisations is an open secret. Sectarian organisations like Sipah Sahaba, Lashkar-e Jhangvi, Tahreek Difah Sahaba, and others had links with Jaish-e Muhammad, Harkat-al Jihad Al-Islami, Harkatul Mujahideen, and Jamiiatul Mujahideen Al-Alami. Ahl-e Hadith Youth Force and Tahreekul Mujahideen are supposed to be two sides of the same coin. Lashkar-e Islam, the Barelvi jihadi organisation, was born from the womb of Sunni Tahreek. The founder of Lashkar-e Ababeel Mujahideen, Choudhury Himayat Ali, was the president of Anjuman Tulaba Islam earlier. In many areas of Pakistan and Azad Kashmir, secretaries and officials of the two kinds of organisations are the same. Jihadi organisations provide military training to the members of sectarian organisations. But they do not want to reveal this linkage. Jaish-e Muhammad denies any links with Sipah Sahaba. However, Maulana Azam Tariq, president of Sipah Sahaba, participated in Jaish-e Muhammad's 'Crush India Rally' in Lahore on 5 February 2000 and said, 'One lakh members of Sipah Sahaba will join Jaish-e Muhammad to fight with the infidels.' Maulana Ziaul Qasmi, chairman of Sipah Sahaba's supreme council, had participated along with other officials of the organisation in Jaish-e Muhammad's Jihad Conference in Jamia Manzoorul Islamia, Lahore, in October 2000. He shook hands with Maulana Masood Azhar and said that Sipah Sahaba would fight shoulder to shoulder with Maulana Masood Azhar's disciples.

In Afghanistan, mujahideen of Jaish-e Muhammad were also given training in the military training camp of Lashkar-e Jhangvi. When Lashkar-e Jhangvi was going to split, the leaders of Jaish-e Muhammad tried to resolve the difference between the two groups. The link between different jihadi and sectarian organisations is also due to the fact that their views on jihad are similar.

Naved Ahmad, an important member of Sipah Sahaba in Jhang said, 'The jihadi organisations are fighting "kufr" outside the country and we are fighting it inside Pakistan. Both are engaged in jihad. But because of some reasons we do not want to make our relation public.'

Members of jihadi organisations were also involved in some incidents of sectarian violence in Pakistan. For example, in 1993 there was a bomb explosion in Kotri that killed seven people. Among the criminals arrested were Kazim, Nazim, and Abdul Qadir who were students of Quotul Islam Madrasa and were associated with Harkatul Mujahideen. They were trained in its training camps in Afghanistan.

One regrettable fact is that some members of jihadi organisations were found to be involved in incidents of robbing and dacoity. After an incident in Karachi in February 2001, the station house officer (SHO) of Latifabad, Section B, Sardar Mengal, conducted a raid and rounded up two robbers with weapons. Their names were said to be Atif and Kashif, and they were said to have admitted that they were associated with Jaish-e Muhammad. Maulana Abdul Hafiz Faisalabadi, leader of Ahl-e Hadith, has accused Lashkar-e Tayyaba of bank robbery a couple of times in his addresses.

Above all, the sectarian element seems to be in ascendance in most jihadi organisations.

Chapter VII
A GRAVE DANGER

The madrasas have not probably contributed as much to the growth of jihadi organisations as the sectarian groups. The fault lies in the managers and teachers of madrasas, in addition to the obscurantist syllabus. One role of jihadi and sectarian organisations has been that they provided employment for students passing out of madrasas. Most of the jihadi organisations pay reasonable monthly salaries to district-level officials and to the mujahideen involved in military training. Sectarian organisations provide employment to them in new mosques and madrasas established to propagate their particular school of thought.

However, the situation is changing now. Throughout Pakistan there are 10,000 madrasas where ten lakh students are studying. In general, about five to seven thousand students pass out from the senior stages every year. The problem of their employment is going to reach a crisis point. After a detailed survey of twenty-nine big madrasas it was found that apart from jihadi organisations, the students from madrasas find employment in the following areas:

1. Department of education: Madrasa students have a special quota in the recruitment of teachers and lecturers in Arabic, Islamic studies, and Urdu. But

very few madrasa students succeed in the selection committee where they have to compete with competent students from government colleges and universities. Besides, the opportunity of employment in the department of education is also meagre.

2. The ideal job for madrasa students is considered to be employment as teachers and instructors in the army. Here also, very few madrasa students succeed in competition.

3. It is not easy to find employment in big madrasas. Even if they succeed, the salary and perks given them are minimal. I was surprised when I was told by teachers of big madrasas in Karachi, Multan, and Peshawar that they got only 3,000 rupees as monthly salary. Among the perks some got two meals a day while others got a place to stay. In small madrasas, the salary is shamefully low – as little as 500 rupees to 1,500 rupees. This situation creates discontent among teachers and they cannot impart education of a reasonable standard. It came out in the survey that the teachers getting minimum salaries were more prone to extremism.

4. All students who pass out every year cannot establish new madrasas. Only those who have financial backing or who have a flair for raising public contribution can succeed in founding new madrasas. From the experience of teachers it was evident that the task was not easy. If the madrasa does not run, monthly rent (of the building) and other expenses cannot be met and borrowings increase. The aid that small madrasas get from zakat and *ashar* fund is not enough for them for the whole

year. Now, the number of madrasas has increased so much that there is no further scope for new ones. The new government policy is also not conducive to the establishment of new madrasas. Quite a bit of resource is necessary to fulfil the conditions that have been set by the government for founding new madrasas. Earlier, a sum of only twenty-five rupees were needed for affiliation to Deeni Wafaqi Board that gave permission for admission to even senior stages.

5. It has never been a preferred option for madrasa students to be teachers or imams in mosques, unless the mosques are big and Waqf-aided. The scope of employment here also is very limited now.

In the light of the above, it is not difficult to imagine the state of things in future. What is the future prospect of 7,000 students coming out of madrasas each year? Because of restrictions on jihadi organisations they cannot find employment there; other employment opportunities are also shrinking. Will not the sectarian organisations use these students for their own ends? Unemployment among them may very well engender another protest movement.

PART TWO

PART TWO

Chapter VIII
RELIGIOUS ORGANISATIONS IN PAKISTAN

In Pakistan 237 religious organisations are working. Among them eighty-two are of sectarian persuasions, and twenty-four duly participate in the political process. Some organisations claim that they work on non-sectarian lines, but people of a specific persuasion are dominant in them. For example, Jamat-e Islami claims that its basis and principles of functioning are non-sectarian, but it has deep imprint of Hanfi-Deobandi school of thought. Similarly, Barelvi school of thought is dominant in Pakistan Awami Tahreek. There are 104 organisations of jihadi nature, and eighteen are of pure *tablighi* persuasion.

Hanfi-Barelvi organisations are the largest in number. This school of thought has a total of forty-four big groups and organisations. If one takes small organisations into account, this number will exceed 100. Among them twenty-two are of sectarian, thirteen jihadi, six semi-political, and two of *tablighi* nature. Hanfi-Deobandi organisations are more effective. The organisations of Deobandi persuasion number forty-six; among these thirty-three are of sectarian, five jihadi, four of religio-political, and three of *tablighi* nature. Organisations belonging to Ahl-e Hadith school of thought have also their influence. They number twenty; among these ten are of sectarian, four of semi-political, three of jihadi, and one of *tablighi* nature. Big Shia organisations number twenty-three; among these sixteen are of sectarian, three of semi-political, three of jihadi, and one of *tablighi* nature. Fourteen organisations owe their origin/allegiance to Jamat-e Islami; among these seven are of education-*tablighi*, four of jihadi, and three of political nature.

Madrasas in Pakistan

The number of madrasas working in Pakistan and Azad Kashmir is 6,761. This number does not include preliminary madrasas for reading and memorising the Holy Koran, mosques, and maktabs. The break-up of the madrasas based on their sectarian persuasions are: Deobandi 1,869, Barelvi 1,616, Ahl-e Hadith 717, Shia and others ninety-seven. These numbers are according to the data collected by the Institute of Policy Studies. Till date, data about madrasas have not been collected in an organised and methodical way.

There are five education boards related to madrasa education in Pakistan. However, all madrasas are not affiliated to these boards or any other central agency. The boards are:

1. Wafaq Al-Madaris Al-Arabiya, Multan (Board for Madrasas of Hanfi-Deobandi school of thought)
2. Tanzeem Al-Madaris, Lahore (Board for Madrasas of Hanfi-Barelvi school of thought)
3. Wafaq Al-Madaris Salafiya, Faisalabad (Board for Madrasas of Ahl-e Hadith school of thought)

4. Tanzeem Shia Wafaq Al-Madaris, Rawalpindi
5. Rabeta Al-Madaris (Board for Madrasas associated with Jamat-e Islami)

Apart from the madrasas under these boards, several big madrasas with branches in particular provinces or areas also function. For example, Jamia Al-Dawa (owing allegiance to Ahl-e Hadith) has ten branches in Pakistan. Darul Uloom (University) Mohammadiya Ghausiya Baseera (owing allegiance to the same Barelvi school of thought) has fourteen branches in different parts of Pakistan.

Welfare Organisations of Religious Groups

Twelve big welfare organisations are working in Pakistan (Table II) under the aegis of religious groups. Among them the Al-Rasheed Trust has the widest network.

Table II: *Classification of Religious Organisations in Pakistan*

of thought	Political	Sectarian	Jihadi	Educational/ tablighi others	Total
Hanfi/Deobandi	4	33	5	3	45
Hanfi/Barelvi	6	22	13	2	43
Ahl-e Hadith	4	10	3	3	20
Shia	3	16	3	1	23
Allied to Jamat-e Islami	3	–	4	7	14
Others	4	1	76	10	91
Total	24	82	104	26	236

Note: In these organisations I have not included those small ones whose influence is localised. Besides, I have not included many groups that will be given in a separate table.

123

Chapter IX
HANFI-DEOBANDI ORGANISATIONS

Forty-six groups of Deobandi school of thought are working in Pakistan (Table III). There are differences among them on questions of faith. Political and approach-based differences are secondary to them. On the question of faith, Deobandis are divided into two groups: *hayati* (life-affirming) and *mamati* (death-affirming). The first group believes in the Prophet's life after death and is close to the Barelvi Naqshbandi school of thought. The second group believes that the Prophet has no presence in the world after his death; rather he is in paradise in his specific place. This group is closer to Ahl-e Hadith (non-followers) in this regard. Such differences on questions of faith are also present in Deobandi organisations. For example, the now-defunct Sipah Sahaba has majority of *hayatis* and they are ready to combine even with the Barelvis to achieve their objective. As opposed to this, Tahreek Difah Sahaba has the majority of *mamatis* who are not ready to associate with the Barelvis under any circumstances. Rather, they claim that they are fighting on two fronts: with Shiism and Barelvism (Address by Ataullah Bandyalui, amir, Tahreek Difah Sahiba, 27 June 1997, Amir Maviah Masjid, Godha).

In religio-political organisations, no importance is given to *hayati-mamati* differences. However, Jamiat

Ulema Islam (Ajmal Qadri group) is regarded as a purely *hayati* Deobandi organisation. The other two groups of Jamiat Ulema Islam contain both *hayatis* and *mamatis*. Politically, the difference between Jamiat Ulema Islam (Samiul Haq group) and Jamiat Ulema Islam (Fazlur Rahman group) is one of approach that has taken personal colours. JUI, (Fazlur Rahman group) supports alignment with leftist organisations for democracy, whereas JUI (Samiul Haq group) sees itself as the protector of sharia. Sectarian organisations of Deobandi persuasion work independently, but on political plane they have support of these two groups. Sipah Sahaba (defunct) also participates in electoral politics; beyond its own orbit it also supports these two groups.

Deobandi sectarian organisations are active on three fronts: against Shiism, against Barelvism, and against Qadianism. The following organisations are more active than others:

1. Sipah Sahaba (defunct)
2. Tahreek Difah Sahaba
3. Tahreek Khuddam Ahl-e Sunnat
4. Lashkar-e Jhangvi (defunct)

The following organisations are working against Barelvism:

1. Jamiat Ishaat O Tauheed Wal-Sunnah
2. Jamiat Ahl-e Sunnat
3. Sawad Azam Ahl-e Sunnat

The following big organisations are working against Qadianism:

125

1. Alami Majlis Khatm-e Nabuwat
2. Pasban Khatm-e Nabuwat
3. International Khatm-e Nabuwat Movement
4. Tahreek Tahaffuz Khatm-e Nabuwat

Jamiat Ulema Islam

Jamiat Ulema Islam is counted among the larger religio-political parties of Pakistan that had become successful in forming governments in two provinces – Frontier Province and Baluchistan. Now, it has split into three parts.

FOUNDATION AND BACKGROUND

Jamiat Ulema Islam was born from the womb of Jamiat Ulema Hind. After Pakistan came into being Maulana Shabbir Ahmad Usmani laid its foundation. Jamiat Ulema Islam, West Pakistan was formed in 1952. Maulana Ahmad Ali Lahori was elected its first amir. The election was held again in 1954 in which Mufti Mohammad Hasan became its amir. Because of sickness, Mufti Mohammad Hasan appointed Maulana Mufti Mohammad Shafi Ahl-e Sunnat as the officiating amir. In 1956, Jamiat's convention was held in Multan in which Maulana Ahmad Ali was elected amir and Maulana Ghulam Ghaus Hazarwi was elected general secretary. Meanwhile, Jamiat Ulema Islam ran a campaign for getting the anti-Islamic articles struck off from the constitution. In 1958 martial law was imposed and General Ayub Khan imposed a ban on political activities. When this ban was lifted in 1962, Maulana Abdullah Darkhasti became the amir of Jamiat Ulema Islam. The Jamiat opposed the dictatorial policies of Ayub Khan.

In the general election of December 1970, Jamiat Ulema Islam got a substantial number of seats as a parliamentary party in Frontier Province and Baluchistan. It formed a coalition government with NEP. Maulana Mufti Mahmood became the chief minister of Frontier Province. But the united government suspended Baluchistan's governor and the chief minister and the governor of Baluchistan. In protest, Mufti Mahmood resigned from the chief ministership of Frontier Province. In the Khatm Nabuwat Movement of 1974, Jamiat Ulema Islam played a vital role. In the general election of 1977, nine political and religious organisations formed a united front, Qaumi Ittihad, to fight election under the leadership of Mufti Mahmood. Qaumi Ittihad announced a nationwide campaign against electoral malpractices which took the form of Nizam-e Mustafa movement. According to the brochure published by Jamiat Ulema Islam (F):

> As a result of this campaign, the government engaged in discussions with People's Party. In these discussions, the Qaumi Ittihad delegation was led by Maulana Mufti Mahmood whereas the government delegation was led by late Zulfiqar Ali Bhutto. These discussions were taking a conclusive shape when power-hungry generals and some incompetent politicians combined to impose martial law again. On 5 July 1977, Chief of Staff General Ziaul Haq took the reigns of power in his hands in the name of Islam.

Table III: *Hanfi-Deobandi Organisations in Pakistan*

Sr. No.	Organisation/Group	Central Leader/ Secretary/ Patron	Founded	Nature	Central Office
1.	Jamiat Ulema Islam (F)	Maulana Fazlur Rahman	1949	Political	Dera Ismail Khan
2.	Jamiat Ulema Islam (S)	Maulana Samiul Haq	1981	Political	Aqora Khatak, District Naoshera
3.	Jamiat Ulema Islam (Q)	Maulana Ajmal Qadri	1981	Political	Anjuman Khuddamuddin, Sheranwala Gate, Lahore
4.	Majlis Ahrar Islam	Syed Ataul Mobin Bukhari	1939	Political/ Sectarian	Daar Bani Hashim, Meherban Colony, Multan
5.	Jamiat Ishaat Tauheed O Nisa	Maulana Ziaullah Shah Bukhari	1939	do	Lala Moosa, Gujarat district
6.	Pakistan Ulema Council	Maulana Qazi Abdullatif	2000	do	Aqora Khatak, District Naoshera
7.	Majlis Sianatul Muslimeen	Maulana Obaidullah	1944	*Tablighi*	Jamia Sharafiya, Ferozepur Road, Lahore
8.	Tablighi Jamat	Maulana Abdul Wahab		do	Raiwind
9.	Sipah Sahaba (defunct)	Maulana Azam Tariq	1985	Sectarian	Jama Masjid Faruqiyah, Shahdara, Lahore
10.	Tahreek Difah Sahaba	Maulana Ataulla Badyalui	1987	do	Jama Masjid Muavia, Water Supply Road, Sargodha
11.	Wafaq Al-Madaris	Maulana Salimullah Khan	1987	Educational	Jamia Faruqiyah, Shah Faisal Colony, Karachi

Sr. No.	Organisation/Group	Central Leader/ Secretary/ Patron	Founded	Nature	Central Office
12.	Alami Majlis Khatm-e Nabuwat	Maulana Khan Mohammad	1949	*Khatm Nabuwat*	Huzuribagh Road, Multan
13.	Pasban Khatm-e Nabuwat	Allama Mumtaz Awan	1949	do	
14.	Tahaffuz Khatm-e Nabuwat	Syed Ataul Mohsin Bukhari	1949	do	Meherban Colony, Multan
15.	Jamiat Ahl-e Sunnat	Maulana Mufi Mohammad Isa Gurmani		Sectarian	Masjid Sadiqa, Satellite Town
16.	Sawad Azam Ahl-e Sunnat	Maulana Safnadyar		do	Gujranwala
17.	Tahreek Khuddam Ahl-e Sunnat	Maulana Mazhar Hussain		Sectarian	Jamia Masjid Madani, Chakwal
18.	Majlis-e Ulema	Maulana Abdul Qadir Azad		Political	Lahore
19.	Lashkar-e Jhangvi (defunct)	Akram Lahori	1896	Sectarian	Do
20.	Lashkar-e Jhangvi (Qari group)	Qari Abdul Hai	2000	do	Karachi
21.	Anjuman Khuddam Deen	Maulana Ajmal Qadri		Welfare trust	Shiranwala Gate, Lahore
22.	Pakistan Shariat Council	Maulana Zahid al-Rashidi			Hashmi Colony, Kangniwala Gujranwala
23.	Majlis Taisiq Al-Islami	Maulana Fazlur Rahman/ Maulana Nafidurrahman Darkhasti	2001	Educational/ Particular Persuasion	Peshawar

Gateway to Terrorism

Sr. No.	Organisation/Group	Central Leader/ Secretary/ Patron	Founded	Nature	Central Office
24.	Jaish-e Muhammad (defunct)	Maulana Masood Azhar	2000	Jihadi	F-16, Ehsan Colony, Bahawalpur
25.	Harkatul Mujahideen	Maulana Fazlur Rahman Khalil	1983	do	Awan School, Muzaffarabad, Azad Kashmir
26.	Harkat-al Jihad Islami	Maulana Abdussamad Sayyal	1980	do	3, Basharat Plaza, 1 9, Markaz, Islamabad
27.	Jamiat Al-Mujahideen Alami	Shaikh Abdul Basit	1983	do	Centreplate Nazd, Qila Muzaffarabad, Azad Kashmir
28.	Lashkar Umar		2001	do	Karachi
29.	Majlis Tawun Islami	Mufti Nizamuddin Shamzai		Sectarian	Jamia Islamia Banuriya, Gurumandar, Karachi
30.	Mashaikh Pakistan	Maulana Syed Sher Ali Shah		do	Peshawar
31.	Mutamar Al-Muhajiroon	Maulana Adeel			Malakand
32.	Tahreek Nifaz Shariat	Maulana Sufi Mohammad	1990		
33.	Majlis-e Amal Ulema Islam	Mujahideen Mohammad Sarfaraz Khan	1998	Council of Deobandi Organisations	Jamia Nusratul Islam, Satellite Town, Gujranwala
34.	Majlis Ulema Ahl-e Sunnat	Maulana Abdul Karim Nadeem		Sectarian	
35.	Tanzeem Ahl-e Sunnat, North	Maulana Qazi Nisar Ahmad			Gilgit

130

Sr. No.	Organisation/Group	Central Leader/Secretary/Patron	Founded	Nature	Central Office
36.	International Khatm Nabuwat Movement	Maulana Manzoor Ahmad Chenoti		*Khatm Nabuwat*	*Chenot*
37.	Jamiat Tulaba Islam (Q)			Student Wing	
38.	Jamiat Tulaba Islam (S)			do	
39.	Sipah Sahaba Students	Maulana Iqrar Abbasi	1987	Sectarian	Hasan Chowrangi, Karachi
40.	Muttahida Ulema Forum	Mufti Ferozuddin Hazarwi			Karachi
41.	Tahreek Ansarul Islam	Abdurrasheed Ansari			do
42.	Tanzeemul Ulema	Qari Alladad			do
43.	Mutmar Al-Ansar Al-Alami	Maulana Mohammad Amin			do
44.	Tahreek Taliban				Ozkazai Agency
45.	Muttaheda Ulema Council	Maulana Abdurraf Mulk (General Secretary)			84 A, Habibullah Road, Garhi Shaho, Lahore

Rift in Jamiat Ulema Islam

A serious rift took place in Jamiat Ulema Islam in 1980 as a result of which it was split into two. The cause of this rift was that one group supported Ziaul Haq's policies while another group wanted to align with the People's Party for restoration of democracy. After the rift, the two groups came to be known as Fazlur Rahman group and Darkhasti group.

Jamiat Ulema Islam (F)'s position on this rift is as follows: In the central general meeting of Jamiat Ulema Islam held in Lahore, Mufti Mahmood was authorised to form a united front with other parties including People's Party for the restoration of democracy. With this end in view Mufti Mahmood formed Movement for Restoration of Democracy (MRD). But before the declaration of the united front could be signed, Mufti Mahmood died in Karachi on 14 October 1980. However, the view of Jamiat Ulema Islam (S) is that Mufti Mahmood was given no such authorisation, nor could he go along with the People's Party. This was Maulana Fazlur Rahman's decision after the former's death. Maulana Ajmal Qadri has told me in an interview that Mufti Mahmood was among the first to congratulate Ziaul Haq on his assumption of power, and asserted in a public meeting in Mochi Gate, Lahore: 'He (Ziaul Haq) is such a person who will work for Islam.' Then Mufti Mahmood had come to Maulana Obaidullah Anwar with the offer of ministership and participation in Shura which he had declined. However, immediately after Mufti Mahmood's death, Maulana Fazlur Rahman formed the MRD.

When Maulana Fazlur Rahman decided to participate in MRD, the amir of Jamiat Ulema Islam, Maulana Abdullah Darkhasti declared the division of the Jamiat in the meeting at Khanpur in 1981. But Maulana Fazlur Rahman did not agree to pull out of the MRD. After this, there were efforts to bring the two groups together. But they were not successful because Darkhasti group always insisted that Fazlur Rahman should first pull out of the MRD. Thus Jamiat Ulema Islam (F) aligned with the People's Party and Jamiat Ulema Islam (Darkhasti) took part in Ziaul Haq's Shura.

Jamiat Ulema Islam (Fazlur Rahman Group)

Maulana Fazlur Rahman, the son of Mufti Mahmood, is the leader of Jamiat Ulema Islam (F). After the division of Jamiat Ulema Islam and till the death of Abdullah Darkhasti, Maulana Fazlur Rahman remained the general secretary while Darkhasti was considered to be the amir, although he supported the Maulana Samiul Haq group. After Darkhasti's death, Maulana Fazlur Rahman became the supreme leader of his own group.

Maulana Fazlur Rahman faction is the largest group of Jamiat Ulema Islam which is more effective in Frontier Province and Baluchistan. It has a large vote bank in both the states, especially in Baluchistan where it has always played a vital role in different governments.

The network of Jamiat Ulema Islam is spread through the four provinces and Azad Kashmir. But there is lack of close coordination. The local ulema give more importance to their individual and local agenda rather than the central policies. But they owe allegiance to one leadership and one religious persuasion.

Madrasas of Jamiat Ulema Islam (F)

In Pakistan, there are more than 1,500 madrasas either run by or affiliated to Jamiat Ulema Islam (F). Out of them 550 are in Frontier Province, 500 in Sindh, 400 in Punjab, and seventy in Baluchistan. There is a department of Jamiat Ulema Islam to supervise the working of these madrasas and offer coordination among them, but it is not very active.

Ansarul Islam

This is the military wing of Jamiat Ulema Islam (F) consisting of madrasa students. Its main responsibility is to provide security to the ulema and leaders of the Jamiat and management of large gatherings of people. It has no strict organisational structure. Mujahideen of other jihadi organisations also work in it.

Majlis Tanseeq Islami

Majlis Tanseeq Islami was established in 2001 in the conference of the Jamiat at Peshawar. Its chairman is Maulana Fazlur Rahman. Its objective is to establish linkages with various educational and intellectual institutes in the Islamic world and found institutes of similar kind with their help.

Jamiat Ulema Islam (Samiul Haq Group)

The leader of this group is Maulana Samiul Haq, the

principal of Darul Uloom Haqqania, Akora Khatak. He became the amir after the death of Abdullah Darkhasti. As opposed to the former group, this group is considered a natural ally of Muslim League and Jamat-e Islami. Apart from Qaumi Jamhoori Ittihad, Jamiat Ulema Islam (S) shared platform with Jamat-e Islami's Pakistan Islamic Front at the time of election. In the days of MRD's campaign this group was spearheading the cause of the Shariat Bill.

Madrasas of Jamiat Ulema Islam (S)

According to Allama Izhar Husain Bukhari, central secretary (information) of Jamiat Ulema Islam (S), the number of madrasas run by this group is 595, where religious teaching is being combined with modern education like English and computer training. According to Izhar Husain, about 500 students of these madrasas have joined jihadi organisations, which they have done at their own will.

Unity Among Religious Organisations and Maulana Samiul Haq

Maulana Samiul Haq has played an important role in bringing about unity among religious organisations. He was instrumental in establishing Milli Ekjahti Council, Afghan Defence Council, and Muttahida Majlis-e Amal, to end sectarianism.

Jamiat Ulema Islam (Ajmal Qadri Group)

Maulana Ajmal Qadri, the patron of Anjuman

Khuddam al-Deen is the leader of Jamiat Ulema Islam
(Q). This is the smallest group of Jamiat Ulema Islam
whose network is limited to Punjab, particularly in
Multan, Shujaabad, Bahawalpur, Okara, and in parts of
Lahore. It does not have much political clout either.
This group supports the *hayati* view of Deobandi
school of thought. However, on the political plane it is
thought to be against the other two groups and Sipah
Sahaba. It does not regard Jaish-e Muhammad or
Harkatul Mujahideen as the right jihadi organisations
and lends it support to Jamiat al-Mujahideen al-Alami.

Anjuman Khuddam al-Deen

Anjuman Khuddam al-Deen was founded by Maulana
Ahmad Ali Lahori, and its objective was to establish
madrasas, to help the destitute, and to participate in
welfare activities. Its current chairman is Maulana
Ajmal Qadri and according to him the Anjuman is
running welfare schemes to the tune of five hundred
crore rupees.

Sectarianism and Jamiat Ulema Islam

The foundation of Jamiat Ulema Islam is based on
purely Deobandi school of thought. And its record of
following and propagating this way of religion is
commendable. Though it has remained more active on
the political front, its relation with sectarian
organisations and its patronage of them are no secret.
Many officials of Sipah Sahaba, Lashkar-e Jhangvi,
Tahreek Khuddam Ahl-e Sunnat, and Tahreek Difah
Sahaba are also the office bearers of Jamiat Ulema

Islam. Moreover, the Deobandi sectarian organisations not only consider Jamiat Ulema Islam as their patron but also participate in its assemblies and gatherings along with their leaders.

Jamiat Ulema Islam's position in this regard is that these organisations cannot be called sectarian because they are working for protecting the honour of the Prophet's companion, and their own way of religion. As far as the involvement of these organisations in sectarian violence is concerned, all the groups of Jamiat Ulema Islam including Milli Ekjahti Council take the stand in public that the violent incidents were taking place because of the involvement of secret services and foreign agencies that have no link with these organisations.

The patronage from such a big religious organisation embolden sectarian groups. Several local leaders have been involved in incidents of sectarian violence. Details about it will come in a chapter on Sipah Sahaba.

Jihadi Organisations and Jamiat Ulema Islam

Jamiat Ulema Islam considers jihad as the soul of its organisation, and is the patron of jihadi organisations of Deobandi persuasion. It is the standing instruction of Jamiat Ulema Islam (F) that it should help Harkatul Mujahideen, Harkat-al Jihad, and Jaish-e Muhammad in Pakistan and Azad Kashmir in all possible ways. This kind of patronage facilitates the growth of sectarian differences among the organisations. According to Yahya Khan, an important member of Al-Badr, Muzaffarabad: 'In the Deobandi madrasas and mosques, they do not cooperate with those jihadi organisations which do not pertain to the Deobandi school of thought, a fact that is a cause of discouragement for many other jihadi organisations.' Yahya Khan referred to an incident in Rawlakot mosque: 'The mujahideen from Al-Badr had gone there to preach their jihadi objectives to people. Members of Harkatul Mujahideen were already there. The *khateeb* (sermon-reader) of the mosque not only allowed them to preach but also to procure funds from the people. But he refused to cooperate with us saying that he does not have JUI's permission to have any truck with Al-Badr. We requested him that others have already preached after the *asar namaz*, and that we should be allowed to preach after *maghrib namaz*; that the mosque is Allah's house and its doors should be open to all. In spite of this we were not allowed (to preach); after *maghrib namaz* when people came out of the mosque we stopped them on their way and gave a discourse.'

It came to our notice both in Pakistan and (more) in Azad Kashmir that Jamiat Ulema Islam has instructed its office bearers to extend help to all the three organisations. But the local management may extend its sincerest help to some specific Deobandi organisation. For example, the *khateeb* of the Hajera central mosque in Azad Kashmir, Maulana Kamal Azad is the patron of Harkat-al Jihad and is opposed to other organisations, particularly Jaish-e Muhammad. His reason for this is: 'I personally patronise Harkat-al Jihad as I think it has been/is working more competently in Occupied Kashmir. Jaish-e Muhammad has engendered discord among mujahideen.' Said Bazdad, an office bearer of Harkatul Mujahideen in Lia district,

Punjab, said: 'Jamiat Ulema Islam helps us more because we had a special role in jihad in Afghanistan and in helping Taliban, and because we dare to look the Americans in the eye. As far as the way of belief is concerned, every individual has his own way; there is no harm if a group has its own way of belief. A particular way of belief accentuates one's identity. The leadership of Jamiat Ulema Islam is even-handed in this regard.'

On the whole, as far as its jihadi policy is concerned, Jamiat Ulema Islam always displayed softness towards Afghanistan and the Taliban. Statements of Maulana Fazlur Rahman like the following have been published several times: 'The battle in Kashmir is for land. We prefer jihad in Afghanistan than in Kashmir.'

Tablighi Jamat

The founder of Tablighi Jamat was Maulana Ilyas of Mewat who founded it to draw ordinary Muslims to religion. Now this Jamat has spread to different parts of the world. Tablighi Jamat claims itself to be non-political and non-sectarian, but most of its adherents are from Hanfi-Deobandi persuasion. However, most Deobandi political and sectarian organisations support its activities, even though many ulema from Deoband are opposed to the way it functions. It is quite popular among common people. The leaders of Tablighi Jamat are against participation in politics, and prefer *tablighi* jihad (self-purification) to military jihad. They have condemned militant jihad in Afghanistan and Kashmir on several occasions. But Tablighi Jamat is proving to be an unwitting ally of jihadi and sectarian organisations. There is no doubt that because of its efforts, ordinary Muslims come to mosques in large numbers where they are exposed to mujahideen from sectarian and jihadi organisations. I have come across many mujahideen whose first association was with Tablighi Jamat. When they join jihadi/sectarian organisations, they severe their connection with Tablighi Jamat and come to regard Tablighi Jamat's works as secondary.

Tablighi Jamat has a six-point agenda that must be followed rigorously by each member:

1. *Kalma* (Profession of faith)
2. *Namaz* (Prayer)
3. *Zikr* (Special prayers/mutterings)
4. *Ikram Walidain* (Services to parents)
5. *Ikram Muslimeen* (Services to Muslims)
6. *Dawat O Tabligh* (Invitation to religion, and Preaching)

Many ulema from Deoband do not agree with Tablighi Jamat's elders when they describe the merits of *dawa* and *tabligh* in exaggerated terms and they criticise it on this count.

The durations of *tablighi* journeys (when people leave their home and go preaching in the company of Maulanas) may be three days, ten days, forty days (*chilla*), four months, six months, one year, and the entire life. The composition of *tablighi* groups is done by the *markaz* (centre) at Raiwind. Generally, the groups doing a journey of four months to one year are sent abroad. The entire expense is borne by the participating members.

Majlis Siyana al-Muslimeen

Majlis Siyana al-Muslimeen is the *tablighi* organisation of Hanfi-Deobandi school of thought in Pakistan. Its founder was Maulana Ashraf Ali Thanwi. It was founded in 1929 (in undivided India). According to Maulana Wakil Ahmad Sherwani, 'Majlis Siyana al-Muslimeen is not a political organisations but a reform movement that invites people to become true Muslims and follow religious tenets in their pristine form. It teaches people to be true human beings so that they can do good to other human beings.' The position of Majlis Siyana al-Muslimeen regarding Tablighi Jamat is that Tablighi Jamat is concentrating on a limited number of points whereas Majlis Siyana al-Muslimeen encompasses the entire sharia.

Majlis Siyana al-Muslimeen was born in Pakistan twenty-six years ago, founded by Maulana Jalil Ahmad Sherwani under the patronage of Mufti Mohammad Amar Tasari who was the founder of Jamia Ashrafiya. Now, its president is Maulana Abdullah, principal of Jamia Ashrafiya, Lahore. Its vice-president is Maulana Nazir Ahmad, principal, Jamia Islamia Imdadiya, Faisalabad. Its branches are working in the madrasas of Jamia Ashrafiya in Multan and Peshawar.

Majlis Siyana al-Muslimeen publishes *tablighi* literature. It also arranges for discourses. *Tablighi* journeys are also organised. It also publishes a monthly, *Al-Siana*. The Majlis tries to appoint at least one preacher in each Deobandi madrasas who should do only preaching and be paid a salary. It organises an annual gathering, generally in March, in Jamia Ashrafiya, Lahore, for three days. Though the crowd here is smaller than in the annual gathering of Tablighi Jamat, important Deobandi ulema from India and Pakistan, particularly the disciples of Maulana Ashraf Ali Thanwi, participate in it.

Fundamentally, Majlis Siyana al-Muslimeen is working to propagate the thoughts of Maulana Ashraf Ali Thanwi. As opposed to Tablighi Jamat, it has a political angle that is expressed from time to time. Its stand is different from that of Jamiat Ulema Islam in that, rather than sharing power it stresses the reform of politicians as a means to establish an Islamic state. With this end in view it writes letters to politicians. The editorials of its mouthpiece, *Al-Siana*, can help one know its political, social, and religious positions.

The first issue of *Al-Siana* came out in 1990 on the theme 'Reform of the government'. The editorial exhorted: 'The current government should change its approach and turn towards God. If the government moves in the right direction, common people will automatically follow the right path.' The editorial of June 1992 issue is on the tension between Ahmad Shah Masood and Gulbuddin Hikmatyar: 'Janab Gulbuddin Hikmatyar is a strong and wise leader. The people of Afghanistan need a leader like him. But because of his stay in Pakistan and being influenced by Pakistani politics, he thought that he would be able to conquer Kabul all by himself. However, Commander Ahmad Shah Masood, because of his experience and military

strength, was more deserving of this honour.' The
October 1996 issue was on Taliban: 'Among the different
political configuration that formed government in
Kabul from time to time, Taliban is the only entity that
came to power not as a result of some agreement but
on the basis of its strength. That is why they are free to
take any decision.'

Jamiat Isha't Al-Tauheed Wal-Sunnah, Pakistan

Jamiat Isha't Al-Tauheed Wal-Sunnah, Pakistan, is an
important religious organisation of Deobandi school of
thought, based on sectarian values. It is the biggest
organisation of the *mamati* group of Deobandi school.
Its foundation was laid in 1957 in Mianwali, Punjab,
by one Maulana Husain Ali who was an alumnus of
Deoband. However, Jamiat Isha't Al-Tauheed Wal-
Sunnah was given an organised structure by Maulana
Syed Inayatullah Shah Bukhari, who spread its area of
influence to upper Punjab and Frontier Province. Its
objective is revealed in its name. It not only regards the
Barelvis as apostates, but also casts aspersions on the
hayati group of Deobandis. Its current amir is Maulana
Syed Ziaullah Shah Bukhari. Following is an extract
from his address that points to the aims and objectives
of this organisation:

> If those who are a stain on the Deobandi school of
> thought cast arrows at us, Jamiat Isha't Al-Tauheed
> will raise a tumult that would soon turn into a storm.
> I will draw your attention to the fact that in this
> country members of 'Ahl-e Sunnat Wal-Jamat' are
> busy leading people ashtray. There was a time when

this organisation was known as the 'caravan of truth', but now it has become a den of grave-worshippers, grave-traders and evil-doers. Deoband's fame had spread because it had become a byword for disseminating awareness and education among the masses. But a time came when some Deobandi scholars had to form Jamiat Isha't Al-Tauheed Wal-Sunnah to let people know what Deobandism is. These elders had their stints in Ahrar (party) and Jamiat Ulema, Deoband. When they felt that some people were misusing the name of Deoband for un-Islamic ends, they founded Jamiat Isha't Al-Tauheed Wal-Sunnah. Hazrat Shahji (Syed Ataullah Shah Bukhari) had said once: 'When members of Ahrar made a heretic the president of the Jamiat, we protested and said that we who were the disciples of Husain Ali could not accept him as the president. And that is why we pulled out.' In the past, our elders pulled out from the organisation because there were elements there who could not put up with elders. The situation is the same even today. Several Deobandi organisations like Tahaffuz Khatm Nabuwat, Sipah Sahaba, Tablighi Jamat have so much aversion to us that they do not even invite anyone from Jamiat Isha't Al-Tauheed Wal-Sunnah to their meetings and conferences.

It is evident from the above extract how extreme they are in their sectarian views. Jamiat Isha't Al-Tauheed does not take part in politics directly, but plays some role in its area of influence at the time of election. What is surprising is that it never supports candidates of any religious group, such as Jamiat Ulema Islam. It normally supports Muslim League candidates or candidates with a greater chance of winning, and uses their political clout afterwards. For example, in Sargodha, for the last four elections it has supported the Muslim League candidate, Choudhury Abdul Hameed (ex-mayor, who has been indicted in corruption charges), and used his clout in its clash with the Barelvis. Jamiat Isha't is always consulted before granting the route of the mourning procession during Muharram.

Jamiat Isha't Al-Tauheed Wal-Sunnah is not in favour of establishing regular offices, but uses mosques and madrasas for this purpose. Its area of influence extends to the districts of Gujrat, Mandi Bahauddin, Sargodha, Khushab, Mianwali, Bhakkar, and Rawalpindi. In Frontier Province it has its presence in Naoshehra and Peshawar. There is no trend of regular membership in it even though membership exists in associations that are allied to it. The following madrasas and mosques are the important centres amongst the fifty mosques and madrasas in Punjab and the fifteen in Frontier Province that the Jamiat is managing.

JAMA MASJID BUKHARI, SHAH FAISAL GATE, GUJRAT

Syed Ziaullah Shah Bukhari, the amir of Jamiat Isha't Al-Tauheed Wal-Sunnah, is the *khateeb* of this mosque. There is also a madrasa, Jamia Ziaul Islam, attached to this mosque. Its manager is Sahibzada Syed Shafaullah Bukhari. There are about a hundred students here.

JAMIA MASJID HANAFIYA, BLOCK NO. 18, SARGODHA

Jamiat Isha't Al-Tauheed Wal-Sunnah has an important centre in the district of Sargodha. Maulana Shamsul Haq Bandyalui is the *khateeb* here. There is also a madrasa, Jamia Ziaul Uloom, attached to the mosque. Its manager is Maulana Ziaul Haq Bandyalui. The madrasa also houses the office of Maktaba Hasina that publishes the Jamiat's literature.

JAMA MASJID AMIR MUAVIA, WATER SUPPLY ROAD, SARGODHA

Jamiat Isha't Al-Tauheed Wal-Sunnah's real strength in Sargodha is evident in this mosque. Its amir is the central leader, Maulana Ataullah Bandyalui. A madrasa is attached to this mosque also which is a branch of Jamia Ziaul Uloom. A large crowd gathers here for the Friday address.

JAMA MASJID ISHA'T AL-TAUHEED WAL-SUNNAH, NAZD GIRLS' NORMAL SCHOOL, LALA MOOSA

The Jamiat's mouthpiece, Naghma Tauheed, Gujrat, is published from here. The editor is Mohammad Abdul Ghaffar.

JAMIA ABI HURAIRA, BRANCH POST OFFICE, KHALIQABAD, NAOSHEHRA DISTRICT, FRONTIER PROVINCE

The Jamiat has an important madrasa in Naoshehra.

MADRASA JAWAHARUL QURAN, RAWALPINDI

This madrasa is an important centre of the Jamiat at Rawalpindi. Its manager is Maulana Mohammad Afzal who is also the assistant secretary of Jamiat Isha't Al-Tauheed Wal-Sunnah.

Allied Organisations

Jamiat Isha't Al-Tauheed Wal-Sunnah has two important allied organisations.

Naojawanan Tauheed O Sunnat, Pakistan

This organisation works among the youth, particularly among the students of madrasas. Its chief secretary is Maulana Shakir Mahmood. It has the same aims and objectives as those of Jamiat Isha't Al-Tauheed Wal-Sunnah. There is just one difference – this organisation works at the very grass roots and arranges for lessons in the Holy Koran and religious assemblies. It works more efficiently in Gujrat, Mandi Bahauddin, and Lala Moosa and plays dominant role in providing human resource for central conferences and rallies. It has a troupe of armed guards that provide security to its office bearers.

Besides young ulema and students, ordinary people can also participate in its activities and become regular members. However, one has to be an Islamic scholar to be a member of Jamiat Isha't Al-Tauheed Wal-Sunnah. Common people cannot become its members. There have been allegations against Naojawanan Tauheed O Sunnat of trying to occupy the mosques of other persuasions. Rival organisations characterise it as the militant wing of Jamiat Isha't.

Tahreek Difah Sahaba

The amir of Tahreek Difah Sahaba is Ataullah Badyalui who is from Sargodha. Its important centres can be found in Sargodha, Khushab, and Mianwali. Among its main objectives are preventing publication of literature maligning the Prophet's companion by the Shias and stopping their 'atrocities'. One important thing about Tahreek Difah Sahaba is that it was

147

founded in 1987; it was the period when Sipah Sahaba had gained in strength in Jhang, the neighbouring district of Sargodha. Sipah Sahaba had the same objectives as Tahreek Difah Sahaba. But Sipah Sahaba had the majority of *hayati* members and for achieving their ends they were ready to align with other organisations, particularly Barelvis. But Tahreek Difah Sahaba gave the slogan that it would fight on two fronts: against Shiism and against Barelvism, which according to it were two sides of the same coin. Tahreek Difah Sahaba is the prominent organisation of the *mamati* group of Deobandis, and in the districts of Sargodha, Mandi Bahauddin, Gujrat, Khushab, and Mianwali, this group is in majority. That is why Sipah Sahaba could not spread fast in these areas. For a long period Tahreek Difah Sahaba had a strong hold in these areas, and proved itself to be a strong rival to the Shia organisations. It gained greater and faster acceptability amongst the people than Jamiat Isha't Al-Tauheed Wal-Sunnah. It was run in a very organised way, down to the neighbourhood level in different districts. It had its students' wing in colleges. Lessons in the Holy Koran and assemblies were organised with great fanfare and the headquarters of Tahreek Difah Sahaba in Jama Masjid Amir Muavia buzzed with fierce activity. It also got the support of various political powers.

According to a local journalist in Sargodha, behind the considerable influence and thorough organisational structure of Tahreek Difah Sahaba lay the hands of foreign agencies. The objective was to save the neighbouring districts from the influence of Sipah

Sahaba, and to divide the Deobandis and erode their strength. Like its meteoric rise, this Tahreek had a rapid decline. According to a member of Jamiat Isha't Al-Tauheed Wal-Sunnah, Hafiz Abdul Ghaffar of Sargodha, the Jamiat gained from this decline and grew stronger.

The jihadi view of Jamiat Isha't Al-Tauheed Wal-Sunnah is similar to that of other Deobandi organisations. It supports all Deobandi jihadi organisations. However, it extends strongest support to Harkatul Mujahideen as most of its members belong to the same religious persuasion.

Tanzeemul Ikhwan, Pakistan

Tanzeemul Ikhwan, Pakistan, is an organisation that pertains to the Deobandi-Naqshbandiya school of thought. It was founded in 1986. Maulana Akram Awan, its amir, is known for his emotional speeches. In 1998 he vowed death for the imposition of sharia in Pakistan, and in 2000 he had gathered his disciples to march together to Islamabad and lay a siege of the government till sharia was announced. However, he had a discussion with the federal minister, religious activities, Ahmad Ghazi, after which he changed his position.

BACKGROUND

Tanzeemul Ikhwan is different from other Deobandi organisations in that it stresses self-purification through muttering of prayers and meditation. It not only lays importance on loud, collective prayers; in fact, this special feature has become its identity. A vast majority of Hanfi-Deobandi school of thought (particularly *mamati* group) does not approve of loud prayer (*zikr*) and declares it un-Islamic. For this, and for other mystical predilections, this organisation is not very popular among Deobandi ulema and organisations. For every member of Tanzeemul Ikhwan, initiation by amir is essential. After initiation, the person gets inducted into the Owaisia Naqshbandiya sect. This sect was founded in Pakistan by Maulana Allah Yar from Chakwal. He gave permission to Maulana Akram Awan for mass initiation. This sect became popular in Chakwal, Jhelum, and their surrounding areas. This area being the nursery of Pakistani army, the disciples of Owaisia sect can be found in large numbers in the army. In the beginning it was a non-political organisation so that along with the retired army men, in-service officers also became its members. In 1995, during the Benazir Bhutto regime when Major General Mustansar and Major Zahir Abbasi started a movement within the army for imposition of sharia, Tanzeemul Ikhwan supported it. It had a role to play in that revolt.

In 1998, Maulana Akram began to reorganise it on the plane of a political organisations and started paying attention to popular struggles to bring about Islamic revolution.

ISLAMABAD MARCH

With this end in view Maulana Akram gathered six thousand disciples in Manara, Chakwal, in October 2000, and warned General Musharraf through a letter: 'If you do not implement sharia, I shall march to

Islamabad with thirty lakh disciples. We shall be unarmed. We shall have the Holy Koran in our hands, rosary in our neck and *kalma* on our tongue. But if anyone attempt to aim his gun at us we shall snatch it and shall enter the city by force.' At first, 26 December 2000 was set as the deadline for imposing sharia. Then, according to the organisation sources, it was postponed to 7 March 2001, at the request of the corps commander at Rawalpindi. The government made arrangements to stop the march and a reconciliation committee was formed. According to a report published in the organisation's monthly journal, *Al-Murshid*:

> In the last ten days of the month of Ramzan when the government did not give any positive reply, Amir Akram Awan ordered his disciples to spread out through the length and breadth of the country to prepare for marching towards Islamabad. 25 December was set as the date for the proposed march. The members were instructed to have copies of the Holy Koran hanging from their neck, have rosaries in their hands, and mutter prayers as they marched to Islamabad and lay siege to it till the time sharia is announced.
>
> Amir Akram Awan had offered such training to his disciples that they were ready to lay down their lives for the imposition of sharia. They had decided that either sharia will be imposed in the country or they will become martyrs for it. Seeing the support of the people the government had to get in touch with Amir Akram Awan. The government realised that these people were not hungry for power; and if the storm broke out, it would be difficult for the government to

151

control it. Helpless, a team of the federal government reached Manara on 24 December. The team had a four-hour-long meeting with Amir Akram Awan. After mutual discussions, the committee, with the permission of General Musharraf, reached an agreement about the imposition of sharia. A committee was formed to give it the final form. It was decided that a Qaumi Ulema Council will be formed to suggest practical measures towards implementation of sharia in all walks of life. The representatives of the government and Tanzeemul Ikhwan conducted negotiations in a very cordial atmosphere. Both expressed their sincerest wishes for national security. Meanwhile, the participants in the discussions said their prayers led by Amir Akram Awan. In the light of the undertakings by the government, Amir Akram Awan suspended the 26 December march.

OBJECTIVES

According to its published charter, Tanzeemul Ikhwan has the following structure:

Political Structure

The Islamic *shura* shall be restored; representatives will be selected through adult franchise; changing any Islamic article or any fundamental Islamic principle through the method of constitutional amendment will be considered treason.

Economic Structure

Islamic Economic Advisory Board shall be constituted which in turn will propose measures of investment without stocks and shares. Steps will be taken to do away with interest at the national and international level.

Legal Structure
A perfectly independent legal framework shall be put in place based on the Holy Koran and Sunnah. Qazi courts will be founded.

Educational Structure
An institute shall be established at the national level to prepare syllabi from a Pakistani perspective for different levels within one year. It will apply throughout the country without any exception. Provision for Arabic learning shall be made from the primary level to facilitate the study of Quran.

Social Structure
The centrality of mosques shall be restored, honour for the ulema and their social status will be increased. An elaborate inventory of 'dos' and 'don'ts' will be made.

Agricultural Structure
Peasants will be informed about the latest agricultural research and will be provided subsidies. The owners of land and the tenants will be made aware of their rights and duties.

Industrial Structure
All efforts will be made for industrial growth. The monopoly of a few families on industrial borrowings will be abolished. A national policy, based on Islamic principles, shall be framed for better relations between the owners and the workers.

Defence Structure
The army shall be imbued with the ideal of jihad. They will be trained not in view of war but of their spiritual uplift. The standard of living of army men at all level shall be improved.

Administration
All federal and provincial administration shall be freed from the colonial legacy and reorganised so that it can serve in the best interest of the people.

External Affairs
The external policy of the country shall be made bold and courageous. No external pressure shall be entertained. Relation with Islamic countries shall be strengthened.

ORGANISATIONAL STRUCTURE
Tanzeemul Ikhwan has no strong organisational structure. Most of its activities centre around assemblies of religious prayers and meditation. The time for these is set throughout the country. Tanzeemul Ikhwan pays considerable interest to education, and founded a few educational institutions. The whole organisation revolves around the personality of Maulana Akram Awan. Owaisa Housing Society and Darul Irfan, Manara, Chakwal, are the nerve centre of the organisation. Its general secretary is Colonel (Retd) Matlub Husain.

The following departments of Tanzeemul Ikhwan are important:

Al-Falah Foundation
The major part of Tanzeemul Ikhwan's expenses are disbursed through Al-Falah Foundation. Its welfare schemes are concentrated on the northern areas. The Foundation's schemes are as follows:

- To provide medical facilities in far-flung areas. The Foundation organises medical camps in different

areas.
- To provide medicines, warm clothes, etc., to the needy.
- To provide scholarships and books to needy students.

'One reason why Al-Falah Foundation is so active in the northern areas is that Agha Khan Foundation of the Ismaili sect and foreign missionaries are active in those areas and draw people to their faith by providing odd services to them. Al-Falah Foundation is trying to redress this.' (Introductory Brochure, Tanzeemul Ikhwan)

In this context, the in charge of Tanzeemul Ikhwan in Lahore, Mohammad Tahir, said that as the resources increase, they will widen the scope of the Foundation's activities.

Al-Ikhwaat

Al-Ikhwaat is the women wing of Tanzeemul Ikhwan whose centre is situated in Lahore Defence area, Phase III. Its secretary is Bashari Ejaz. It is an effective department of Tanzeemul Ikhwan that tries to draw women from the influential strata to it. Several film actresses and poetesses are among its members.

It is said that the main objective of Al-Ikhwaat is to restore the lost dignity of women. According to a published brochure of Al-Ikhwaat, it exhorts women to come to the way of the Lord. Muttering of prayers is prescribed as a means to this end. There is a regular course for that. The preachers of Al-Ikhwaat make rounds of homes, schools, and colleges to spread their message. The brochure states that Al-Ikhwaat's lowest unit consists of thirteen members. The total members of Al-Ikhwaat in entire Pakistan, is supposed to be around seven thousand. It is obligatory for each member to pay ten rupees as admission fee and contribute 100 rupees annually to it. It plays a major role in collecting funds for Tanzeemul Ikhwan.

Al-Ikhwan Jihad Force
The founding of Al-Ikhwan Jihad Force was announced by Maulana Akram Awan in 1999. This is the jihadi wing of Tanzeemul Ikhwan. Its base camp is situated in Rawlakot and Bagh, and Lashkar-e Tayyaba provides training to its members. While laying its foundation, Maulana Akran Awan had said: 'By the grace of God, we have played an extremely crucial role in the war in Afghanistan which was not publicised because we did not take part in any organised jihad. We sent people for extremely sensitive work in Kashmir, but it was not known because we have no organisation there. We lent our best human resource to the organisations that are working there. Now we are beginning work in this area with Al-Ikhwan Jihad Force.'

However, Al-Ikhwan Jihad Force could not shape up as an independent organisation. It has remained a source of material and human assistance to Lashkar-e Tayyaba. According to Major (Retd) Maqbool Ahmad Shah, deputy amir of Tanzeemul Ikhwan, 'We coordinate with Lashkar-e Tayyaba to provide human and material resource for jihad in Kashmir.'

Saqara Education System

Saqara Education System is an affiliated organisation of Tanzeemul Ikhwan whose central office is located in

Darul Irfan, Manara, Chakwal. According to Saqara's brochure, 'It is an ideal educational system, combining the old and the new, for the making of a better Muslim and a better Pakistani.' The following institutes are working under it:

1. Saqara Academy (High School), Darul Irfan, Manara
2. Saqara Academy (for girls), Darul Irfan, Manara
3. Saqara High School Township, Lahore
4. Saqara College Township, Lahore

INFORMATION AND PUBLICATION DIVISION

Tanzeemul Ikhwan has a publication division under which a printing house, Idara Naqshbandiya Owaisia, works and it has published more than a hundred books so far in Urdu and English. It has been printing the monthly, *Al-Murshid*, for the last eighteen years. Choudhury Ghulam Sarwar is in charge of this division.

TREASURY DEPARTMENT

The members make contributions to the organisation according to their capacity, apart from the annual fee. Saqara Education System and the publication division are profit-making concerns. Non-resident Pakistanis also contribute generously. This well-organised department pays special attention to raising funds through contributions. The amir of the organisation has the discretion to use fund as he deems fit.

NETWORK

The disciples of Maulana Akram Awan are spread out all over the country, particularly in army and civil bureaucracy. These disciples are regarded as members of Tanzeemul Ikhwan. Tanzeem's central office is located in College Road Township, Lahore. The network of Tanzeemul Ikhwan is not well organised and the records are not up to date. The number of disciples is larger in Lahore, Gujrat, Kharian, Boreywalah, Jhelum, and Rawalpindi in Punjab; in Naoshehra and Chatral in Frontier Province; and in Karachi and Hyderabad in Sindh. One can find Tanzeem's offices in these places. Apart from Manara, Chakwal, the following are some other important centres:

1. Askari Masjid, South Colony, Khariyan
2. Jamia Anwarul Quran, Chowk 142/E-B, Wahari
3. Masjid Cantonment Board, Tufail Road, Naoshehra
4. New Masjid Darul Irfan, Mabrit, Chatral
5. Darul Irfan, Behind Abdullahpur Wagon Stand, Railway Colony, Faisalabad
6. Central Jama Masjid, Toba tek Singh
7. Owaisa Safariyat, Al-Karam Square, Liaqatabad, Karachi
8. Masjid Tubi, Phase I, Maler Cantt, Karachi
9. Jama Masjid Abu Bakr, Phase II, Defence Housing Authority, Karachi
10. Masjid Al-Khizr, Old Ghallamandi, Gojrah
11. Owaisa, College Road Township, Lahore
12. Masjid Shaan al-Islam, 2 Gulbarg III, Lahore
13. Al-Ikhwan Jihad Force, College Road, Nazd al-Noor Hotel, Bagh, Azad Kashmir.

Darul Irfan, Chakwal District

Darul Irfan is located near Manara, Chakwal. Besides

being the spiritual centre of the Owaisa Naqshbandiya sect, it is also the centre of Tanzeemul Ikhwan where its offices are located. Attached to it is also a residential area meant for the members of Tanzeemul Ikhwan. The annual meeting of Tanzeemul Ikhwan takes place here, usually from 13 July to 13 August.

Owaisa Housing Society, Lahore

Owaisa Housing society which is located in College Road Township is affiliated to Punjab Cooperative Housing Society. Its management is structured on the same line as that of Markaz Mansoora of Jamat-e Islami. Apart from residential blocks there are provincial offices, the publication division, and the offices of Saqara Education System. There is also a Jama Masjid.

MEMBERSHIP FORM

The membership form of Tanzeemul Ikhwan is notable for its general declaration and for conditions it stipulates for the members. The following declaration is printed on it:

> I want to be a member of Al-Ikhwan. I shall obey its Charter fully. My only objective is the pleasure of God. I and my family will abide by the sharia, and I will request my friends and relatives to do the same. In all matters of conflict or dispute, I will abide by the decision taken by Al-Ikhwan.

Tahreek Nifaz-e Shariat Muhammadi (Banned)
(Movement for Imposition of Muhammadi Sharia)

Maulana Sufi Muhammad and his thirty companions

of Tahreek Nifaz-e Shariat Muhammadi were awarded a seven-year jail sentence by the special court established in the Central Jail, Dera Ismail Khan. This was because, despite the government's orders to the contrary, he had led six thousand tribal Pathans to Afghanistan to help the Taliban. Most of them either died or were taken prisoners. Sufi Muhammad had managed to return to Pakistan with only seventy companions. Before this, restrictions were imposed on Tahreek Nifaz-e Shariat Muhammadi (Malakand) on 13 January 2002.

BACKGROUND

For the historical background of the founding of Tahreek Nifaz-e Shariat Muhammadi, we shall have to go back to Malakand division's history and politics since 1969. Till 1969, Sawat, Dir, and Chitral functioned as princely states governed by rulers who were independent about all internal matters of administration. They had their own legal system. Sharia laws operated in Sawat through Qazi. But according to Maulana Zahid al-Rashidi, 'With the passage of time the institution of Qazi was corrupted by bribes and personal influences. One did not hear good things about many Qazis. But people got cheap justice, and cases were disposed of promptly.'

In 1969, when the independent status of the three above states came to an end, and they were merged with the state of Pakistan, the Constitution became operative there and the administrative and legal structures changed according to the Constitution. The three former states were given the status of districts. In

Dir, an armed movement against the government broke out in 1975 regarding the royalty of the forests. To make the movement more effective, restoration of the earlier legal system, according to which the right to royalty and illegal felling of trees went in favour of timber merchants, was included in the charter of demands. This made the movement massively popular, and Zulfiqar Ali Bhutto had to impose a new legal system through FATA regulations in Malakand division encompassing the three districts of Sawat, Dir, and Chitral, and beyond.

The lawyers of Malakand challenged this regulation in the Peshawar High Court on the plea that it was against the fundamental rights and legal protection of citizens. They demanded that the same legal system functioning in entire Pakistan should operate here also. In the first phase of the rule of Aftab Sher Pao, chief minister, Frontier Province, the High Court declared the regulation null and void. The government of Aftab Sher Pao challenged the High Court's decision in the Supreme Court which upheld the decision of the High Court.

It was at this time that Sufi Muhammad had begun his Tahreek Nifaz-e Shariat Muhammadi which demanded that the gap created by the Supreme Court's decision to annul FATA regulations should be filled in by imposing sharia in place of modern legal system. He demanded its immediate implementation in Malakand division.

Tahreek Nifaz-e Shariat Muhammadi was founded on 10 May 1989 from Dir district. In the first election of the organisation, Sufi Muhammad became the amir and Abdul Wahid al-Maruf, the president. The initial objective of the Tahreek was to establish peace and harmony in the people of the area who had turned into one another's enemy because of fierce political divisions and disagreements.

The background of Sufi Muhammad, its leader, is that he had been associated with Jamat-e Islami for a long period; he was also the District Council chairman at one time. But he has remained unattached to any organisation since 1981. Rather, he had decreed that establishment of religious organisations and vote politics were not only impermissible (haram) but a stumbling block in the way of the imposition of sharia. He had been the principal, Darul Uloom Miran, Lal Qila, Dir, and was known as a conservative maulana in religious circles.

On 9 May 1990, the members of Tahreek Nifaz-e Shariat Muhammadi pitched a camp in Tamargira, Dir district, and demanded imposition of sharia. However, even after their agitation for twelve days when the government did not pay any attention to them they declared imposition of sharia in the area on their own. After this agitation, they built their office and began to extend their area of influence. Muhammad Khalid Syed Ali Shah from Sawat joined the movement and played a vital role in spreading the movement in all corners of Sawat. The influence of the movement began to be felt in the entire Malakand division and the members began to work in mosques secretly.

Then members of the Tahreek Nifaz-e Shariat Muhammadi arranged a demonstration (dharna) on the GT Road. The Frontier Province government formed a consultative committee but Sufi Muhammad and other leaders refused to participate in any discussion. They stood firm on their one point agenda of sharia imposition. In this demonstration, about 30,000–40,000 people lay down on the road for seven consecutive days. The arrangements of the demonstration were done by the organisers on the same footing, as must have been done in times of jihad in earlier times.

On 17 May 1994, the governor of Frontier Province issued an ordinance declaring imposition of Muhammadi sharia in Malakand division. The ordinance was to remain in force for four months. After the expiry of this period when it was being made into an Act, members of Tahreek Nifaz-e Shariat Muhammadi again came out for a massive demonstration. But this time the government did not allow them to gather at one place. As a result, the crowd gathered at different places in many districts and demonstrated against the government. At some places they turned violent and targeted the army. A Badiuzzaman, MP, People's Party, died in a clash. The members of the Tahreek occupied many government buildings including airports. Eventually Maulana Sufi Muhammad surrendered himself to the army and agreed to cooperate with it. With army officers he made rounds of all the Tahreek centres and asked members to return home. An agreement was arrived at between the government and Tahreek Nifaz-e Shariat Muhammadi according to which the Tahreek's demand for sharia was accepted. On 26 November 1994, the law secretary of Frontier Province wrote a letter of confirmation to

Maulana Sufi Muhammad that also bore the signature of the state home secretary, Ayub Khan. The letter ran as follows:

Respected Maulana Sufi Muhammad bin Al-Hazrat Hasan Sahib,

Assalamu alaikum!

You will remember that there was a discussion in Timargira between the State Chief Secretary, Home Secretary and you regarding sharia regulation 1994 in Malakand Division. In this regulation, 'shariat' has been defined as it was defined in the Imposition of Shariat Act 1991. That is, the orders are according to the letters and spirit of Quran and Sunnah. All Islamic laws will be applied in this area under this regulation. Moreover, an Islamic legal framework will be instituted for administering Islamic laws. In this regard, the post of Qazi will be introduced according to this regulation.

During the meeting you had stressed that a Qazi should be appointed in each tehsil and these appointees should be well versed in Islamic jurisprudence.

After due consideration the government has agreed to the proposal of tehsil Qazis who will administer both civil and criminal laws, and that students passing out of Islamic university will be qualified for this job. To facilitate this, suitable changes are being made in the recruitment laws. The life and duties of the Qazi will be according to Quran and Sunnah. In urgent cases, those legal officers will be appointed Qazis who have completed an approved course of sharia laws. The Qazi has been invested with all powers that will enable him to decide cases from the police and the administration according to Islamic laws and award punishment or reward as warranted.

To bridge the legal gap in Malakand Division is our collective responsibility. I am sure that in the new draft of Shariat Regulation Act (PATA), 1994, all provisions have been made that will ensure that the area becomes an abode of prosperity and peace. I implore you to show the moral courage that the nation expects from you, and cooperate with us to implement the new system. In the light of experience, if changes are needed in it from time to time, suitable steps will be taken in this regard.

The government has further decided to implement the system, put in place in Malakand Division, in the district of Kohistan as well, concurrently.

In the light of the above governmental decision, the governor of Frontier Province promulgated the ordinance on 1 December 1994. After its implementation Maulana Ahd Al-Rashdi, general secretary, Pakistan Shariat Council went for a survey of Malakand division. The monthly *Al-Sharia*, Gujranwala, published a detailed account of his visit written by him. An extract from it is being presented here that throws light on several aspects of the Tahreek:

It was greatly disturbing for me to meet four important members of the Advisory Committee (Majlis-e Shura) of Tahreek Nifaz-e Shariat Muhammadi from 10–12 December. None of them had yet read the regulation. They reported that it was not read out even in the Advisory Committee's meeting. This was not an encouraging sign.

ANOTHER EXTRACT

To unduly stress secondary or marginal issues during the movement to such an extent that they become identified as its main concern or motto may cause more harm than good to the movement. For example, it was stressed so much during the movement that right-hand drive is preferred according to sharia that a member proudly said to me that he had insulted the English laws by resorting to right-hand drive for a full day in Mangora. It is not necessary; even if any sharia angle is involved here, it is of a very minor nature. To emphasise such things results in trivialising the movement. Similarly, the issue of beard comes up again and again. To keep beard is a tradition of the Prophet (Sunnah) and every Muslim should respect it. It is also our responsibility to save this tradition from the target of ridicule and insult. It was heard a couple of days ago that on the demand of leaders of Tahreek Nifaz-e Shariat Muhammadi, the government was looking for officers with beard so that they could be appointed in Malakand division. We feel that this is a sure way of making the Sunnah ridiculous. The administrative and legal system remained colonial; only the officers will be bearded so that all the dirt and filth of the system will be hidden behind this holy screen.

SOME IMPORTANT FACTS

When Tahreek Nifaz-e Shariat Muhammadi resorted to agitation in April 2001, the governor of Frontier

Province, Lieutenant General R Syed Iftikhar Hussain gave the following statement: 'In Malakand Division, the issue is not of sharia, but of non-custom-paid cars, illegal felling of trees and tax evasions.' (*Mashriq*, daily, Peshawar, 3 May 2001)

When I ascertained the opinion of people in Malakand division, the following facts came to light:

1. Whenever Tahreek Nifaz-e Shariat Muhammadi gives a call for agitation, the first to support it are the unions of transporters and timber merchants. Transporters stop plying vehicles and timber merchants declare a holiday for labourers.
2. There is a large number of non-custom-paid vehicles in Sawat, Chitral, Bajora Agency, Dir, and Boniar.
3. Agitations are normally held in tourist season resulting in considerable fall in the number of visiting tourists.
4. Because of lack of tourists, other money-making activities, i.e. felling trees and smuggling to Afghanistan and China get a fillip.
5. Transporters, timber merchants, and tribal chiefs do not want to pay taxes. They demand sharia so that they do not have to pay taxes. An office bearer of Al-Sawat Transport Foundation, Haji Ataullah, told me in Mengora: 'We will not give any tax as provided in the English law, as it is against sharia. If an Islamic government imposes *ashar* and *zakat*, we will certainly pay.'
6. The Hotel Association feels that these agitations are engineered by smugglers and timber merchants so

that they can conduct their dubious business when all the routes remain open. Zahid Ali Khan, a member of Al-Sawat Association, said: 'Tahreek Nifaz-e Shariat Muhammadi was the handiwork of agencies. We are very happy that restrictions have been imposed on it. Their agitations caused much harm to tourism and travel industries. In the last season, we could not even pay our staff. This movement had the backing of smugglers who took full advantage of the agitations. We are ready to pay tax. But the smugglers do not want to pay tax for the fear that the government will come to know their real trade.'

7. Azam Khan, an inhabitant of Mengora who worked as a woodcutter, said: 'Whenever there is an agitation, our master declares a holiday and asks us to go for demonstration. We do not get any work/wages for days. If the government agrees to their (the movement's) demand, thousands of poor people will be saved from dying.' On restrictions imposed, he said, 'Such restrictions were imposed so many times earlier. Many people died, but they do not give up. Let the season come, they will again come out.'

Tahreek Nifaz-e Shariat Muhammadi and Elections

Tahreek Nifaz-e Shariat Muhammadi has always opposed democracy and elections. However, in the municipal elections of 2000 it showed a different face. Aqeel Yusufzai, a senior reporter of the daily *Mashriq* from Peshawar, said: 'The Tahreek always called democracy a regime of the infidels, but some relatives of its central leaders participated in the last elections. As I come from Sawat I get to know the situation there. The son of Abdul Wahid Khan, considered the right hand of amir Sufi Muhammad, was running the campaign for the candidates supporting him. Jameel, the nephew of another leader of the Tahreek, Sultan Muhammad, fought the election. Another leader who was part of the Tahreek's discussion team fought the election and won. Malik Naobahar, their important leader, also fought the election. In this municipal election, the secretaries were elected from Jamat-e Islami, for both lower and upper levels, and they had the support of the victorious candidates of Tahreek Nifaz-e Shariat Muhammadi.'

Sufi Muhammad's expedition to Afghanistan proved a disaster, bringing down his popularity graph in Malakand and Dir. But the roots of Tahreek Nifaz-e Shariat Muhammadi are still deep in this area.

After Sufi Muhammad, Maulana Muhammad Alam has been made the officiating amir. Haji Nagin Khan, the Secretary General, Haji Gulfaraz, secretary from Dir, and Maulana Abdullah Haq, secretary from Sawat are all in jail.

Tahreek-e Taliban, Pakistan

This organisation was formed on the structure of Taliban in Afghanistan. Its leader is Mulla Muhammad Rahim. Its influence is limited to the tribal areas, especially Orkazai Agency. This Tahreek came to public notice when on 13 December 1998, its sharia court in Orkazai Agency sentenced a murder accused, Khayal Ghaffar, to death publicly. Before this, it had already put a ban on TV, VCR, and music. Hardly a week after sentencing Khayal Ghaffar to death, Taliban's posters appeared in the main markets of Peshawar and Cantt, where its Islamic agenda was articulated for Pakistan. According to the January issue of the monthly, *Newsline*:

> This posters also carried an insignia that showed two crossed swords, with the picture of The Holy Quran and kalma Tayyaba under it. The government had been criticised in the posters for taking an un-Quranic decision. The Tahreek's objectives have been spelt out through the objectives of sharia. It was written in the poster that punishment for crimes is a religious duty. But here murderers are not punished because of which murder has become a daily occurrence. Similarly, thieves do not have their hands chopped and that is why people's possessions are unsafe. This is an open revolt against the Quran. The objective of Tahreek-e Taliban is to make efforts for the imposition of Islamic laws and to remove all sources of obscenity and shamelessness from society. The poster contained no address or any other information.

The leaders of Tahreek-e Taliban have been successful in taking the movement to eighteen tribes who live in Orkazai Agency, and in some semi-tribal areas as well. Mulla Rahim denies any linkage of his organisation with the Taliban in Afghanistan. Of course, he says that he supports Taliban in their struggle in Afghanistan, and wishes to bring about an

Islamic system like them in the entire Pakistan, including the tribal areas.

Majlis Ahrar Islam, Pakistan

The objective of Majlis Ahrar Islam is evident in their slogan: 'God's rule, zindabad; democracy murdabad!' The written charter also corroborates this.

> All power emanates from God. Tauheed (belief in one Allah), Khatm Nabuwat (end of prophethood) and honour for the Prophet's Companions constitute our religion. Khilafat, consultation and consensus constitute our politics. Jihad is our pursuit. Allah's Pleasure and the Prophet's mediation constitute our aim.

Majlis Ahrar Islam is working in Pakistan according to the above charter. It is regarded as a very important non-political organisation of Deobandi school of thought.

ORGANISATIONAL NETWORK

Majlis Ahrar Islam's founder was Syed Ataullah Shah Bukhari who was a supporter of Indian nationalism. After the formation of Pakistan, it remained dormant for fifteen years. After the death of Syed Ataullah Shah Bukhari, his son Syed Ataul Mohsin became his successor and reorganised it in 1962. The management of the Majlis is in the hands of an eight-member consultative committee whose leader is called amir. Currently, Syed Ataul Memon Bukhari is its amir, and the secretary is Maulana Muhammad Ishaq.

Majlis Ahrar's network is spread throughout Pakistan, especially Punjab. Its presence is felt in the areas of Multan, Lahore, Toba tek Singh, Muzaffargarh,

Ohari, and Khanpur.

Two departments of the Majlis are effective:

1. Tabligh
2. Madrasas

Tahreek Tahaffuz Khatm Nabuwat (Department of Tabligh)

Tahreek Tahaffuz Khatm Nabuwat is the department of *tabligh* of the Majlis Ahrar Islam which is very active, so much so that it has become its identity marker.

Wafaq Al-Madaris Al-Ahrar

Syed Ataul Mohsin Bukhari had laid the foundation of this madrasa board under which thirty-four madrasas are working in Punjab. The central madrasa is located in Mamoora, Multan, and has its affiliation with the board. The examination system in all madrasas is based on the system followed here. The expenses in the madrasas (the list of madrasas given elsewhere) amount to thirty lakhs of rupees are borne and by the centre. These madrasas are the centres of activities of Majlis Ahrar and Tahreek Khatm Nabuwat.

Majlis Ahrar supports Sipah Sahaba. It not only endorses its point of view but also extends full cooperation to it. The Majlis claims that it had started the first jihadi movement in Kashmir against the Dogra regime. That is why it supports all jihadi organisations of Deobandi persuasion. Several teachers and students of Mamoora Madrasa are associated with jihadi organisations. Several students of this Mamoora

Madrasa, Meherban Colony, Multan, have been martyred in Occupied Kashmir.

Sipah Sahaba (Banned)

Sipah Sahaba is the biggest sectarian organisation of the Deobandi school of thought that was banned on 12 January 2002. But as an organisation, it is still active. It has the full patronage of Jamiat Ulema Islam. Since its inception to the point of being banned, 200 of its members and leaders were killed, while they have been involved in 1,200 incidents of sectarian clashes.

BACKGROUND

Sipah Sahaba was founded on 6 September 1985. Among its founders were Maulana Haq Nawaz Jhangvi, Maulana Ziaur Rahman Faruqi, Maulana Isarul Haq Qasmi, and Maulana Azam Tariq.

At the time of its inception it was christened 'Anjuman Sipah Sahaba', and Maulana Haq Nawaz Jhangvi, who was the deputy amir of Jamiat Ulema Islam in Punjab, was its supreme leader. Before the founding of Anjuman Sipah Sahaba, Maulana Haq Nawaz's fame rested on his fierce anti-Barelvism that reverberated through his eloquent speeches in Jhang and Punjab. He was given the title, 'Shahanshah of Addresses'. Many reasons are attributed to the founding of Sipah Sahaba. Among them the following three are the most important:

Founding of Tahreek-e Nifaz Ja'fariya

The march that Wafaq Ulema Shia and Imamia Students' Organisation had arranged in Islamabad on 6 July 1980 on the issue of a different set of laws for Shias

173

had compelled the martial law government to accede to their demands. This success encouraged Mufti Jafar Husain to lay the foundation of Tahreek-e Nifaz Fiqh Ja'fariya. The revolution in Iran and Iran government's patronage facilitated the growth of this organisation.

The emergence of a Shia organisation was noted with alarm in Sunni circles. As a reaction, Jamiat Ulema Islam and Jamiat Ulema Pakistan organised two big 'Ahl-e Sunnat Conferences' where discussions were held about the best ways to counter this. For three years, Deobandi and Barelvi organisations reflected over this. Finally, the deputy amir of Jamiat Ulema Islam (F) in Punjab, Maulana Haq Nawaz, laid the foundation of Sipah Sahaba in Jhang, even though at that time Jamiat Ulema Islam (F) and Tahreek-e Nifaz Ja'fariya were fighting together on the platform of MRD for the restoration of democracy.

Sunni Businessmen's Front Against Shia Landlords
The feudal system has been prevalent in Jhang for centuries. The majority of the feudal lords here is Shia whereas the business class and industrialists come from the Sunni sect. In Jhang and Cheneot the interests of these two sects come into direct conflict. A small instance of this is: In Jhung there is a transport company owned by a Sunni; to offer competition the Shia landlords founded a transport company. The two groups had tensions; they quarrelled at bus stations and robbed one another's buses. When the buses owned by the Sunni passed through the areas owned by Shia landlords, they were attacked. The Shia landlords were also active in politics. When Sipah Sahaba was formed the Sunni bus owner became its

strongest supporter and an office bearer.

Independent sources and police records confirm the fact that there were eighteen traders of Jhang behind the formation of Anjuman Sipah Sahaba. After its formation Maulana Haq Nawaz was invited and they discussed the organisation's aims and objectives with him. The traders wanted to give the organisation a religious colour that will ensure support of the Sunni majority against the Shias.

Maulana Haq Nawaz's fame rested on his ability to deliver virulent and provocative speeches. He was greatly suited to the post. The traders invested hugely in Anjuman Sipah Sahaba and it became successful. In his speeches, Maulana Haq Nawaz now made Shiism and feudalism his targets in place of Barelvism. A little after the founding of Anjuman Sipah Sahaba, the famous businessman of Jhang, Shaikh Yusuf became a member of the provincial assembly (MPA) with its support. After this the famous industrialist, Mian Iqbal's younger brother Mian Abid, became MPA from Sipah Sahaba's platform.

A Part of Ziaul Haq's Programme against the People's Party
According to a study, after assuming power, Ziaul Haq encouraged the formation of the Mohajir Qaumi Movement (MQM) in Karachi and Hyderabad, and Anjuman Sipah Sahaba in Punjab in order to scuttle the influence of the People's Party. Sipah Sahaba came out openly against the 'feudal' and 'Shia' Bhutto, and in this it was also helped by the secret services during Ziaul Haq's regime. According to the study, Ziaul Haq was unhappy about the Islamabad march by the Shias, and their attitude during the Pakistan visit of the

Iranian president in 1980 when they raised the slogan, 'Imam Khomeini zindabad; Ziaul Haq murdabad'. That is why he had resolved to undercut their strength.'

Meanwhile, in September 1980, war broke out between Iran and Iraq. The sympathy of Pakistan's Shia community was with Iran, and hundreds of youth from ISO went to Iran to help. On the other side, the anti-Shia ulema supported Iraq. This led to increased tension between the two groups. During haj that year the Iranian pilgrims demonstrated in Mecca against the Saudi government, and they had the support of Pakistani Shias. This led to a deterioration of relationship between Iran and Saudi Arabia. The Saudi government offered economic assistance to the anti-Shia organisations in Pakistan, while Shia organisations got assistance from Iran. Thus, the battle for the Gulf states was fought in Pakistan. This led to grave sectarian tensions and the enemies of Pakistan took full advantage of this.

Anjuman Sipah Sahaba and Sectarian Conflict

After its founding, Anjuman Sipah Sahaba had taken the position that the books published by the Shias contained scurrilous writings about the Prophet's companions, and that this was done at the instance of the Iranian government that wants to turn Pakistan into a Shia state. In the light of this, the aims and objectives of Sipah Sahaba contained the following:

1. To impose the tradition of Khilafat in Pakistan.
2. Pakistan should be declared a Sunni state.
3. The books that contained defamatory writings

about the Prophet's companions should be banned.

4. Shia ulema defaming the Prophet's companions should be punished.

Sipah Sahaba's aims and objectives provoked the Sunnis and the organisation grew in strength. The Shia-Sunni conflict in Jhang further inflamed the atmosphere in Punjab and that slowly spread throughout entire Pakistan. Maulana Haq Nawaz's virulent speeches and Shia ulema's provocative attitude added fuel to the fire. Sectarian violence started. During the years 1986–89 in Jhang district alone, there were about three hundred victims of sectarian violence.

Assassination of Maulana Haq Nawaz Jhangvi

In February 1990, Maulana Haq Nawaz was killed in Jhang, and that led to sectarian clashes of the worst kind. The Sipah Sahaba leadership held the Shia landlords, especially Abida Husain, and the Iranian government responsible for this. As a result, several Shia ulema and the Iranian counsellor, Sadiq Ganji, were killed. To avenge the death of Maulana Haq Nawaz, Sipah Sahaba formed an underground group called 'Jhangvi Tigers'. According to an important ex-leader of Sipah Sahaba, in Madrasa Mahmoodiya of Jhang, a list of Shia ulema suspected of being involved in the murder of Maulana Haq Nawaz was drawn up. All of them were killed between 1990 and 1991. According to this leader, Maulana Haq Nawaz provided Sipah Sahaba with a martyr figure that helped them rise to power in Jhang. The National Assembly seat lost in the election by Maulana Haq Nawaz in 1988 was won by Sipah Sahaba in 1990.

Assassination of Maulana Isar Qasmi and Maulana Ziaur Rahman Faruqi

By the time elections were held in 1990, Sipah Sahaba had consolidated its position in Jhang. In this election Maulana Isar Qasmi of Sipah Sahaba was elected member of the National Assembly from Jhang. When he was killed in 1991, Maulana Azam Tariq was elected in the by-election from this seat. After the murder of Isar Qasmi, Maulana Ziaur Rahman was elected amir of Sipah Sahaba who reorganised it on a national level. But dissensions in Sipah Sahaba began in his tenure. The president of the Punjab branch resigned because of disagreement and said in a press conference that Sipah Sahaba was playing in the hands of secret services. A group broke away from Sipah Sahaba to form Lashkar-e Jhangvi. On 18 January 1997, when Maulana Ziaur Rahman Faruqi, along with other leaders of Sipah Sahaba, were on their way from jail to the session court for an appearance, a bomb exploded in their car. Maulana Faruqi, along with twenty-five others, died on the spot.

Maulana Azam Tariq's Tenure as Amir

Sipah Sahaba's current amir is Maulana Azam Tariq who had already been elected twice to the National Assembly from Jhang. He tried to redefine Sipah Sahaba as a moderate religio-political organisation, and earned the support of Deobandi organisations.

According to the English monthly *The Herald*:

> After being elected as MNA, Azam Tariq concentrated on politics and tried to weed out terrorist elements from Sipah Sahaba. To give it a broad base he declared that establishment of peace is the primary aim of Sipah Sahaba. This not only resulted in the reduction of violence, but Sipah Sahaba was able to have two ministers in the Punjab cabinet in 1995. Riyaz Hashmat Janjua and Shaikh Hakim became state ministers and hundreds of jailed Sipah Saha ba members were released.

It was at this time that Lashkar-e Jhangvi was founded, and the old enmity with Tahreek-e Ja'fariya continued. Thus Sipah Sahaba could not really shake off its sectarian character.

In an interview with the English daily *News*: Maulana Azam Tariq said on 23 August 2001:

> Sipah Sahaba was formed as a reaction to Tahreek -e Ja'fariya. To fight against Sipah Sahaba, Tahreek -e Ja'fariya formed Sipah Muhammad. We have massive evidence to show that members of Sipah Muhammad were involved in killing our workers. The terrorists of Sipah Muhammad are given shelter in a religious institute which is the headquarters of Tahreek -e Ja'fariya. The same country helps both Tahreek -e Ja'fariya and Sipah Muhammad which enables them to spread sectarian bloodshed in Pakistan.

He further said, 'Let there be investigation into both Sipah Sahaba and Tahreek-e Ja'fariya to ascertain who among them gets foreign funding. Whoever is found guilty should be banned.' The Maulana also clarified Tahreek-e Ja'fariya's relationship with Lashkar-e Jhangvi by saying that Lashkar-e Jhangvi should have been banned much earlier, and that his workers have no truck with it. He also said: 'There are hundreds of Lashkar-e Jhangvi members in prison. Not even one of them could confirm his relationship with us. We have asked them on different occasions to give up violence, as that creates problems for us, and that there is no place for such violence in Islam.'

Talibanisation Programme of Sipah Sahaba

In the VII International Difah Sahaba Conference in Karachi on 22 October 2000, Maulana Azam Tariq presented a proposal of converting twenty-eight big cities of the country as model cities. The initial five steps were spelt out:

1. The shops must close with azan (call for prayer).
2. Friday should be a general holiday.
3. Bribes and impermissible business must be stopped.
4. Cable network must be terminated.
5. Any decision should be taken in consultation with ulema.

Maulana Tariq said in his address:

> Let all the shops be closed with the calling of azan. If any trader does not obey, let other traders boycott him and thus compel him to fall in line. The traders must be persuaded that they should not allow sale of adulterated goods, narcotics, wine, and other impermissible items. The traders in these cities, in

conjunction with ulema and other individuals, should prevent fixing of dish antennae and operation of cable network. For resolving their disputes they should not go to the court or the police but approach the mosque where the ulema would resolve them according to Islamic laws, as it is done in Jhang. And all this must be publicised in newspapers.

ORGANISATIONAL STRUCTURE OF SIPAH SAHABA AND NETWORK

Sipah Sahaba is managed by a supreme council whose leader is the chairman. The current chairman is Maulana Ziaul Qasmi. Maulana Azam Tariq is the president and Shaikh Hakim Ali is the vice-president. The following are members of the Shura: Khalifa Abdul Qayyum, Maulana Yahya Abbasi, Syed Muzammil Shah, Qari Ali, Akbar Mengal, Dr Khadim Husain, Maulana Abdul Ghani (central General Secretary), Maulana Mujibur Rahman Inqilabi (secretary, broadcasting and publishing), Maulana Masoodur Rahman Usmani, Maulana Muhammad Ahmad Ludhianwi, Maulana Niaz Muhammad, Maulana Khaliq Rahmani, Hafiz Abdul Hamid (central commander, UK), Maulana Muhammad Ahmad Madani (Karachi), Maulana Abdul Ghafoor Nadeem, Maulana Muhammad Ilyas Balakoti, Qazi Muhammad Israil, Sahibzada Izharul Haq, Arshad Mahmood (USA), Maulana Muhammad Sadeeq Hazarwi (Dubai), Maulana Abdul Hafiz Makki (Saudi Arabia), Qari Amanullah (Saudi Arabia), Abdurrahman (New York), Maulana Abdul Latif Nomani (Canada), and Maulana Habiburrahman (Bangladesh).

The headquarters of Sipah Sahaba is located in Jamia Faruqiya, Jia Moosa, Shahdara, Lahore. All organisational controls are exercised from there. The second headquarters is Madrasa Mahmoodiya in Jhang from where the international units are controlled.

Sipah Sahaba has paid considerable attention to district-level and tehsil-level units. Before it was banned, Sipah Sahaba had seventy-four district-level and 225 tehsil-level units working in entire Pakistan. Before it, only Jamat-e Islami had such a wide organisational network.

For the efficient working of the organisation, Sipah Sahaba had different departments, among which the department of *dawa* (inviting people to the way of God) and reform, the department of management, and, the department of broadcasting and publication were the most active ones.

The two of its affiliated organisations were also very active:

SIPAH SAHABA WELFARE TRUST

The objective of this trust is to fight the cases of the prisoner members, bear the expenses of the prisoners and their families, help the families of martyrs and poor members. Till 2001, this trust has borne the expenses of 1,500 cases of its members, including cases related to killings. Its central office is located at Jama Masjid Haq Nawaz, Jhang Sadar, and its chairman is Dr Khadim Husain.

SIPAH SAHABA STUDENTS

When Anjuman Sipah Sahaba was founded, there was strong condemnation from ISO. Keeping this in mind,

Sipah Sahaba Students was founded in 1990 whose objective was to induct student members and to scuttle the influence of ISO from schools and colleges. Its branches were opened throughout the country. Malik Umar Farooq was its first central president. Till 1997 Sipah Sahaba Students was very active in the educational institutions of Frontier Province, Baluchistan, and Punjab and added substantially to the sectarian tension in Pakistan. Its central office is located in Jama Masjid Sadeeq, North Karachi, and its current president is Hafiz Iqrar Ahmad Abbasi.

MADRASAS OF DEOBANDI SCHOOL OF THOUGHT AND SIPAH SAHABA

Sipah Sahaba got utmost help from the madrasas of Deobandi school of thought. In most of the Deobandi madrasas it was evident that the teachers and students, whether they supported any other jihadi organisation or not, had great sympathy for Sipah Sahaba and contributed to its human and organisational strength.

Keeping the importance of madrasas in mind, Sipah Sahaba also established many madrasas. Those that were established in Lahore, Jhang, Faisalabad, and Samandari became active centres of Sipah Sahaba's activities. These madrasas are listed below:

1. Jamia Madnia Talimul-Quran – Ameen Town, Naimat Abad Road, Faisalabad
2. Jamia Umar Farooq Islamia (Regd), Samandari Faisalabad, Manager: Rehan Mahmood Zia
3. Jamia Mahmoodiya Gulshan Jhangvi, Jhang
4. Jamial-uloom-ul-Islamia Alfaridia, Islamabad
5. Madrasa Furqania, Ali Khail Khalagi, Qila Saifullah

6. Madrasa Miftahul Uloom, Sadiq Shaheed Road, Quetta
7. Madrasa Ishatul-Quran, Hazro, Atak, Manager: Maulana Abdul Salam
8. Jamia Farooqia Maingalabad, (Baluchistan)
9. Jamia Farooqia, Shah Faisal Colony, Karachi
10. Jamia Asharfia Haqania, Landhi, Karachi
11. Jamiat-uloom-al-Islamia, Allama Banouri Town, Karachi
12. Madrasa Talimul Quran, Sohrab Goth, Karachi
13. Jamia-Al-Rasheed, Ahsanabad, Karachi
14. Darul-uloom Farooq Azam, North Karachi
15. Jamia Islamia Muhzanal-uloom, Banaras Colony, Karachi
16. Jamia Anwar-ul Quran, Adam Town, Karachi
17. Darul-Uloom Haseeniah, Shahdadpur, Sangarh
18. Madrasa Anwar-ul Uloom, Shikarpur Road, Sakkur
19. Jamia Miftahul uloom, Hyderabad
20. Jamia Arabia Siddique Akbar, Colony Bakhira, Hyderabad
21. Jamia Islamia, Sybtada Town, Sakardoo
22. Jamia Talimul Quran, Dagar, Buniar
23. Jamia Usman Bin Affan, Khuwazahkhilah, Sawat
24. Darul Uloom Siraj-ul-Islam, Kahi Kohat
25. Jamia Darul-uloom-ul-Islamia, Darwesh Masjid, Peshawar
26. Darul-Uloom Osmania, Bairoon Aasya Gate, Peshawar
27. Jamia Nizam-ul Uloom, Androon Maki Gate, Banno
28. Jamia Siddique Akbar, Abdali Masjid, Multan
29. Jamia Khairul Madaris, Multan

30. Jamia Mukhzanul-uloom, Khanpur
31. Jamia Farooq Azam, Jia Moosa, Shahdara, Lahore
32. Madrasa Bilal, Sabza Zar, Lahore
33. Jamia Darul-uloom, Idgah Kabirwala, Khanewal
34. Jamiatul-Manzoor-ul-Islamia, Idgah Sadar, Lahore
35. Jamia Osmania, Model Town, Lahore
36. Jamia Madinah, Karim Park, Lahore
37. Pracha Jamia Islamia, Tehsil Janairatak
38. Madrasa Mairajul-Uloom, Tabi Qaisrani, Dera Ghazi Khan

MATERIAL RESOURCES

Sipah Sahaba had never adopted any other popular means to raise funds except for the proceeds from the sale of hides of animals sacrificed on Eid. According to a local leader of Sipah Sahaba in Jhang: 'People contribute voluntarily. The treasury department does not get any substantial amount as monthly fee from members. Some businessmen with sympathy for Sipah Sahaba contribute liberally to it. They are from Jhang, Faisalabad, Cheneot, Lahore, and Karachi. The foreign branches of Sipah Sahaba also make their own contributions.' About funding from Saudi Arabia and other Arab countries, he said that only senior leaders would be aware of that. 'But the general impression is that the Saudi government has been funding the madrasas; in 2000, it has contributed 170 lakh rupees to the treasury department for madrasas in Jhang only.'

Financial irregularities in Sipah Sahaba have also come to light from time to time. For example, the secretary of Madrasa Jamia Qasimia, Faisalabad, Maulana Zahid Mahmood (son of Sipah Sahaba's former amir Ziaur Rahman Faruqi) who was the chairman of the Supreme Council of Sipah Sahaba, left it on 10 March 2001, and joined Jamiat Ulema Islam (Q). He revealed that the leaders of Sipah Sahaba embezzled the funds. He accused Maulana Azam Tariq of embezzling funds to the tune of one crore rupees. According to a news item:

> Zahid Mahmood Qasmi, son of late Maulana Ziaul Qasmi, chairman of Sipah Sahaba's Supreme Council, broke away from Sipah Sahaba, and accused the leadership of embezzling funds worth about one crore rupees that was meant for orphans, widows and prisoners. He said that he was leaving the Supreme Council of Sipah Sahaba established by his own father. He said that the leaders of Sipah Sahaba, most of whom possess Land Cruisers and other comforts, must have misused funds worth at least one crore rupees out of which 70 lakhs came from the proceeds of hides of sacrificed animals, and funds from London, Dubai and Saudi Arabia. All the above money was meant for families of martyrs, widows, orphans, and prisoners whose cases were fought in the court.
>
> *Pakistan*, daily, Lahore, 11 March 2001

DISSENSIONS IN SIPAH SAHABA

After the assassination of Maulana Haq Nawaz, Sipah Sahaba has never been free of dissensions. But these have rarely come out in the open. On the whole, there were three groups within Sipah Sahaba:

1. One group is dedicated to the ideals of Maulana Haq Nawaz and is ready to take to terrorism for the

fulfilment of those ideals.

2. The second group feels that Sipah Sahaba should be pragmatic and try to fulfil its ideal by becoming a reckonable political force. The military wing should be separated and offered patronage only from a distance.

3. The third group is strongly against sectarian violence. But this group is the smallest among the three.

Besides these ideological dissensions, there was also discontent about financial irregularities. Some leaders accused some others of corruption and of being the stooges of some foreign power. A similar charge was levelled against Maulana Azam Tariq by Maulana Izharul Haq, the son of Maulana Haq Nawaz, who broke away from it in 2002. Maulana Izharul Haq was a member of Majlis-e Shura of Sipah Sahaba. Similarly, Maulana Zahid Mahmood Qasmi accused the leadership of financial irregularities in a press conference in Lahore Press Club, resigned from Sipah Sahaba, and announced the dissolution of its supreme council. Earlier also, some leaders had left Sipah Sahaba. According to a leader of the organisation in Jhang: 'Those who leave Sipah Sahaba are, in fact, agents of secret services, sent here to demoralise us. Or, the secret agencies buy them over. Some also leave Sipah Sahaba to save their lives, and indulge in giving statements against the leadership.'

The leadership of Sipah Sahaba is now dominated by the second group, though the first group is also active in the areas of its preference and encourages establishment of affiliated organisations.

THE TERRORIST GROUP OF SIPAH SAHABA

Members supporting violence broke away from Sipah Sahaba from time to time and formed various organisations. Besides Lashkar-e Jhangvi, six other organisations were formed:

1. Jhangvi Tigers
2. Al-Haq Tigers
3. Al-Farooq
4. Al-Badr Federation
5. Allahu Akbar
6. Tanzeemul Haq

Different leaders of Sipah Sahaba extend their patronage to either of these organisations and, according to Sipah Sahaba, Jhang, indicate targets as well. Except for Al-Badr Federation, all the other groups have been active in Jhang, Cheneot, Samandari, and Faisalabad. Al-Badr Federation was formed in Karachi. Jhangvi Tigers, Al-Haq Tigers, and Allahu Akbar later merged with Lashkar-e Jhangvi.

Lashkar-e Jhangvi was founded in 1996. Riaz Basra was its chief commander who had been the secretary, broadcasting and publication of Sipah Sahaba earlier. He was of the view that Maulana Haq Nawaz's ideals should be disseminated through the use of force and his complaint against the leadership of Sipah Sahaba was that they had forgotten the ideals of Maulana Haq Nawaz. It is also claimed from some sources that Lashkar-e Jhangvi was formed by the leadership of Sipah Sahaba to divert attention from itself as a militant party.

The position of Sipah Sahaba on this issue is that it has no relationship with Lashkar-e Jhangvi. But both the organisations had links and Lashkar-e Jhangvi's members had always been seen in Sipah Sahaba's offices and madrasas. Moreover, their disagreement is not about aims and perspective but organisational. Even this organisational disagreement has been looked upon with suspicion. It is suspected that Sipah Sahaba had formed this group so that its political agenda suffers no setback. To support this argument, it is pointed out that members of Lashkar-e Jhangvi stayed in the same mosques and madrasas that are regarded as important centres of Sipah Sahaba. It is also no secret that leaders of Sipah Sahaba have been visiting members of Lashkar-e Jhangvi in jail.

Lashkar-e Jhangvi began its operation in 1996 and made important Shia government officers its target. Its organisational network was strong and complicated. The leader was called supreme commander under whom were twelve commanders. A consultative committee was formed to lead the management of Lashkar-e Jhangvi. Every member and leader of Lashkar-e Jhangvi gave up his original name, took up an assumed name, and fake identity cards were made in the new name. According to an important leader of Sipah Sahaba in Jhang, Riaz Basra had twelve fake identity cards in different names. For supply of arms, a network was formed between Afghanistan to Punjab, and from Punjab to Karachi. The members of Lashkar-e Jhangvi did not go beyond 500, but they have added a bloody chapter in the history of terrorist violence. Its small number is said to be due to the fact that for admission to Lashkar-e Jhangvi, one had to take an oath of death, and severing the ties from all worldly relationships one had to dedicate oneself to the cause. Lashkar-e Jhangvi had divided its area of operation into separate units. According to this division, the areas of Gujranwala, Rawalpindi, and Sargodha were under the command of Riaz Basra. Faisalabad, Multan, and Bahawalpur divisions were under Malik Ishaq and Karachi was under Qari Abdul Hai.

Till 2001, Lashkar-e Jhangvi had been involved in 350 incidents of terrorist violence. It suffered great damage during the second phase of the rule of Nawaz Sharif when, between 1998 and 1999, dozens of its members were killed in police encounters. It was also heard that Lashkar-e Jhangvi had already been paid a sum of 13.5 crore of rupees to assassinate Nawaz Sharif, Mian Shahbaz Sharif, chief minister, Punjab, and Syed Mushahid Husain, the federal minister for information. The bomb explosion on 2 January 1999, in Raiwind Road, Lahore, is said to be a part of this scheme.

Lashkar-e Jhangvi Breaks Up

The Majlis-e Shura of Lashkar-e Jhangvi was held on 27 December 2000, in its centre near Kabul in Afghanistan. Among the participants were top leaders like Riaz Basra, Qari Abdul Hai, Akram Lahori, Zakaullah, Sajid Pathan, Athar Rahman, Tanvir Urf, and Asif Ramzai. Asif Ramzai presented a blueprint of the future agenda that included efforts to get the leaders of Lashkar-e Jhangvi released from jail, and decapitation of Shia organisations. Qari Abdul Hai and Tanvir Urf opposed this, arguing that as long as the military government was there, such steps would invite more trouble for the organisation, and that the country was at a crossroads and such violent agenda at this moment would not be beneficial for Pakistan. When this disagreement threatened to turn into fisticuffs, Qari Abdul Hai demanded to see the accounts from Riaz Basra claiming that he had the records proving that the funds of Lashkar-e Jhangvi have been embezzled. This was the first public revolt against Riaz Basra. However, Qari Abdul Hai had already consolidated himself in the organisation; he was the chairman of the Majlis-e Shura and was in charge of Lashkar-e Jhangvi's military training camps in Afghanistan. After this dissension, Qari Abdul Hai alias Qari Asadullah alias Talha met important members of Lashkar-e Jhangvi and with their help took charge of Lashkar-e Jhangvi's leadership. He occupied the training camps and snatched away the cars of Riaz Basra's supporters. Under these circumstances, armed confrontation between the two groups began in which several people from both the groups were wounded. Seeing this, the Taliban interfered in the matter and appointed Jaish-e Muhammad's Mufti Abdul Sagar to arbitrate between them. Mufti Sagar called a meeting between the two groups for a compromise, but Riaz Basra refused to take part in it saying that he had already expelled Qari Asadullah from the organisation. The Qari group also alleged that it was because of Riaz Basra's imprudent policies that Noor Gul, who was a close friend of Qari Abdul Hai, was killed in a police encounter. Noor Gul was an instructor in the training camp in Afghanistan and was an ammunition/explosive expert. In February 1999 he was involved in a conspiracy to kill Nawaz Sharif by bombing his car in Raiwind, Lahore. He was arrested later and killed in an encounter near Multan. The police claimed that some of his companions had come to release him from police custody that led to the encounter in which he died.

Riaz Basra's End

Riaz Basra, the supreme commander of Lashkar-e Jhangvi, remained a challenge for the police for twelve years. Eventually, he was killed in a police encounter in Wahari district on 14 May 2002. He was wanted in 300 cases and there was a reward of fifty lakh rupees declared on his head. Besides the charge of killing the Iranian councillor, Sadiq Ganji, he was accused of killing Sikandar Shah, chairman, Shia Political Party, Syed Tajammul Husain, ex-commissioner, Sargodha, Syed Zulfiqar Husain Naqvi, Mohsin Ali Naqvi, Muhammad Ashraf Marth, SSP, and of killing twenty-five people in a bombing in Mominpura, Lahore.

When he was a fugitive from police, Riaz Basra kept in touch with newspapers through telephone and gave several interviews. He used at least ten fake names: Shahji Abdurrahman, Ashraf Bhatt, Sajjad, Pir Sahib, Bawaji, Choudhury Sahib, Haji Sahib.

Riaz Basra was born in a peasant family of Qasba Khursheed in Jharoya police station area of Sargodha.

His father was Ghulam Muhammad who was a farmer. He was educated first in the school at Jharoya, then at Sargodha, and finally in a madrasa in Lahore. He joined Sipah Sahaba in 1986 and soon became one of its most active members. He was also its president at Sargodha. Then he met Maulana Haq Nawaz and began to be counted as one of his close aides. In 1988, he was made central secretary, broadcasting and publication, Sipah Sahaba. In 1988, he fought the provincial assembly election, opposite Nawaz Sharif, and bagged 9,000 votes. He built the Sipah Sahaba's office at Lotton Road, Lahore. He also participated in the war in Afghanistan. He was wounded in the war and walked with a limp. He founded Lashkar-e Jhangvi in 1996 and made its base camp in Afghanistan.

In 1994, his name was known in the international media in connection with Sadiq Ganji murder case. The police arrested all the accused, but came to know of Riaz Basra from an accused after eight days of the incident. On 30 April 1994, he was presented before the Special Court for Terrorists. He wanted to go to the toilet. The policemen accompanied him to the toilet where his companions had already put arms for him. He began to fire at the police and, still handcuffed, fled on the motorcycle with his companions. After that he fled to Afghanistan and the responsibility of Lashkar-e Jhangvi fell on Akram Lahori. After that, Riaz Basra kept on visiting Pakistan from time to time and was involved in many incidents of sectarian violence. Many suspect that the police encounter in which he was alleged to have been killed was a fake one. They argue that he was arrested four months earlier and was under the custody of the Intelligence Bureau (IB), Faisalabad. He was not handed over to the police because the legal process would have taken a long time and he could have even escaped. After him, Akram Lahori became the leader of his group. But he was arrested in July 2002. According to his statement, about a hundred Lashkar-e Jhangvi members are still at large.

Qari Abdul Hai alias Qari Asadullah alias Talha
(Commander, Lashkar-e Jhangvi)
According to police record, the real name of Qari Asadullah was Qari Abdul Hai, and he was known in the organisation as Talha. He was a resident of Alipur in the district of Muzaffargarh and obtained his madrasa education from Madrasa Abdul Fatah, Abu Bakr Masjid, Chowrangi, Karachi. He joined Lashkar-e Jhangvi in 1997 at the age of thirty. He participated in violence for the first time in Shahr Sultan in Muzaffargarh in which fourteen Shias were killed. He left for Afghanistan in 1996 and took the charge of Lashkar-e Jhangvi camps. He soon progressed in the organisation and challenged the leadership of Riaz Basra. When he made his own group, he had the support of most of the leaders of Lashkar-e Jhangvi, including Shakil Ahmad from Fort Abbas and Tanvir Khan from Kabirwala. Both of them had an award of five lakh rupees individually on their heads. Traces of Qari Asadullah's group still exist in Pakistan, Karachi being the centre of its activities. It also works under the names of Harkatul Mujahideen and Lashkar Umar.

Sipah Sahaba's Character and Current Situation

Sipah Sahaba always received the support of the two large groups of Jamiat Ulema Islam. Maulana Haq Nawaz himself was associated with Jamiat Ulema Islam. Many of the leaders of Jamiat Ulema Islam not only supported it but spearheaded a movement for its establishment. Especially, Maulana Hasan Jan, leader of JUI (F) in Peshawar was very active in this regard. In many districts the office bearers of Sipah Sahaba and JUI are the same. Several leaders and members of Jamiat Ulema Islam are involved in the sectarian clashes on behalf of Sipah Sahaba. Jamiat Ulema Islam has played a vital role in the growth of Sipah Sahaba and strengthening its network. The mosques, madrasas, and offices of Jamiat Ulema Islam are used by Sipah Sahaba for its own activities.

As the violent incidents spearheaded by Sipah Sahaba increased, several Deobandi organisations of similar nature were founded. Organisations like Tahreek Difah Sahaba and Tahaffuz Namoos Sahaba widened their network. Many Deobandi ulema opposed the violence perpetrated by Sipah Sahaba and Lashkar-e Jhangvi, but remained silent for fear of Sipah Sahaba. On 7 February 2001, the weekly, *Takbeer*, from Karachi published a report of sectarian clashes in Karachi. An excerpt from this report:

> Sometime ago when Maulana Yusuf Ludhianwi died, a famous teacher of Darul Uloom (Banwari Town) who also teaches Prophet's Traditions, said, on condition of anonymity, in a tearful voice that such irreparable damage was inflicted because of their own

lack of moderation and criminal stubbornness. His clear indication was to the Sipah Sahaba. He did not want to be on record, but somehow he wanted to send this message to the Sipah Sahaba that if it continued with its agenda, then such incidents would occur in future also.

Taking advantage of its growing popularity, Sipah Sahaba wanted to bring about a Taliban-type revolution in Pakistan. However, when Sipah Sahaba and Lashkar-e Jhangvi were banned on 14 August, it had to put this agenda on the back burner. Rather, it concentrated on saving its members from being arrested. After 11 September 2001, the pressure from the government increased on Sipah Sahaba. This can be gauged from the following letter written by Maulana Azam Tariq in reply to a communication from the home ministry:

Respected Janab Munir Bhatt,
Section Officer, Federal Home Ministry, Pakistan,
Assalamu alaikum,

I hope you are fine. We received your letter dated 24 October 2001 [No. 1(2) POLL, 3 March 2001], in which you have made allegations against Sipah Sahaba and served a warning for future. I thank you for your letter and proceed to deal with the charges one by one so that situation becomes clearer to you.

Charge 1:   Sipah Sahaba is registering 50,000 youths for military training in Afghanistan.

Charge 2:   When they will return after training, these youths may be used in Pakistan.

Charge 3:   In Peshawar, on the pretext of protesting against American oppression, talks about causing harm to the life and property of the Shias are going on.

Charge 4:   Leaders of Sipah Sahaba are giving irresponsible speeches.

Dear sir, about the first charge, let me state that no such resolution has ever been taken in any of Majlis-e Shura, and no instruction has been sent to this effect to the units by any leaders. Being the president of Sipah Sahaba, I am writing this with full responsibility that the information received by you is based either on a newspaper report (you know better about their reliability), or the personal opinion of an individual that might have been expressed in a rally or meeting. On the whole, this charge is false. There is no place in the country where such registration is going on. We have no such policy.

As far as the 2nd charge is concerned, it is based on mere conjecture. Sipah Sahaba is a patriotic and peace-loving organisation. Its leaders and members are not behind any other Pakistani in patriotism. You know that when our government, through the blessings of USA, was active against the Russians in Afghanistan, thousands of Pakistanis took part in the jihad. But after returning, no one used his military training against his own country, nor those who receive training for Kashmir jihad do this. Then why should Sipah Sahaba be suspected of it?

As for the 3rd charge, I have probed the entire area of Peshawar. None from our organisation has said anything about harming the life and property of the Shias during the demonstrations against American oppression. To my knowledge, Sunnis, Shias and even

Christians are collectively protesting against American atrocities. This charge must be some mischief on the part of a prejudiced officer whose only objective is to defame Sipah Sahaba. Yes, it is possible that the Iranian policy against the Taliban could have been condemned, and people have the right to do so.

About the 4th charge, I must say that our leaders are fearless in condemning American brutality and barbarism. They consider it against Islam and the country to support the Americans, and reject the policy of facilitating American attack on the Taliban. Sipah Sahaba keeps itself within the limits of peaceful and permissible protest against oppression and brutality in the world. However, we consider it a sin to use even a single word against peace and tranquillity in our own land. My effort will be to ensure that the members of the organisation observe the best norms, speak with responsibility and support their stand with evidence.

I hope, after these clarifications, you will be reassured. In any case, we are not far from one another. We are travellers in the same boat, and rather than denigrating one another, we should try to solve problems through mutual understanding. Our effort will be not to create any misunderstanding in future. Mutual rapport can solve a lot of problems. May Allah help and support Pakistan and Muslims.

With regards,
Maulana Muhammad Azam Tariq
Sipah Sahaba, Pakistan

Sipah Sahaba was banned on 12 January 2002 and 1,600

of its members were rounded up. But Sipah Sahaba is not only a part of many political fronts, but plays a vital role in some. Its offices (that have now been shifted to mosques and madrasas) are working in different cities and various programmes are held by it. The network of the organisation in Pakistan is detailed in Table IV.

Table IV: *Sipah Sahaba's (banned) Network in Pakistan*

Sr. No.	District/ Tehsil	Amir/Secretary/President	Office/Centre
1.	Lahore		Jamay Farooq Azam, Jia Moosa, Shahadra, Lahore
2.	Gujranwala	Hafiz Saqlain Bipharwi	Ghanta Ghar Gujranwala
3.	Shaikhupura	Rana Ayub	Sargodha Road, Shaikhupura
4.	Okarah	Qari Ghulam Mahmood Anwar	Gole Chowk, GT Road, Okarah
5.	Gujrat	Qari Farooq/Riaz Ahmad Khan	
6.	Sialkot	Maulana Ahsan-ul Haque Farooqi	
7.	Khushab	Ghulam Yahya	Sargodha Road, Khushab
8.	Bhakkar	Muneer Ahmad	Jamia Qadriya, Rahimabad, Bhakkar
9.	Mianwali	Sultan Mahmood Aawan	
10.	Sahiwal	Maulana Abdul Ghafoor	Jamia Uloom-al Shariah, Sahiwal
11.	Multan	Maulana Abdul Rasheed	Jamia Siddique Akbar, Abdali Masjid, Multan
12.	Jhang	Rana Ayub	Jama Masjid Haq Nawaz, Jhang Sadar
13.	Sargodha	Qari Fateh Muhammad	Jama Masjid Block No. 1, Sargodha
14.	Dera Ghazi Khan	Habib Chingwani	Jamia Farooqia, Quetta Road, Dera Ghazi Khan
15.	Hasilpur	Haji Mohammad Sharif	
16.	Sadiqabad		Circular Road, Sadiqabad

Sr. No.	District/ Tehsil	Amir/Secretary/President	Office/Centre
17.	Rahim Yar Khan	Maulana Masoodur-Rahman Khamani	Markazi Jamia Masjid, Rahim Yar Khan
18.	Toba Tek Singh	Hafiz Mohammad Owais	
19.	Gojrah	Maulana Syed Sarfaraz-ul Hasan	
20.	Kamaliah	Maulana Peerji Abdul Hakim	
21	Cheneot	Hafiz Abu Baker	Jamia Mahmudiya, Cheneot
22.	Peshawar	Maulana Darwesh	Namak Mandi, Peshawar
23.	Chitral	Maulana Sher Aziz	Jamia Masjid Siddique Akbar Saryan, Nazd Sadai Bazar, Abbottabad
24.	Kohat	Abid Pracha	
25.	Dera Ismail Khan	Niaz-ullah/ Abdul Qayyum	Madrasa Nomania, Dera Ismail Khan
26.	Laki Maroot	Jumma Khan	
27.	Karachi		Buffer Zone, Hasan Chorangi, Karachi
28.	Hyderabad	Maulana Muhammad Farooq Azad	
29.	Jacobabad	Ahmad Ali Samru	
30.	Meerpur Khas		Madina Masjid Shahi Bazar, Meerpur Khas
31.	Quetta	Hafiz Mohammad Qasim Siddique	Daftar Gualmandi Chowk Jamia Miftahul uloom, Quetta

Tahreek Khuddam Ahl-e Sunnat

The founder of Tahreek Khuddam Ahl-e Sunnat is Maulana Qazi Mazhar Hussain who is the *khateeb* of Madani Jama Masjid, Chakwal. This is one of the first among those organisations, founded in 1980, working against the Shias. Maulana Qazi Mazhar Husain is regarded as the spiritual deputy (*Khalifa*) of Maulana Syed Ahmad Madani. Among its aims and objectives, three are prominent:

1. Reviving the *Khalifa* system
2. Protecting the honour of Prophet's Companions
3. Proving the rightness of Hanfi-Deobandi school of thought

This Tahreek is seen as the representative organisation of the *hayati* sect of Deobandis. It casts aspersion on the belief of *mamati* sect. It is not a big organisation so far as its structure and network are concerned. But its branches are to be found in the Punjab districts of Chakwal, Mianwali, Bhakkar, Khushab, and Jhelum. The *khateebs* of a few mosques in the Achchra area of Lahore are associated with it. However, Chakwal is its main centre.

Tahreek Khuddam Ahl-e Sunnat holds the same view about the Shias as those of Sipah Sahaba. But it does not support its way of functioning. It claims to be the first organisation to give the call for protection of the honour of the four *Khalifas* (just after Prophet Muhammad) and the Prophet's Companions.

Jaish-e Muhammad (Banned)

Jaish-e Muhammad is an important jihadi organisation of Deobandi persuasion. It has been banned by the Government of Pakistan on 12 January 2002. After this, it is supposed to have taken on a new name, Al-Furqan, on which no consensus has been reached yet. Some sources say that after his release, Maulana Masood Azhar, amir of Jaish-e Muhammad (who is under house arrest at this moment) will declare its new name. Even after the ban, it is working freely in many areas of Pakistan and Azad Kashmir.

FOUNDATION

Jaish-e Muhammad was founded on 31 January 2000, by Maulana Masood Azhar who is its supreme leader. Before 31 December 1999 Maulana Masood Azhar was in jail in Occupied Kashmir. In December 1999 five hijackers hijacked the Indian Airlines flight IC814 and took the aircraft to Kandahar airport. For freeing the passengers, the hijackers demanded the release of Maulana Masood Azhar, Mushtaq Zargar, and Umar Shaikh. This was agreed to by the Indian government on 31 December 1999. After his release Maulana Masood Azhar was given a grand welcome and the Deobandi ulema gave him great honour. Earlier, Maulana Masood Azhar was associated with Harkatul Mujahideen, but after his release he announced the end of this relationship and started planning to lay the foundation of a new jihadi organisation.

About Jaish-e Muhammad's formation, a detailed report was published in the fortnightly, Jaish-e Muhammad, Karachi in its few initial issues. Following are a few excerpts from this report:

> One issue that exercised the mind of jihadis at this time was the organisation that enjoyed Maulana's blessings. The fact is – Maulana Masood Azhar, along with his friends, Commander Sajjad Khan Shaheed, Commander Langaryal, Commander Maulana Abu Jangal and Hafiz Ilyas, had alienated himself from all groups on 22 May 1998...

The honour of spearheading the Kashmir cause in Pakistan goes to three spiritual figures: Honourable Mufti Azam Mufti Rasheed Ahmad (late), Shaikhul Hadith Hazrat Dr Maulana Sher Ali Shah, and Hazrat Mufti Nizamuddin Shamzai. These three personalities were saddened by the circumstances, and looked forward to some changes in the prevailing organisations. When the circumstances did not change even after their best efforts, the three leaders declared publicly their disassociation from these organisations.

Under these circumstances, Hazrat Maulana went into meditation for some days and then sent for those sincere mujahideen who were at higher posts in big organisations in those days but were unhappy with the leadership (of those organisations). Shaikh Maulana Masood Azhar sought their opinions on three possible situations:

a.   All of them should join just one organisation and work for its reform.

b.   The Harkatul Ansar experiment should be repeated. That is, both the big organisations may be invited to merge and work together.

c.   To form a new organisation on the structure of Taliban, and ask all the sincere mujahideen of the two organisations to join it.

After consultation, it was decided that the first situation was not desirable, because the members of both the organisations had come to him (Maulana Masood Azhar) with the invitation to join their organisations. Whichever organisation the Maulana joins will be a cause for great jubilation for the members of that organisation, but it will be difficult for the members of the other organisation to come to join their rival organisation merely for him. The insurmountable barriers of hate and enmity stand between them. This hatred and enmity has (*sic*) even divided the martyrs and prisoners. The decree of martyrdom is also being changed at the instance of some people. And even if one member shifts to the other organisation because of personal conviction, the problem of security will haunt him. Finally, Maulana's hitherto neutral position vis-à-vis the two organisations will be compromised, and the other group will harbour a grudge against Maulana just as they harbour grudge against the leaders of their rival group. In this way, the hopes reposed on the maulana by the mujahideen for the reform of the community will be belied. The second situation had already been tried and its result was there for everyone to see. Even if the leaders were invited to join, and their status was ensured, they would still not accept one another from heart. Even while sitting together, they would still think about their personal interests and old ties. This happened at the time of the founding of Harkatul Ansar. One group had resolved, on the very foundation day, that they would remain faithful to their earlier organisation, and if instructed, would return to it. The failure of that experiment had left a deep scar in the heart of the Muslim community. To repeat the same experiment would be like adding insult to injury. The third option might, however, be considered by the amir taking the requirements of the sharia into account. Then all the jihadi groups might be invited to join it unconditionally. Absolute obedience to the amir should be ensured and all kinds (*sic*) autonomy and individualism be removed, that were the root cause of two organisations splitting into eleven splinter groups. As the consultation with the elders was required, no definitive decisions were taken in the meeting. But this much was certain that a new organisation was going to be formed for the betterment of the Muslim community. After this, Maulana Masood Azhar left for Karachi to consult with the leaders.

The three leaders supported the proposal. Honourable Mufti Rasheed Sahib welcomed it and read a special prayer. Honourable Mufti Shamzai also welcomed it very enthusiastically. After the Friday prayer at Abdul - Falah mosque, Karachi, the name 'Jaish-e Muhammad' was announced and a press conference was arranged. Global broadcasting agencies publicised the fact that Maulana Masood Azhar is the amir of all Mujahids of Pakistan, and all the mujahideen should come under the same banner. After declaring its birth, Maulana Muhammad Yusuf Ludhiani (late) took initiation from him. In that emotionally charged atmosphere Mufti Nizamuddin Shamzai Sahib, Mufti Jamil Khan Sahib, Maulana Abdul Jabbar Sahib, Maulana Sajid Usman Sahib, and several other mujahideen took initiation from the amir. Thus Jaish-e Muhammad was born amidst auspicious circumstances.

Background of Maulana Masood Azhar

Maulana Masood Azhar is the son of a teacher of Islamic studies, Allah Bakhsh Shabbir, of Bahawalpur. He has five brothers and six sisters. Masood Azhar's grandfather was the headmaster of Sadat Middle School at Amirpur. Allah Bakhsh Shabbir who is known as Alwi Amirpuri married the daughter of Mufti Muhammad Husain Chughtai who was an active member of the Ahrar Party. Three of Maulana Masood Azhar's brothers and four sisters are married. One sister, Rabia Bibi, worked in Kabul during the Taliban regime. Tahir Anwar, his elder brother, works in a computer centre in Bahawalpur, and had made several rounds of Afghanistan in connection with jihadi activities. Another brother, Muhammad Ibrahim Azhar was the district amir of Harkatul Ansar in Bahawalpur. Ibrahim Azhar had gone to Afghanistan for the first time with a friend, Jamilurrahman, when he was nineteen years old, and later he also took his father there. The Indian authority feels that he was one of the hijackers who had hijacked the Indian plane for the release of Maulana Masood Azhar. Maulana Masood Azhar's younger brother, Abdul Rauf Asghar, has recently passed out from Jamiatul Uloom Islamia, Banwari Town, and looks after the Idarah Khairul Amn along with his elder brother, Ibrahim Azhar. Among the two other younger brothers, Jahangir Akbar is studying in Darul Uloom, Kolangi, and Aurangzeb Alamgir is studying in Darul Iftah, Nazimabad, Karachi.

Maulana Masood Azhar who is now thirty-five years old was born in Bahawalpur in 1968. He passed out from Jamiatul Uloom Islamia, Banwari Town (1980–89) and then taught in the same madrasa for two years. When and how was he associated with jihad? He says: 'When I was studying at Jamiatul Uloom Islamia, Banwari Town, I heard about jihad for the first time. Some students of this madrasa had gone to Afghanistan and joined Maulana Irshad Rasheed's movement... I had appeared in my last exam and was awaiting the result when I got ready for jihad. At the advice of Maulana Abdul Sami Shaheed I went to Afghanistan. When I returned, I got associated with jihad.'

Maulana Masood Azhar has written twenty-nine

books on jihad. He has also been the editor of Harkatul Mujahideen's journal, *Sada-e Mujahid* and *Soot-e Kashmir*. The fortnightly, *Jaish-e Muhammad*, used to be published under his supervision. After it was banned, *Al-Islah* is coming out in its place. He has been associated with the department of *dawat* of Harkatul Mujahideen, and travelled to many foreign countries to collect funds for it. During such a travel, he was arrested at Jeddah airport on the charge of keeping counterfeit dollars. He had played a vital role in the merger of Harkatul Mujahideen and Harkat Al-Jihad Al-Islami to form Harkatul Ansar. As a result of this merger, Maulana Shahadatullah had become its leader and the commander-in-chief was Maulana Abdul Jabbar. Maulana Masood Azhar himself had become its information secretary. The concept of Harkatul Ansar was his. After the arrest of many members in Kashmir, Harkatul Ansar broke up, which has saddened him deeply.

In November 1993 Maulana Masood Azhar had played an important role in the return of Pakistani troops from Somalia where they had gone as a part of United Nations Peacekeeping Force. On the one hand, he had reassured the Pakistani army officers that Somali Muslims would not oppose them or attack them; on the other hand, he went to Kenya in November 1999, and reassured the current Somali Muslim leadership that the Pakistani peacekeeping troops were returning, and that they should continue their jihad against the infidels. His companions in this mission were the senior Pakistani journalist, Mujiburrahman Shami, Altaf Husain Quraishi, and

Mustafa Sadiq.

On 11 February 1994, Maulana Masood Azhar was arrested from the city of Anantnag in Occupied Kashmir. The objective of his visit to Kashmir was to meet the Harkatul Ansar commanders. Holding a Portugal passport he had reached Delhi from Dhaka. This passport was managed by the Pakistani jihadi known as 'Hafiz', based in London. The passport contained the seals of India, Pakistan, and Bangladesh; he had earlier reached Saudi Arabia and from there to Dhaka on Pakistani passport. Before reaching Kashmir he had stayed in Delhi for twelve days; he had also visited Lucknow, Varanasi, Kanpur, Deoband, Saharanpur, and Jalalabad (UP) and participated in many gatherings.

The arrest of Maulana Masood Azhar in Occupied Kashmir was entirely unexpected. He was on an important mission there. A very important member of Harkatul Mujahideen, who had been ostensibly 'underground' in Dera Ghazi Khan till February 2002, said to me: 'We came to know much later that Maulana Masood Azhar had developed close rapport with Osama bin Laden, and he was working at his behest. Harkatul Ansar management did not know this. He had gone to Occupied Kashmir on an important mission, even though the leaders of Harkatul Ansar advised him to the contrary. I have no idea what that mission was. Because of him, our commander, Sajjad Afghani, was arrested there and killed. Both had a quarrel inside the jail which was arbitrated by the leaders. Only later we came to know about his secret meetings with Osama. He had met him once in Kenya, and a second time in the Prophet's mosque (in Saudi Arabia) where both had reached in disguise. I think, Osama intended to bring Harkatul Ansar under Al-Qaida management, and Maulana Masood Azhar seemed to him to be the most suitable person for its leadership. But one cannot say definitely whether Maulana Masood Azhar was sincere to Osama. Now he is spreading dissension in the name of unity.

'After his release, when Maulana Masood Azhar reached Pakistan, he immediately engaged himself in the task of building an organisation. At this time the delegations from Harkatul Mujahideen and Harkat-al Jihad Islami tried to meet him and offered him the leadership of their organisations. But he rejected these offers. According to *The Herald* (February), "An important source from Harkat told us that as soon as Maulana Masood Azhar reached Bahawalpur after his release, a delegation from Harkatul Mujahideen tried to meet him, but he refused to meet it; and after two weeks announced the formation of Jaish-e Muhammad that hit Harkatul Mujahideen directly."'

Quarrel with Harkatul Mujahideen for Resources

When Jaish-e Muhammad was formed, several leaders of Harkatul Mujahideen and Harkat-al Jihad Islami joined it. Among them are:

1. Maulana Abdul Jabbar, chief secretary, Harkatul Mujahideen and ex-secretary, Amoor Hizb
2. Maulana Sajid Usman, ex-deputy amir, Harkat-al

Jihad Islami
3. Maulana Qari Sadiq, ex-finance secretary, Harkatul Mujahideen
4. Qari Zarar Urf Qasai, ex-chief commander, United Harkatul Ansar
5. Mufti Owais, ex-member, Majlis-e Shura, Harkat-al Jihad Islami
6. Maulana Ghulam Murtaza, ex-chief secretary and amir (Punjab), Harkatul Mujahideen
7. Maulana Abdullah Shah Mazhar, ex-secretary, Harkat-al Jihad Islami, Karachi

Most of the members of Harkat-al Jihad Islami and Harkatul Mujahideen from Lahore, Gujranwala, Bahawalpur, Faisalabad, Sahiwal, and Okara joined Jaish-e Muhammad. According to the fortnightly, Jaish-e Muhammad:

Ninety-five per cent of the Pakistani jihadis fighting for Islamic state in Afghanistan joined Jaish-e Muhammad. From the district Kupwara of Occupied Kashmir, an ex-commander of Harkatul Mujahideen joined Jaish-e Muhammad. After a few days, the famous Guerrilla Commander, Mufti Muhammad Asghar Khan (ex-member Majlis-e Shura, Harkatul Mujahideen) joined Jaish-e Muhammad with his companions. He has been in charge of the launching pad for a long time; in other words, the entire set-up of Harkatul Mujahideen inside Occupied Kashmir has come under its (Jaish-e Muhammad's) control. Commander Sajid Jihadi has declared this. The amir of Sipah Sahaba in Pakistan, Maulana Azam Tariq has pledged complete support to it (Jaish-e Muhammad).

Right after the founding of Jaish-e Muhammad, quarrels started between it and Harkatul Mujahideen about resources. Harkatul Mujahideen alleged that Jaish-e Muhammad had occupied seventy-four of its offices. Jaish-e Muhammad argued that as most of the members had joined it, it had a right on those offices. A commander of Harkatul Mujahideen has claimed that the Harkat property occupied forcefully by Jaish-e Muhammad would amount to more than three crores of rupees. There were fierce fights over distribution of resources in which Sipah Sahaba supported Jaish-e Muhammad. In the fights, two members of Harkatul Mujahideen died and many were injured. Jaish-e Muhammad's condition was similar. Finally, the issue was brought before the ulema of Jamiatul Uloom Islamia, Banwari Town, and Darul Iftah, Karachi, for arbitration. Harkatul Mujahideen was represented by Maulana Faruq Kashmiri, and Jaish-e Muhammad by Maulana Abdul Jabbar. The arbitration committee consisted of Mufti Rasheed Ahmad, Mufti Nizamuddin Shamzai, and Dr Sher Ali Shah of Oziristan. Its decision was: the Harkat offices occupied by Jaish-e Muhammad shall be returned to Harkatul Mujahideen; in return, Harkatul Mujahideen shall pay forty lakh rupees to Jaish-e Muhammad. After this decision, quarrels between the two organisations broke out again. Harkatul Mujahideen alleged that all the valuables had been removed from the offices that had been returned to it, the rest had been vandalised. This quarrel reached Afghanistan as well and one *mujahid* from Jaish-e Muhammad killed a member of Harkatul Mujahideen. This case was sent to sharia court, and finally to Osama bin Laden. Osama gave Harkatul Mujahideen fifty lakh rupees and twelve new double-cabin pick-ups, and thus the matter was resolved. He extracted a promise from Maulana Fazlur Rahman Khalil (general secretary, Harkatul Mujahideen) that he would not come in conflict with Jaish-e Muhammad again.

After the fight over resources, now they began to fight over division of 'martyrs', and that continues till today. Both the organisations lay claim on the martyrs who were killed in Afghanistan and Occupied Kashmir. The situation can be gauged from a report published in the May 2001 issue of the monthly, *Sada-e Mujahid*, Karachi:

> Sometime ago, a current journal, *Jaish-e Muhammad* published an interview with a *mujahid* Commander, Shahin. There are several things in this interview that do not help the cause of jihad or the related organisation. They appear to be in the nature of a negative invitation to jihad, and a betrayal of journalistic ethics, because the interviewee not only disassociates himself from these negative tendencies, but declares his joining of Harkatul Mujahideen whose ulema always pretend to fly high the flag of Truth and Righteousness. It is a pity that our youths respond to the call of jihad and sacrifice their lives and the ulema leadership use them for their own interest and mutual revenge. You can hear the Truth from the truth-teller Commander Shahin. He received his initial training from the training camp of Harkatul Mujahideen, Khalid bin Walid, in 1998, spent about two months in Bagram and came back. Then he went to Kargil front where he engaged with

Hindu 'sheep', after that he insisted on entering the valley; finally he went to the border and entered the Poonch valley, and participated in several missions in Banihal, Islamabad, and Doda to get the occupied valley freed of Hindu occupation forces. In this way, he attained the status of a *ghazi* (crusader) and came back.

My name is Muhammad Akmal, code name Shahin. I am from Alladitta tehsil in Multan. In the published interview in the journal, Jaish-e Muhammad whatever has been attributed to me with reference to Harkatul Mujahideen or its leadership is pure falsehood. I never said any of the things. I found the leaders of Harkatul Mujahideen to be true Muslims, following the sharia to the letter. Seeing them, I decided to join the organisation. I would like to work as a *mujahid* from the platform of Harkatul Mujahideen. My conscience supports it. I do not want to enter into any anti-jihad quarrels among the mujahideen, but want to fight wholeheartedly on behalf of Harkatul Mujahideen. I pray to God to give me strength and patience.

For confirmation, the audio cassette of the above is available with Harkatul Mujahideen. We always wanted to keep ourselves protected against malign allegations. This write-up is basically to make our readers aware of the reality. Now, when the religious groups are coming closer, people who make such allegations will lose any moral authority to talk about jihad.

As regards fight over martyrs, the following extract from the May 2000 issue of *Sada-e Mujahid* can be noted. Its title is 'An Important Clarification'. Here is how it goes.

213

As you know, Harkatul Mujahideen has been engaged in fighting infidels in Afghanistan and Kashmir over a long time. Thousands of youth from Harkatul Mujahideen have laid down their youthful lives on the front, and continue to do so till today. But today some people want to appropriate the sacrifice and hard work of Harkatul Mujahideen to gain cheap popularity. For example, they claimed *mujahid* Muhammad Faruq Arshad who became a martyr in the Occupied Kashmir, as their member. *mujahid* Muhammad Faruq Arshad was associated with Harkatul Mujahideen. His father has confirmed this through a fax message that Muhammad Faruq Arshad was associated with no other organisation except Harkatul Mujahideen.

Structure of Jaish-e Muhammad

The structure of Jaish-e Muhammad is based on both *tablighi* and militant considerations. Its militant structure is not based exactly on that of the army. In Occupied Kashmir, the chief commander is in overall charge of all activities. He is assisted by a deputy chief commander. For every district there is a district commander who is responsible for the activities in that district. The district commander may divide the district into several zones. The chief commander is directly accountable to the amir.

For preaching and publicity, there is a department of *dawat* and *irshad* that organises different jihadi programmes. This department is assisted by central, state-and district-level organisations. The state amir looks after the programmes in the province. The district amir looks after the organisations at the tehsil and area levels, and the tehsil amir has the authority to build units at the ward levels. Before it was banned, Jaish-e Muhammad had seventy-eight district-level and 390 tehsil-level offices working in Pakistan. After banning, these offices, particularly in big cities were closed. However, the offices in small towns and all the offices in Azad Kashmir are working. In every district-level office, three officials are working on salary.

CHARTER

Maulana Masood Azhar clarifies the objective of Jaish-e Muhammad in his editorial of the June 2001 issue of Jaish-e Muhammad in the following words:

Jaish-e Muhammad is a World Islamic movement/ organisation based on the principles of sharia. After just one year of its inception it has progressed much, by the grace of God. This movement will remove apostasy and strive for the implementation of sharia. For this, it has first reorganised its internal management. This organisation is conducting jihad against the enemies of religion and the country, and trying to bring Muslims closer to the Prophet. In simple words one can say 'Jihad against infidels, and fight against apostasy'. It has just two targets: the enemies of Islam are its military targets, whereas the non-Islamic elements among Muslims are its *tablighi* target. In this age of distortion, this movement talks about pure Islam and, by God's grace, its voice is being heard and accepted. This movement is free from any unwanted emotionalism. It does not talk of raising arms against everyone and at all times. Where sharia unequivocally decrees, it goes to kill; where reformation is needed, it uses words, spoken and written, instead of swords. Since this movement has been started merely for the Pleasure of God, to establish His religion, to protect Muslims... and to bring to the right path those who have gone astray, to work in this movement is a great opportunity. What else Muslims should want except that they should invite people to the way of God and should be ready to make all kinds of sacrifices for Islam?

Organisational Structure of Jaish-e Muhammad

Jaish-e Muhammad has seven departments, looked after by a twelve-member Central Consultative Committee (Markazi Majlis-e Shura). The amir can take any decision but he has to get endorsement (prior/ex post facto) from the Majlis-e Shura. The departments are as follows:

MILITARY DEPARTMENT

The responsibility of this department is training the mujahideen and launching them inside Occupied Kashmir. Besides, it also selects targets for the mujahideen there. Maulana Abdul Jabbar is the amir of this department, and Mufti Muhammad Asghar is the launching commander. Four big camps are working under this department:

1. Madrasa Syed Ahmad Shaheed Balakot
2. Camp Muzaffarabad
3. Camp Hajera
4. Camp Mansehra

After the end of the Taliban regime in Afghanistan, the jihadi camps located there have folded up. People say that a camp has been shifted to Waziristan.

Department of Prisoners (*Aasireen*)

This department strives to get the prisoners released from the jails of enemies. This department is directly under the supervision of the amir. Mufti Rafiq Ahmad is in charge. So far, this department has remained dormant.

Department of *Dawat* and *Irshad*

The head of this department is Maulana Muhammad Owais Khan Kashmiri. Besides chalking out *tablighi* (preaching and publicity) programmes, officials of this department meet the relatives of martyrs to offer them consolation and assistance and organise events to commemorate the martyrs.

Madrasa Syed Ahmad Shaheed, Balakot

The largest of Jaish-e Muhammad's training institute is Madrasa Syed Ahmad Shaheed which was established just after the founding of Jaish-e Muhammad. This madrasa is directly under the supervision of Maulana Masood Azhar. Qari Shah Mansoor is in charge of the madrasa.

This madrasa is located at a place to which access is very difficult. There is a village, Atr Sheesha, located on the road from Mansehra to Balakot Town. Five kilometres away from this village a pathway goes up the hill. This path is so steep and uneven that no ordinary car can ply on it. Even if a person manages to reach there, he is not permitted to enter the madrasa. Even Jaish-e Muhammad members can enter only after thorough search and registration. My journalist friend from Swat, Sayeed Khan, had visited the place to have a look at it. He was not permitted to enter even after half an hour of interrogation about the object of his visit. From outside, it appears to be a massive institute, the gate in front is like that of a castle. The flag of Jaish-e Muhammad flutters atop the gate. Behind the gate, among the tall trees is hung the platform for the watchmen from where they can oversee the whole campus.

Apart from the training of mujahideen, the yearly conference of the office bearers in the country is also held in the madrasa. Different programmes are held here throughout the year. It is also an educational and religious institute. According to Jaish-e Muhammad's records, seven thousand students passed out from here in the year 2000 alone. It is a kind of refresher course of three-months' duration, and every Jaish-e Muhammad Mujahid must undergo this course. Madrasa Syed Ahmad Shaheed is equipped to accommodate and feed 2,000 mujahideen at a time.

Martyrs Department

This department was opened on 31 January 2001. The man in charge here is Maulana Abdul Jabbar, and Khalid Jatoi is the secretary. A four-member committee helps them. The committee members are: Anwar Ali, Qari Abdul Ghafoor, Hafiz Muhammad Ashraf Jatoi, and Maulana Muhammad Akram. This department maintains the record of the martyrs killed in Afghanistan, Kashmir, and India; it also maintains the record of all outgoing mujahideen and those who manage to return from their areas of action. The following activities are carried out by this department:

1. To inform the families of martyrs immediately.
2. To give the families the initial grant of fifteen thousand rupees. If the families are poor, they are granted a monthly grant of 1,500 rupees. According to the department records, 130 families are being given this grant.
3. To send the journal, *Jaish-e Muhammad*, and other jihadi publications to these families. Five hundred thirty-five such families are sent complimentary copies of *Jaish-e Muhammad* (after Jaish-e Muhammad was banned this journal has been renamed, *Al-Islah* and is published fortnightly).
4. To award titles and shields of honour to martyrs.
5. To send the martyr's will and other belongings to his family.
6. To supervise the payment granted to the families of martyrs.
7. To maintain a record of the resources.

Apart from these, to pay homage to the martyr, this department organises a programme commemorating him within twenty days of his martyrdom.

Department of Grievance Redressal (*Sho'ba Amr bil Maroof O Nahi an-il Munkar*)

This department is working under the supervision of Maulana Ghulam Murtaza. According to a brochure of Jaish-e Muhammad, this department is responsible for the following activities:

1. To supervise the working of other departments and individuals to ascertain whether any of their actions was un-Islamic or against the principles of the organisation. If anyone violates the principles, the department can proceed against him.
2. To receive the proposals/complaints of members, send them to amir or relevant individuals. It will also investigate cases where such investigation is called for.
3. To protect the by-laws of the organisation. The amir's messages also will be declared through this department.
4. To look into the cases of arrest of its members, look after their cases and their belongings. Communication with the front line and the training of members are also the responsibilities of this department. A board of thirty ulema oversee the working of this department.

In 2001, this department did the following:

1. Organised 2,000 programmes in Pakistan and Azad Kashmir.
2. Prepared 500 new mujahideen.
3. Persuaded the principals of madrasas to send students for training. Students from 1,000 madrasas took military training.
4. Did remarkable work to build affiliated organisations.

Matrimonial Department

This department arranges alliances for mujahideen. Its secretary is Qazi Umar Farooq Abbasi. According to the June 2001 issue of *Jaish-e Muhammad*, this department arranged the following alliances up to June last year:

Total	409
Punjab	270
Sindh	84
Frontier Province	36
Baluchistan	12
Foreigners	7
Girls	148
Boys	261
Bachelors	321
Second Marriage	88
Families facilitating alliances	75

In the same issue of the journal it is observed:

> We had thought that only those involved in jihad will take interest in this department. But this department is attaining such popularity that it is taking international dimensions. All sorts of people – jihadi, non-jihadi, religious, political, businessmen – approached this department. As it is a religious duty, our services are available to all, provided that they are true Muslims.

Department of Broadcasting and Publication

This department of Jaish-e Muhammad is very active. Besides keeping in touch with newspapers and other media, publication is one of its major activities. This department has so far published about seventy books and more than two hundred jihadi pamphlets. Besides, it publishes the fortnightly, *Jaish-e Muhammad* (renamed *Al-Islah*), and the weekly, *Shamsheer*, which is printed in both Urdu and English. A monthly journal for women, *Banaat Ayesha*, is also published. Muhammad Maqsood Ahmad is in charge of this department. Its central office is located in Jama Masjid, Bathi Bafrozon, Karachi. The annual budget of this department is eighty lakh rupees. It is a profit-making department of Jaish-e Muhammad. Before the ban, the circulation of *Jaish-e Muhammad* was said to be thirty thousand. The circulation of *Banaat Ayesha* is seventeen thousand.

The First Split in Jaish-e Muhammad (Founding of Tahreek Al-Furqan)

The first breakaway group from Jaish-e Muhammad was led by Shah Mazhar who was the amir of Jaish-e Muhammad in Sindh Province. He broke away from Jaish-e Muhammad in October 2001 and formed Tahreek Al-Furqan. Before coming to Jaish-e Muhammad, he was the amir of Harkat-al Jihad Islami, Karachi, and had joined Jaish-e Muhammad with his entire group. Jaish-e Muhammad welcomed him and he had made a place for himself in it because of his fiery speeches. He was counted among the close aides of Maulana Masood Azhar. The reason for his disagreement with Jaish-e Muhammad is said to be that Maulana Masood Azhar had formed this organisation to unite all Deobandi organisations, which did not happen. On the contrary, disagreement among these organisations grew in intensity. A member of Jaish-e Muhammad in Lahore, however, felt that Shah Manzar was unhappy with the fact that everything in Jaish-e Muhammad had the seal of Maulana Masood Azhar and there was no sharing of power. Shah Manzar's name also figures in the American list according to which four Jaish-e Muhammad members were designated as 'dangerous'. He broke away from Jaish-e Muhammad with his entire group that is said to have about a thousand members. His separation from Jaish-e Muhammad is considered to be the breaking up of the Jaish-e Muhammad, Sindh Branch, from the centre. A week after founding the new organisation, Maulana Abdullah Shah Manzar was arrested in Karachi. Maulana Ejaz Mahmood is officiating in his place.

JAISH-E MUHAMMAD'S NETWORK

Jaish-e Muhammad's network extends to seventy-eight districts of Pakistan. The details of district branches are given in Table V. The biggest centre is in Karachi where about a hundred offices work. After Karachi, other big centres are in Multan and Bahawalpur. It has fifty-five offices in Bahawalpur and forty in Multan. In Frontier Province, it has big centres in Oziristan Agency, Malakand, Kohat, Banno, and Dera Ismail Khan. In Azad Kashmir, the largest centre is in Muzaffarabad. Here, its offices are located in the residence of the ex-chief minister of Azad Kashmir, Mumtaz Ahmad Atoi. In Baluchistan, Chajgora is an important centre. Jaish-e Muhammad has paid special attention to build its organisational network inside Sindh. It has its offices in every district there. After Hizbul Mujahideen, the largest network in Pakistan belongs to Jaish-e Muhammad. However, in terms of human resource it has an edge over Hizbul Mujahideen. Moreover, in some districts, the offices of the weekly, *Zarb-e Momin*, and those of Al-Rasheed Trust are also used as offices of Jaish-e Muhammad. In fact, they act as better substitutes, after the ban. This writer has collected most of his materials about Jaish-e Muhammad from the offices of *Zarb-e Momin* in Dera Ghazi Khan, Multan, Sangrha, and Hyderabad.

Madrasas Providing Human Resource to Jaish-e Muhammad

Jaish-e Muhammad gets its members from government schools and colleges, and madrasas. It is easier for Jaish-e Muhammad to get human resource from the government institutions where units of Jamiat Tulaba Islam and Sipah Sahaba Students exist. The department of dawat and irshad organises jihadi lectures and other programmes in these institutions, and prepares the students for training during the summer vacation. Maulana Muhammad Salim Khan of Ofaq al-Madaris al-Arabiya (a madrasa board) claims that in madrasas, students are not allowed to go for jihadi training during the course of study. Despite this claim many students of madrasas not only acquire military training but also take part in practical jihad.

According to a student, Mansoor, of Jamia Ehteshamiya, Jacob Line, Karachi, he was a student at the third stage (*salis*) and had visited Afghanistan twice during summer vacation for jihadi training in Kabul. He had several friends with him as well. He said that younger students from his madrasa are not allowed to go for jihadi training. He and his friends are allowed to go for training, but are not permitted to go for jihad till they have finished their studies. But some students are 'seduced' by mujahideen to go to jihad. On their return, they are given a reprimand by the madrasa authorities and then taken back. Mansoor further said that normally students are sent for training in the camps at Mansehra and Balakot located in Pakistan. The teachers in different madrasas are also directly involved in jihadi activities. The list of these madrasas is too long. Only Jaish-e Muhammad's important madrasas are as follows:

1. Jamiatul-uloom Islamia Banoriah, Karachi
2. Darul-uloom Farooqiah, Karachi
3. Darul-uloom Hamadiah, Karachi
4. Jamia Haqqaniah, Akora Khatak, Naoshehra
5. Jamia Ashrafiya, Lahore
6. Khairul Madaris, Multan
7. Jamia Islamia, Dera Ghazi Khan
8. Madrasa Boonistan, Panjgour, Baluchistan
9. Jamiatur-Rashid, Ahsanabad, Karachi
10.Jamia Miftahul uloom, Hyderabad
11.Madrasa Jaish-e Muhammad, Shikarpur
12.Jamia Mukhzanul-uloom, Khanpur
13.Jamia Imdaya Babul-uloom, Kehrorika
14.Jamia Asharfiah, Lahore
15.Jamia Manzoorul Islamia, Lahore
16.Jamia Islamia, Kashmir Road, Rawalpindi
17.Madrasa-e-Khalidia, Chechawatani
18.Jamia Usmania, Shorkot

19. Jamia Rahmiah Tarteelul Quran, Rahim Yar Khan
20. Jamia Farooqiah, Shujaabad
21. Madrasa Abu Hurairah, Naoshera
22. Darul-uloom Azazil, Naoshera
23. Jamia Noumania Sualehiyah, Dera Ismail Khan
24. Darul-uloom Islamia, Muzaffarabad (Azad Kashmir)
25. Jamia Farooqiah, Maingalabad (Baluchistan)

Important Fund-raising Forums

Jaish-e Muhammad's department of material resources is quite active in raising funds. Its fund-raisers keep on visiting mosques throughout the year. Fund-raisers are also sent to foreign countries for this purpose. Despite the ban, Jaish-e Muhammad was able to raise funds to the tune of one-and-a-half crore of rupees from the sale of hides of sacrificed animals. The following organisations also provide material assistance to Jaish-e Muhammad:

Al-Rasheed Trust

Al-Rasheed Trust is working as a welfare trust. The USA has already banned it. The Government of Pakistan has also frozen its account. Despite this, it is an active organisation that have been engaged in making welfare schemes and founding institutes during the Taliban period. It does not provide funds directly to the jihadi organisations. But its department of prisoners (*Asiraan*) provides funds for the release of mujahideen jailed in different countries. Jaish-e Muhammad also takes advantage of this fund.

Al-Akhtar Trust

Al-Akhtar Trust International is working under Maulana Hakim Muhammad Akhtar. It has started several welfare schemes inside Sindh. It does not compete with Al-Rasheed Trust, but it also raises funds for the mujahideen which is distributed among different jihadi organisations, including Jaish-e Muhammad.

Jaish-e Muhammad's Militant Activities

The first militant incursions by Jaish-e Muhammad in Occupied Kashmir was by Commander Sajid Jihadi alias Baba Ghazi. This was in March 2000. He had engineered an explosion in the compound of Srinagar Jail, and thus opened the account of Jaish-e Muhammad. Till date, 179 Jaish-e Muhammad members have been killed in Occupied Kashmir. It claims to have killed 1,496 Indian army men including brigadiers, colonels, majors, captains, and soldiers. Jaish-e Muhammad has also mounted eighty-nine fidayeen attacks.

Majority of Jaish-e Muhammad's youths come from Punjab, specifically, Multan, Bahawalpur, and Rahim Yar Khan. Waziristan, Peshawar, Naoshera, and Kohat in Frontier Province, and Karachi and Shikarpur in Sindh are the towns and cities that send maximum number of youths to Jaish-e Muhammad. After Lashkar-e Tayyaba, Jaish-e Muhammad began fidayeen attacks in Occupied Kashmir and India. According to Jaish-e Muhammad sources, it has mounted thirty-five fidayeen attacks in Occupied Kashmir in 2001, in which twenty-three of its own members and 250 officers and soldiers of the Indian army were killed.

One target of Jaish-e Muhammad's militant agenda is the Shiv Sena leaders, and those Hindu leaders who were involved in the demolition of the Babri Masjid. It claims to have killed fifteen Shiv Sena and other Hindu leaders who were involved in the demolition of the Babri Masjid.

Jaish-e Muhammad had promptly claimed the responsibility of attacking the Indian Parliament, but contradicted it the following day. Important sources say that Jaish-e Muhammad wanted to compete with Lashkar-e Tayyaba by mounting an attack on the Red Fort. And when the incident occurred, it promptly claimed responsibility, but it had to contradict it under pressure from some agencies. Some Jaish-e Muhammad sources say that the incident was a surprise for them as they had sent no such mission, although some members, to establish superiority, had issued the statement claiming responsibility. This harmed not only Jaish-e Muhammad but Pakistan also.

Attack on the Assembly of Occupied Kashmir

Jaish-e Muhammad accepted the responsibility of attacking the assembly house of Occupied Kashmir. It was also confirmed in a report published in the issue dated 15 October 2001 of the weekly, *Zarb-e Momin*:

> It happened last Monday. The puppet state assembly members of Occupied Kashmir were just coming out after concluding the day's work when a government car appeared on the road in front of the assembly. A handsome youth in police uniform was sitting in it.

The onlookers must have thought him to be an officer on duty. Who knew that this devotee of God was going to meet his Lord. As it reached close to the assembly house, a loud explosion rent the atmospher e. In a few moments, the entrails of the supporters of the oppressive regime in Kashmir were on the road. This incident has shaken the Indian government, and has served the message to the slogan-mongers of Akhand Bharat that it would be better for them to free Kashmir. Otherwise they will continue to receive such gifts.

Jaish-e Muhammad, After the Ban

On 12 October 2001, America announced freezing of Jaish-e Muhammad bank accounts. In December 2001 he was put under house arrest. In January 2002, Jaish-e Muhammad was banned. After the ban, the accounts of Jaish-e Muhammad were frozen and raids were conducted to arrest its members. In the raids conducted between January and May, only forty-five mujahideen of Jaish-e Muhammad were captured, most of whom are ordinary members. Jaish-e Muhammad sources said that early in December 2001, it had sent away its important leaders and mujahideen to such places where they could not be captured. Jaish-e Muhammad's offices were working in Azad Kashmir till May 2002. I met quite a few mujahideen in the offices at Kotli, Muzaffarabad. From Kotli office we got to know that those mujahideen who were in Karachi, Rawalpindi, and Peshawar were sent away on holiday in January. Some of them had reached Azad Kashmir. Offices in Dera Ghazi Khan, Leh,

Muzaffargarh, Rajanpur, and Laodhran operated till March 2002, though the signboard had been taken off. Several Jaish-e Muhammad offices had shifted to the offices of *Zarb-e Momin* and Al-Rasheed Trust.

In the new jihadi set-up, Jaish-e Muhammad has been attached to Al-Jihad. Now, Jaish-e Muhammad will not be able to conduct any activities in Occupied Kashmir in its own name. Its organisational structure has been handed over to Al-Jihad. In Azad Kashmir, its offices will continue to work. Jaish-e Muhammad sources say that it is working in Pakistan and will soon emerge with a new name. It will reappear as a welfare organisation in Pakistan.

LEADERS OF JAISH-E MUHAMMAD

Maulana Abdul Jabbar

Maulana Abdul Jabbar is the Deputy amir of Jaish-e Muhammad and in charge of its militant wing. Earlier, he was the chief secretary of Harkatul Mujahideen and the secretary of its militant wing. He has played a vital role in bringing the office bearers of Harkatul Mujahideen to Jaish-e Muhammad. He fought in Afghanistan against the Soviet army and the Northern Alliance.

Maulana Asmatullah Muavia

He is the amir of Jaish-e Muhammad in Azad Kashmir. Earlier, he was an active member of Sipah Sahaba. He joined Jaish-e Muhammad at the behest of Mufti Owais Khan, and made a place for himself in Jaish-e Muhammad because of his fiery speeches.

Maulana Sajid Usman

Before joining Jaish-e Muhammad he was the deputy

amir of Harkat-al Jihad. He is known to have great organising abilities. He is in charge of Jaish-e Muhammad's department of material resources, and lives in Karachi.

Maulana Qari Sadiq
He was the former director of resources in Harkatul Mujahideen. He looks after the management of Jaish-e Muhammad. He played a vital role in spreading the network of Jaish-e Muhammad in Punjab.

Mufti Owais
He is the amir of Jaish-e Muhammad's department of *dawat* and *irshad*. Before joining Jaish-e Muhammad, he was the member of the Majlis-e Shura of Harkat-al Jihad. He is a great orator.

Qari Zarar Urf Qasai
Before joining Jaish-e Muhammad he was the chief commander, United Harkatul Ansar. He is a member of Jaish's military department.

Maulana Ghulam Murtaza
Maulana Ghulam Murtaza is the head of the department of grievance redressal. Before joining Jaish-e Muhammad, he was the chief secretary of Harkatul Mujahideen in Punjab. He played an important role in occupying the offices of Harkatul Mujahideen in Punjab. He is close to Maulana Masood Azhar. He lives in Kausar Colony, Bahawalpur.

Maulana Qari Umar Faruq Abbasi
He is in charge of Jaish-e Muhammad's matrimonial Department. He is the principal, Jamia Rahimia Tarteel al-Quran, Rahim Yar Khan. He is also the *khateeb* of the central Idgah in Rahim Yar Khan.

Mufti Muhammad Asghar
He is Jaish-e Muhammad's launching commander.
Two of his brothers have been martyred in Kashmir.
He was associated with Harkatul Mujahideen before
joining Jaish-e Muhammad. Madrasa Syed Ahmad
Shaheed is his permanent residence.

Table V: *Jaish-e Muhammad: District Branches*

Sr. No.	District	Amir	District/Tehsil Offices
1.	Multan	Mehtab Nafees	1) Masjid Khuda Baksh Wali Muhalla Aslamabad, Kachchi Sarai Stop, Masoom Road, Multan
			2) Jama Masjid Rasheedia, Rasheedabad, C/o Sadiq Book Centre, Multan
2.	Maan Kot		Jamia Asharfiah, Adda Maan Kot, C/o Hakim Saheb, Multan
3.	Tehsil Jalalpur	Mujahid Shakeel Ahmad	Adda Jalalpur Peerwala, Near Nirala Sweets, Tehsil Jalalpur, Multan
4.	Lodhran		Purani Sabzi Mandi, Near Rehman Masjid, Multan Road, Lodhran,
5.	Khanewal		Gali No. 2, Colony No. 3, Khanewal
6.	Tehsil Mian Chunnoo	Amanullah	Makki Masjid, T Chowk, Mian Chunnoo
7.	Tehsil Jahaniyan		First Floor, Abdul Ghani Pinsari, Sadar Bazar, Jahaniyan
8.	Tehsil Abdul Hakim		Near Bab Umar, Multan Road, Abdul Hakim, Khanewal
9.	Khushab	Umar Hayat	Railway Road First Floor, Zia Electronics, Nawan Lari Adda, Khushab
10.	Bhakkar		Furniture Market, Near Bismillah Furniture, Jhang Road, Bhakkar
11.	Lahore	Ahsanullah/ Naved Farooqui	Jamia Masjid Usmania, Quarter Railway General Store, Near Engine Shed, Mughal Pura, Lahore

Gateway to Terrorism

Sr. No.	District	Amir	District/Tehsil Offices
12.	North Lahore		Aamir Road IAS School System, Bagh, Lahore
13.	Lahore		Milad Chowk Near Jama Masjid Mehmood, Nishat Colony, Lahore
14.	Rahim Yar Khan	Rizwan Hameed	House No. 108, Bano Bazar, Rahim Yar Khan
15.	Tehsil Sadiqabad	Maulana Abdul Latif Siddiqui	Allama Iqbal Road, East Ghalla Mandi Gate, Sadiqabad
16.	Tehsil Liaqat Pur		Abbasia Road, Chowk Ghanta Ghar, Liaqatabad
17.	Tehsil Khanpur	Qari Mukhtar Ahmad	Near Jama Masjid Abdullah Bin Masood, Rahim Yar Khan, Khanpur
18.	Tehsil Kher Pur Tamiwali		Main Bazar, Maqbool Market, Kherpur Tamiwali, District Bahawalpur
19.	Chakwal	Asad Ali	Panwal Road, Tehsil Chowk, Chakwal
20.	Tehsil Tila Gang		Opposite Zahid Hardware, Chakwal Road, Tehsil Tila Gang
21.	Naruwal		Darman Road, Near Azim Public School, Shakar Garh, District Naruwal
22.	Wahari	Mujahid Abdullah	1 Floor, Usamah Medicine Company, Opp. Thana Sadar Wahari
23.	Tehsil Boreywalah		1 Floor, Marghoob Market, College Road, Boreywalah
24.	Mailsee		Madrasa Jamal-ul-Quran Colony, Chowk Mailsee, District Wahari
25.	Leh		1 Floor, Rais Jewellers, Lalli Lal Road, Leh
26.	Jhang	Abid Hussain	Gali Faran Model School, Near Girls College Chowk, Gojrah Road, Jhang
27.	Tehsil Shor Kot	Sher Ahmad Khaki	Near Rafiqi Chowk, Shor Kot Cantt, District Jhang

234

Sr. No.	District	Amir	District/Tehsil Offices
28.	Sialkot		Rais Chowk, Hameeda Plaza, Flat No. 18, Sialkot
29.	Tehsil Daska		Marhaba Market, Basant Road, Diska, District Sialkot
30.	Tehsil Pasarwer		Main Road Qila Colarwala, Tehsil Pasarwer, District Sialkot
31.	Gujrat	Qamaru-uz-Zaman Siddiqui	Near Dadar Gulab Shah Qabristan, Sargodha Road, Gujrat
32.	Tehsil Kharian		1 Floor, Sangam Plaza, Main Bazar, Kharian
33.	Sargodha	Maulana Ghulam Haider	Opp. Chowdhary Hotel, 1 Floor, Hafiz Morh, Sagodha
34.	Tehsil Sahiwal		Near Utility Store, Sahiwal, District Sargodha
35.	Shaikhupura		Near Masjid Sadar Thana Road, Shaikhupura
36.	Mureed Key		Tankey Bazar, Near Malik Hotel, GT Road, Mureed Key, District Shaikhupura
37.	Tehsil Nankana		Main Bazar, Syed Wala Road, Bachaykee, Tehsil Nankana, Shaikhupura
38.	Okarah	Naved Farooqi	Jamia Usmania, 1 Floor, Gole Chowk, Okarah
39.	Tehsil Renalah Khurd	Qari Ghulam Abbas (Deputy secretary)	Kamyab Building, Ghalla Mandi, Renalah Khurd, District Okarah
40.	Deepalpur		Lorry Adda Deepalpur, Okarah
41.	Haveli Lakha		Al-Farid Book Depot, Railway Road, Haveli Lakha, Okarah
42.	Sahiwal	Bhai Sheerazi	Behind Bank Of Punjab, Rashid Minhas Road, Sahiwal
43.	Faisalabad	Qari Hamad-Ullah Farooqi	Afghanaaabad No. 2, Gali No. 12, Opp. Jamia Masjid Ayyubia, Faisalabad

Gateway to Terrorism

Sr. No.	District	Amir	District/Tehsil Offices
	Tehsil Juranwalah		
44.			1 Floor, Dawakhana, Ghalla Mandi, Juranwalah
45.	Samandari	Hakim Muti-ullah Aawan	Faisalabad Road, Near Wapda Daftar Samandri, District Faisalabad
46.	Mianwali	Maulana Abdur Rasheed	Gali M C High School Wali, Main Bazar, Mianwali
47.	Peelan		Near Muhajreen Masjid, Zameen Bazar, Peelan, District Mianwali
48.	Klorekot		Beside Jama Masjid, Old Lorry Adda, Opp. Muslim Commercial Bank, Klorekot
49.	Tehsil Pindi Bhatiyan		Lahore Road, Near Thana Pindi Bhanyan, District Hafizabad
50.	Gujranwala		Near Bhai Bhai Tractors House, Lorry Adda, Behind Yusuf Plaza, Gujranwala
51.	Tehsil Wazirabad		Near Masjid Darah Kabootranwali, Main Bazar, Wazirabad
52.	Attock		Arsalan Plaza, Committee Chowk, Pindi, Kheb
53.	Rajanpur	Maulana Abdul Jabbar	Opp. Habib Bank, Rajanpur
54.	Tehsil Jampur		Near Albaina School, Jampur
55.	Rojhan		Jamia Muhammadia, Rojhan
56.	Behawalanger	Ismail Zabeekh	College Road, Milad Chowk Chishtiyan, District Behawalanger
57.	Fort Abbas	Rana Shehzad	Awami Bazar Fort Abbas, District Behawalanger
58.	Manchanabad		Baldiya Road, Manchan, District Behawalanger
59.	Haroonabad		Chaman Bazar, Haroonabad, District Behawalanger
60.	Dera Ghazi Khan	Maulana Bashar-ul-Haq	Near Purani Sabzi Mandi, Sadar Bazar, Block No. 3, Dera Ghazi Khan

236

Sr. No.	District	Amir	District/Tehsil Offices
61.	Pakpatan		Near Ar-Rahman Bakery, Inside Ghalla Mandi, Pakpatan
62.	Tehsil Aarif Wala		Jamia Masjid Usmania Quboolah Chowk Aarif Wala, District Pakpatan
63.	Qusoor	Mohammad Yunus Azhar	Opp. Wagon Stand, Near Lorry Adda, Qusoor
64.	Mandi Bahauddin		Chowk Alvi Hospital, Jamboo House, Mandi Bahauddin
65.	Toba Tek Singh		Gali Dhobiyan Wali, Kasheedakari Bazar, Shorkot Road, Toba Tek Singh
66.	Rawalpindi	Umar Hayat Farooqi	House No. K34, Katariyan, Satellite Town Bazar, Wahari
67.	Muzaffargarh	Nasim Aijaz	District Office, Near Baldiya Office, Multan Road, Muzaffargarh
68.	Texla	Kamran Akhtar	Tehsil Office, Opp. Iqbal Market, Muhalla Shabbirabad, Alipur, Muzaffargarh

Baluchistan

Sr. No.	District	Amir	District/Tehsil Offices
69.	Khazdar		Near State Life Office, Hospital Road, Khazdar
70.	Dera Murad Jamali		Phatak Road, Derah Murad Jamili, Baluchistan
71.	Pajgour	Hafiz Ehtasham-ul-Haq	Madarsab Bunistan, Pajgour, Baluchistan

Sindh

Sr. No.	District	Amir	District/Tehsil Offices
72.	Larkana	Bhai Abdul Hafiz	Madrasa Rouzatul-Uloom, Muhammadi Colony, Near Shaikh Zaid Hospital, Chowk Qamar Road, Larkana
73.	Sanghar	Maulana Muhammad Afzal Chishti	Near Rehmat Shah, M A Jinah Ros, Sanghar

Gateway to Terrorism

Sr. No.	District	Amir	District/Tehsil Offices
74.	Naushero Firoz		Opp. Madrasa-e-Haseeniah Taleemul-Quran, Station Road, District Naushero Firoz
75.	Sukkur	Maulana Muhammad Naim Siddiqui	Near Abdul Ghaffar Chole Wala, Gali No. 1, Ghantaghar, Sukkur
76.	Hyderabad	Maulana Jalil-ur-Rahman	Selawatpara, Near Avon Chowk, Hyderabad
77.	Meerpur Khas	Mufti Abdullah Anwar	
78.	Shikarpur	Abdul Hafiz	Shopping Centre, Near Lakhi Dil, Shikarpur Masjid Aqsa, Aarain Mohalla Khanpur, District Shikarpur
79.	Kherpur Meerus	Maulana Ubaidullah Khaki	Madrasa Talimul Quran Jeelani, Mohalla, District Khairpur, Nawab Shah Road Pakka Chang Tehsil Faizganj, Kherpur, Meerus
80.	Nawab Shah	Maulana Afzal Chishti	1 Floor, Munir Printing Press, Jakrah Bazar Nawab Shah
81.	Ratoo Derah		Near Muhammadi Masjid Bus Stop, Ratoo Derah
82.	Jacobabad	Noor Hasan	Near Ghantaghar, Shikarpur Road, Kandhkot, District Jacobabad
83.	Ghotaki	Maulana Muhammad Tayyab	Rehamwali Road, Ghotaki
84.	Pano Aqil		Opp. Tariq Tent Service, Balaji Road, Pano Aqil
85.	Dharki		Haji Allah Rakhiyo Sharma Circuit, Reti Road, Dharki
86.	Tando Adam	Hafiz Hasan Sheikh	Station Road, Near Markazi Qaomi Bachat, Tando Adam
87.	Kot Ghumal Muhammad		Near Town Committee Chowk, Kot Ghulam Muhammad, Sindh
88.	Karachi		Flat No. 12, Adda D Fashion, Near Regal Chowk, Chowk Sadar Karachi

Sr. No.	District	Amir	District/Tehsil Offices
Frontier Province			
89.	Peshawar		Khan Plaza, Sunehri Masjid, Peshawar Sadar
90.	Mansehra	Muhammad Yusuf Azhar	Chinar Road, Near Masjid Taqwa, Lorry Adda, Mansehra Shakbari Road, Madni Masjid Stop, Office, District Health Officers
91.	Abbottabad	Umar Farooq Abbasi	Mount View Hotel, Opp. No. 3, Government High School, Abbottabad
92.	Kohat	Doctor Alam Bangash	Shah Faisal Masjid Bairoon, Shah Faisal Gate, Kohat
93.	Gilgit		Behind Park Hotel, Muhalla Karot, Gilgit
94.	Naoshera		Mumtaz Building, Near High School No. 1, GT Road, Naoshera
95.	Dera Ismail Khan	Maulana Hamadullah Farooqi	Opp. Haq Nawaz, Near Tahir Air Condition, Post Office, Dera Islmail Khan
96.	Mardan		Gojargarhi Road, Sufbedar Ayub Road, Baghdad Mardan
97.	Hari Pur Azad Kashmir		Chowk Sheranwala Gate, Bilal Plaza, Flat No. 1, Haripur
98.	Meerpur	Maulana Hasan Mehmood	Nabeel Haneef Plaza, Sarrafa Bazar, Tangi Meerpur, Azad Kashmir
99.	Daddyal		Sayyidai Gali, Near Maqbool Bhat, Shehad Chowk, Daddyal, Azad Kashmir
100.	Muzaffarabad	Shehbaz Khan Basharat	49-B, Mumtaz Rathore House, Upper Chattar, Muzaffarabad

Harkatul Mujahideen

Harkatul Mujahideen is an important organisation of Deobandi school of thought. The USA banned it in October 2001. It is considered a big jihadi formation in view of its militant activities in Afghanistan and Occupied Kashmir. Harkatul Mujahideen was born from the womb of Harkat-al Jihad. Among its founder members are Maulana Fazlur Rahman Khalil, Maulana Muhammad Masood Alvi, and Saifullah Shaukat.

Before Harkatul Mujahideen was founded, Harkat-al Jihad was the only Deobandi organisation fighting against the Soviets in Afghanistan. Its leadership was purely Pakistani and the majority of its members were students of Deobandi madrasas. Maulana Irshad was the leader of this organisation who, in 1984, died fighting in Afghanistan along with twelve of his Pakistani companions. Then Maulana Saifullah Akhtar became its new amir. But some members did not consent to his leadership. One group was led by Maulana Masood Ali and he had the support of the mujahideen from the madrasas of Mianwali and Kundiyan. He gave his group the name, Jibba Khalidiya. Meanwhile, he met Maulana Fazlur Rahman Khalil, who had the support of the *mujahid* students from Dera Ismail Khan, in a front and sought his suggestions. After mutual consultations the new formation was given the name Harkatul Mujahideen. Maulana Fazlur Rahman became its amir and Maulana Masood Alvi its central commander.

By the end of 1984, Harkatul Mujahideen had built

its organisational structure and it began jihad under the leadership of the Afghan commander, Jalaluddin Haqqani. It also kept in touch with Maulana Yunus Khalis's Hizbul Islami. The greatest responsibility of Harkatul Mujahideen was to gather human resource from Pakistan. It played a vital role in the conquest of Khost. In the Khost front, Harkatul Mujahideen's first supreme commander, Abdul Rasheed, was killed. Commander Maulana Shabbir, Mufti Abu Ubaida, and Nurul Islam were the other casualties.

Having played their role in Afghanistan, Harkatul Mujahideen turned its attention to Occupied Kashmir where the movement for independence was in its initial stages. Some youths from Occupied Kashmir had come to Maulana Masood Alvi for military training. Maulana Masood laid the foundation of a jihadi organisation for Kashmir named Jamiatul Mujahideen (he had founded Jamiatul Mujahideen in 1972, but during Afghan war he did not use this name) and gave the Kashmiri youths its responsibility. However, the Maulana died in the cantonment in Paktia state in 1988 when his legs hit a landmine.

Maulana Fazlur Rahman Khalil took up the entire responsibility of Harkatul Mujahideen and built up the formation's network in Kashmir. Commander Sajjad Rashid was launched in Occupied Kashmir. The first band of Harkatul Mujahideen entered Occupied Kashmir in 1991 and established their centres in Baramula, Anantnag, and Poonch.

Meanwhile, Harkatul Mujahideen was reorganised in Pakistan and its branches were opened in most of the districts. Till 1991, Harkatul Mujahideen got its human resource mainly from madrasas. Then a separate department was opened to draw students from government schools and colleges, and youths from other walks of life. By 1995, the latter group, whose background was not religious, had outnumbered the students from madrasas by several times.

Founding of Harkatul Ansar

After the end of the Afghan War, Harkatul Mujahideen and Harkat-al Jihad started the militant campaign in Occupied Kashmir separately. They competed with each other in publicising their jihadi activities in exaggerated terms. This led to mutual tension and bitterness. To come to grip with this situation, a number of leaders like Maulana Rasheed, Maulana Hafiz Yusuf Ludhianwi, Maulana Dr Sher Ali, and Maulana Samiul Haq began rigorous efforts. Eventually, in June 1993, both the organisations agreed to merge with each other. Thus, Harkatul Ansar was founded. Maulana Shahadatullah of Harkat-al Jihad was appointed the chief commander.

After Harkatul Ansar came into being there was a fillip in militant activities in Occupied Kashmir. One reason for this was its commander, Sajjad Afghani. But he was arrested in February 1994 along with Maulana Masood Azhar. Harkatul Ansar began efforts to get both of them released. After Sajjad Afghani's arrest, Commander Sikandar (Javed Ahmad Dabra) was made the chief commander of Occupied Kashmir. He kidnapped two British tourists in April 1994 and demanded the release of Sajjad Afghani and Maulana

Masood Azhar in return. According to Maulana Masood Azhar, the Indian government had agreed to release them, and the leadership of Harkatul Ansar had ordered the release of the tourists. Meanwhile, on 11 November 1994, a number of Americans and Englishmen were kidnapped in Delhi at Commander Sikandar's behest. An organisation named, Al-Hadeed claimed responsibility. The name 'Al-Hadeed' was used so that the Pakistani leadership of Harkatul Ansar might not bring pressure for their release. But this effort went in vain. Not only that Maulana Masood Azhar and Sajjad Afghani were not released, Harkatul Ansar found itself in a mess because of this misadventure.

Rift in Harkatul Ansar

Harkatul Mujahideen had agreed to merge in Harkatul Ansar on the condition that in case of any disagreement, it would return to its own organisation. In other words, Harkatul Ansar had already two groups. In 1995, when a formation named Al-Faran kidnapped some tourists to get Maulana Masood Azhar and Sajjad Afghani released, the leadership of Harkatul Mujahideen once again came under pressure and the USA imposed a ban on it. The leaderships of Harkatul Mujahideen and Harkat-al Jihad blamed each other for this. Eventually, both the organisations reverted to their pre-merger identities. However, a third group also emerged that called itself, United Harkatul Ansar. Qari Zarar Urf Qasai became its commander. It later merged in Jaish-e Muhammad.

Who Formed Al-Faran?

In 1995, in the Pahalgam area of Occupied Kashmir, some American, British, and German tourists were kidnapped. A formation called Al-Faran claimed responsibility. According to an important member, Akbar, of Jaish-e Muhammad in Sargodha, Commander Sikandar and Commander Abdul Hamid Turki had formed Al-Faran to get Maulana Masood Azhar released. As both of them were earlier associated with Harkatul Mujahideen, Harkatul Ansar squarely blamed it saying that its erstwhile members were repeatedly indulging in activities forbidden by the central command. In the beginning, Harkatul Mujahideen defended the duo, but when the two organisations separated, Maulana Fazlur Rahman Khalil began to say that Al-Faran was floated by RAW. He said in an interview:

> Al-Faran has been formed by RAW with the calculated purpose of defaming the mujahideen as terrorists, particularly in the eyes of the West, and they engineered some bogus incidents. Al-Faran has no existence in Kashmir. The European tourists were kidnapped by RAW, and through the fictitious name Al-Faran, they shifted the blame to Harkatul Mujahideen. Today, there are only two great jihadi organisations in the world – Hamas in Palestine and Harkatul Mujahideen in Kashmir.
>
> *Sada-e Mujahid*, monthly, Karachi, March 2000

The tourists could not be released, because Commander Sikandar and Commander Abdul Hamid, who had made this scheme, died in a mission and this matter came to a standstill. After the commanders died, Harkatul Mujahideen publicly disassociated itself from Al-Faran. According to Akbar, there was no doubt about the intentions of the two commanders; they had resorted to this after being disappointed by their leadership. If Harkatul Mujahideen had not ordered release of the British tourists in April 1993, they would not have felt the need to form Al-Faran.

From Harkatul Mujahideen to Jaish-e Muhammad

Maulana Masood Azhar was released as a result of the hijacking of the Indian Airlines plane in December 1999. Barely two months after his release, Maulana Masood Azhar declared the forming of his new organisation. Many *mujahids* of Harkatul Mujahideen and Harkat-al Jihad joined Jaish-e Muhammad. Its formation dealt a severe blow to Harkatul Mujahideen. Many of its offices in Punjab and Sindh were taken over by Jaish-e Muhammad.

The strongest opposition to Jaish-e Muhammad came from Harkatul Mujahideen. An important leader of Harkatul Mujahideen in Dera Ghazi Khan says: 'We were most delighted by his (Maulana Masood Azhar) release. But when we went to meet him, he was a changed man. He was not ready to consider himself a part of Harkatul Mujahideen, even though our journal *Sada-e Mujahid* was continually singing his praises. According to Fazal Muhammad, another leader of Hizbul Mujahideen:

Some of our known thinkers and intellectuals offer a new philosophy by making a fine distinction between 'jihad' and 'qital' (slaughter) which is a deep conspiracy against jihad. They say that they tried their best to dissuade Maulana Masood Azhar from making a new organisation, but the Maulana was insistent on it. After the organisation was formed, differences between the *mujahids* and the blame-game have accentuated. This sin must be visited on him.

Sada-e Mujahid, April 2000

A leader of Harkatul Mujahideen from Kotli told me that Maulana Hafiz Yusuf Ludhianwi and Maulana Mufti Nizamuddin Shamzai had an important role in breaking Harkatul Mujahideen. 'On the one hand, they reassured us that they would not allow forming of a new organisation, even while they were in the process of forming it. He referred to an issue of *Sada-e Mujahid* that published the report of a programme that took place in the Mansehra training camp in February 2000. Mufti Shamzai Sahib had come there and declared support for Harkatul Mujahideen. Following is an excerpt from his speech:

Harkatul Mujahideen has its own military wing and the whole world knows about its name and achievements. The youth from these organisations have made untold sacrifices for the oppressed Muslims. Maulana Masood Azhar is one of our companions whose contributions to the cause of jihad cannot be overemphasised. Through God's special grace, he was released from the jails of Hindus, and the circumstances of his release are known to everyone. I do not know why (and I do not have any misconception about anyone) he now refuses to work with his former colleagues. He said clearly, 'I cannot go along with those colleagues, neither can I leave jihad.' He has also consulted the ulema in this regard. We tried our best to persuade him to work with former companions. But he said that he wanted to work for jihad with a new name.

Harkatul Mujahideen has not folded up. We do not want to gladden the heart of Clinton, Vajpayee, Jews of Israel and the communists of Russia by declaring the death of this organisation. This organisation was established by our elders and it is working efficiently in the cause of jihad. We will patronise it as long as it remains steadfast on its jihadi agenda. It is mere false propaganda that this organisation is being folded up.

We have always patronised Harkatul Mujahideen, and will continue to do so. I am saying it in clear words that it is our and our elders' organisation. Fact is – I am the supporter of jihad and want to serve Islam wherever it is possible, and doing so, by the grace of God, to the best of my abilities.

Sada-e Mujahid, monthly, Karachi, March 2000

Organisational Structure of Harkatul Mujahideen

Despite its fame, the organisational structure of Harkatul Mujahideen is not very well knit, compared to other such organisations. It has four central departments:

Military Department	Secretary, Maulana Faruq Kashmiri
Department of Dawat and Irshad (Preachings and Commands)	Secretary, Maulana Nurul Haq

| Department of Resources | Secretary, Qari Muhammad Sadiq |
| Department of Communications and Publication | Secretary, Maulana Fazal Ahmad |

However, there is no close coordination among all these departments, due to which disagreements often crop up in the organisation. The hold of Maulana Fazlur Rahman Khalil is quite strong on the organisation. He is the general secretary, but practically he has all the powers. Maulana Faruq Kashmiri is the amir, but his influence is limited to the activities related to military training.

Apart from the above four, there is also a department of administration looked after by Maulana Allah Osaya. This department supervises organisational management throughout the country. However, the department of *dawat* and *irshad* has precedence over this department inasmuch as it plays a dominant role in providing human resource to Harkatul Mujahideen. The military department and the department of communications and publication are also very active ones. Apart from training the *mujahids*, the military department makes arrangement for launching them in Occupied Kashmir and keeps in touch with the organisational set-up there. It had even a tank in its camp in Afghanistan. The department of communications and publication publishes jihadi literature, the monthly *Sada-e Mujahid*, and the weekly *Al-Hilal*, and keeps in touch with the media.

A Harkatul Mujahideen member associated with the publication of *Al-Hilal* in Karachi said that before

Jaish-e Muhammad came into being, the organisational structure of Harkatul Mujahideen was quite strong. But it had grown considerably weaker after some important leaders had crossed over to Jaish-e Muhammad. But things were coming back to normal again, and coordination among different departments was being established. The same member said that for lack of coordination earlier, leaders often issued statements in their individual capacity that ran counter to the policy of the organisation.

At this moment ten offices of Harkatul Mujahideen are working in Azad Kashmir. In Pakistan, it had forty-eight offices out of which twenty-four are working irregularly. After the crackdown, the offices at Karachi, Islamabad, and Muzaffarabad have become centres from where the organisation is being controlled.

HARKATUL MUJAHIDEEN'S NETWORK

Harkatul Mujahideen's network is still intact in Pakistan and Azad Kashmir. Earlier, it had a strong network in Afghanistan that included Afghans as well. Harkatul Mujahideen derives most of its human resource from Punjab, especially from Gujranwala, Rahim Khan, Khanewal, Multan, Dera Ghazi Khan, and Jhang. In these districts, Harkatul Mujahideen has its units down to the ward level. Gilgit, Dera Ismail Khan, Naoshehra, and Kohat are important in Frontier Province. Among the cities, Karachi provides the largest number of members. Harkat has good network here. A detailed list of branches of Harkatul Mujahideen is presented in Table VI.

CAMPS

Harkatul Mujahideen had four training camps in Afghanistan and one each in Pakistan and Azad Kashmir. The camps in Afghanistan folded up after the decimation of Taliban. These camps were in Barij, Ghand, and Kabul. The Mansehra camp in Pakistan is temporarily closed, whereas the Muzaffarabad camp in Azad Kashmir is still working.

SHAH ISMAIL SHAHEED CAMP, MANSEHRA

On the road from Mansehra to Muzaffarabad is a village, Barasi. From Barasi runs a dusty road up the hill. After thirty minutes of risky ride on car one can see the silhouette of a wall like that of a castle. This is the biggest camp of Harkatul Mujahideen in Pakistan. It is equipped to train and feed 700 *mujahids* at a time. Mufti Muhammad Asghar has been in charge of this camp. A *mujahid* from Multan, Muhammad Iqbal, who is now working in the office at Kotli said that the camp was closed in March. But as the situation gets back to normal it will resume work. He said that American commanders and Pakistani agencies raided the camp several times, and dozens of *mujahids* were captured. Iqbal felt that they were looking for Arab *mujahids*, but no Arab *mujahids* were there at the time of raid. There were, of course, Pakistani *mujahids* who had fought along with the Taliban in Afghanistan. There were some Afghans among those captured. Iqbal did not know where they were at present.

HARKATUL MUJAHIDEEN AND AL-QAIDA

Harkatul Mujahideen is the first Pakistani jihadi

organisation to be banned by the USA in 1999. The most serious allegation against it is that it had close links with Osama bin Laden, and it frequently warned the USA. The US cruise missile attack on Afghanistan in August 1998 had seriously harmed Harkat's two camps, Khalid bin Walid and Muwavia, and killed twenty-one of its mujahideen. After this, Harkat's Maulana Fazlur Rahman Khalil had said: 'We will take revenge on America for this.'

What was the nature of Harkatul Mujahideen's linkage with Al-Qaida and Osama bin Laden? This is still a question mark. Harkatul Mujahideen denies any links with Al-Qaida. Maulana Fazlur Rahman Khalil had said this in an interview:

> Osama bin Laden has his own mission and we have ours. We are simply fighting the war of independence in Kashmir. We do not have any organisational or jihadi links with Osama bin Laden. As for Osama's struggle, it is the struggle of the entire Muslim community. His demand is that the American soldiers must get out of the sacred land. It was our Prophet's command that the Jews and Christians should be turned out of Arabia. This is not Osama's stand but the command of our Prophet. In this sense, the whole Muslim community is with Osama in his mission.
>
> *Nida-e Millat*, weekly, Lahore, August 1998

As opposed to this claim, Arab mujahideen have been trained in the camps of Harkatul Mujahideen. This has been corroborated by one of the former officers of Mansehra camp. Besides, Harkatul Mujahideen never denied the fact that after the formation of Jaish-e

Muhammad, Osama bin Laden had made Harkatul Mujahideen a gift of twelve double-cabin pick-ups and substantial funds.

In the current US-Taliban war, the fighters of Harkatul Mujahideen had gone to Afghanistan for jihad under the leadership of Maulana Fazlur Rahman Khalil. Sixty-five of them died at the hands of the US army, including some important leaders like Ustad Faruq and Baba Lahori who were among Harkat's best commanders. A journalist from Peshawar told me that Arab mujahideen were hiding in Mansehra camp, and they were rounded up in a raid by the American secret agency, FBI. The journalist claimed to have met Maulana Fazlur Rahman Khalil a couple of times. 'He is an emotional man, often contradicting his earlier statements.' As an instance of this he said that the Maulana admitted his links with Osama bin Laden a couple of times and later denied it.

Harkat's Concept of Freedom in Kashmir

An interview of Maulana Fazlur Rahman Khalil was published in the daily, *The Nation*, from Lahore on 23 February 1999, in which he had said, 'Harkat has no objection to an autonomous Kashmir.' He simply wanted the return of the Indian army from Kashmir which was the object of the jihad. This was something that I asked each *mujahid* of Harkat that I ran into. Some just refused to believe in the statement. But two *mujahids* among them had said, 'This issue has come under discussion in jihadi circles several times – what will the status of Kashmir be after it is freed from

India. Every time the proposal came that Kashmir should be an independent Islamic state. But Abu Saleh from Kotli said it was a mere proposal, not a plan.'

Institutes Supplying Human Resource to Harkatul Mujahideen

It is a common impression about Harkatul Mujahideen that it is dominated by students of madrasas. My personal observation and the records of Harkatul Mujahideen indicate to the contrary. I have met more than two dozen members of Harkatul Mujahideen in their offices at Kotli, Rawlakot, Dera Ghazi Khan, and Karachi. Out of them, only five were from madrasas. Out of 800 martyrs of Harkatul Mujahideen, only 118 were from madrasas.

Three *mujahids* from Gilgit – Hazrat Gul, Asim, and Quddus – told me that they joined Harkatul Mujahideen together in December 2001. Hazrat Gul had done his middle school and was unemployed; Asim and Quddus were at leisure after the matriculation examination. They came in touch with Harkat through its mobile jihadi preachers who had come to the mosque of their area and had given a discourse after *namaz*, and asked people to join the jihad. Iqbal from Multan said that he began to go to the prayers in mosque after he got in touch with Tablighi Jamat; then he came across the jihadis. Sulaiman Gilani, a student of Jamia Faruqiya, Karachi, joined jihad on his own.

Among the madrasas, Kora Khatak, Jamia Abu Huraira, Naoshehra; Jamia Nomania, Dera Ismail

Khan; Jamia Makhzanul Uloom, Khanpur; Jamia Faruqiya, Shujaabad; Jamia Islamia Banooriya, Jamia Ihtishamiya, and Jamia Faruqiya, Karachi have sent the maximum number of students to Harkatul Mujahideen.

It is also important to note about Harkatul Mujahideen that its leadership is in the hands of individuals passing out from madrasas.

Material Resources of Harkatul Mujahideen

There are three sources of income for Harkatul Mujahideen.

FOREIGN ASSISTANCE

Pakistanis leaving abroad and the sheikhs of some Arab states contribute funds to Harkatul Mujahideen. The representatives of Harkatul Mujahideen make rounds of foreign countries to collect funds.

ASSISTANCE FROM INSIDE THE COUNTRY

Funds are collected from mosques in cash; during the harvesting season funds are also collected in kind.

HIDES OF SACRIFICED ANIMALS AND PUBLICATIONS

The Taliban government had made a gift of fertile tracts of land in Afghanistan to Harkatul Mujahideen. Mujahideen grow harvest there with the help of peasants. A member of Harkatul Mujahideen in Dera Ghazi Khan told me that in 2001, Harkatul Mujahideen had collected funds to the tune of fifty-five lakh rupees from Pakistan. Despite the ban, Harkat raised seven lakh rupees from the sale of hides of sacrificed animals. He told me that the major source of income was foreign funding. He also gave me a pamphlet prepared for fund-raising. It was written there in bold letters:

> Please deposit zakat, charity, and gifts to Jihad fund, and send a clear message to the world-bully America that the youths of Harkatul Mujahideen are not alone.

On 26 September 2001, the Pakistani government ordered freezing of all Harkatul Mujahideen bank accounts in Pakistan. At this, Ammar Mehdi, an office bearer of Harkat said that Harkat had just one joint account, the rest of the accounts are in the name of individual leaders. Following are the details of some of these accounts:

1. Qari Muhammad Sadiq, Current Account No. 1236–9, Allied Bank, Khayaban-e Sir Syed, Rawalpindi
2. Mazhar Husain, Current Account No. 1440–1, Allied Bank, Khayaban-e Sir Syed, Rawalpindi
3. Maulana Farooq Kashmiri, Current Account No. 1440–1, Allied Bank, Khayaban-e Sir Syed, Rawalpindi

Important Activities of Harkatul Mujahideen

From 1984 to 2001, Harkat's 840 mujahideen have become martyrs in Afghanistan and Occupied Kashmir. The record of all these mujahideen are there in the office of Harkatul Mujahideen in Islamabad. According to these records, among the martyrs, 566 were from Pakistan, eighty-nine from Occupied Kashmir and Azad Kashmir, and seventeen from

Afghanistan. Fifty-five mujahideen died during the US attack on Afghanistan. Seventy mujahideen had gone to Afghanistan under the leadership of Maulana Fazlur Rahman Khalil; of them only fifteen had come back along with the Maulana.

The following is the state-wise break-up of martyrs:

Punjab	352
Sindh	64
Frontier Province	72
Baluchistan	13
Azad Kashmir	45
Total	566

The following is the district-wise break-up of martyrs in Punjab:

Gujranwala	36
Rahim Yar Khan	22
Lahore	18
Khanewal	14
Multan	25
Dera Ghazi Khan	10

Among the martyrs from Sindh province, forty-six were from Karachi, eleven from Sukkur, and twelve from Shikarpur. Among the martyrs from Frontier Province, twenty-nine were from Gilgit, fifteen from Mansehra, eighteen from Sawat, and eight from Kohat. Among those from Azad Kashmir, eighteen were from Muzaffarabad and nine from Bagh. Among those from Baluchistan, six were from Quetta. In Kargil, twenty-nine mujahideen from Harkat were killed, while in 1988, in the attack on Harkatul Mujahideen camps twenty-nine had died. In India, five members of Harkatul Mujahideen had died in an operation in the state of Arunachal Pradesh. It is also to be noted that among the martyrs there were also seventeen from Afghanistan, two from Turkey, two from Iran, and one each from the USA and the UK.

Among Harkatul Mujahideen's missions, the most spectacular ones were – the siege of Dargah Hazratbal, occupation of Charar Sharif, Zangli Camp Expedition, Qila Murad Beg Expedition (Afghanistan), and exploding a bridge in Assam (India). According to its own record, the following are the details of these incidents:

SIEGE OF DARGAH HAZRATBAL

'Among the expeditions taking place in 1999, Siege of Dargah Hazratbal was one that had given a new lease of life to the movement in Kashmir. Because of this expedition, Harkat was praised all over the world. Imposing a ban on Hindu yatras, Harkat's youth gave ample proof of their grip on Kashmir. Hindustan was brought on its knees, but the Harkat made a list of demands and kept the ban on yatra intact which holds till now. The credit for the ban goes to Commander Nasir, Harkat's amir who, till date, is taking God's name in Indian jail.'

OCCUPATION OF CHARAR SHARIF

'The expedition to Charar Sharif was carried out under the leadership of Commander Shaokat Zubair and Commander Abu Jandal. It is regarded as one of the finest achievements of the mujahideen. It is said that the mujahideen kept it under their control for three months, and kept the Hindu brutes on tenterhooks. Finally, the Hindu oppressors put to fire the entire Charar Sharif and showered bullets on the mujahideen. Thus this expedition came to an end. Commander Shaokat Zubair has achieved martyrdom, and Commander Abu Jindal is in Indian jail.'

ZANGLI CAMP EXPEDITION

'The Zangli Camp Expedition is unique in the history of Kashmir that sent the headquarters buildings, one helicopter, and hundreds of soldiers to hell. No *mujahid* was killed. The central figure of this expedition was Commander Uqab who later achieved martyrdom.'

FORT MURAD BEG EXPEDITION

'This expedition continued for seven consecutive days. Sixty of Harkat's valiant fighters defended the fort against an attack mounted on it in the darkness of the night. The enemies had to take to their heels leaving scores of their companions dead. In this encounter, nineteen of Harkat's youths were martyred. Amirul Mumenin had sent a special message for Maulana Abdul Jabbar, and the defence minister made a gift of a tank. Seeing its defensive strategy and agility, the defence of Bagram area was entrusted to the responsibility of Harkatul Mujahideen. It gave fitting replies to dozens of attacks on the Fort Murad Beg and Kabul was made invincible. Ilyas Baba and Maulana Salim Malik, the famed scholar, died in an attack. In another attack Commander Osama and Commander Salman achieved martyrdom.'

ASSAM EXPEDITION

'Harkatul Mujahideen carried out a mission in Assam where a strategic bridge was destroyed that disrupted communication with seven Indian states. It resulted in the loss of several hundred crore of rupees for the Indians.'

ATTACK ON CIVIL SECRETARIAT, SRINAGAR

'It conducted two raids on the secretariat in Srinagar within a week in broad daylight. Thus it dealt a crushing blow on the Indian security forces without any loss to itself.'

TALIBAN-US WAR

In the US attacks on Afghanistan meant to destroy Taliban and the Al-Qaida network, Harkatul Mujahideen helped the Taliban. Till December 2001, more than seventy Harkat members had been killed in the war, including Ustad Faruq, Baba Lahori, and Shamsheer who were important leaders of Harkatul Mujahideen.

IMPORTANT LEADERS OF HARKATUL MUJAHIDEEN

Maulana Fazlur Rahman Khalil

Though Maulana Fazlur Rahman Khalil is formally the general secretary of Harkatul Mujahideen, he is, practically, the amir. He was a student of Madrasa Jamia Nomania in Dera Ismail Khan when he went to Afghanistan for jihadi training. He received training in the camp of Harkat-al Jihad and remained in this organisation till the founding of Harkatul Mujahideen. It is said about him that he has close links with Osama bin Laden. After the US cruise missile attack on the training camps in Afghanistan, Maulana Fazlur Rahman Khalil began to issue statements against

America, and his name was included in the list of FBI. During the recent US raids against the Taliban, he had gone to Afghanistan along with seventy mujahideen, and returned to Pakistan safely in January 2002. Since then he was in Islamabad and there was no restrictions on his movements. However, from August 2002, he has been put under house arrest.

Maulana Faruq Kashmiri
Besides being the amir of Harkatul Mujahideen, he is also the secretary of its military department. He is a veteran of the Afghan War. He was formerly associated with Harkatul Ansar. When Harkatul Ansar broke up, he joined Harkatul Mujahideen. It is said that he is unhappy with Maulana Fazlur Rahman Khalil's dictatorial ways, and wants to use Harkat's full strength in Occupied Kashmir.

Maulana Fazal Muhammad
Maulana Fazal Muhammad is considered to be the ideologue of Harkatul Mujahideen. He is from Karachi. After receiving his education from Jamia Banooriya, he has become a teacher there. He has had a vital role in collecting human resource from Sindh and Karachi. He is considered to be strongly opposed to Maulana Masood Azhar. He is also a veteran of the Afghan war. He is the secretary of Harkat's Communications and Publication department.

Maulana Allah Osaya
He is in charge of Harkat's management. His fame is in being an emotional orator. The annual fund-raising campaign is conducted under him. He is close to Maulana Fazlur Rahman Khalil in his views, and does not want to

limit jihadi activities only to Occupied Kashmir.

The Current Position of Harkatul Mujahideen

After it's ban by America and the birth of Jaish-e Muhammad, Harkatul Mujahideen had grown considerably weaker. The end of Taliban in Afghanistan has dealt another severe blow to it, and it is under great pressure now. Reliable sources from Harkat say that on the one hand, ISI wants to finish it off, and on the other, there is considerable confusion in the organisation itself.

Harkatul Mujahideen is being asked to disband itself and merge into Jamiatul Mujahideen which is an important Deobandi jihadi organisation in Kashmir. In that case, the management of Harkat in Azad Kashmir and Pakistan will remain in the hands of its leaders. Maulana Fazlur Rahman Khalil does not endorse this proposal, though Maulana Faruq Kashmiri has expressed his consent to it.

Table VI: *Branches of Harkatul Mujahideen in Pakistan and Occupied Kashmir*

Sr. No.	District	Amir/ Secretary	Centre/Office
1.	Lahore	Syed Muzammil Hussain	Near Thana Garhi Shaho, Lahore
2.	Qusoor		Railway Road, Qasoor
3.	Rawalpindi		House No. 154-B, Sector 1, Khyaban-e-Sir Syed, Near CDA Stop, Rawalpindi
4.	Mianwali		Committee Chowk, Mianwali
5.	Dera Ghazi Khan		1 Floor, Al-Ghazi Machinery Store, New College Road, Dera Ghazi Khan

Sr. No.	District	Amir/ Secretary	Centre/Office
6.	Sargodha		Near Jama Masjid, Bhool Chook, Sargodha
7.	Rahim Yar Khan		5-Shahi Road, Rahim Yar Khan
8.	Khanpur		Tahir Peer Road, Near Deenpur Chowk, Khanpur
9.	Jhelum		Madrasa Talim-ul-Quran, Machine Muhalla No. 1, Jhelum
10.	Kot Adoo		Madrasa Madinal-Uloom, Dera Deen Panah, Tehsil Kot Adoo
11.	Attock		Aslam Plaza, Flat No. 401, Fountain Chowk, Attock
12.	Bahawalpur		Koocha Gul Hussain Muhalla Imam Shah, House No. 735–3/13, Bahawalpur
13.	Ahmadpur Sharqia		Near Telephone Exchange, Chowk Nayyer Shaheed, Ahmadpur Sharqia
14.	Peshawar	Haffa Umar	Near Board Staff, Gali F Khan, Khalil Town, Peshawar
15.	Abbottabad		Muhalla Nurooduddin, Near Abu Baker Siddique Chowk, Abbottabad
16.	Banno		Old Chai Bazar, Masjid Haq Nawaz Khan, Banno
17.	Batgram		Kachehri Road, Khaiber Hotel, Batgram
18.	Taimergrah		Bus Adda, Taimergrah
19.	Gilgit		C/o Sher Zaman General Store, Airport Chowk, Gilgit
20.	Chitral		Shahi Bazar, Chitral
21.	Dera Ismail Khan		Near Farooq Shahid Chowk, Commisionery Bazar, Dera Ismail Khan
22.	Sawabi		Waris Khan Market, Jehangeer Road, Sawabi
23.	Sawat		Green Chowk, Airport Road, Mangoorah, Sawat

Sr. No.	District	Amir/ Secretary	Centre/Office
24.	Mansehra		Bedrah Road, Near Dawood, Mansehra
25.	Sakardoo		Rah, Near Chashma Masjid, Sakardoo
26.	Mardan		Iqbal Market, Near Nehar Chowk, Mardan
27.	Karachi		Jama Masjid, Mustafa Haroonabad, Sher Shah Road, Karachi
28.	Sukkur	Hafiz Muhammad Andher	Madrasa Arabia Irshad-ul-Quran, Chowk Bus Stop, Panoon, Aaqil Sukkur
29.	Panjgour	Ehtasham-ul-Haq	Madrasa Misbah-ul-Uloom Sarikoran, Panjgour
30.	Muzaffarabad		Near Aawan High School, Upper Chattar, Muzaffarabad
31.	Simahni	Maulana Sajjad	Madrasa Arabia, Madinia Achmanabad, Simahni
32.	Rawlakot		University College, CMH Road, Rawlakot
33.	Bagh		Madrasa Imdad-Ullah, Post Office, Hari Guhal, Bagh
34.	Kundal Shahi		Camp Abu Huraira, Kundal Shahi, Aathmuqam
35.	Mirpur		The Book Bank, Zahid Market, Sector 2-B, Mirpur, Azad Kashmir
36.	Kotli	Muhammad Zubair	Al-Razzaq Plaza, Shahid Chowk, Kotli
37.	Abbaspur		Markazi Jamia Masjid, Maind Bazar Abbaspur, District Poonch
38.	Dadyal		Sharif Plaza, Room No. 8, Bhatti Chowk, Dadyal.

Note: The offices in Punjab and Sindh had been working till February 2002, and those in Azad Kashmir and Frontier Province had been working till 15 April 2002.

Harkat-al Jihad al-Islami, Pakistan

Harkat-al Jihad al-Islami which is also known as

Harkatul Ansar is the first regular jihadi organisation born in Pakistan. It has a strong and well-knit organisational structure and apart from Pakistan and Occupied Kashmir, its network is spread out in Chechnya, Uzbekistan, Burma, and Bangladesh. It had planned to open its branches in Palestine in 2002, but the plan was changed after 11 September 2001.

BACKGROUND

Harkat-al Jihad was founded in 1979 by Irshad Ahmad. When the Soviet army entered Afghanistan, the first delegation of ulema from the Frontier Province went to Afghanistan to participate in the war under his leadership. There, the ulema took military training and later played a decisive role in providing human resource to the Taliban from Pakistan. They even succeeded in getting a fatwa issued by the Pakistan ulema in favour of participation in war.

In the Afghan War, Harkat-al Jihad came in touch with Maulana Muhammad Nabi Muhammadi and his group, Harkat-e Inqilab Islami. This group adhered to the Deobandi school of thought. It is also said about Harkat-al Jihad that it provided assistance to Ahmad Shah Masood. However, its amir Qari Saifullah Akhtar says:

> When our first caravan got ready to go to Afghanistan in 1980, we first collected information about the jihadi organisations there. As per our knowledge, Maulana Nasrullah Mansoor Shaheed's Harkat-e Inqilab Islami was the only organisation that was totally composed of Deobandi ulema and students. That is why when we reached Peshawar we met Nabi

Muhammadi Sahib first. Our relationship with Harkat-e Inqilab Islami remained close till the advent of Taliban. The Chancellor of Kabul University, Maulana Peer Muhammad Rohani, and the Deputy Minister, Hajj and Wakf, Maulana Commander Arsalan Khan Rahmani are witness to this. We were with Commander Arsalan Khan and assisted him. Our 21-years stint in jihad is witness to the fact that we had never any truck with any other organisation except Harkat-e Inqilab Islami. I have not met Masood till today.

When Maulana Irshad Ahmad was killed in Afghanistan in 1985, Maulana Qari Saifullah Akhtar became the central amir. There was disagreement among the mujahideen about his leadership, and Maulana Fazlur Rahman Khalil and Maulana Masood Avi founded a separate organisation named Harkatul Mujahideen.

MERGER WITH HARKATUL ANSAR AND BREAKING AWAY

No great change in the organisation resulted from its merger in Harkatul Ansar and then breaking away from it, except that Qari Zarar broke away from Harkat-al Jihad and formed United Harkatul Ansar. But he did not get the support of the majority of mujahideen in Harkat-al Jihad. Moreover, as the Taliban came to power, Harkat-al Jihad got a new lease of life and many of its members got jobs in the Taliban army and administration.

IMPORTANT MEMBERS OF HARKAT-AL JIHAD JOINED JAISH-E MUHAMMAD

After the founding of Jaish-e Muhammad, rumours

were floated to the effect that Maulana Qari Allah Akhtar had declared support to Jaish-e Muhammad, and the entire management of Harkat-al Jihad was merging in it. Such rumours confused the members of Harkat-al Jihad. Jaish-e Muhammad further declared that the central deputy amir of Harkat-al Jihad, Maulana Muhammad Umar had also joined Jaish-e Muhammad. Harkat-al Jihad contradicted it immediately, and formed a committee to scotch such rumours, prevent Jaish-e Muhammad from occupying Harkat-al Jihad's offices, and to take steps that could save Harkat-al Jihad from all kinds of schism and confusion – internal and external. Maulana Said Ahmad Awan, Zafar Shah, and Maulana Ustad Ajmal were members of this committee.

Harkat-al Jihad's amir, in his speech at the Mansehra camp on 13 April 2000, had mounted a scathing criticism on Jaish-e Muhammad:

Today, it is of utmost importance for mujahideen to unite against apostasy. But a certain lobby is now spreading the worst kind of confusion instead of forging unity. Irshad Ahmad Shaheed was the first to begin jihad in Pakistan. Maulana Fazlur Rahman Khalil was his central commander. Harkatul Mujahideen and Harkat-al Jihad were the two organisations that made unforgettable sacrifices in the jihad in Afghanistan and Kashmir. Harkatul Mujahideen is the biggest jihadi organisation. But other organisations are being formed nowadays that are minting money. We fight war by our faith in Allah. There were differences between Harkatul Mujahideen and Harkat-al Jihad, but none of it came out in public in the written or oral form. Now some people have landed in the arena with a bang and want to appropriate the contributions made by Harkatul Mujahideen and Harkat-al Jihad for the last fifteen years. They are taking resort to false propaganda just to publicise their names, by pretending to be greater *mujahids* than others. I want to make it clear that it is a specific lobby that has a surfeit of wealth. We know where that money has come from, and at whose behest they are working.

ORGANISATIONAL STRUCTURE

The organisational structure of Harkat-al Jihad is as strong as that of Hizbul Mujahideen and Lashkar-e Tayyaba. As it is engaged in jihad, apart from Kashmir, in Afghanistan, Myanmar, Chechnya, Uzbekistan, and Tajikistan, its structure is wider. During the time of the Taliban its central secretariat worked in Kabul and Kandahar which are now being shifted to Oziristan and Boniar. One secretariat has already been working in Islamabad.

In Occupied Kashmir, Harkat-al Jihad is named Harkat-al Jihad Brigade 111. Though its management is in the hands of the central leaders of Harkat-al Jihad, it is semi-autonomous. Its centre is in Kotli, Azad Kashmir, and it has a base camp office at Muzaffarabad. The following of its departments are important:

1. Department of Dawat and Irshad (Preaching and Commands)
2. Military Department
3. Management Department

4. Department of Communications and Publications

The following are the important office bearers:

1. Chief Patron: Syed Anwar Husain Nafees Shah
2. Patron: Maulana Qari Saifullah Akhtar
3. Central Amir: Maulana Muhammad Ahmad Umar
4. Amir: Maulana Adeel Jehadyar
5. Secretary to Chief Patron/Resources: Maulana Muhammad Amin Rabbani
6. Amir, Jammu and Kashmir: Maulana Abdussamad Sayyal
7. Deputy Amir: Maulana Muhammad Ahmad Mansoor
8. Secretary, Department of Dawat and Irshad: Maulana Syed Habibullah Shah/Maulana Junaidullah Akhtar
9. Deputy Secretary: Maulana Muhammad Idris Abbas
10. Chief Commander, Jammu and Kashmir: Muhammad Ilyas Kashmiri
11. Secretary, Militant Activities: Commander Mahboob Ahmad
12. Secretary, Martyrs and the Physically Handicapped Committee: Maulana Said Ahmad Awan
13. Secretary, Management Committee: Maulana Ustad Ajmal
14. Launching Commander: Qari Owais Mansoor
15. Secretary, Al-Jihad Students Movement: Syed Bedar Husain Shah Gilani
16. Amir, Harkat-al Jihad, Arakan, Burma: Maulana Abdul Quddus
17. Amir, Harkat-al Jihad, Uzbekistan: Shaikh Muhammad Tariq Al-Farooq

18.Amir, Harkat-al Jihad, Afghanistan: Commander Sajjad Ahmad
19.Chief Commander, Harkat-al Jihad, Tajikistan: Commander Khalid Irshad Tawana (Ex)
20.Secretary, Harkat-al Jihad, Chechnya: Commander Hedayatullah

Institutes Providing Human Resources

Harkat-al Jihad is the only jihadi organisation of Deobandi school of thought that receives the majority of its members from madrasas. Harkat-al Jihad also receives students from madrasas in foreign countries for training, swelling its ranks. Harkat-al Jihad is also different in the sense that unlike other jihadi organisations it does not criticise the Tablighi Jamat. On the contrary, it appreciated its efforts and took advantage of its members. In Raewind, in madrasas and *tablighi* gatherings, Harkat-al Jihad can distribute its literature also offer discourses.

Some of the big madrasas providing human resource to Harkat-al Jihad are in Punjab and Frontier Province. The principals of several madrasas are also the office bearers of Harkat-al Jihad. Why is there such a preponderance of madrasa students in Harkat-al Jihad? When I asked this question to the mujahideen, they came up with the following three reasons:

1. Harkat-al Jihad stresses on observance of sharia and the sectarian school of thought.
2. As it was close to the Taliban, it managed to give employment to many madrasa students in Afghanistan. After the end of the Taliban, this factor

will certainly affect Harkat-al Jihad.
3. Harkat-al Jihad has a large jihadi network and a *mujahid* does not have to wait long before launching.

Department of Material Resources

The secretary of this department is Maulana Muhammad Amin Rabbani. There is a central finance committee composed of Maulana Mufti Hyder Ali, Maulana Qari Abu Hamza, Master Abdul Hamid, and Maulana Said Ahmad Awan. Besides raising funds from the public in Pakistan, Harkat-al Jihad also raises income by selling arms to smaller jihadi groups. Its fund-raisers in foreign countries are very active. The accounts of Harkat-al Jihad are in the name of the following individuals:

1. Zahid Iqbal, Current Account No. 1442, Allied Bank, Industrial Area, I 9, Islamabad
2. Maulana Muhammad Amin Rabbani, Current Account No. 2900, Allied Bank, Abparo Market Branch, Islamabad

NETWORK

As pointed out earlier, Harkat-al Jihad is the biggest jihadi organisation in terms of its network. Its motto is – 'Every Muslim Country's Second Defence Line – Harkat-al Jihad al-Islami.'

Harkat-al Jihad's network is spread through twenty-four countries. According to one of its publicity brochures:

After the jihad in Afghanistan, the valiant fighters of Harkat-al Jihad al-Islami (al-Alami) are scripting accounts of their valour in Kashmir, Burma, Tajikistan, Chechnya, Palestine and the states in the Middle East. Harkat-al Jihad has the singular honour of uniting the mujahideen of India, Bangladesh, Burma, Iran, Philippines, Malaysia, Africa, the UK, Ireland, Fiji, America and the different states of the Middle East, under the green banner of jihad and providing them an opportunity to participate in the arena of practical jihad.

In Pakistan, it has its network in forty districts. Punjab and the Frontier Province are the most important in this regard. In Punjab, Sargodha, Dera Ghazi Khan, Multan, Khanpur, Gujranwala, Gujrat, Bhakkar, and Mianwali; and in Frontier Province, Banno, Kohat, Oziristan Agency, Dera Ismail Khan, Sawabi, and Peshawar are the most active centres of Harkat-al Jihad.

CAMPS

During the Taliban regime in Afghanistan, Harkat-al Jihad had six camps in Kandahar, Kabulm and Khost. Most of the mujahideen were trained there. It has also one camp in Occupied Kashmir.

Mahmud Ghaznawi Camp, Kotli
Haji Khan Amin is in charge of this camp. This camp is located about 20 kms away from Kotli. It is equipped to accommodate and train 800 mujahideen at a time. After the camps in other parts of Pakistan folded up, the pressure on this camp has increased. Safe sites for new camps are being searched in the Frontier Province.

IMPORTANT MISSIONS

Harkat-al Jihad has engineered a string of militant activities in Occupied Kashmir, Chechnya, Burma and Uzbekistan. The largest number of its mujahideen were killed in Occupied Kashmir. In 1999, 102 of its mujahideen died in Occupied Kashmir, and nine in Afghanistan. Of the 102 killed in Occupied Kashmir, fifty-eight were from Occupied Kashmir, ten from Azad Kashmir, twenty-one from Punjab, four from Sindh, and nine from Frontier Province. According to the February 2001 issue of the monthly *Al-Irshad* (Islamabad), in 2000, Harkat-al Jihad lost seventy-eight mujahideen; of them sixty-nine died in Occupied Kashmir, seven in Afghanistan, and two in Chechnya. A greater number of Harkat-al Jihad's encounters in Afghanistan and Occupied Kashmir were of a military nature, and a lesser number of them were of the guerrilla kind. According to *Al-Irshad*:

> The founder of Harkat-al Jihad and its first amir, Hazrat Maulana Irshad Ahmad was martyred in Shirana in 1985 while leading the mujahideen, and thus left a glorious history behind him. Hazrat Maulana Khalid Zubair Shaheed was awarded an honorary medal by the Afghan Mujahideen government for conquering the famous Argon military camp in the Paktika province of Kabul. Harkat-al Jihad has set the tradition of snatching arms from the Indian army. Harkat-al Jihad's Chief Commander and Amir-e Hind, Nasrullah Mansoor Langyal has the singular achievement of a siege by 40,000 Indian army men for 72 hours. Harkat-al Jihad has also the distinction of establishing a training

camp in Occupied Kashmir to train Kashmiri youths, amidst 7 lakh soldiers of the Indian army.

Harkat-al Jihad's Track Record in Kashmir

In Occupied Kashmir, the mujahideen of Harkat-al Jihad are known in common parlance as 'Afghani'. The first group of sixteen mujahideen from Harkat-al Jihad entered Kashmir in 1991. Of them twelve were Pakistani and four Kashmiri. All of them had already participated in jihad in Afghanistan. Commander Amjad Bilal was the first commander-in-chief of Harkat-al Jihad who initiated action there. Till date, as many as 650 mujahideen of Harkat-al Jihad have been killed in Occupied Kashmir. Of them 200 were from Punjab, 190 from Azad Kashmir and Occupied Kashmir, forty-nine from Sindh, twenty-nine from Baluchistan, and seventy from Afghanistan. In addition, five were Turk, and forty-nine were Uzbek, Arab, and Bangladeshi.

When Harkat-al Jihad began its missions in Occupied Kashmir, Ahl-e Hadith and other organisations carried out propaganda against it saying that it was a *tablighi jamat* and it had nothing to do with jihad; that the letterhead they carried was merely to collect contribution from people. According to Ikramullah, an important member of Harkat-al Jihad who had taken part in militant activities in Occupied Kashmir: 'The situation was volatile in Occupied Kashmir. This propaganda had affected Harkat-al Jihad. But when some Arab and Turkish mujahideen reached Kashmir and Harkat-al Jihad began its missions, this propaganda slowly died away. We try not to interfere in sectarian

273

affairs, as instructed by our leadership. But there (Occupied Kashmir), seeing worship and rituals in dargahs and graveyards, the mujahideen lose their cool and get into a rage. But the management sends back such mujahideen to the training camp.'

Track Record in Uzbekistan

Shaikh Muhammad Tahir Faruq is the amir of Harkat-al Jihad in Uzbekistan. There, Harkat-al Jihad's missions are focussed on establishing an Islamic state. It has a different management there. As for jihadi activities, it conducts its scheme in conjunction with Noman Ghani's group, Uzbek Tahreek. So far, twenty-seven of Harkat-al Jihad's youth have been killed in Uzbekistan. Harkat-al Jihad started its militant activities there in 1990. Its youth were trained in Harkat-al Jihad's camp in Afghanistan. The Uzbek Harkat-al Jihad gets full cooperation from Harkat-al Jihad in Pakistan.

Why did the Uzbek Harkat-al Jihad decide to take recourse to militancy? Shaikh Muhammad Tahir Faruq said in a speech in the office of Harkat-al Jihad in Islamabad:

We have made all arrangement to prepare ourselves on the lines of the sharia to fight Karimov and his infidels. The enemy wanted it time and again that we should jump to battle without sufficient prepa ration. But we acted with restraint, despite internal and external pressures. We are in a position to strike whenever and wherever we want.

a. The Karimov administration has rounded up the

known ulema and thrown them in jail. To defame them before the public, they have accused the ulema of such detestable crime as dealing in drugs. Among these ulema are Shaikh Abdul Wali, Shaikh Muhammad Rajab, Shaikh Abdul Ahad, Shaikh Abdullah, and other known scholars.

b. The Karimov administration has closed all madrasas. They have closed four thousand mosques and turned them into centres of brainwashing through a heretic education system among school children. There is a ban on azan on loudspeakers, purdah and keeping beard. All this means that the country is being pushed again to the Lenin era. Mujahideen and ordinary prisoners are given only pork-stew which they cannot eat. All the prisoners have become weak. Over and above this, they are exposed to the extreme heat of the desert, and they are often subjected to violence. This is a desert area where Russia used to dump its atomic and chemical waste. In these circumstances, every week 15–20 Muslims are embracing slow death.

c. The Russian Communist army stopped a bus, took down the Muslim women from it and tore their veils to shred before everyone. This terribly upset people and Harkat-al Jihad in particular.

d. If Harkat-al Jihad delayed action, the un-Islamic groups like Khawarij, Takfir, Qadiani, Bahai, and secular formations would have got the upper hand and mounted attack on it. In practice, these groups had started working along these lines. Under the above circumstances, Harkat-al Jihad decided to take recourse to militant activities.

Track Record in Afghanistan

The mujahideen of Harkat-al Jihad gave active support

to the Taliban against the Northern Alliance. In Afghanistan, its members were called 'Punjabi Taliban'. The closeness of Harkat-al Jihad's relationship with the Taliban can be gauged from the fact that three of its ministers and twenty judges were associated with Harkat-al Jihad. Its patron, Qari Saifullah was among Mullah Umar's advisers. He lived in Kandahar till the US attacks on Afghanistan.

About 300 members of Harkat-al Jihad died fighting against the Northern Alliance. In return, Mulla Umar had given Harkat-al Jihad special permission to start six training camps in Afghanistan that were known as the cantonment of the Taliban government. Besides the mujahideen, members of the Taliban police had also been trained there.

Track Record in Pakistan

Harkat-al Jihad had tried to bring about a revolution in Pakistan several times. In 1995 when Major General Zahirul Islam Abbasi and Major Mustansar Billah made plans to revolt against the general headquarters (GHQ), Harkat-al Jihad's (at that time, Harkatul Ansar) amir, Qari Saifullah Akhtar was with them. In case of revolt, he was to provide both human and material resource. But when the plan did not succeed, Qari Saifullah became the government witness. This affected Harkatul Ansar in the sense that serious differences cropped up among its leaders. It received a further jolt when Maulana Fazlur Rahman Khalil reverted to the erstwhile Harkatul Mujahideen.

Track Record in Chechnya

Dozens of Harkat-al Jihad members have died in Chechnya. Even the Islamabad office does not have the exact numbers. The Pakistani Harkat-al Jihad continues to extend assistance to Chechnya. According to *Al-Irshad*:

> God be praised! Dozens of Harkat-al Jihad's mujahideen have achieved their objective (we are the second defence line of all Islamic countries) by participating in jihad at Qafqaz (Chechnya) just as they did in Afghanistan. Its commander, Maulana Hedayatullah Sahib who had been in Maura al-Nahr area for a month, is not only imparting military training to the mujahideen, but several mujahideen commanders in the neighbouring states are engaging the Russian forces under his leadership.

Current State of Harkat-al Jihad

After the end of the Taliban regime in Afghanistan, many mujahideen of Harkat-al Jihad have taken refuge in Uzbekistan, Tajikistan, and Chechnya. Its members in Pakistan have been advised to lie low and wait for further instructions from the leadership. The mujahideen currently present in Kotli camp, Kotli office, and Muzaffarabad can be launched in Occupied Kashmir. After the ban on some jihadi organisations, Harkat-al Jihad Brigade 111 has been merged with Jamiatul Mujahideen, for jihadi missions. According to this decision, its leadership in Kashmir will be in the hands of Jamiatul Mujahideen whereas its (Harkat-al

Jihad) leadership in Pakistan and Azad Kashmir will be in the hands of its former leaders. Maulana Nazim Ahmad Sayyal will act its secretary in Pakistan, and in the camps of Harkat-al Jihad, mujahideen from other organisations can also be trained.

The central command of Harkat-al Jihad has not been totally dismantled, although the instruction has been sent out that the local people in different countries where Harkat-al Jihad has its units should take the lead and the Pakistani mujahideen should be called back. Some details of the organisation of Harkal-al Jihad al-Islami in Pakistan and Azad Kashmir are presented in Table VII.

Table VII: *Harkat-al Jihad al-Islami: In Pakistan and Azad Kashmir*

Sr. No	District/ Tehsil	District/Tehsil Secretary	Office/Centre
1.	Lahore	Maulana Muhammad Yaqoob Faiz	Near Chowk Chouberji, Shamnagar, Lahore
2.	Gujranwala		Aftab Market, Behind Regent Cinema, GT Road, Gujranwala
3.	Dera Ghazi Khan	Maulana Abdul Hameed Dervi	Jamia Islamia, Near Nabalari Adda, Dera Ghazi Khan
4.	Rawalpindi	Maulana Mohammad Twarsi	Kashmir Road, Rawalpindi
5.	Texla	Qari Abdullah	Near Sharif Hospital Stop, GT Road, Waah Cantt.
6.	Attock	Maulana Khan Muhammad	
7.	Multan	Maulana Muhammad Akram	Jamia Ashrafiya, Maankot, Multan
8.	Marri	Maulana Muneer Ahmad	Siddique Chowk, Marri

Sr. No	District/ Tehsil	District/Tehsil Secretary	Office/Centre
9.	Kahota	Hafiz Zubair Ahmad Madni	Kachehri Road, Kahota
10.	Toba tek Singh	Maulana Allah Bakhsh	Madina Market, Near Railway Gate, Toba tek Singh
11.	Bahawalpur	Maulana Abdullah	Near Fareed Gate, Circular Road, Bahawalpur
12.	Waah Cantt.		Sharif Hospital Stop, GT Road, Waah Cantt.
13.	Peshawar	Abu Mugheerah Hazarvi	Madrasa Muaz Bin Jabal, Peshawar
14.	Chaar Sadda	Maulana Idris	Darul-Uloom Islamia, Chaar Sadda
15.	Naushara	Maulana Habib-Ullah Shah	Near Jamia Tehseen-ul-Quran, Naushara
16.	Mansehra	Qari Abdullah	Near Markazi Jamia Masjid Hanfia, Mansehra
17.	Sawaat	Maulana Mufti Mohammad Umar	Green Chowk, Mengora, Sawaat
18.	Karachi	Ghaffan-Ullah Khan, Maulana Mufti Hammad-Ullah, Maulana Nurul Hasan	Gulshan Iqbal, Karachi
19.	Tando Adam	Maulana Nurul Hasan	
20.	Dadoo	Imran Khan Korai	Dadoo, Sindh
21.	Hyderabad		Office, Opposite Muhammadi Masjid, Plot 35, Liaqat Colony, Hyderabad
22.	Quetta	Abu Zubair	Gualmandi Chowk, Quetta
23.	Muzaffarabad	Shahid Masood Kashmiri	Apar Chattar, Muzaffarabad
24.	Kotli	Naseem Iqbal Qureshi	Near District Hospital, Kotli, Azad Kashmir
25.	Jandalah	Maulana Sayyed Habibullah Shah	
26.	Lodhran	Maulana Abdul Jabbar	Jamia Islamia, Babul-Uloom, Kehrorpacca

Sr. No	District/ Tehsil	District/Tehsil Secretary	Office/Centre
27.	Sargodha	Khalid Irshad Towana	Bans Bazar, Near Ghalla Mandi, Sargodha
28.	Shujaabad		Jamia Farooqia, Shujaabad
29.	Faisalabad	Maulana Abdul Qayyum	202, Rab Gatti Sharqi, District Faisalabad
30.	Samandari	Mohammad Hanif	Jamia Masjid Tauhid, Samandari

Harkat-al Jihad al-Islami, Arakan

In Karachi, there is a large concentration of Burmese Muslims from Arakan. The Korangi area is also known as the Burmese town and is called 'Mini Arakan'. Thirty Arakani madrasas are working here. Through the efforts of the teachers and students of these madrasas, the Pakistani branch of Harkat-al Jihad, Arakan, has been formed.

BACKGROUND

It was founded in 1988 with the objective of uniting the Muslim majority areas of Arakan and start jihad for freedom. The Lahore weekly, *Zindagi*, published an interview with Maulana Abdul Quddus, amir, Burma issue of Harkat-al Jihad, in its 25–31 January 1998, which throws light on the background of this organisation:

> Arakan is a Muslim majority state. There are seventy lakh Muslims here. Burma got its independence in 1948. Prior to that, Arakan was an independent state. As the British, while leaving India, left the Kashmir question unresolved, similarly, by including Arakan state in Burma, they have left Muslims saddled with a

huge problem. The British had earlier included one part of Arakan to the subcontinent which is now known as Chittagong in Bangladesh. You may not know that currently there is a communist government in Burma that has prohibited religious education for Muslims. They made a survey of the Muslim areas and were furious to see that religious education was being imparted there. They expressed their strong disapproval of it and punished the Muslims. They ordered us to send our children to the communist schools where they teach apostasy. They began to oppress the ulema. They said that they did not have the time to manage the departure of such a large number of people for pilgrimage (haj), and cannot allow them to spend so much foreign exchange. They also do not allow collective prayer (namaz) and Friday congregations. They say that we waste time on the pretext of religion. They were not even prepared to allow Eid congregation and declare holiday on the occasion of Eid. To them, it is sheer waste of time. Under these circumstances, it had become difficult to live there. Who does not love his own country? But one also wants honour for one's religion. It is precisely because of this that my father had to migrate to Bangladesh when President Ziaur Rahman was in power. Four lakh Burmese Muslims have already migrated to Bangladesh.

As a result of Bangladesh's efforts, there has been a pact between Burma and Bangladesh according to which we were sent back to Burma in 1979. But as soon as my children began to go to madrasa, the soldiers came to beat me and then they closed the madrasas. Finally, I took permission from my parents and came to Bangladesh. From there, through India, I arrived in the Islamic country of Pakistan. In Karachi, I began my education in Jamia Faruqiya and Jamia Anwarul Quran. Meanwhile, war in Afghanistan broke out and I went there several times at the invitation of Harkat-al Jihad and participated in jihad. I lived in Afghanistan from 1982 to 1988.

Q: Were there other Burmese students participating in jihad in Afghanistan?

A: Yes, many of my brothers from Burma were participating in jihad. We have also established a branch of Harkat-al Jihad in Burma. Our objective was that as soon as the jihad came to an end in Afghanistan we would begin jihad in Burma.

Q: Did you try to build up the organisation there?

A: Yes. We have built up the organisation. Its base is in Bangladesh. As the war in Afghanistan came to an end, we shifted to Bangladesh. Other Burmese organisations were also working there. We could not unite, but pursued our objective in our own ways. The hilly regions of Bangladesh were the centre of our activities. Jihadi missions were also carried out inside Burma from there. This went on till 1991. In the process, hundreds of Burmese soldiers died; some of our members also achieved martyrdom. On 10 November 1991, the Burmese Muslims migrated to Bangladesh once again. The UNO gave them refugee status and issued permits to them. Our organisation began to train the youth coming from Burma. Our members are engaged in the adjoining border areas of Cox's Bazar.

AIMS AND OBJECTIVES

The aims and objectives of Harkat-al Jihad, Burma, are

as follows:

1. To impart military training to the youth from Arakan
2. To conduct raids inside Arakan
3. To work for the welfare of refugees inside and outside Arakan
4. To help the families of prisoners and mujahideen
5. To extend all possible help to the Burmese refugees in Bangladesh

ORGANISATIONAL STRUCTURE

In Pakistan, Maulana Ahmad Hussain, principal, Madrasa Islamia, Aurangi Town, is the patron of Harkat-al Jihad, Burma. Its central amir, Maulana Abdul Quddus, is also in Pakistan. The deputy amir is Maulana Rauful Alim Wafa. All the three are Arakani Muslims. They are establishing the following departments in Pakistan:

1. Military Department: Secretary, Maulana Abdul Quddus
2. Department of Communication and Publication: Maulana Sadeeq Arakani
3. Department of Management and Bangladesh-Burma Relations

This management has no relation with Harkat-al Jihad, Pakistan. Rather, it is related to the Harkat-al Jihad al-Islami al-Alami (World Harkat-al Jihad). Of course, Arakani mujahideen receive training at Harkat-al Jihad's camp at Kotli. But most Arakani mujahideen complain that members of Harkat-al Jihad, Pakistan, do not cooperate with them fully. They have to gather their own resources. Most Arakanis in Karachi are very poor and they cannot contribute much resources. Whatever fund is collected is spent on the refugees in Bangladesh and on madrasas. This directly affects jihadi activities in Arakan, and it is due to this that for the last two years, no significant mission could be undertaken.

NETWORK

The network of Harkat-al Jihad, Burma, is there in Arakan, Bangladesh, and Pakistan. In Pakistan, Karachi is the biggest centre. In Lahore, Maulana Syed Shah Habibullah was the representative of Harkat-al Jihad, Burma. But when I tried to establish communication with him on 29 March 2002, I was told that he had left Lahore after the ban on jihadi organisations.

Madrasa Khalid bin Walid, Karachi

This madrasa was founded in 1988, and it is quite influential in the area of Korangi. Its chief secretary is Maulana Abdur Rahman Mujahid. Apart from the Burmese and Bangladeshi refugee children, students coming from Arakan and Bangladesh also study here. The education is free up to the graduate level. This madrasa is known as the camp of Harkat-al Jihad. But it has no facility for practical training, though it imparts jihadi instructions. Students from this madrasa acquire training from the camps in Afghanistan and Jammu and Kashmir. They are employed as *mujahids* either in Afghanistan or in Burma. From 1988 to 2001, eighty-six students of this madrasa have acquired military training. Out of them sixty-five have been employed in the front. The total number of students in the madrasa is 500.

Very few students passing out from the madrasa

return to Arakan. They prefer to live in Pakistan or Bangladesh. They are encouraged by their teachers to return to Arakan and initiate jihad there.

Other Burmese Madrasas in Karachi
There are thirty madrasas in the Burmese colony, whereas in Karachi, there are forty-eight madrasas. These madrasas pay special attention to impart jihadi education to students so that they can take part in militant activities. To unite all these madrasas, there is a board known as Wafaqul Madaris. Its secretary is Maulana Abu Bakr Siddiq.

Ma'hadul Faruq, Cox's Bazar, Bangladesh
Harkat-al Jihad, Arakan, established this madrasa in 1994. It is fulfilling the educational needs of the children of Rohangiya Burmese refugees. Apart from this, four other madrasas of Harkat-al Jihad are working in Cox's Bazar.

Jamiat Khalid bin Walid Al-Khairita
This is the welfare wing of Harkat-al Jihad which is working for the welfare of the Rohangiya refugees in Bangladesh. Its central office is in Madrasa Khalid bin Walid, Karachi.

Jamiatul Mujahideen Al-Alami

Jamiatul Mujahideen Al-Alami is a jihadi organisation of Deobandi persuasion. It carries out jihadi missions in Occupied Kashmir. It has no relation with General Abdullah's jihadi organisation, Jamiatul Mujahideen.

Its founder was Maulana Masood Alvi, and according to its printed literature, it was founded in March 1973. In this sense, it is the first jihadi organisation to be born in Pakistan. Its objective was to raise an army of Muslim youth who, firm in their conviction in Islam, should emulate the Arabs who rose from humble status and conquered the whole world. They would implement sharia in their daily life and go out for jihad wherever needed. They would love death more than life.

With this object in view, Maulana Masood Alvi gathered his friends in Jama Masjid, Khairul Madaris, Multan, in March 1973 and founded Jamiatul Mujahideen Al-Alami. In 1973, a camp was put up in the jungles of Alipur Jatoi for the training of the youth. Meanwhile, Khatm Nabuwat movement began and its armed youth played a decisive role in Multan. When Khatm Nabuwat movement came to an end, Maulana Masood Alvi left for Kundiyan in the Mianwali district. Here he appealed to the known Deobandi scholar, Khwaja Khan Muhammad, for assistance. Khan Muhammad promised to make arrangements for martial arts along with the traditional system of education in his madrasa. And thus, the youth began to receive martial training here.

In 1979, when the Russian army entered Afghanistan, Maulana Masood Alvi, along with some companions, went to Afghanistan for jihad. It is claimed that he was the first Pakistani to go to Afghanistan to participate in war, and the instruction for this had come from Mufti Mahmood. (Harkat-al Jihad claims that it was Maulana Irshad Ahmad who was the first Pakistani to go to Afghanistan for jihad.) It was at this time that Maulana Masood Alvi had established the first jihadi madrasa in Pakistan so that manpower for the Afghan

War could be provided. Maulana Masood Alvi laid the foundation of Harkatul Mujahideen along with Maulana Fazlur Rahman Khalil in Afghanistan and merged Jamiatul Mujahideen in it. But in 1987, these organisations broke away again.

Maulana Masood Alvi had died on 29 July 1988 in a landmine explosion. After him, Maulana Saifullah Shaokat became the central amir, and it was in his leadership, that Jamiatul Mujahideen started militant activities in Occupied Kashmir in 1989. In 1990, the first group of Jamiatul Mujahideen entered Occupied Kashmir.

In September 1991, Maulana Saifullah Shaokat died along with six mujahideen in an encounter with the Indian army in Karan sector. Among the dead was also the central commander, Yaqub Tariq. After this, Mufti Shabbir Ahmad became the central amir.

According to the literature of Jamiatul Mujahideen Al-Alami: 'Jamiatul Mujahideen Al-Alami only believes in the Pleasure of God and not in fame or publicity. That is why people are not aware of even a fraction of its sacrifices.' After this it presented a long list of its martyrs killed in Occupied Kashmir.

ORGANISATIONAL STRUCTURE

The chief patron of Jamiatul Mujahideen Al-Alami is Mufti Bashir Ahmad. Its amir is Maulana Abdullah from Dera Ismail Khan. There is a twenty-one-member committee to look after its management. It supervises the following departments:

Military Department

This is the most important department of the

organisation. Its central commander is Abdur Rahim. The training camp in Zawar works under the aegis of this department. After the Taliban regime, the camp is closed now. Jamiatul Mujahideen Al-Alami is trying to build a camp in Kotli.

Department of Dawat and Jihad
Maulana Abdul Wahid Jalali is the secretary of this department. The function of this department is to publicise the activities of the mujahideen in the front and inspire readers to join jihad. It also organises assemblies and conferences in different parts of the country.

Department of Communications and Publication
Its secretary is Abdul Sattar Malik. Apart from publishing jihadi literature, this department also deals with the media. It also publishes the jihadi journal, *Al-Masood*.

Department of Resources
Besides collecting funds for jihad, this department also helps poor mujahideen and the families of martyrs. It is under the direct supervision of the central amir.

NETWORK

As for networking, it is limited to a few districts in southern Punjab, Dera Ismail Khan in the Frontier Province, and Muzaffarabad and Bagh in Azad Kashmir. It is small in comparison with other Deobandi jihadi organisations. It has the support of Jamiat Ulema Islam (Q). Its central office is located in Jama Masjid, inside Sheranwala Gate, Lahore. Its leadership has cordial relations with Sipah Sahaba and Lashkar-e Jhangvi. The network of Jamiatul Mujahideen Al-Alami is presented in Table VIII.

CURRENT SITUATION

In the new set-up for jihadi organisations, Jamiatul Mujahideen Al-Alami has an important role. Harkatul Mujahideen and Harkat-al Jihad will now work under Jamiatul Mujahideen Al-Alami in Occupied Kashmir. In Azad Kashmir and Pakistan, these organisations will rename themselves. But the training of their members will be common.

Table VIII: *Network of Jamiatul Mujahideen Al-Alami*

Sr. No.	District	Amir	Centre/Office
1.	Muzaffarabad	Maulana Habibur-Rehman	Near Nare, Chehla Pul, Chehla Bandi, Muzaffarabad Town-5528
2.	Bagh (Azad Kashmir)		Islam Plaza, Final Floor, Kachahri Road, Bagh
3.	Rawalpindi		Jama Masjid King Mandi, Near Pauri Pul, Sadar Rawalpindi
4.	Islamabad		Jama Masjid Farooq Azam, Gali No. 72, G-93, Islamabad
5.	Jhelum	Hakim Mohammad Usman	Usmania Dawakhana, Main Bazar, Jhelum
6.	Mandi Bahauddin		Madina Masjid (Chongi Wali) Railway Road, Mandi
7.	Faisalabad		Jama Masjid, Salbeel, Outside Karkhana Bazar, Faisalabad
8.	Kabirwala		Near Saleem Ainak House, Shirt Bazar, Kabir Wala, Khanewal
9.	Lahore	Maulana Iqbal	Jama Masjid, Outside Sheranwala Gate Lahore,
10.	Multan	Islam Tahir	Jama Masjid Sahaba, Nau Bahar Nehar, Wahari Morh, Multan
11.	Rahim Yar Khan	Maulana Khadim Qasmi	Alimgir Hotel, Railway Road, Rahim Yar Khan

Sr. No.	District	Amir	Centre/Office
12.	Dera Ismail Khan	Maulana Amir Abdullah	Madina Hotel, New Khan Adda, Dera Ismail Khan
13.	Karachi	Malik Fazlur-Rahman	House No. 251, Fatima Jinnah Colony, Jamshed Road, Karachi
14.	Checha Watni		College Road, Near M C High School, Checha Watni
15.	Panjgour	Ehtasham-ul-Haq	Madrasa Misbahul-Uloom Sarikoran, Panjgour, Bluchistan

Lashkar-e Umar

Lashkar-e Umar is a jihadi organisation whose name was first heard in 2001 when newspaper offices in Rawalpindi and Islamabad received fax messages from a hitherto unknown organisation that declared Pakistan as an irreligious country (Darul Mukaffar) and jihad against Musharraf regime as the bounden duty of each Muslim. Later, it sent fax messages by the name 'Al-Saeqa' and distributed pamphlets against the government in Islamabad. One of the pamphlets claimed that the attack mounted on the frontier constabulary at Takutkutgram in Frontier Province was by this organisation. This was the beginning of guerrilla warfare against the government. According to sources, when the government began to collect data on the organisation it had renamed itself as Lashkar-e Umar.

Lashkar-e Umar's name surfaced again when it mounted an attack on the Saint Dominic Catholic Church at Bahawalpur on 28 October 2001, in which sixteen Christians and one Muslim died. On 29 October 2001, the office of the daily *Nawa-e Waqt* in Multan received a fax message in which Lashkar-e Umar claimed responsibility for attacking the church. In the message it was said, 'We accept the challenge of the crusade declared by the American President, George W Bush. This is our first gift to Bush. If he does not stop raids in Afghanistan, we will continue to do this.' This fax was sent from Shujaabad by one Shafiq who was an active member of Harkatul Mujahideen. His father is an imam in a mosque. The police arrested Shafiq, and with the help of clues given by him arrested eighteen more from Bahawalpur, Yezman Mandi, Alipur, and Uj Sharif areas. Of them, four were associated with Jaish-e Muhammad, twelve with Harkatul Mujahideen, and one with Lashkar-e Jhangvi.

Four days before the attack on the church, an Anti-US demonstration was organised in Karachi by Tahreek Al-Furqan, and Americans in Pakistan were served a warning against their life in Pakistan. Maulana Abdullah Shah Manzar, amir of Tahreek Al-Furqan, the breakaway group from Jaish-e Muhammad, had also threatened to start a civil obedience movement. It is conjectured that Lashkar-e Umar has the support of Tahreek Al-Furqan, or it is just another name for it. It is also conjectured that Lashkar-e Jhangvi (Qari Asadullah Group) may have changed its name, and it may have been involved in the explosion in Masjid Ali in Rawalpindi in February 2002. The first suicide attack was carried out in Karachi on 8 May 2002, in which five Frenchmen were killed. It was suspected to be the handiwork of Lashkar-e Umar. It was known from the home ministry sources that members of Lashkar-e Jhangvi, Jaish-e Muhammad, Harkatul Mujahideen, and Harkat-al Jihad are there in Lashkar-e Umar. It is said that Umar Shaikh, arrested in the Daniel Pearl case, is the leader of this group. Some sources in Karachi said that this formation (Lashkar-e Umar) is a breakaway group from Harkatul Mujahideen whose leader is Imran. This formation is also supposed to be working in the name of Harkatul Mujahideen al-Alami.

Al-Mansoorin

This organisation has emerged only recently in Occupied Kashmir. According to Harkat-al Jihad, the friends of its ex-commander, Mansoor Langyal (now in Indian jail) have broken away from Harkatul Mujahideen and Harkat-al Jihad and formed this group. The objective of this organisation is to get Mansoor Langyal and other mujahideen released from Indian jails. In Azad Kashmir this formation has links with Harkat-al Jihad, but nothing is known about its organisational structure and network.

Al-Intiqam

This name first came to light when, in August 2000, some terrorists attacked a foreign missionary school at Murree. It is supposed to have been formed by the breakaway members of Jaish-e Muhammad and Harkatul Mujahideen. It has sent the message, 'America's decimation of the Taliban will be avenged.' Some other sources have asserted that Al-Intiqam has the support of Al-Qaida, and it is not a permanent name. Rather, in the ensuing terrorist strikes against foreigners in Pakistan, different names will be used.

Anjuman Ahl-e Sunnat, Bultistan

The Sukardo and Ghanche districts are inhabited by the Ismaili and Noor Bakhshi sects. Sunni population is only 5 per cent here. Anjuman Ahl-e Sunnat is a Hanfi-Deobandi organisation that has considerable hold on its Sunni population. Basically, it is a non-political organisation which builds madrasas and mosques and works for the religious rights of the Sunnis. This has been active for the last sixty years. Its current management is as follows:

Chairman	Mufti Suroor Ahmad
Patron	Syed Tahir Ali Shah
Deputy Chairman I	Maulana Ibrahim Khalil
Deputy Chairman II	Hafiz Muhammad Hilal Zuberi
General secretary	Haq Nawaz
Deputy General secretary	Abdul Karim Arif

Under the aegis of Anjuman Ahl-e Sunnat, there are eleven Jama masjids (the total number of mosques being twenty-five) and twenty-four madrasas in the Sukardo and Ghanche districts. The biggest of the madrasas is Jamia Islamia in Sukardo. Besides religious education, it also imparts general education up to the middle school level. The total number of students here is 300, taught by ten teachers. The principal is Maulana Muhammad Umar and Maulana Abdur Rahman is the secretary. It has also a Darul Ifta run by Mufti Sharifullah, a former student of Jamia Banooriya, Karachi. The other madrasas are as listed in Table IX.

Table IX: *Madrasas in the Sukardo and Ghanche Districts*

Sr. No.	Name of Madrasa and Place	Teachers
1.	Madrasa Talimul Quran Sherthang	Maulana Mohammad Umar Saheb
2.	Madrasa Talimul Quran, Sherthang	Headmistress
3.	Madrasa Talimul Quran, Akramabad	Qari Ghulam Haider
4.	Madrasa Talimul Quran, Mathal	Hafiz Liaqat Ali
5.	Madrasa Talimul Quran, Hameedgarh	Maulana Abdul Khaliq
6.	Madrasa Talimul Quran, Kharpee Touk	Maulana Abdul Ghafoor
7.	Madrasa Talimul Quran, Jinah Town	Maulana Abdul Rashid Jauhar
8.	Madrasa Talimul Quran, Aliabad	Maulana Karim Baksh
9.	Madrasa Talimul Quran, Purana Bazar	Maulvi Mohammad Shafee
10.	Madrasa Talimul Quran, Umarabad	Hafiz Mohammad Bashir
11.	Jamia Aisha Lilbanat Sakardo	
12.	Madrasa Talimul Quran, Sarmak	
13.	Madrasa Talimul Quran, Sheigerkhas	Maulvi Abdul Qayyum
14.	Madrasa Talimul Quran, Sagaldushegar	
15.	Jamia Siddiqiya Hanfiah Barra	Maulana Ehsanullah
16.	Madrasa Talimul Quran, Barah Gond	Maulvi Abdul Hakim
17.	Madrasa Talimul Quran, Bhatong Khaploo	Maulana Sana-Ullah
18.	Madrasa Talimul Quran, Sharooni	Maulana Rehmat-Ullah
19.	Madrasa Talimul Quran, Mulla Ali Wakanomi Khaploo	Qari Mohammad Yusuf
20.	Madrasa Talimul Quran, Kawas Chorbhat	Maulana Mohammad Ashraf
21.	Madrasa Talimul Quran, Kharkoh	Maulana Mohammad Shafi
22.	Madrasa Talimul Quran, Hyderabad (Daghooni)	Maulana Inayat-Ullah
23.	Sultan-ul-Madaris, Daghooni	Hafiz Mohammad Kaseer
24.	Madrasa Talimul Quran, Kharang Daghooni	Maulvi Abdul Khaliq

The Anjuman runs a charitable medical dispensary in Sukardo which is an extension of the Siddiqui Trust in Karachi. This trust is one major source of funding for the Anjuman.

During the Kargil War, the madrasas of the Anjuman provided help to different jihadi organisations, putting up the mujahideen in mosques and madrasas. The Anjuman claimed that the people of other sects did not cooperate with the mujahideen and even fired at them.

Jamiat Ahl-e Sunnat, Gujranwala

Jamiat Ahl-e Sunnat is a non-political organisation of Deobandi persuasion that has the support of Jamiat Ulema Islam. Its important leaders are Mufti Muhammad Isa Khan Gurmani, Maulana Hafiz Gulzar Ahmad Azad, and Maulana Qazi Abdul Rasheed. Its central office is located in the Jama Masjid Siddiqia, Satellite Town, Gujranwala. Apart from Gujranwala, it has its network in Rawalpindi.

Most of the leaders of Jamiat Ahl-e Sunnat are also the office bearers of Jamiat Ulema Islam (S). The basic reason for this is that the main objective of Jamiat Ahl-e Sunnat is the promotion of Hanfi-Deobandi school of thought. It advocates unity among all organisations of Deobandi school of thought and sharing the same platform. Pakistan Shariat Council has also made several efforts in this regard, but they were in vain.

Jamiat Ishat al-Quran Wal-Hadith (Lawa, Chakwal District)

Jamiat Ishat al-Quran Wal-Hadith is a non-political

organisation whose main objective is promoting learning of Quran and Hadith. Its amir is Qazi Muhammad Arshad al-Husaini. Three madrasas are working in Chakwal under the aegis of this organisation. It has a substantial presence in Chakwal. It publishes religious literature and distributes it freely. Its central office is at Lawa, Chakwal.

Sawad-e Azam Ahl-e Sunnat

This is supposed to be a big organisation of Deobandi ulema. It has a strong network in Karachi and it has remained involved in several sectarian clashes.

Its leader is Maulana Asfanadyar Khan. The teachers of more than 300 madrasas in Karachi and Frontier Province are its members. Among the main objectives of this organisation is to establish links between the ulema of Ahl-e Sunnat (Deobandi) and safeguard their rights. To strengthen religious belief among people is another of its objective.

Though Sawad-e Azam is a non-political organisation, its links with Jamiat Ulema Islam are very strong and it supports its political agenda. It is also a part of Afghan Defence Council and Milli Ekjahti Council.

Tanzeem Ahl-e Sunnat, Sindh

The founder and chairman of Tanzeem Ahl-e Sunnat is Faiz Muhammad Faiz Naqshbandi. He is the principal, Jamia Qasim Hashimiya, north Karachi. It is a small organisation that wants to save Ahl-e Sunnat from misguided beliefs (Barelvism). Its presence is limited to a few madrasas in Karachi.

Tanzeemul Ulema, Pakistan

The chairman of Tanzeemul Ulema, Pakistan, is also Maulana Faiz Muhammad Faiz. Its objective is to work for unity among Deobandi ulema. Its network is also very limited.

United Ulema Council

This organisation was formed to unite Deobandi organisations and religious groups. But it took on a personal dimension later. Its amir is Maulana Fazlur Rahman Darkhasti, principal, Jamia Makhzanul Uloom, Khanpur, and its general secretary is Maulana Abdur Rauf Malik (Lahore). The leaflet that was published at the time of its formation indicates its objectives:

> The foremost need of the hour in Pakistan is the prominence of sharia and the end of non-religious governments. For this, all religious groups must unite. All organisations of Ahl-e Sunnat persuasion should recognise this fact sooner than later. Otherwise, the wave of apostasy will sweep away everything, and the religious leaders will be equally responsible for it.

Motamar Al-Muhajiroon

The leaders of Motamar Al-Muhajiroon are Maulana Adeel and Maulana Iftikhar Ahmad Siddiqi. This organisation is limited to the areas of Peshawar,

Naoshehra, Mansehra, and Kohat. Its objective is to promote jihadi environment and provide help to jihadi organisations. Motamar Al-Muhajiroon is also part of Afghan Defence Council. Basically, it is the ulema wing of Harkat-al Jihad.

Mashaikh Pakistan

Mashaikh Pakistan is a representative organisation of the ulema and shaikhs of Deobandi (*hayati*) school of thought. Its chief leader is Maulana Syed Sher Ali Shah, Shaikhul Hadith, Jamia Haqqania, Kora Kharak. Among its other leaders are Qazi Muhammad Arshad Al-Husaini, Maulana Qazi Anwaruddin, Maulana Syed Pir Asghar Ali Shah, Maulana Ubaidullah (Lahore), Maulana Najibullah (Quetta), Maulana Pir Saifullah Khalid (Lahore), and Maulana Zarooli Khan (Karachi).

The objective of Mashaikh Pakistan is to establish links among the teachers of Hadith from Deoband so that they can take a common stand on issues. Though it is a non-political organisation, it supports Jamiat Ulema Islam (S). The scholars of Mashaikh Pakistan play a crucial role in the social, religious, and political affairs because of their status in society. It is supposed to be a prosperous Deobandi organisation that runs hundreds of madrasas and shrines in Pakistan.

Majlis Tawun Islami

The patron of Majlis Tawun Islami is Maulana Mufti Nizamuddin Shamzai, and its primary objective was to maintain links with the teachers and alumni of Jamia Banooriya, Karachi. But new madrasas are being established by it in Karachi, Quetta, and Sindh. The organisational structure and network of Majlis Tawun Islami are not strong.

Khatm Nabuwat Groups of Deobandi Persuasion

There are four Khatm Nabuwat groups of Deobandi persuasion:

1. Alami Majlis Tahaffuz Khatm Nabuwat
2. Pasban Khatm Nabuwat
3. Tahreek Tahaffuz Khatm Nabuwat
4. International Khatm Nabuwat Movement

Basically, these are splinter groups formed because of mutual disagreements from time to time.

Alami Majlis Tahaffuz Khatm Nabuwat

The foundation of Alami Majlis Tahaffuz Khatm Nabuwat was laid by Syed Ataullah Shah Bukhari in 1949. In 1954, he was made its amir. Among the succeeding amirs are – Qari Ahsan Ahmad Shujabadi, Maulana Muhammad Ali Jalandhari, Maulana Lal Husain Akhtar, Maulana Muhammad Hayat, and Maulana Allama Muhammad Yusuf Banooriya. The current amir is Maulana Shah Nafisul Husaini, and the current patron is Maulana Khan Muhammad.

Fifteen madrasas are working in Pakistan under the supervision of Alami Majlis Tahaffuz Khatm Nabuwat. It has fifty offices in Pakistan. The most important department of Alami Majlis Tahaffuz Khatm Nabuwat is the *tabligh* department that distributes literature worth lakhs of rupees in Urdu, Arabic, English, German, and other languages freely. Its central offices are located in Huzoori Bagh and Multan.

Pasban Khatm Nabuwat

The amir of Pasban Khatm Nabuwat is Mumtaz Husain. Its network is not so wide.

Tahreek Tahaffuz Khatm Nabuwat

Tahreek Tahaffuz Khatm Nabuwat is the *tablighi* department of Majlis Ahrar Islam, Pakistan. Its leader is Maulana Syed Ataul Memon Bukhari. This organisation also regards Maulana Khwaja Khan Muhammad as its patron. Its network is wider than other Khatm Nabuwat groups.

International Khatm Nabuwat Movement

The amir of International Khatm Nabuwat Movement is Maulana Manzoor Ahmad Cheneoti. Its central secretariat is at Cheneot. The network of this organisation is also wide.

Islami Mission Pakistan, Bahawalpur

Islami Mission is working in Pakistan for the implementation of sharia. Its patron is Maulana Syed Abdul Qadir Azad, and Haji Abdul Majid Khan is the general secretary. It was founded in 1962, but its activities are limited to Bahawalpur. Its main objectives are:

1. Dominance of sharia

2. Preaching Islam
3. Fighting false beliefs

Islami Mission has built a mosque in Model Town in Bahawalpur. A madrasa is attached to it. There is also a dispensary. It has acquired 10 acres of land in Bahawalpur where Jamia Darool Uloom, Jamia Banat al-Islam, Islami Public School, College, and Library are being built, spending five crore rupees. Its central office is located in Model Town, A-Block, Bahawalpur.

Majlis-e Amal Ulema Islam

This is a united front for Deobandi groups that was founded in March 1998. Its amir is Maulana Muhammad Sarfaraz Khan Safdar who is associated with Madrasa Nusratul Uloom at Gujranwala. The deputy amirs are Dr Maulana Sher Ali Shah and Maulana Abdur Razzaq of Darul Uloom Haqqania, Kora Khatak.

It is not a permanent organisation, but a front for Deobandi organisations, whose objectives are:

1. Implementation of Islamic state
2. Confronting the challenges of Western culture
3. Ending of American interference
4. Protecting independence of madrasas
5. Establishing harmony in place of terrorism

After remaining active for a few months this organisation has become dormant.

Ulema Council

After the failure of Majlis-e Amal Ulema Islam,

another front of Deobandi ulema, Ittihad Ulema Council was formed in September 2000, with the same objectives that were: to unite Deobandi organisations (of ulema) on the basis of a common code of conduct, and to end differences among them, or at least discourage them to air their differences in public making the Deobandi sect everyone's laughing stock. Maulana Zahid al-Rashidi played a prominent role in establishing this front.

Jamiat Ulema Islam (S)'s Maulana Qazi Abdul Latif is its amir while the deputy amir is Ziaul Haq Qasmi of the now banned Sipah Sahaba. This front represents eighteen organisations, including Harkatul Mujahideen and Harkat-al Jihad.

The model code of conduct prepared by the council for the organisations has the following important points:

1. Ulema Council will work as a common forum for the organisations of Deobandi ulema and establish links among them.
2. The groups will invite the leaders of other groups in their assemblies.
3. In the assemblies, sloganeering for particular personalities will be avoided.
4. Mutual differences need not be aired in public in general assemblies.

Pakistan Shariat Council

The amir of Pakistan Shariat Council is Maulana Fidaur Rahman Darkhasti, and its general secretary is Maulana Zahid al-Rashidi. This is a notable political organisation of Deobandi persuasion, which is working for the implementation of sharia and unity among the Deobandi groups. Its central office is in Hashmi Colony, Kangniwala, Gujranwala. Madrasa Makhzanul Uloom, Khanpur, is one of its very active centres. Apart from Pakistan and Azad Kashmir, the network of Pakistan Shariat Council is spread out in the UK and other countries of Europe. It wants to bring about a change in the syllabi of madrasas to bring it in line with the demands of the modern time. A committee has been formed to look into this, which is led by Maulana Muhammad Sarfaraz Khan Safdar. A sharia academy has also been formed in Gujranwala.

However, the central figure of Pakistan Shariat Council is Maulana Zahid al-Rashidi. He also writes a column in an Urdu newspaper in Islamabad. He has special status among the members of the Deobandi religious, sectarian, and jihadi organisations, and is called to all forums. He extends special patronage to Harkatul Mujahideen, and has a role in its management. He wants to unite Deobandi organisation on a single platform and has succeeded partially in his endeavour. He had an important role in the founding of Ulema Council and Majlis-e Amal Ulema Islam.

Pakistan Shariat Council brings out a monthly journal, *Al-Sharia*.

Chapter X
ORGANISATIONS OF AL-HADITH PERSUASION

Ahl-e Hadith accounts for the smallest number of religious organisations in Pakistan. One reason for this is that Ahl-e Hadith sect is more organised than any other sects, though the number of people adhering to this way of belief is smaller than those of other sects. However, in the last decades, this number has gone higher.

Currently, there are seventeen regional and national groups of Ahl-e Hadith persuasion working in the country. Of these, six groups also participate in practical politics, six are sectarian, three are *tablighi*, and three are jihadi groups. There is also an educational board that organises examinations, etc., of Ahl-e Hadith madrasas. A list of organisations of Ahl-e Hadith persuasion in Pakistan is presented in Table X.

These groups have differences on finer points of belief. All of them are non-following (*ghair muqallid*) *salafis*, but have differences among them about ways of ablution, *namaz*, rituals, etc., that come in the way of their sharing the same platform. Most of them also differ on political grounds – some groups are opposed to participation in active politics and want to devote all of their energy on matters of belief. For example, Jamat Ghurba Ahl-e Hadith has the view that when the majority of the people will turn into *salafis*, the political power will automatically come into their hands. However, Jamatul Mujahideen's view is that the current democratic system is wrong, and they should not participate in this process till an Islamic government is established for which they will continue to struggle. Jamat Al-Dawa had the same view before it decided to take part in active politics.

Unlike other Ahl-e Hadith groups, the Central Jamiat Ahl-e Hadith does not consider democracy to be a heretical form of government and is in favour of changing the system by participating in the process. Apart from differences on political perspective, they also differ on their views about jihad. Some consider it more obligatory than others, while some other groups consider military activities as the lesser jihad and exhort its members to concentrate on self-purification which is the greater jihad. Some groups do not consider jihad in Afghanistan and Occupied Kashmir permissible at all.

Points of Difference About Jihad

1. Is jihad absolutely obligatory, or is it a lesser obligation?
2. Can jihad be conducted only at the instruction of *khalifa* or *amir*?
3. What is the importance of self-purification?
4. Militant jihad cannot be conducted without effective management and resources.
5. Is taking part in jihad in Kashmir simply permissible under certain conditions, and not obligatory?

Keeping the above in view, let us look at the stand taken by different organisations on this issue:

Jamat Ahl-e Hadith's Stand

The stand taken by Jamat Ahl-e Hadith, Pakistan, is clear: it gives precedence to self-purification. This stand is elaborated in the journal, *Siratul Mustaqeem*, in its June 1995 issue:

> Our difference with the advocates of limited jihad is obvious. To go out to jihad with an organisation 75 per cent of whose members are ignorant, infirm and ineffective, is not salutary. Our Prophet declared jihad against one's self as superior precisely because, as long as one cannot conquer his own self (baser emotions/urges), he cannot fight external evil. In this context, the Prophet compared jihad with human body, saying that as long as the body cannot fight internal ailments, it cannot conquer external powers. That is why, at this point of time, the best jihad will be to make people healthy and to remove their ignorance and inertia. We must prepare the youth by educating them, by inculcating moral values in them so that they can fulfil the objectives of jihad. As long as we are not able to do this, our dream of refurbishing the image of Islam will not be realised. Excessive emotionalism has already brought the community to the brink of destruction. We cannot be a party to this process of destruction. Now, it has become inevitable to recognise the demands of the time. However much one runs after a mirage, one cannot achieve his destination. For us, Pakistan is the most appropriate site for jihad. Evils like apostasy, oppression, injustice and obscenity are rampant here.

To leave Pakistan in this state and conduct jihad elsewhere is certainly not an Islamic approach. Such attempts by any organisation create suspicion in the mind of the people as to why members of the organisation are going to other countries to conduct jihad, ignoring the evils that surround them in their own country. If we have absolute certainty about the fact that because of our struggle in Occupied Kashmir, the oppression of the Kashmiri people will be alleviated and an Islamic state will be established there, only then can jihad and our participation in it be justified. However, when it is evident to any sensible person that our struggle will not yield the above results, why should we waste our resources and energy there? It is a measure of our stupidity that after having done an experiment in Afghanistan, and seeing its consequence, we now want to repeat that experiment and waste our resources and energy!

Abu Fattada, 'Open the Lock with the Key'

Jamiat Ghurba Ahl-e Hadith's Stand

Jamiat Ghurba Ahl-e Hadith's stand is close to that of Jamat Ahl-e Hadith. Like the former, it also stresses moral reform of the individual and the society, and adduces instructions from the Koran and Hadith in favour of that stance. However, it is not opposed to militant jihad under certain conditions.

Markazi Jamiat Ahl-e Hadith's Stand

The Deputy Chairman of Markazi Jamiat Ahl-e Hadith, Maulana Muhammad Madani (late) said in an interview published in *Siratul Mustaqeem*, May 1995 issue:

307

Some people are conducting jihad on a commercial basis. Graves are being traded; some elements (of some groups) are trading on martyrs, selling the shrouds of martys to keep their business going. Those who did not have a battered cycle have now acquired Pajero cars through this business. Those who could hardly manage a spartan meal are now feasting on chicken roast. What lucrative business!

Markazi Jamiat Ahl-e Hadith regards the struggle in Occupied Kashmir as jihad proper. According to it, Tahreekul Mujahideen fulfils all the qualifying conditions of jihad.

Jamat Al-Mujahideen's Stand

Jamat Al-Mujahideen supports militant jihad; however, it is in favour of an administration that can issue instructions about jihad. Along with militant jihad, it also gives importance to self-purification.

Jamat Al-Dawa's Stand

Jamat Al-Dawa's stand is different from other Ahl-e Sunnat groups. It is a strong advocate of militant jihad and considers it absolutely obligatory. Its militant wing, Lashkar-e Tayyaba, makes the following declaration again and again:

We have taken an oath!
We will fight for the Word of God morning and evening. We will fight in the sea as on the desert. Be it Israel or India, America or Russia, the UK or Serbia, we will fight against the infidels. We will not

stop jihad in the way of God. Our bodies may fall to pieces, the blood in our veins may drain out, but we will not stop jihad. Because it is God's Command. O youth, come! Acquire training and join this militant army. There is still time. Don't miss this opportunity.

Department of communication and publications of Al-Dawa published a booklet, *Why We Do Jihad?* by Abdul Salam bin Muhammad, in May 1999. This book says that Lashkar-e Tayyaba is doing jihad for eight objectives, and all these objectives (according to it) have been culled from the Koran:

1. Muslims should fight as long as a dispute persists.
2. It is obligatory for Muslims to fight till Allah's kingdom is established in the world.
3. It is obligatory for Muslims to fight till they finish all governments by infidels and extract *jeziya* from them.
4. If oppression is going on in any part of the world, Muslims should fight till it is removed.
5. If any infidel kills a Muslim, we should fight to avenge it.
6. If any nation perpetrates a breach of contract against Muslims, it is obligatory to fight with that nation.
7. When any nation takes an aggressive posture on Muslims, we should fight in self-defence.
8. If the infidels encroach upon any part of a Muslim land, it is obligatory to fight them and restore it. This point has been elaborated further:
   (a) After eight hundred years of rule in Andalusia (Spain), Muslims have been ejected from there up to the last man, and Christians took over. It is obligatory upon us to restore it.

(b) The whole of India, including Kashmir, Hyderabad, Assam, Bihar, Junagarh, Nepal, and Burma were under Muslim rule. It has fallen into others' hands as we had given up jihad.

(c) The Jews have encroached upon Palestine. Our *qibla*, Baitul Muqaddas in Jerusalem, has been captured by them. Apart from them, scores of countries such as Bulgaria, Hungary, Sicily, the Russian Turkistan, and the Chinese Turkistan, etc., were under Muslim rule. It is obligatory upon Muslims to restore them. The area extending up to 90 km from Paris and the forests of Swaziland were the abodes of Muslim mujahideen. Now it is in the hands of infidels.

Jamat Al-Dawa's stand is: as the eight above objectives have not yet been achieved, jihad will continue. It is often pointed out to the Lashkar-e Tayyaba that the above eight objectives have not yet been realised even in Pakistan. The reply to this has been given in the booklet in the following words:

My brothers! You must understand this well. There are two kinds of infidels – one who has not professed the Faith, and one who has professed it. The former fights against us because we have professed the Islamic Faith. The latter will never fight against us because he has become our brother and entered our religion through professing the Faith. However, if he (the latter) is going astray, we will talk to him, persuade him to come to the way of religio n. As long as he does not raise his hand against us, we will not raise ours against him. We will consider him wrong and misguided, and say that he is committing sins of un-belief (*kufr*) and associationism (*shirk*). But we will not declare war against him. Because if we declare war against those who have professed Faith, we cannot do war with those who haven't.

Table X: *Organisations of Ahl-e Hadith Persuasion in Pakistan*

Sr. No.	Organisation/ Group	Amir/ Secretary	Founded	Nature	Central Office
1.	Markazi Jamiat Ahl-e Hadith	Professor Sajid Mir	1956	Political/ Religious	Central Secretariat 106, Ravi Road, Lahore
2.	Jamat-Al-Dawa	Prof. Mohammad Said	1986	Religious/ Political	Markaz Tayyaba, Muridke, District Shekhupura
3.	Jamat-e-Ghurba Ahl-e Hadith	Imam Abdur Rahman	1986	*Tabligh*/ Religious	Bans Road, Karachi, Ph: 2632961
4.	Markazi Jamiat Ahl-e Hadith	Engineer Ibtisam Ilahi	1994	Political	Lowrence Road, Lahore
5.	Muttahida Jamiat Ahl-e Hadith	Maulana Zia-Ullah Shah Bukhari	1994	Political	Multan Road, Lahore
6.	Jamat-Ahl-e Hadith	Maulana Muhammad Hussain Shekhpuri	1919	*Tabligh*/ sectarian	Jamia Masjid Ahl-e Hadith Chowk Dalgiran, Lahore
7.	Jamat al-Dawat-ullil-Quran Wanista Afghanistan	Sheikh Samiullah		Jihadi	
8.	Tahreekul Mujahideen	Maulana Abdullah Ghizali	1989	Jihadi	Shaheed Makki Road, Muzaffarabad

311

Sr. No.	Organisation/ Group	Amir/ Secretary	Founded	Nature	Central Office
9.	Lashkar-e Tayyaba	Zakiur Rahman Lakhwi	1991	Jihadi	Chehella Bandi, Muzaffarabad
10.	Jamiat-Ulema Ahl-e Hadith	Abdul Qadir Khamosh		Sectarian	Lahore
11.	Anjuman Ahl-e Hadith			Sectarian	Lahore
12.	Tahaffuz Harmain Sharifain Movement Pakistan	Maulana Abdul Ghafoor			Jamia Uloom Asria, Jhelum
13.	Ahl-e Hadith Youth Force	Shahid Rafiq	1986		106, Ravi Road, Lahore
14.	Jamat-ul-Mujahideen	Dr Arshad Randhawa	1837	Jihadi	Near Ganga Ram Hospital, Lahore
15.	Tablighi Jamat Ahl-e Hadith	Maulana Abdur Rahman Salafi		Tablighi	Jama Masjid-ud-Tauhid, Court Road, Karachi
16.	Shaan-e Ahl-e Hadith			Sectarian	Bans Road, Karachi
17.	Tanzimul Madaris Salafia	Prof. Sajid Meer		Educational	Faisalabad
18.	Jamiat Tahaffuz-ul Quran Al-Kareen-ul-Khairiya	Qari Abdul Jabbar Rabbani		Educational	Akhtar Colony, Dera Ghazi Khan
19.	Ahl-e Hadith Janbaz Force	Maulana Mohammad Akhtar	1994	Sectarian	Karachi
20.	Ahl-e Hadith Students Federation		1994	Students' Wing	Lawrence Road, Lahore

Markazi Jamiat Ahl-e Hadith

Markazi Jamiat Ahl-e Hadith is the biggest religious and political organisation of the 'salafi' sect. Its amir is Professor Sajid Mir. It also runs Wafaqul Madaris Salafiya which is the representative educational board of Salafia madrasas. Professor Sajid Mir is the chairman of this board.

Markazi Jamiat Ahl-e Hadith traces its beginning from the All India Ahl-e Hadith Conference held in Ara, Bihar province (India), on 23 December 1906. After Pakistan came into being, its centres were established in Lahore and in Mamun Kanjan in Faisalabad district. Jamiat Ahl-e Hadith showed its religious and political strength for the first time by organising an Ahl-e Hadith conference in Mochi Gate, Lahore, on 18 April 1986. Allama Ehsan Elahi Zaheer has played a seminal role in activating Jamiat Ahl-e Hadith. In the eighties of the twentieth century, he opposed the Shariat Bill and charted a different course for Ahl-e Hadith which later became the identity marker of this organisation.

ORGANISATIONAL STRUCTURE

The current leadership of Markazi Jamiat Ahl-e Hadith was elected on 7 November 1997, in Jamia Mahmudiya, Gujranwala. A twelve-member cabinet was formed. Professor Sajid Mir became the amir, Mian Muhammad Jameel became the Secretary General, and Haji Abdur Razzaq became the secretary, resources. Following were the Cabinet members:

1. Mian Muhammad Jameel   Central Secretary

2.	Hafiz Abdur Rahman Madani	Deputy Amir
3.	Maulana Muhammad Azam	Secretary, Education
4.	Maulana Muhammad Naim Bhat	Secretary, Information
5.	Haji Abdur Razzaq	Secretary, Resources
6.	Mian Abdus Sattar	Secretary, Elections
7.	Maulana Muhammad Ishaq Kohri	Secretary, Social Service
8.	Qari Muhammad Hanif Rabbani	Secretary, Tabligh
9.	Maulana Irshadul Haq Asari	Secretary, Publications
10.	Rana Muhammad Shafiq Sarwaru	Asst. Secretary General
11.	Maulana Abdul Rasheed Hijazi	Asst. Secretary General
12.	Professor Abdul Ghafoor Rashid	Asst. Secretary General

OBJECTIVES

Markazi Jamiat Ahl-e Hadith has the following objectives, according to its printed charter:

1. Markazi Jamiat Ahl-e Hadith wants the dominance of the Koran and Hadith
2. Ahl-e Hadith's invitation is an invitation towards God
3. Ahl-e Hadith's invitation is for the observance of Sunnah
4. Ahl-e Hadith's invitation is from the Salafi school of thought

5. Ahl-e Hadith's invitation is an invitation for true mysticism/spiritualism

Markazi Jamiat Ahl-e Hadith has full endorsement of the concept of Pakistan which, according to it, means the following:

1. To adhere to the two-nation theory which was the basis of Pakistan's formation
2. To establish dominance of the Book and Sunnah in Pakistan

As opposed to its stated views, Markazi Jamiat Ahl-e Hadith is regarded as the 'B' team of the Muslim League (N). There is a recognition to this in its charter as well:

Markazi Jamiat Ahl-e Hadith has opposed the feminine government (Benazir Bhutto's government), and considered it necessary to unite with Muslim League (N) in the larger national interest. This is the reason why Mian Nawaz Sharif has repeatedly admitted the need for high-level actions. Rather, Mian Nawaz Sharif who was, at one time, eager for the support of Jamat-e Islami, has now forgotten the road to Mansoora.

NETWORK

The network of Markazi Jamiat Ahl-e Hadith is spread over the four provinces and Azad Kashmir. Its important centres are in Faisalabad, Lahore, Dera Ghazi Khan, Khanpur, Rahim Yar Khan, and Islamabad. Most of its manpower comes from these districts of Punjab. The madrasas under the Aafaqul

Madaris Salafia, spread over the whole of Pakistan, are also important centres of Markazi Jamiat Ahl-e Hadith. In most of the districts, its offices are located in these madrasas.

AFFILIATED ORGANISATIONS

Markazi Jamiat Ahl-e Hadith has eight affiliated organisations. Among them, a few important ones are described here.

Ahl-e Hadith Youth Force

Ahl-e Hadith Youth Force is the youth wing of Markazi Ahl-e Hadith which works from the ward level up to schools and colleges. Its chairman is Hafiz Shahid Amin, and Hafiz Atiqullah Umar is the general secretary. Its network is wide and it is considered to be the mainstay of Markazi Jamiat Ahl-e Hadith. Its charter and programmes are in consistence with those of Markazi Jamiat Ahl-e Hadith. An important feature of this organisation is its involvement in a number of sectarian clashes. It not only distributes literatures against other sects like the Shias and the Barelvis but also gets involved in mutual bickering. A teacher of Markaz al-Tauheed in Dera Ghazi Khan told me that AYF was a naked sword against the enemy groups. 'We have had several skirmishes with Shia organisations in Dera Ghazi Khan. Last year, the Shias had filed a case of terrorism against Qazi Abdur Rahim Kalim, the patron of the Youth Force. But they could not prove anything. In reply, we also filed cases against them. We support Sipah Sahaba's stand against the Shias.' Referring to the Barelvis, the teacher said that they never occupied their mosques, and tried to counter their false belief through legal means. Many cases have been filed against leaders of the Youth Force at different places. It also supplies human resource to Tahreekul Mujahideen.

Tahreekul Mujahideen

Tahreekul Mujahideen is an important jihadi organisation of Ahl-e Hadith persuasion which was formally affiliated to Markazi Jamat Ahl-e Hadith in 2000. The position of the general secretary of United Jihad Council is with this organisation. Shaikh Jamilur Rahman represents it in the Council.

BACKGROUND

In 1989, when militant activities began in Occupied Kashmir, the Jamat Ahl-e Hadith declared founding of a military wing there named Tahreekul Mujahideen. In the beginning, its area of operation was very limited. Maulana Abdullah Ghazali extended it to Azad Kashmir and Pakistan, and with the help of Jamat al-Mujahideen, made arrangements for the training of its members in Afghanistan. Later he built a training camp near Muzaffarabad. Tahreekul Mujahideen began militant activities in 1994.

Tahreekul Mujahideen got formally affiliated to Jamat Ahl-e Hadith in 2000. Markazi Ahl-e Hadith extended patronage to it and appointed Maulana Shahabuddin Madni as its supervisor in Azad Kashmir. Maulana Abdullah Nasir Rahmani who was its patron from the beginning and also the amir of Markazi Jamiat Ahl-e Hadith in Sindh, was made its patron in Pakistan.

Markazi Jamiat Ahl-e Hadith regards it as a representative jihadi organisation of the *salafi* persuasion and has been trying for Lashkar-e Tayyaba's merger in it. Regarding its background, Maulana Shahabuddin Madni said in an interview published in the July 2000 issue of the Muzaffarabad monthly, *Shahadat*:

> Actually, the first organisation of Ahl-e Hadith persuasion to be founded was Tahreekul Mujahideen. At that time there was no other organisation of Ahl-e Hadith persuasion here. In 1990, we organised the Kashmir Conference attended by such great personalities as Hafiz Said Sahib, Professor Sajid Mir Sahib, Maulana Fazlur Rahman Sahib and so on. The conference was held under the banner of Tahreekul Mujahideen. It was a jihad conference organised by Tahreekul Mujahideen and Jamiat Ahl-e Hadith. The then Prime Minister of Azad Kashmir, Sardar Abdul Qayoom had also participated in it. These two organisations were the known ones at that time. We will try to rectify the inadequacy of the past and further activate the movement. Tahreekul Mujahideen is the military wing of Jamiat Ahl-e Hadith, and our identity. In this connection, we have established links with Pakistan's Ahl-e Hadith ulema and my father had stressed it in the meetings of Shura and the general assembly that we will cooperate with Tahreekul Mujahideen. Now if the ulema do not admit it, it is up to them. They will be asked whether they know that there is a single organisation inside Kashmir that worked for the Faith as well as for jihad, and if they know it, why they do not cooperate with it? We will try to take this message to our brothers in Pakistan who do not assist us or show lack of

enthusiasm in assisting us. As far as Azad Kashmir is concerned, my father's message is that all our sympathies lie with Tahreekul Mujahideen. As for Pakistan, as we are associated with Ahl-e Hadith, we will request them to help Tahreekul Mujahideen as much as they can. This is our group and our identity.

ORGANISATIONAL STRUCTURE

The organisational structure of Tahreekul Mujahideen is composed of two central departments: management and military. There are three more departments whose activities are important:

1. Department of dawat and tabligh: It works in Occupied Kashmir to preach Salafia school of thought and get young men inducted to the organisation. In Pakistan, it gets support from Markazi Jamiat Ahl-e Hadith and Ahl-e Hadith Youth Force. Its amir is Shaikh Jamilur Rahman.
2. Department of management: Besides planning the management of the organisation in entire Pakistan and Azad Kashmir, it works to maintain links among local offices and the central secretariat. It also organises different jihadi programmes.
3. Department of relief: It works to help the families of Tahreekul Mujahideen martyrs and maintaining contact with them.

Important office bearers of the organisation are as follows:

1. Central Amir   Maulana Abdullah
                         Ghazali
2. Amir   Shaikh Jamiluddin

3.	Deputy Amir	Abdullah Mubarak
4.	Patron	Shaikh Abdullah Nasir Rahmani
5.	Secretary, Communications (Rabeta Al-Amoor)	Abdul Shakur Azad
6.	Secretary, Communications, Pakistan	Do
7.	Secretary, Department of Relief	do
8.	Secretary, Department of Resources	Hafiz Abdus Sattar Hamad
9.	Secretary, Department of Publications	Shakir bin Abdullah
10.	Secretary, Department of Dawat	Shaikh Jamilur Rahman
11.	Launching Commander (Secretary, Abdullah bin Mubarak camp)	Abu Hamza
12.	Chief Commander	Abdur Rahman Adil

Department of Resources

This department raises resources for jihad fund from Pakistan and Azad Kashmir. It also tries to get funding from different Islamic welfare organisations of the world. In 2000, it raised fifty-five lakh rupees in cash from Pakistan besides contributions in kind.

Al-Harmain Islamic Foundation is an important welfare organisation of Saudi Arabia which is engaged in missionary and welfare activities in different parts of the world. This foundation provides substantial funds to Tahreekul Mujahideen. The general secretary of this foundation had visited Pakistan in 2000. In an interview with *Shahadat*, the mouthpiece of Tahreekul Mujahideen, he had said that it provides funding to both Tahreekul Mujahideen and Jamiat Ahl-e Hadith. Following is an excerpt from this interview:

> As for the Kashmir problem, I am glad to say that we have been in touch with different institutes and groups there from the beginning, especially those groups like Tahreekul Mujahideen that are following the footsteps of *salafi* reformers. In Occupied Kashmir, this organisation is known as Ahl-e Hadith or Tahreekul Mujahideen. They are involved in missionary and jihadi activities which are very close to our heart. Ten years ago, when the Kashmiris had begun jihad, we have been constantly thinking about how best to help them. Whether these Muslims are aged or small children, women or students or common people, they are immensely deserving of our help. But we have not yet been able to reach them because of strict vigilance and interrogation by the Indian army. But we have not despaired. We are trying our best; God will certainly help us. Anyway, we are offering our services in Occupied Kashmir through Jamiat Ahl-e Hadith and Tahreekul Mujahideen.

Tahreekul Mujahideen is also working through the 'Welfare Organisation for Kashmiri Muslims' that is playing an important role in collecting funds from foreign countries.

From the point of view of resources, Tahreekul Mujahideen is considered to be the king of all other organisations. All office staff, down to the tehsil level are paid and given transport (cars, motor cycles).

NETWORK

Tahreekul Mujahideen has its network in forty districts of Pakistan. In 2001, five more district offices have been opened. According to a report of the department of communications of Tahreekul Mujahideen: 'Last year, the network of Tahreekul Mujahideen (Jammu and Kashmir) in Pakistan has been much more strengthened than earlier years. Besides the district management, now management has been formed at the tehsil and sector levels too. Thousands of mujahideen have received training from Abdullah bin Mubarak camp, and hundreds of them reached Kashmir and took part in jihad. Last year, more than 1,500 missionary and jihadi programmes were held.'

Tahreekul Mujahideen has substantial impact in Khanpur, Rajanpur, Jampur, Dera Ghazi Khan, Mian Channo, Faisalabad, Gujranwala, Karachi, Haripur, and Abbottabad. Details of the organisations network of Tahreekul Mujahideen are presented in Table XI.

Abdullah bin Mubarak Camp

The training camp of Tahreekul Mujahideen, located in Muzaffarabad, is known as Abdullah bin Mubarak camp. Its amir is Commander Abu Hamza. The deputy amir is Commander Muhammad Shafi who is an expert in military training. Maulana Muhammad Afzal Alvi is a teacher here. For moral instruction of the mujahideen, an eight-day *tablighi* course is also taught here.

Track Record in Occupied Kashmir

As far as militant activities are concerned, Tahreekul

Mujahideen is one of the important jihadi organisations in Kashmir. It claims to have first used landmines against the Indian army. According to its own record, 500 of its mujahideen have already been killed in Occupied Kashmir so far. Of them, seventy were from Occupied Kashmir, 215 from Punjab, forty-five from Azad Kashmir, forty-nine from Sindh, and nineteen from the Frontier Province. It also claims to have killed 3,000 Indian army men, including senior officers. It got a severe jolt when its commander, Abu Wasim Salafi was killed in 1999. And, after the arrest of Maulana Abdullah Ghazali in February 2002, there was a significant reduction in its militant activities. After the death of Ghazali, Abdullah Mubarak has been made the officiating amir of Tahreekul Mujahideen.

Tahreekul Mujahideen is also vigorously involved in sectarian clashes in Occupied Kashmir. It was born of Jamat Ahl-e Hadith of Occupied Kashmir. Earlier, it was regarded as a sectarian *tablighi jamat*. Tahreekul Mujahideen also claims to be the only organisation in Occupied Kashmir that is working as a *salafi* religious group in addition to conducting jihad.

According to Saif Lulabi, a Kashmiri refugee living in Gulpur Kotli, Tahreekul Mujahideen has its impact in Kupwara and Poonch. They have changed several Barelvi mosques into Ahl-e Hadith mosques there.

IMPORTANT LEADERS

Shaikh Abdullah Ghazali
Shaikh Abdullah Ghazali is the central amir of Tahreekul Mujahideen and one among its founders. He is from Srinagar, Occupied Kashmir. He was

earlier associated with Jamat Ahl-e Hadith, Occupied Kashmir. He has been accused in several sectarian cases. He was arrested in Occupied Kashmir in February 2000.

Shaikh Jamilur Rahman

Besides being the base camp amir of Tahreekul Mujahideen, Shaikh Jamilur Rahman is also the general secretary of United Jihad Council. He is from Occupied Kashmir, and has been living in Pakistan since 1994. He played an important role in consolidating Tahreekul Mujahideen in Pakistan.

Commander Owais Sajjad

Commander Owais Sajjad is the secretary of communications in Pakistan. In March 2000, he was given the charge of the office at Islamabad. The reason for this is said to be that he had started to interfere in the organisational affairs of Markazi Jamiat Ahl-e Hadith. His sympathies were more with Jamat al-Mujahideen than with the Jamiat (Ahl-e Hadith).

Shaikh Abdullah Nasir Rahmani

Besides being the patron of Tahreekul Mujahideen, Shaikh Abdullah Nasir Rahmani is also the amir of Markazi Jamiat Ahl-e Hadith, Sindh. It is because of his efforts that Markazi Jamiat Ahl-e Hadith has made Tahreekul Mujahideen its military wing. Even before this affiliation, he was the patron of Tahreekul Mujahideen. He tries to persuade Ahl-e Hadith organisations to help Tahreekul Mujahideen instead of Lashkar-e Tayyaba.

Maulana Shahabuddin Madani

Maulana Shahabuddin Madani is the supervisor of Tahreekul Mujahideen in Azad Kashmir. He is the son of Maulana Muhammad Yunus Asari, amir of Markazi Jamiat Ahl-e Hadith in Azad Kashmir. He is an alumnus of Madina University. He is the vice principal of Jamia Mahmudiya, Muzaffarabad. He has not yet participated in practical jihad. His main job is the promotion of Tahreekul Mujahideen in Azad Kashmir.

Abdul Shakur Azad

Abdul Shakur Azad has been appointed in March 2002 as secretary, communications (Pakistan), in place of Commander Owais Sajjad. Abdul Shakur Azad has also been associated with Ahl-e Hadith Youth Force, and is thought to be close to Professor Sajid Mir.

Table XI: *Tahreekul Mujahideen – District-wise Details*

Sr. No.	District and Tehsil	District/ Tehsil Secretary	Office
Punjab Province			
1.	Lahore	Shakeel-ur Rahman	Offices Markazi Jamiat Ahl-e Hadith, 106, Ravi Road, Lahore
2.	Sialkot	Tahir Abdul Razzaq	i) Kotli Behram Khadim Ali Road, Near Hari Masjid, Sialkot ii) Office Tehrikul Mujahideen, Kaunagarh, District Sialkot
3.	Bahawalpur	Mohammad Khalid Ameer	Tanveer Iqbal, Lock Maker, Near Jama Masjid Ahl-e Hadith, Multan Road, Bahawalpur
4.	Khanewal		Jama Masjid Ahl-e Hadith, Block No. 11, Khanewal
5.	Shekhpura	Abu Owais Shehbaz Abdul Wahid	Chak No. 5, Badda Post Office Nankana, District Shekhpura
6.	Multan	Abu Baker Saeed	Hazoori Bagh Road, Near Kotwali, Baker Mandi, Multan City
7.	Jahaniyan	Abdul Khalique Chowdhery	Chak No. 138, Jahaniyan

Sr. No.	District and Tehsil	District/ Tehsil Secretary	Office
8.	Rajanpur	Maulana Liaqat Ali Siddiqui	Tehrikul Mujahedeen, Circular Road, Rajanpur
9.	Jampur	Maulana Ismail Sajid	Jamia Mohammadia, Irfanabad, Jampur
10.	Kot Radha Kishan	Miyan Abdul Jabbar	Markazi Jama Masjid Ahl-e Hadith, Gandhiyan Road, Kot Radha Kishan, Tehsil and District Qasoor
11.	Okara	Qari Abdul Maqeeat Mujahid	Office Tehrikul Mujahideen (Main Bazar Akhtarabad) District Okara
12.	Naruwal	Bhai Ghulam Murtaza	Office Tehrikul Mujahideen, Al-Qamar Clinic, United Bank Shakargarh, Naruwal
13.	Attock	Arif Mahmood Hussain Salafi	Camp Pole Agency Lorry Adda Pindi Khep, District Attock
14.	Rahim Yar Khan	Reyaz Mahmood Bat	Asif Electronics, Banno Market, Near Moti Masjid, Rahim Yar Khan
15.	Gujranwala	Miyan Iftikhar Ahmad Zaheer	
16.	Faisalabad	Maulana Tayyab Rabbani	Office Mumtaz Kabar Market, Opp. Sheel Petrol pump, Islamnagar, Sargodha Road, Faisalabad
17.	Dera Ghazi Khan	Miyan Abdul Jabbar Rabbani	Chowk Churhatta, Block No. 60, Dera Ghazi Khan
18.	Sahiwal	Qari Zulfiqar Mujahid	Bhato Nagar, Sahiwal
19.	Qasoor	Khalid Mahmood Kashmiri	Qasoor
20.	Sargodha		Jama Masjid Ahl-e Hadith, Block No. 19, Sargodha
21.	Saadiqabad	Hafiz Aijaz Ahmad	Jamia Islamia, Gali No. 6, Arif Wala, Sadiqabad
22.	Tehsil Deepalpur	Maulana Hafizur Rahman	Jamia Tadreesul Quran, Deepalpur
23.	Wahari	Qari Sayed Ahmad Zia	Mubarak Masjid Ahl-e Hadith, Jinnah Road, Wahari
24.	Jhelum	Mohammad Akbar Salfi	Machine Mohalla, Jhelum

Sr. No.	District and Tehsil	District/ Tehsil Secretary	Office
25.	Tehsil Abdul Hakim	Abu Maviah Mahmoodul Hasan	1 Floor, Zum Zum Medical Store, Multan Road, Abdul Hakim, District Khanewal
26.	Tehsil Gagumandi	Hafiz Abu Baker Siddique Tahir	Tariq Dawakhana, Masjid Market, Gagumandi, Wahari
27.	Talundi	Shafiq Anwar	Karyana Merchant Tauhid Chowk, Main Bazar, Talundi, Qasoor
28.	District Lodhran	Mohammad Idris Jami	
29.	District Muzaffargarh		Markazi Jama Masjid Ahl-e Hadith, Chowk Saroor Shahid, District Muzaffargarh
30.	Boreywalah	Qari Umar Farooq	Jama Masjid, E Block, Boreywalah, District Wahari
Frontier Province			
1.	Peshawar	Abu Khalid Rabbani	Jamia Ashrafiya, Peshawar
2.	Mansehra	Khurshid Anwar Khan	Office Tehrikul Mujahideen, Rakhnai, Mansehra
3.	Balakot	Qari Fazl-ullah (patron)	Jamia Masjid Ahl-e Hadith, Balakot
4.	Aibatabad	Qari Aurangzeb	Jamia Masjid Ahl-e Hadith, Haveliaya, Aibatabad
5.	Abbottabad	Qari Abdul Hafiz (district amir)	Office Mount View Hotel, 1 Floor, Idgah Road, Abbottabad
6.	Abbottabad		Mushtaq Salfi, Leather Merchant Alam Market, Near Harini Vegetable Market, Abbottabad
7.	Haripur	Abu Osama Mohammad Wisalat	Malik Shopping Centre, Main Bazar, Misripura, Hazara
8.	Kohat	Abdullah Jaan	Peshawar Market, Kohat
Azad Kashmir			
9.	Muzaffarabad	Maulana Rafiq Akhtar Kashmiri	Darul-Hujrah, Pajgaran, Shahid Gali Road, Muzaffarabad
10.	Kotli		Rahnou Goi, District Kotli
11.	Islamabad	Commander Owais Sajjad	Office Quran Institute Plaza, Flat No. 2, Street 7, 1–81, Islamabad

Wafaqul Madaris Salafia

This is a board of Ahl-e Hadith madrasas, supervised by Markazi Jamiat Ahl-e Hadith. Professor Sajid Mir is the chairman of this board.

Disputes Between Markazi Jamiat Ahl-e Hadith and Jamat Al-Dawa

The weekly, *Ahl-e Hadith*, Lahore, published a statement against Lashkar-e Tayyaba in its issue of 12 January 2001 which is reproduced below:

Hooliganism in the Name of Jihad

We have received a report from Pasroor tehsil that there is a deluge of jihadi organisations in the country today. Many of them are indulging in hooliganism, and instead of conquering Kashmir they have now concentrated on conquering Ahl-e Hadith mosques and the Ahl-e Hadith ulema. A recent instance of this is the mischief by the mujahideen of Lashkar-e Tayyaba. On Monday, 28 Ramadhan (25 December), Maulana Kifayatullah Shakir, the secretary of Markazi Jamiat Ahl-e Hadith in Pasroor who is also President, AYF, Pasroor, had gone to meet Rana Muhammad Shafiq Khan, central leader, Markazi Jamiat Ahl-e Hadith. After the meeting when the two ulema came out on the road, 10–12 youth of Lashkar-e Tayyaba began to harass them. As a crowd gathered there, they kidnapped Maulana Kifayatullah, took him to Masjid Darul Huda, Pasroor, and badly manhandled him when he was on fast. Then they took him to the adjoining village, Basiwala and subjected him to further violence. When the Maulana wanted to say *namaz*, they did not allow him. They went on hurling abuses at him, and at other leaders like Maulana Rafiq Khan Pasroori, Sajid Mir (respected amir) and Rana Shafiq Khan. When this was brought to the notice of the government administration, these youth were taken to the police station but they said on oath of the Holy Koran that they knew nothing about Maulana Kifayatullah. But, after a few minutes, they agreed to bring the Maulana there by the time of the isha *namaz*. Throughout this episode Rana Shafiq Khan showed exemplary restraint while the other group subjected the Maulana to extreme violence and threatened in public to kill him and raid his house. Maulana Kifayatullah showed his determination by saying that he could not leave Markazi Jamiat Ahl-e Hadith which is the inheritor of the traditions of the ulema and the teachers of Hadith, till the last drop of blood in his vein. This incident led to great unrest and discontent in the area. All the people of the area cutting across sectarian groups said that it was sheer terrorism, and wondered whether this is the jihad they always preached about. Does the sharia permit such violence? Should those who are living on *zakat* and the doles of the secret agencies be allowed to engineer such violence? In the light of the above report, the jihadi organisations, particularly the leaders of Jamat Al-Dawa, should reflect on what their members are doing and what the implication of their actions will be.

This is a small example of the dispute between

Markazi Jamiat Ahl-e Hadith and Jamat Al-Dawa. The dispute had begun right at the time when Professor Hafiz Said and his friends had founded a new Ahl-e Hadith formation with the name, Markaz Al-Dawa al-Irshad. Professor Said was also invited to join Markazi Jamiat Ahl-e Hadith. But his stand was that Markazi Jamiat Ahl-e Hadith was a divided house and did not have the support of the majority of the sect. Apart from disagreements on political matters, there are also differences between the two groups on matters of Faith. Jamat Al-Dawa thinks that Markazi Jamiat Ahl-e Hadith has deviated from the pure Salafia school of Faith, and by associating with non-salafis, it has caused harm to the sect.

Breakaway Groups of Markazi Jamiat Ahl-e Hadith

So far, Markazi Jamiat Ahl-e Hadith has four splinter groups:

1. Jamiat Ahl-e Hadith (Maulana Lakhwi Group)
2. Jamiat Ulema Ahl-e Hadith (Maulana Qazi Abdul Qadir Khamosh)
3. Markazi Jamiat Ahl-e Hadith (Allama Zubair Zaheer)
4. Markazi Jamiat Ahl-e Hadith (Ibtisam Ilahi Zaheer)

The main reasons for this dissension in Markazi Jamiat Ahl-e Hadith are said to be the frequent changes in its stand, particularly its nexus with Muslim League (N), scramble for positions, and embezzlement of funds.

Jamat Al-Dawa

Jamat Al-Dawa is an important organisation of Ahl-e Hadith school of thought that has recently decided to participate in politics. Earlier, its name was Markaz Al-Dawa al-Irshad, but after the crackdown in 2002, it has changed its name. However, more than its real name, it is known as Lashkar-e Tayyaba that was banned on 12 January 2002. Jamat Al-Dawa has separated the management of Lashkar-e Tayyaba and confined it to Azad Kashmir. The leader of Jamat Al-Dawa is Prof. Hafiz Muhammad Said who is now under house arrest. Jamat Al-Dawa, in the form of Lashkar-e Tayyaba, has remained the biggest jihadi group in Pakistan.

BACKGROUND

Jamat Al-Dawa was founded in 1986 when the teachers of Islamic studies (of Ahl-e Hadith persuasion) associated with the Engineering University, Lahore, decided to participate in the Afghan War. Among these teachers were Professor Hafiz Muhammad Said, Professor Zafar Iqbal, Hafiz Abdur Rahman Makki, Hafiz Abdus Salam bin Muhammad, Shaikh Jamiluddin, and Mufti Abdur Rahman. This decision was also catalysed by a promise of help from Saudi Arabia, by a few teachers of Madina University. It was the concluding phase of the Afghan War. Markaz Al-Dawa al-Irshad formed Lashkar-e Tayyaba to send the youth to jihad, and jihadi camps were established in Paktia and Kantar, the provinces where the majority of people are of Ahl-e Hadith persuasion. After the establishment of the camps Lashkar-e Tayyaba began to receive help from the USA and Saudi Arabia, and from the ISI. In 1989, Lashkar-e Tayyaba left the Afghan front and proceeded towards Kashmir.

In an interview with *The Herald*, Karachi (February 2002), Professor Hafiz Muhammad Said remarked, 'We kept ourselves aloof from the groups engaged in civil war in Afghanistan and concentrated on jihad in Kashmir.'

In the Afghan War, only five mujahideen of Lashkar-e Tayyaba were killed. They are:

1. Abdul Rauf Janbaz   Okara
2. Nazeer Abu Bakr   Bahawalpur
3. Muhammad Aslam   Karachi
4. Khalid Saifullah   Lahore
5. Muhammad Qasim Sajid   Faisalabad

Lashkar-e Tayyaba got the opportunity to show its clout in Occupied Kashmir, where it began operation since 25 January 1990. Within two years it started bagging headlines in newspapers. Lashkar-e Tayyaba was in dire need of manpower, and to fulfil this need it activated Markaz Al-Dawa al-Irshad that spread its network throughout Pakistan. But after a short time Markaz al-Dawa al-Irshad began to face difficulties. Ahl-e Hadith mosques and madrasas cooperated in the beginning, but that cooperation gradually fizzled out. There were two reasons for this:

1. Most of the Ahl-e Hadith madrasas in Pakistan represented the views of Markazi Jamiat Ahl-e Hadith and Jamiat Ghurba Ahl-e Hadith, and they are registered with Wafaq al-Madaris Salafia. They were afraid of the growing strength of Lashkar-e Tayyaba. Further, the irresponsible and anti-sharia

behaviour on the part of the members of Lashkar-e Tayyaba had defamed the Ahl-e Hadith school of thought.

2. Professor Hafiz Muhammad Said and his friends adhered to the Ahl-e Hadith school of thought, but on some issues they differed with the ideologues of Ahl-e Hadith. One example of this was the excessive stress on jihad, while one group of ulema of Ahl-e Hadith felt that the government's permission and support was necessary for jihad.

Because of the above differences, members of Lashkar-e Tayyaba found their support dwindling in Ahl-e Hadith mosques. Against this background, in 1994, Lashkar-e Tayyaba decided to establish new mosques and madrasas. A centre was opened in Muridke and offices were opened in different cities. Department of dawat was established to offset lack of cooperation from Ahl-e Hadith. By 1998, Markaz al-Dawa al-Irshad had been fully organised.

After the incident of 11 September 2001, and subsequent US attacks on Afghanistan and extreme pressure on jihadi organisations in Pakistan, Markaz al-Dawa al-Irshad changed its name to Jamat Al-Dawa. It was further declared that Lashkar-e Tayyaba will be confined to Azad Kashmir. Jamat Al-Dawa also declared its decision to take part in active politics.

NETWORK

Before the birth of Jamat Al-Dawa, Markaz al-Dawa al-Irshad, and Lashkar-e Tayyaba had already built their wide network in Pakistan. Jamat Al-Dawa had concentrated in Sindh and southern Punjab. It received good response in Sindh. Shahdadpur, Nawab Shah, Sangarh, Larkana, and Hyderabad had become its active centres. This is indicated by the participation of the youth from Sindh in Lashkar-e Tayyaba. Among Lashkar-e Tayyaba's 1,016 mujahideen killed in Kashmir, 365 were from Sindh. In Baluchistan, Jamat Al-Dawa made its presence felt in Quetta, Zob, and Turbat. In Punjab province, Lahore, Shekhupura, Gujranwala, Sialkot, Multan, Lodhran, Dera Ghazi Khan, and Bahawalpur are its main centres. Before 13 January 2002 Jamat Al-Dawa had 1,150 offices in Pakistan and Azad Kashmir. Of them, 116 are still working actively. Jamat Al-Dawa is facing difficulties after the ban on Lashkar-e Tayyaba. People are more familiar with Lashkar-e Tayyaba than Jamat Al-Dawa. As the two are too intimately associated, the detailed network of Jamat Al-Dawa is being presented along with that of Lashkar-e Tayyaba later.

ORGANISATIONAL STRUCTURE

The management of Jamat Al-Dawa is run by a Shura. After the arrest of Professor Hafiz Said, now the officiating amir is Hafiz Abdus Salam bin Muhammad who is from Saudi Arabia. Among other important members of the Shura are Professor Zafar Iqbal, Professor Abdur Rahman Makki, Maulana Masoodur Rahman Janbaz, Maulana Abdul Ghaffar Razamirani, Maulana Abdul Ghafoor Damani, Hafiz Abdus Salam bin Muhammad, Syed Qasim Shah, Maulana Amir Hamza, Maulana Abdur Rahman Hafiz, Hafiz Masood Alam, and Hafiz Saifullah Mansoor. Jamat Al-Dawa has been divided into four provincial sectors. Before

the ban on Lashkar-e Tayyaba, Jamat Al-Dawa had
1,150 organisational offices in Pakistan, out of which
seventy-four were district-level offices. After the ban
on Lashkar-e Tayyaba, many of the offices have closed
down; and some have converted into offices of Jamat
Al-Dawa. According to one survey, till March 2002,
forty district-level and seventy-six tehsil-level offices of
Jamat Al-Dawa were working regularly in Pakistan.

The departments working under the aegis of Jamat
Al-Dawa are listed in Table XII.

Table XII: *Departments Working Under the Aegis of Jamat
Al-Dawa*

Sr. No.	Department	Amir	Objectives	Office
1.	Jihad (Lashkar-e Tayyaba)	Maulana Abdul Wahid Kashmiri	Jihad	Chehla Bandi, Muzaffarabad, Azad Kashmir
2.	Education	Professor Zafar Iqbal	New education System	Muridke, District Shekhupura
3.	Doctors, hospitals, dispensaries	Dr Zafar Iqbal	Welfare activities	do
4.	Journals, pamphlets	Naved Qamar	Propaganda	do
5.	Preaching and reform	Amir Hamza	do	do
6.	Ulema and teachers	Hafiz Abdul Ghaffar Madani	do	do
7.	Students	Tanvir Ahsan Hashmi	do	do
8.	Social Service	Dr Zafar Iqbal	do	do
9.	Women	Umm Hamad	Activating women	do

Sr. No.	Department	Amir	Objectives	Office
10.	Peasants and labour wing	Haji Maqbool Ahmad	Collecting contributions from peasants	do
11.	Public relations	Yahya Mujahid	Communications and publications	do
12.	External affairs	Hafiz Abdur Rahman Makki	Relations with foreign countries	do
13.	Darul andalus	Abdus Salam bin Muhammad	Publication of books	4, Lake Road, Chaubarji, Lahore

Markaz Jamat Al-Dawa (Jamat Al-Dawa Centre), Muridke

Markaz Jamat Al-Dawa is located in a place called Muridke which is 30 km to the south-west of Lahore. It is spread out in a 200-acre tract of land. The basic model of this centre has been borrowed from Jamat-e Islami's centre in Mansoora. It has residential, organisational, jihadi, and educational structures. Because of the recent crackdown, most people related to press and publication have gone underground, and I could not manage to get permission to visit it. The following facts have been culled from the feature written by Kamal Siddiqui in the daily *Dawn*, 7 May 2000, and a number of issues of *Mujalla Al-Dawa*.

Apart from being a hub of jihadi programmes, Markaz Al-Dawa is also the centre of organisational activities. The residential block is also large, intended to accommodate members so that they can get an ideal environment. It has provision for education from the primary level to college for both men and women. There is a madrasa too where instruction is available for undergraduate levels. Professor Zafar Iqbal, who is in charge of this *markaz*, said that students there are imparted jihadi education, not jihadi training. For the latter, they go to Muzaffarabad camp. 'Allah has ordained jihad. Those who are following it are right, and those who are preventing it are wrong. In our campus we have provision for physical exercises and the games permitted by sharia.' He said to the feature writer of *Dawn*: 'Taliban is a group of misguided elements. We have higher ideal than them.' (The reference to Taliban came here because Jamat Al-Dawa has made a volte face on its Taliban policy.)

Besides a hospital, there is a market on the campus in which anti-sharia goods like cigarettes, pictures, music records, etc., cannot be sold. Professor Zafar Iqbal clarified to *Dawn* that it had become a world centre for education and upbringing, and students from Europe were coming for education there. There is a fishery in the *markaz* which is a profit-making concern. The agricultural land yields good harvest. After the harvest is gathered, the same wide grounds are used for assemblies and conferences.

The security arrangement is tight in the campus and gun-totting watchmen are visible here and there. This is the opposite of what one finds in Mansoora. Markaz al-Dawa has almost turned it into a military camp.

IMPORTANT DEPARTMENTS

After the department of jihad, the following departments of Jamat Al-Dawa are important:

Department of Preaching and Reform (Dawat O Islah)
The head of this department is Amir Hamza. Besides conducting ordinary and special courses on preaching, it also sends out groups for *tabligh*. It also organises different *tablighi* and jihadi programmes, through the help of local and district-level management. The local office bearers conduct the monthly programmes and send their report to the centre. The activities of this department are published in the journals *Al-Dawa* and *Jihad Times*. In the August 2002 issue of *Al-Dawa* there is the report of a Jihad Conference, among other reports, which is significant for several reasons. The text of the report is as follows:

> Yesterday the Jihad Hind conference was organised in a village Bhini Jhata near the border. The mujahideen had invited villagers of the border areas to come and listen to their messages. The mujahideen fixed powerful loudspeakers towards the Indian direction so that their clarion call can reach India. Bhai Khalid Saiful Islam made a fiery and emotional speech in which he challenged the Indian officers saying that that day is not far when their defeated army will be driven out of Kashmir and the mujahideen will drown them in the Indian ocean, and reach Kashmir, Delhi, Agra and Kathiawad. It should be remembered that during the Kargil conflict, mujahideen at the Wagha border assembled in groups to challenge the enemy, and chanted the following verse on megaphone:
>
> Run away, bania, run away.
> Tucking the tail between your legs.

Anyway, when the mujahideen finished their programme and came back, the youth from Pakistan Rangers reached the village the next morning and congratulated the elders. They said, 'As a result of your programme, one of our crucial problem has been solved. The Indian BSF wanted to have a door through the fence so that whenever there was need for violence they could get the RAW agents infiltrated from this side. We wanted to prevent the BSF from making the door, but they insisted on it. The issue had reached a boiling point. After your programme, they have sent word this morning that they did not want to have the door anymore and that they are shifting the post from here. They requested us not to call the Lashkar-e Tayyaba here because they know that if the members of Lashkar-e Tayyaba arrive, mujahideen will be born in every house and they will enter Kashmir through this door and carry out their fidayeen missions. The Indian army thought it wise to give up the idea of the door.'

Department of Ulema and Teachers
The head of this department which is working among madrasas, schools, and colleges, is Professor Zafar Iqbal. The membership of this department is said to be 400.

Students Department
This department plays a crucial role in initiating movements in schools and colleges. Jihadi programmes involving students are also organised by this department. The Head of this department is Tanvir Ahsan Hashmi. In 2001, this department has organised 500 jihadi programmes throughout Pakistan.

Department of Education
The most effective of Jamat Al-Dawa's departments is the department of education. This department is instrumental in getting the Lashkar-e Tayyaba sufficient manpower. It is also a profit-making concern of Jamat Al-Dawa. This department runs about 200 Al-Dawa model schools, two science colleges, and eleven madrasas. Its central secretariat is in Muridke, and Professor Zafar Iqbal is the head of the Department.

The syllabi taught in Al-Dawa schools are much different from those in other educational institutions. Arabic, Urdu, and English are compulsory, and the rest of the syllabus is based on Islamic belief and teachings. According to Professor Zafar Iqbal: 'For this purpose we have written an *Elementary Reader* replacing the secular perspective of the earlier *Reader*. In the earlier *Reader* we had *Alif* for *anar* (pomegranate), *Bé* for *bakri* (goat) and so on. This has been replaced by the concept of *Alif* for Allah, *Bé* for *bandooq* (gun), *Té* for *tope* (cannon) and so on.'

In an Al-Dawa school, it is necessary for each teacher to go to jihad once, or at least he should have jihadi training. Professor Iqbal says, 'It is not we who declare jihad obligatory, Allah Himself ordained so. When students read the Holy Koran, they will certainly follow this path. The teachers carry out all their religious duties with utmost sincerity. They also have a pre-service training that goes a long way in predisposing them to jihad. So, when they enter our school they are perfect in all aspects.'

The department of education has a good organisational set-up. There is a secretary of education for the whole country. After that, each province has a secretary. Thus, there is one secretary each for Sindh, Baluchistan, Punjab, the Frontier Province, Northern Regions, and Kashmir. There are coordinators who assist the secretary. Writing and printing of syllabi are the responsibility of syllabus department. One principal looks after at least five schools.

Following is the province-wise break-up of Al-Dawa schools:

Punjab	60 (Boys)
Punjab	35 (Girls)
Frontier Province	14
Sindh	30
Baluchistan	
Azad Kashmir	12

The monthly hostel fee in Al-Dawa schools is up to 1,600 rupees.

Jamat Al-Dawa al-Islamia

A network of madrasas is working under the aegis of Jamat Al-Dawa. There are ten madrasas in this network. The central office is located in Muridke. Maulana Abdullah Salafi is the head of this department. The total number of students in all these madrasas is around 1,500; the teaching in six of the madrasas is up to the graduate (alia) level. The details of these madrasas are as follows:

1. Al-Muhid al-Ali lil-Dawa al-Islamia: Markaz Tayyaba, Muridke, District Shekhupura
2. Al-Muhid al-Ali lil-Dawa al-Islamia: Markaz

Tabuk, Shujaabad Road, Ladh, Multan
3. Al-Muhid al-Ali lil-Dawa al-Islamia: Markaz Yarmuk, Arain Model Farm, Multan Road, Pattuki
4. Al-Muhid al-Ali lil-Dawa al-Islamia: Markaz Janeen, Railway Godown, Haveli Likha, Okara
5. Al-Muhid al-Ali lil-Dawa al-Islamia: Markaz Ummul Qari, Mohalla Old Orphanage, Mianwali
6. Al-Muhid al-Ali lil-Dawa al-Islamia: Markaz Khaibar, Tatharakhi, Tehsil: Diska, District Sialkot
7. Al-Muhid al-Ali lil-Dawa al-Islamia: Masjid Ummul Qura, Kohat, Frontier Province
8. Al-Muhid al-Ali lil-Dawa al-Islamia: Markaz Aqsa, Jama Masjid Taqwa, New Zaghoon Road, Quetta
9. Al-Muhid al-Ali lil-Dawa al-Islamia: Markaz Al-Qads, Turbat, Baluchistan
10. Al-Muhid al-Ali lil-Dawa al-Islamia: Jalo Park Road, Lahore

For girl students, there is just one madrasa, Markaz Tayyaba, in Muridke. Every year, about fifty-five students graduate from all the madrasas. A twenty-one-day course called *daora safa* is conducted in all madrasas, to teach students ways of *tabligh*.

Department of Resources
This is one of the most important departments of Jamat Al-Dawa. Besides collecting funds for jihad from Pakistan, fund-raisers are sent to foreign countries as well. According to Jamat Al-Dawa sources, about twenty crore rupees were collected under different heads in 2001. The contribution of different departments in this regard has been as follows:

1. External affairs	2.00 crore
2. Profit of Dar-al Andalus	0.80 crore
3. Students' department	0.35 crore
4. Hides of sacrificed animals	2.50 crore
5. Department of women	0.70 crore
6. Department of peasant and labour wing	0.45 crore
7. Miscellaneous	6.00 crore

Jamat Al-Dawa sources said that this year they could not meet the target amount that was to be raised from the hides of sacrificed animals, and they faced much difficulty in raising funds after the government restrictions.

Jamat Al-Dawa gets hefty contributions from Arab states, especially Saudi Arabia, for madrasas and schools. It has also established its units in European countries that send substantial contribution to the jihad fund every year.

It should be noted here that there is a separate branch for raising funds that works under the department of resources. A staff of 500 members worked for this branch in Pakistan, who looked after the boxes of jihad contribution and sent the money to the centre after opening the boxes. These members were entrusted to do only this job and they were directly appointed by the department of resources, and paid salaries. Haji Maqbool Ahmad is now the head of the department of resources.

Martyrs Department
This department helps families of martyrs. Abdul Ghaffar Madani is the head of this department. Such families are paid 1,500 rupees per month. A brochure

of Jamat Al-Dawa claims that till 2001, 175 families were receiving this monthly grant. Moreover, this department also helps those mujahideen who lose limbs in action, and finds them employment. It stays in constant touch with the families.

External Affairs

Abdur Rahman Makki is the head of this department. It tries to establish links with jihadi organisations in foreign countries and provides them manpower. It maintains links with Bosnia, Chechnya, and other countries. It also tries to establish links with foreign governments and political groups to sell its ideological agenda. Between 11 September 2001 and March 2002, this department has sent 3,000 letters and emails to 130 governments in this regard.

Department of Peasants and Labour Wing

Maqbool Ahmad is the head of this department. Its responsibility is to maintain links with peasants and various labour organisations, and unite them on Jamat Al-Dawa's platform. It raises jihad fund and collects tithe from peasants. This department forms special groups specifically for the collection of tithe from entire Pakistan, especially from the villages of Punjab, Sindh, and the Frontier Province.

Dar al-Andalus

Basically, it is the department of press and publication. Abdus Salam bin Muhammad heads this department. It prepares books and pamphlets on jihad. It sells literature worth lakhs of rupees every year earning good profit for the organisation. In 2001, this department has published more than 100 books and pamphlets in Urdu, Arabic, English, and other languages, and made a profit of about rupees eighty lakhs.

Department of Public Relations

This department organises various programmes on behalf of Jamat Al-Dawa, and maintains links with the newspapers and the media. In 2001, it organised sixty national-level programmes and 235 state-level programmes. Yahya Mujahid is the head of this department.

Lashkar-e Tayyaba (Banned)

Lashkar-e Tayyaba is the real identity of Jamat Al-Dawa. In fact, Lashkar-e Tayyaba is often taken to be Jamat Al-Dawa. Lashkar-e Tayyaba was banned in Pakistan on 13 January 2002. But Jamat Al-Dawa had already taken precautionary steps. On 24 December 2001, Hafiz Muhammad Said, the amir of Markaz Dawa al-Irshad and Lashkar-e Tayyaba, addressed a press conference in which he declared renaming of Markaz Dawa al-Irshad and relinquishing the leadership of Lashkar-e Tayyaba. The same day the State Bank of Pakistan issued a circular freezing the accounts of Lashkar-e Tayyaba and Umme Tamir Nao. Professor Said declared that henceforth Markaz Dawa al-Irshad would be known as Jamat Al-Dawa and he could continue to be its leader. He further said that Lashkar-e Tayyaba would be confined to Azad Kashmir. Its new leader would be Maulana Abdul Wahid Kashmiri, and Maulana Zakiur Rahman Lakhwi would be its supreme commander. Jamat Al-Dawa would cooperate with it in Pakistan, and would send (to Azad Kashmir) any contributions (fund) that might be made to it by anyone. A new general council composed of the following people was formed:

1. Abdullah — Anantnag
2. Haji Azam — Poonch
3. Muzammil Bhat — Doda
4. Muhammad Amir — Baramula
5. Choudhury Abdullah Khalid — Bagh
6. Rafiq Akhtar — Muzaffarabad
7. Aftab Husain — Kotli
8. Faisal Dar — Srinagar
9. Choudhury Yusuf — Amirpur
10. Maulana Shariful Qari — Baluchistan
11. Raja Irshad Advocate — Muzaffarabad
12. Masood Lone Advocate — Muzaffarabad

Lashkar-e Tayyaba is working freely in Azad Kashmir. In Pakistan, many offices of Jamat Al-Dawa are doubling as offices for Lashkar-e Tayyaba. In the operation against jihadi and sectarian organisations, forty-five people belonging to Lashkar-e Tayyaba and Jamat Al-Dawa have been arrested, but they are mostly ordinary members. The leaders had already shifted to Azad Kashmir. The network of Lashkar-e Tayyaba along with that of Jamat Al-Dawa in Pakistan is presented in Table XIII.

According to Lashkar-e Tayyaba sources, among the 10,000 trained mujahideen of Lashkar-e Tayyaba, 6,000 are engaged in operation in Occupied Kashmir. Dr Manzoor Ahmad, an important member of Jamat

Al-Dawa, has compiled the records of Lashkar-e Tayyaba's eleven-year long history of militant activities. According to these records, in eleven years, Lashkar-e Tayyaba's 1,016 mujahideen have been killed, and they have killed 14,369 soldiers and officers of the Indian army.

Lashkar-e Tayyaba began its mission from Rawalpura on 25 January 1990. Ravi Khanna, the squadron leader of Indian Air Force, and three other pilots were killed in that incident in the bus station. According to Dr Manzoor Ahmad's report: 'During those days of 1990 mujahideen from Kashmir had gone to Afghanistan for military training in Tayyaba camp. A different camp, called Aqsa camp, was established near Tayyaba camp for their training. In Muzaffarabad, Baitul Mujahideen was established. Here Pakistani and Kashmiri mujahideen received training together.'

In the beginning of 1991, the first batch of mujahideen trained in Aqsa camp reached Muzaffarabad. To refine their training, Badar Post was founded and a camp named Ummul Qura was established in Muzaffarabad. In 1992, the first batch of Lashkar-e Tayyaba mujahideen was launched in Occupied Kashmir, and it had its first engagement on the morning of 26 August 1992. The mujahideen were led by Abu Khalid Aftab Ahmad, and they killed nineteen Indian army men. In the beginning, they sought help from other jihadi organisations. The first amir of Lashkar-e Tayyaba in the Kashmir Valley was Abu Hafs who was killed in Baramula in 1993. After that Lashkar-e Tayyaba carried out several missions. In those years, another camp known as Abdullah bin Masood was established in Muzaffarabad. In 1995, Lashkar-e Tayyaba first established its base in the districts of Jammu. Till 1995, about a hundred of Lashkar-e Tayyaba's commanders and officers were killed. It claims to have played an important role in the Kargil War.

Lashkar-e Tayyaba began its fidayeen mission on 12 July 1999, by mounting an attack on the BSF headquarters in Bandipura, Baramula. Thirteen Indian army men, including DIG (Brigadier) S A Chakravarty and Deputy Commandant Mohan Raj were killed in that attack. This first suicide bomber was Abu Sulaiman Muhammad Akmal from Multan. On 3 November 1999, an attack was mounted on the headquarter of Corps 15 of the Indian army in Badami Bagh, Srinagar. In this attack forty-five Indian Army men were killed, including Col. Bhatia, Major Purushuttom, and Subedar B D Sharma. Abu Mauz Muhammad Amin from Bahawalpur had led the arrack. On 1 January 2000 there was a suicide attack on an Indian army camp in Poonch killing thirty-five army men, including two officers. In 1999, there were eleven fidayeen attacks in which 258 Indian army men and officers died. In 2000, there were forty-five fidayeen attacks in which 891 army personnel were killed.

Attack on the Red Fort

The most spectacular of Lashkar-e Tayyaba missions so far is the attack on the Red Fort. This was carried out on 22 December 2000. The February 2000 issue of the journal, *Al-Dawa* records this report with pride:

> The entry was from Lahore gate at 7.30 p.m... two
> soldiers were at the gate... two more soldiers at the
> post near the gate... the two (mujahideen) were
> approaching from the front... no one suspected
> them... there was a function of army families going...
> they went in to buy tickets for the show... when the
> show was in full swing they came out and hid
> themselves... by 8.30 all civilians left, for which they
> had been waiting... at 8.40 a soldier came and looked
> at them suspiciously... at this our brothers hit him
> and started the mission, then they fled from the scene
> and came to the car parking... they killed a soldier
> who was running up and down there... then they
> entered into two rooms of the barrack... one fired the
> gun and the other hurled a grenade... one room was
> vacant, in the other there was a soldier... then they
> came out and proceeded to the civilian residential
> areas... a man was coming on a motorcycle followed
> by a car... our brothers aimed guns at them but did
> not fire as they were civilians... then another car
> came from one side and two soldiers came out... they
> killed them... a watchman came running and he was
> also killed... then firing began from all sides... then
> the fidayeen got separated but they were able to come
> out... after coming out one *mujahid* killed another
> soldier... by that time the army had fanned out on all
> sides... but by the grace of God the fidayeen escaped
> successfully... thus, according to our information,
> twelve soldiers were annihilated.

The second big attack by Lashkar-e Tayyaba was on
Srinagar airport in February 2001. The report of this
incident was also published in the February 2001 issue

of *Al-Dawa*:

On 15 January 2001, the mujahideen of Lashkar-e Tayyaba managed to get the green car of a forest officer. Donned in police uniforms six fidayeen entered the Srinagar airport through the gate. The gate usually remained open. Our brothers (mujahideen) first threw grenades and then began to fire on the Indian soldiers. Two brothers entered the X-ray area of the reception, installed themselves behind the checking machine, and began to fire. Two brothers ran towards the runway and began to fire on the military aircrafts. A jumbo jet was damaged. Two more fidayeen entered the army offices and started firing on the officers present there. Then, one of them entered the shopping area and fired at the soldiers stationed there. By Pakistan standard time, the mission began at 2.15 p.m. and continued for three-and-a-half hours. After fighting for three and a half hours our brothers achieved martyrdom. Eighteen army personnel including an officer were killed in this attack and 15–20 were injured. There was also a member of the Jammu and Kashmir police who are normally composed of Muslims. There are two kinds of police force. As we have Punjab Police or Sindh Police who administer crimes; there is another kind of police known as Task Force. This Task Force is composed of traitors who work for the Indian army for money. Members of this force have been given police posts. The mujahideen of Lashkar-e Tayyaba do not wield arms against the ordinary police, rather they cooperate with them. But they fight with the police of the Task Force and inflict damage on them. During the mission on the Srinagar airport, the mujahideen had donned the uniform of the Task Force. Before the mission, Brother Abu Khazla had made a detailed reconnaissance of the airport from inside. It should be remembered that he had worked with the Air Force for seven years. Normally, all international airports have the same design and structure. So, he knew almost everything. Two other brothers had supplied detailed information about the buildings, roads and entry routes of the adjoining areas. Thus, three brothers were involved in this (recce) work, who knew about every little details and had seen everything with their own eyes.

The success of the above missions not only boosted Lashkar-e Tayyaba's morale, but also made it easy for the organisation to get human resource and raise funds. Muhammad Khalid, an important district-level member of Lashkar-e Tayyaba from Multan said, 'Before 11 September 2001, and even now, we are in a position to get Kashmir freed any moment. But our target is entire India. Then will come the turn of Israel. We want to destroy India. As for the current difficulties, they are temporary. Well, governments will come and go. Whoever is in power – Benazir or someone else – no one can ignore jihadi organisations because we are fighting for the consolidation of Pakistan and Kashmir's independence.'

Lashkar-e Tayyaba's Jihadi Camp

After the closure of the camps in Afghanistan and Mansehra, in the Frontier Province, only five camps of Lashkar-e Tayyaba are now working:

TAYYABA CAMP (MA'SKAR TAYYABA)

This camp is located in Muzaffarabad. It can accommodate and train 500 mujahideen at a time.

AQSA CAMP (MA'SKAR AQSA)

This camp is also located near Muzaffarabad. It can accommodate and train 150 mujahideen at a time.

UMMUL QURA CAMP

This camp near Muzaffarabad was established in 1990. It prepares 500 mujahideen per month.

ABDULLAH BIN MASOOD CAMP

This camp in Azad Kashmir can accommodate 300 mujahideen.

MARKAZ MUHAMMAD BIN QASIM

This centre, built like a fort, is situated in Maldasi, tehsil Shahdadpur, district Sangrhi. It is one hour's drive from Hyderabad. This is one of the three camps in Sindh that is still operating, whereas the camps at Sangarh and Larkana have been closed. This property has been donated by Haji Imran, a *mujahid* of Lashkar-e Tayyaba, and now it is being used as the centre for Jamat Al-Dawa also. Seen from outside, it looks like a fort. Though there is no signboard at the gate, local people know that it is a jihadi camp. Lashkar-e Tayyaba sources claim that it has trained 10,000 mujahideen so far.

Martyrs

Lashkar-e Tayyaba claims to have annihilated more than ten thousand Indian army personnel in the last twelve years from 1990 to 2002. In the same period,

1433 of its mujahideen have been killed. The year-wise break-up is as follows:

Year	No. of Martyrs
1990	01
1991	03
1992	01
1993	20
1994	31
1995	36
1996	84
1997	112
1998	91
1999	253
2000	289
2001	312
2002	200

The largest number of Lashkar-e Tayyaba's martyrs comes from Punjab, and the next from Frontier Province. The number of martyrs from Sindh and Baluchistan works out to 385.

Lashkar-e Tayyaba's Participation in Jihadi Activities in Foreign Countries

Lashkar-e Tayyaba has not kept its jihadi activities confined to Occupied Kashmir alone, but participated in freedom movements in other countries as well. In the invitation for the annual conference at Muridke, a brief report is printed on it. The following is an extract from the report attached to the invitation in 1998:

Apart from Pakistani mujahideen, hundreds of mujahideen from other countries like Kashmir, Bosnia, Chechnya, the Philippines, Somalia, and European and American countries have received training from the camps in Afghanistan and are doing jihad at many fronts in the world. Hundreds of youth are receiving training everyday. Several of our aid groups and camps are operating in Kashmir. The Ummul Qura camp is like a thorn in the enemy's flesh. The Lashkar-e Tayyaba mujahideen, trained in our training camps in Kashmir, are sounding the death knell for Hindus in India and Jews in Israel. More than a hundred youths from Lashkar-e Tayyaba have already attained martyrdom in the Kashmir valley, and they have sent hundreds of Hindus to hell. In Bosnia, the commander of Marakaz al-Dawa al-Irshad, Abu Abdul Aziz, laid the foundation of jihad with four of his comrades. Now their number has increased to thousands and the whole of Europe is trembling in fear (of them). In sum, wherever you go in the world, you will find mujahideen from Markaz al-Dawa al-Irshad fighting against apostasy and injustice.

The Lashkar-e Tayyaba sources in Muzaffarabad accepted that mujahideen from all countries gather in Lashkar-e Tayyaba's camps. After receiving training from these camps they go back to their own countries and participate in jihad. Some of the mujahideen from the European countries (where there is no jihadi front) are sent to Occupied Kashmir, though ordinarily, it is not Lashkar-e Tayyaba's policy to send them there.

On 22 October 2000, Professor Muhammad Said, in his address to Lashkar-e Tayyaba mujahideen at

Gulshan, Karachi, asserted that it had already initiated jihad against the Jews.

Lashkar-e Tayyaba and Sectarianism

Lashkar-e Tayyaba is often alleged to have spread sectarian clashes in Pakistan. It has played a vital role in promoting Ahl-e Hadith school of thought in Pakistan. The majority of youths joining Lashkar-e Tayyaba is from the Hanfi (both Deobandi and Barelvi) sect. Before military training, the mujahideen have to undergo two courses of Ahl-e Hadith school of thought:

1. General Course: This is a twenty-one-day course in which basic principles of Ahl-e Hadith school of thought are taught.
2. Specialised Course: This is a three-month course that elaborates the above principles and establishes the superiority of this school of thought over others.

In this regard, the opinions of two of Lashkar-e Tayyaba's members are important. One of them comes from Shahdadpur (Sindh) which is one of the prime centres of Lashkar-e Tayyaba. Here we met Imran (jihadi name: Abu Osama) who received training in a Lashkar-e Tayyaba camp in the province of Kandahar in Afghanistan. We met Abu Osama (who is in hiding nowadays) through a friend from Mirpur Khas, Abu Muhammad Salim. Abu Osama confirmed that Ahl-e Hadith tenets are preached in jihadi camps. Abu Osama said, 'If they preach truth, it is perfectly all right. When I went there for training, I had no idea

355

what my sect was. Earlier, there was no facility for religious education in Shahdadpur. I passed class III and was content to become a tailor. After joining the camp I realised that I belong to the Barelvi school of thought. There, my teachers, and specially my friend Haji Bashir guided me. There is no coercion to change one's way of belief. One is given a jihadi environment, and one's mind changes automatically.'

The second opinion is that of Akbar Khan from Sargodha. He has passed his BA and is associated with Jaish-e Muhammad. He is on 'holiday'. (After training, and after returning from a mission, mujahideen are allowed a holiday.) Earlier, he was with Lashkar-e Tayyaba. Akbar said, 'I am from the Hanfi persuasion. My elder brother is also associated with a jihadi organisation. First, I was friendly with Lashkar-e Tayyaba. Two years ago I had gone to Tayyaba camp in Muzaffarabad for training. I kept performing namaz in the Hanfi way. First, they tried to persuade me with sweet words to change my ways, but I countered their arguments. It was a twenty-one-day course. About the tenth day I bandied words with them and our teacher, Abu Tantala took a sarcastic tone (against my ways). Things were made too difficult for me to stay there. On the fifteenth day, I tried to leave the camp, but I was not allowed. They became aggressive, and then they softened up and behaved very gently with me. But I left the camp on the eighteenth day.' Akbar further said, 'They can bear with Deobandis if they have to, but they just hate the Barelvis and consider them infidels. They are very hard on Barelvi boys, even beat them occasionally.'

Such things are heard about Lashkar-e Tayyaba in Occupied Kashmir too. Many people in Muzaffarabad – *muhajirs* and mujahideen – corroborated this. Professor Khaliq Ahmed who leads a human rights group said, 'Lashkar-e Tayyaba is one of those organisations that is involved in sectarian clashes in Occupied Kashmir.' Advocate Noorullah Quraishi (a *muhajir* from Srinagar) who practices in Muzaffarabad said, 'They occupy mosques of other sects there, and instead of doing jihad start doing *tabligh*.'

What are the views of Lashkar-e Tayyaba and Jamat Al-Dawa about the Barelvis? Some excerpts from the speeches of Qari Abdul Hafiz Wahabi may give us some idea. Qari Abdul Hafiz Wahabi is associated with Ahl-e Hadith now. The following speech was recorded at Faisalabad and is available in an audio cassette:

They (Lashkar-e Tayyaba mujahideen) are doing jihad for money and making courtesans of the daughters of the Barelvis. This is the group of Abu Jandal who says, 'Lift the daughters of Barelvis as booty.' We have differences with Barelvis and Shias on points of belief, but if a Maulana stands on the pulpit and says, 'Because they are kafirs and sinners, lift their daughters' (God forbid!), I cannot follow such a religion. The religion never allows this. I am not an adherent of such jihad that permits you to lift girls of the other sects. You will ask how much of truth is there in my claim. There is a *mujahid* of Lashkar-e Tayyaba who has a shop at Ferozepur Auto station. He kidnapped the daughter of a Barelvi, and Professor Said performed the ritual for marriage. After that he ran away with the girl. Later, the police caught up with him and he had to cough up forty thousand rupees to save his skin. When he was asked why he did this. He said, 'Professor Said has given the fatwa that the daughters of apostates are legitimate booty for us.'

Whatever the truth in the claim of Qari Abdul Hafiz, at least this much is clear that Lashkar-e Tayyaba and Jamat Al-Dawa are sectarian groups and have a terrible dislike for other ways of belief.

Fidayeen Attacks

Lashkar-e Tayyaba first introduced the concept of fidayeen attacks in Occupied Kashmir. It claims to have mounted ninety-eight fidayeen attacks between 1999 and 2000, including the attack on the Red Fort in Delhi. It claims that 200 Indian army personnel were killed in these attacks, whereas only eleven mujahideen were killed.

After it began fidayeen attacks, Lashkar-e Tayyaba was severely criticised by religious organisations, as committing suicide is a sin in Islam. In this context, Hafiz Abdur Rahman wrote a long article in the May 2001 issue of the journal *Al-Dawa*, supporting suicide attacks. The following is an excerpt from this article:

Fidayeen action is a bright chapter in the history of the Muslim community. Whenever jihad was declared, fidayeens have come forward to be in the vanguard. Not only in the days of the Prophet's Companions, but later also, such fidayeens have appeared on the scene and achieved their targets in the most dangerous situations. They embraced certain death and achieved martyrdom. No *fidayi* has ever killed himself or jumped into fire or strapped explosives on his body with the deliberate intention of killing himself. Of course, there are scores of examples from the early ages when they have attacked enemies, raided army camps, entered the palaces of kings by stealth, confronted enemy hordes single-handedly, but no one has ever designated it as suicide. On the contrary, teachers of the Prophet's Traditions have considered it a desirable activity. Muhammad bin Hasan (Shibani) says, 'If one Muslim mounted an attack on a thousand apostates, it is not objectionable if he felt that he was capable of inflicting damage on them, and if he was desirous of God's forgiveness. If he feels that by doing so he would instil courage in Muslims and they would be inspired to do valorous deeds, there is no harm in such an attack, as it will ultimately benefit Muslims. Alternatively, if he feels that by doing so he would be demoralising the infidels and demonstrate before them the strength of a Muslim's attachment to his religion, then also it is a laudable activity. Allah has praised and encouraged Muslims (for valorous deeds).' He says, 'Verily, Allah has traded the life and property of Muslims for paradise.' We have mentioned these to support fidayeen attacks. These will help us understand the psychology of such mujahideen. Every day and every night we get to know about the fidayeen missions of Lashkar-e Tayyaba mujahideen and their martyrdom. If we put the fidayeen encounters of the earlier ages and those of Lashkar-e Tayyaba mujahideen side by side, we find a lot of commonality. For example, in the fidayeen attacks on the Red Fort, on 15 Corps at Badami Bagh, on the airport and on the police headquarters, groups of two to four mujahideen were involved. They mounted the attacks speedily and with utmost courage killed Hindu army officers.

From Major Purushuttom's office, on his own phone they called up BBC and said, 'We are Lashkar-e Tayyaba's fidayeen and calling from inside the cantonment.' Qari Abu Marsad Abdur Rahman Shaheed's stand is, 'Kill or be subjugated (be killed)'. One has to kill to escape being killed. He took his baby boy on his lap and said, 'I can see what kind of treatment will be meted out to a martyr's son.' Such strength of belief in one's martyrdom!

Table XIII: *Network of Jamat Al-Dawa and Lashkar-e Tayyaba in Pakistan*

Sr. No.	District/ Tehsil	District/ Tehsil Secretary	Office/Centre
1.	Lahore	Hafiz Abdul Hashim	4-Lake Road, Choberji, Lahore
2.	Sargodha	Amjad-Ur-Rahman	Muslim Bazar, Bans Bazar, Sargodha
3.	Faisalabad	Professor Abdul Ghaffar	Zainul Abdin Plaza, First Floor Mainpur Bazar, Faisalabad
4.	Jhelum	Nabeel Shehzad	Baba Sooni Chowk, Opp. Mohammad Hussain Areywalah, Jhelum
5.	Mailsi		Khalil Market Addah Garahmor, Tehsil Mailsi, District Wahari
6.	Sahiwal	Abu Zobaan	
7.	Dera Ghazi Khan	Mohammad Yusuf	Chowk Block No. 3, Dera Ghazi Khan
8.	Multan	Abu Osama	Tareen Road, Near Divisional Sports Ground, Multan
9.	Attock		56-B, Near Habib Bank, Civil Bazar, Attock City
10.	Shekhupura		Shaami Road, Cicil Lines, Shekhupura
11.	Okara		Tayyaba Market, Ghosia Bazar, Near Dr Ghulam Bani's Clinic, Okara Cantt.

Sr. No.	District/ Tehsil	District/ Tehsil Secretary	Office/Centre
12.	Jaranwala		Main Chowk, Mandi Bachyana, Tehsil Jaranwala, District Faisalabad
13.	Boreywalah		Chungi No. 5, Main Gate, Wahari Bazar, Borewalah
14.	Kabirwala		Nialari Adda Near Al-Hafiz Iron Store, Kabir Walah, District Khanewal
15.	Abdul Hakim		1 Floor, Minhas Traders Multan Road, Abndul Halim
16.	Mianwali	Abu Abdul Wahab Anjum	
17.	Bhakkar/ Klorekot	Abu Wiqas	Baitul-Mujahideen, Near Railway Gate, Sadar Chongi, Klorekot
18.	Pindi Bhatiyan		Opp. Lari Adda, Puttan Road, Pindi Bhatiyan, District Hafizabad
19.	Manchanabad		Near Abu Bakar Chowk, Thana Road, Manchanabad
20.	Chakwal	Abu Abdur Rahman	Hospital Road, Chakwal
21.	Jahaniyan	Abu Jihad	Behind Mohammadi Masjid Ahl-e Hadith, Tayyaba Street, Block No. 6, Jahaniyan
22.	Renalah Khurd		Near Jamia Abi Huraira, Ghalla Mandi, Renalah Khurd, District Okara
23.	Kehrorpacca		Behind Waiting Room, Bal Nehr, Amirpur, Sadat Tehsil Kehrorpacca
24.	Tonsa		1 Floor, Kasht Jamil Laboratory, Near Vegetable Market, Tonsa
25.	Leh		Mianwali Road, Hospital Wali Gali, Chowk Azam, Leh
26.	Mian Chunno		Near Shaheen Chowk, Mian Chunno
27.	Rawalpindi	Iqbal Salfi	56/0 Circular Road, Rawalpindi

361

Sr. No.	District/ Tehsil	District/ Tehsil Secretary	Office/Centre
28.	Muzaffargarh	Ghulam Qadir Subhani	
29.	Wahari		Gali No. 9, Zoological Road, F Block, Wahari
30.	Gujranwala		76-A, Satellite Town, Gujranwala
31.	Rahim Yar Khan		Tayyaba Street, Amanat Colony, Rahim Yar Khan
32.	Sialkot		Murabad, Sialkot
33.	Qasoor	Abdullah Adeel	
34.	Jhung		Marzipura, Jhung
35.	Karachi	Abu Osama Yusuf	17/B, Sulaiman Tairus, Hasan Squire, Gulshan Iqbal, Karachi
36.	Hyderabad	Shamsul Haq Chaang	Tilak Chari, Near Alrafey Market, House No. 2880/A, Hyderabad, Sindh
37.	Sukkur	Mujahid Muheeb	
38.	Moro		Near Dawood Chowk, Sayyal Market, Moro, Sindh
39.	Sangarh	Hafiz Razaullah	
40.	Meerpur Khas	Abu Imran	Meerpur Khas
41.	Shehdadpur	Hafiz Abdullah	Near Latif Park, Shehdadpur
42.	Larkana	Abdur Rauf Bhutto	Gajjanpur Chowk, Larkana
43.	Dadoo		Main Road, Meehar, District Dawood
44.	Jacobabad		Azad Manzil, Quetta Road, Jacobabad
45.	Jafarabad	Haji Mohammad Amin Khosa	Jhanda Tadawah, Jafarabad
46.	Badain	Abu Baker Nizamani	Opp. Ayyub Plaza, Tandoo Ghulam Ali Road, District Badain
47.	Jaam Nawaz Ali		Sufi Centre, Main Bazar, Seerani, Tehsil Jaam Nawaz Ali
48.	Obaaro (Ghotaki)		Opp. Miyan Iftikhar Ahmad Zar'i Services, Main Road, Obaaro, District Ghotaki

Sr. No.	District/ Tehsil	District/ Tehsil Secretary	Office/Centre
Lashkar-e Tayyaba, Azad Kashmir			
49.	Muzaffarabad	Rafiq Akhtar	Baitul Mujahideen, Lower Plate, Muzaffarabad
50.	Rawlakot	Haji Azam	Baitul Mujahideen, Opp. SP Office, Near Sabir Shaheed Stadium, Rawlakot
51.	Bhambar		Baitul Mujahideen, Post Office Chowki, Simahni, District Bhambar
52.	Daddyal		Baitul Mujahideen, 1 Floor, Taj Plaza, District Meerpur
53.	Kotli	Aftab Husain	Baitul Mujahideen, Near Post Office, Kotli
54.	Wailamgarh		Baitul Mujahideen, 1 Floor, Yakirah Bakery, Wailamgarh, District Meerpur
55.	Meerpur	Choudhury Mohammad Yusuf	Baitul Mujahideen, Sector B-4, Meerpur, Azad Kashmir

Jamat Al-Mujahideen

Jamat Al-Mujahideen is regarded as the oldest organisation of Ahl-e Hadith persuasion that traces its beginnings to Syed Ahmad Shaheed.

BACKGROUND

Jamat Al-Mujahideen is known for its underground activities and it is taken to be the first regular/proper jihadi organisation in Pakistan that had started working in Kashmir in 1948. However, this is past history now. In Pakistan, it is now known as a big Ahl-e Hadith organisation that works on a three-point programme:

1. Implementation of Islamic Shura in place of democracy

2. Acceptance of jihad (military) in political, social, and individual life
3. Removal of un-Islamic accretions from Islam

Currently, its amir is Ghazi Abdul Karim Khan and deputy amir is Dr Arshad Randhawa. For every member of Jamat Al-Mujahideen, and particularly for the amir, participation in jihad is obligatory. Despite his age, the current amir participated in the Afghan War in Kandahar, Kabul, and Jalalabad fronts. After the movement by Syed Ahmad Shaheed, during the British attack on Afghanistan, Jamat Al-Mujahideen began underground activities there and established its centre at Charqand (Bajora Agency), which continues to be a big centre of Jamat Al-Mujahideen till now. Maulana Ghulam Rasool Mehr has written two books on the activities of this organisation. They are *Jamat Al-Mujahideen* and *Sarguzasht-e Mujahideen*. Since the time of Syed Ahmad Shaheed, the organisation has been in existence and it has had sixteen amirs so far. The outgoing amir selects his successor during his lifetime.

Chronology of the Amirs of Jamat Al-Mujahideen

1.	Syed Ahmad Shaheed	1782–1831
	Maulana Shah Ismail Shaheed	1778–1831
2.	Maulana Wali Muhammad Shaheed	1831–1840
3.	Maulana Syed Nasiruddin Dehlawi	1840
4.	Maulana Syed Abdurrahim Shaheed	1840–1841
5.	Maulana Inayat Ali	1841–1846
6.	Maulana Vilayat Ali	1852–1858

7. Maulana Noorullah	1858–1862
8. Maulana Abdullah	1862–1902
9. Maulana Abdul Karim	1902–1915
10. Maulana Niamatullah Shaheed	1915–1921
11. Maulana Rahmatullah Shaheed	1921–1921
12. Maulana Fazl Elahi	1921–1928
13. Maulana Muhammad Bashir Shaheed	1928–1934
Maulana Fazl Elahi	1934–1951
14. Maulana Sufi Abdullah	1951–1975
15. Maulana Muhammad Sulaiman	1975–1983
16. Ghazi Abdul Karim Khan	1983–

Current Status

Jamat Al-Mujahideen now concentrates on madrasa education. It has its centres in Chamarqand, Lodhran, Karachi, and Mamun Kanjan.

Madrasa Jamia Talimul Islam

The foundation of this madrasa was laid by the fourteenth amir, Sufi Abdullah in September 1938 and its objective was to prepare mujahideen. According to Sarguzasht-e Mujahideen:

> (Sufi Abdullah) consulted Maulana Fazl Elahi and decided that the location for the madrasa should be selected in such a way that it should be far away from human habitation, and access to which would be difficult. Mujahideen should be prepa red there and sent out... With this end in view a spot called Udanwala was selected which was 4–5 miles away from Mamun Kanjan railway station (Faisalabad district). Nowadays, Madrasa Udanwala is known as

Jamia Talimul Islam, Mamun Kanjan, which is close
to the railway station, while the old madrasa is also
working in its old spot.

Jamia Abi Bakr Al-Islamia, Karachi

The foundation of this madrasa was laid by Maulana
Muhammad Sulaiman, the sixteenth amir of Jamat Al-
Mujahideen. The objective of this madrasa was also to
prepare students both for educational and for jihadi
purposes.

Track Record in Afghanistan and Kashmir

Jamat Al-Mujahideen participated actively in the war
that began in Afghanistan after 1979. It was in touch
with Maulana Yunus Khalis's group. It facilitated the
participation of other jihadi organisations in the war in
Afghanistan, including the current leadership of Jamat
Al-Dawa. The current amir, Ghazi Abdul Karim and
other leaders like Professor Choudhury Muhammad
Zafarullah, Dr Muhammad Arshad Randhawa, Maulana
Khalid Garjhaki, and Maulana Hakim Mahmood
participated in the war in Afghanistan.

Jamat Al-Mujahideen played an important role in
the formation of Tahreekul Mujahideen, the first
jihadi organisation of Ahl-e Hadith persuasion in
Occupied Kashmir. It arranged for the training of its
mujahideen in Afghanistan. Before Tahreekul
Mujahideen got formally associated with Markazi
Jamiat Ahl-e Hadith, the offices of Jamat Al-
Mujahideen in Pakistan doubled as offices of
Tahreekul Mujahideen too.

Rift with Markazi Jamiat Ahl-e Hadith

The nature of differences between Jamat Al-Mujahideen and Markazi Jamiat Ahl-e Hadith is both religious and political. The complaint of the leaders of Jamat Al-Mujahideen against the leadership of Markazi Jamiat Ahl-e Hadith was that they (the latter) did not give importance to militant jihad. To blunt this criticism, Markazi Jamiat Ahl-e Hadith extended its patronage to Tahreekul Mujahideen. The second complaint is based on the political stand of Markazi Jamiat Ahl-e Hadith. It supports the current democratic system. The third complaint is about the ownership of a few madrasas. According to a member of Tahreekul Mujahideen, most of these complaints have been sorted out.

Jamat Ghurba Ahl-e Hadith

This is a non-political organisation which works for Markazi Jamiat Ahl-e Hadith in its *tablighi* programme. It is supposed to be an effective organisation of Ahl-e Hadith that has a good network in Punjab and Sindh.

The amir of this organisation is Maulana Abdur Rahman Salafi who is also the principal of Jamia Sitaria Islamia in Karachi. This organisation was founded in 1916 with the basic objective of propagating Ahl-e Hadith school of thought. There are differences within the adherents of Ahl-e Hadith school of thought on matters of belief, and they are divided into nine groups. Jamat Ghurba Ahl-e Hadith follows the views propounded by Maulana Abdul Sattar Dehlawi; they are also nicknamed, 'Sitari'. It has a good organisational structure with the

367

following departments working under it:

1. Department of education – Koran and Hadith and Islamic learning
2. Department of management and construction of mosques
3. Department of press and publication
4. Department of *tabligh* – The Book and the Sunnah
5. Department of social service
6. Department of higher education
7. Department of jihad
8. Department of women's education
9. Department of material resources

Twelve madrasas are working under the aegis of Jamat Ghurba Ahl-e Hadith; of them the following four are important:

1. Jamia Sitaria Islamia, Karachi
2. Madrasa Arabia Dar al-Islam, Karachi
3. Dar al-Hadith Jamia Muavia, Lahore
4. Syeda Fatema al-Zehra al-Islamia Lil-Banat (for women), Karachi

Tablighi Jamat Ahl-e Hadith

It is working as a Tablighi Jamat of Deobandi persuasion. Its centre is located in Jama Masjid Tauheed, Court Road, Karachi.

Shabaan-e Ghurba Ahl-e Hadith

This organisation is working among the youth. Its central office is in Karachi, and its amir is Maulana Abdul Hannan Samroori.

Jamat Ahl-e Hadith, Pakistan

Jamat Ahl-e Hadith, Pakistan, is one of the oldest organisations of Ahl-e Hadith sect whose foundation was laid in 1918. It was reorganised in Pakistan by Maulana Abdul Qadir Rupri, and he remained its amir throughout his life. After his death, Maulana Muhammad Husain Shekhupuri became the leader of Jamat Ahl-e Hadith. Its network is spread in Punjab and Sindh, particularly Karachi. It played an important role in the formation of Milli Ekjahti Council. Its views on jihad are opposite to those of Jamat Al-Dawa. This is the reason why several of its members were harassed by those of Lashkar-e Tayyaba. Its important centre in Lahore is Jama Masjid Ahl-e Hadith, Chowk Dalgiran; in Okara its centre is located in Jamia Mahmudiya Ahl-e Hadith.

The objective of founding Jamat Ahl-e Hadith was to bring all groups of Ahl-e Hadith persuasion on one platform and unite them. Its other objective was to establish Ahl-e Hadith madrasas. Now, thirty big Ahl-e Hadith madrasas are working in Punjab and Sindh.

The management of Jamat Ahl-e Hadith is run by a Majlis-e Shura that has twenty-two members. It has several ancillary departments, the most important of which is Ahl-e Hadith Janbaz Force.

Ahl-e Hadith Janbaz Force

Ahl-e Hadith Janbaz Force was formed on 22 February 1991. It is the youth wing of Jamat Ahl-e Hadith and its leader is Maulana Akhtar Muhammadi. Its objective is to promote Ahl-e Hadith school of thought, to wrok for the welfare of the people of this sect, and to unite the ulema of Ahl-e Hadith. Its network is present in a few districts of Sindh and Punjab. Its main centre is Karachi where it has consolidated itself.

Muttahida (United) Jamiat Ahl-e Hadith

Muttahida Jamiat Ahl-e Hadith was a united front of Ahl-e Hadith organisations that was founded in 1992. But soon dissensions cropped up among the members, a major reason of which was the selection of Professor Sajid Mir as the senator in 1993. The stand of Muttahida Jamiat Ahl-e Hadith was that as this seat was earmarked for Ahl-e Hadith groups, a consensus should have been arrived at among the groups first. But Professor Sajid Mir put forward his own name without taking other groups into confidence. Most of these groups have broken away from the Ittihad, and have formed another Ittihad. At present Maulana Ziaullah Shah Bukhari is the chief secretary and Hafiz Yahya Aziz Mir Muhammadi is its amir.

Jamiat Ahl-e Hadith (Lakhwi Group)

The leader of this group is Maulana Muinuddin Lakhwi who is an ex-MNA. Its presence is there in Okara and adjoining areas. It is basically a breakaway group of Markazi Jamiat Ahl-e Hadith. The differences between Maulana Muinuddin Lakhwi and Allama Ahsan Elahi Zaheer had an old history. Allama Ahsan Elahi Zaheer criticised the former for his support of Ziaul Haq. Maulana Muinuddin Lakhwi reported: 'A couple of days before his death when I was in

Islamabad, Allama Zaheer had sent me a message saying that he considered me as the amir. Whatever was said (by him) earlier was due to Mian Fazal Haq (leader, Markazi Jamiat Ahl-e Hadith).' Later, Maulana Lakhwi had disagreement with Professor Sajid Mir regarding the senate seat and his group broke away. This group remained active in Muttahida Jamiat Ahl-e Hadith and Maulana Lakhwi is considered to be an important leader of the Muttahida.

Markazi Jamiat Ahl-e Hadith (Ibtisam Elahi Group)

The leader of Markazi Jamiat Ahl-e Hadith (Ibtisam Elahi Group) is Engineer Hafiz Ibtisam Elahi Zaheer, who is the son of Allama Zaheer. Its patron/amir is Abdur Rahman Ludhianwi. Its differences with Markazi Jamiat Ahl-e Hadith (Sajid Mir) is both political and organisational. Ibtisam Elahi group was not in favour of Professor Sajid Mir's support of Muslim League (N). Moreover, the two groups fought over the funds received from Saudi Arabia. The Ibtisam Elahi group turned out Sajid Mir group from the centre of Markazi Jamiat Ahl-e Hadith in Lawrence Road, Lahore. This led to violence between the two groups. But the ulema intervened, and Sajid Mir group was granted space for office at Ravi Road during Nawaz Sharif regime.

Ibtisam Elahi group has the support of the majority of Ahl-e Hadith ulema, but it could not establish a coherent network throughout Pakistan. Its student wing, 'Ahl-e Hadith Students Federation' has a strong presence.

371

Markazi Jamat Ahl-e Hadith

The amir of Markazi Jamat Ahl-e Hadith is Allama Zubair Ahmad Zaheer. He formed this organisation after breaking away from Markazi Jamiat Ahl-e Hadith in 1995. His disagreement with Professor Sajid Mir was due to the latter's proximity with Nawaz Sharif and his tendency to use the organisation for personal benefit. He also accuses Professor Sajid Mir of embezzlement of funds. Markazi Jamat Ahl-e Hadith is not an effective organisation. Its presence is limited to Lahore and Okara. Its central office is located at Jamia Gulbarg III, Lahore.

Anjuman Ahl-e Hadith

The president of Anjuman Ahl-e Hadith is Maulana Fazlur Rahman bin Muhammad. It is confined to Lahore. The main objective of this organisation is to work for the welfare of Ahl-e Hadith sect. Its centre is located at Jama Masjid Mubarak, Railway Road, Lahore.

Jamiat Ulema Ahl-e Hadith

The leader of this formation is Maulana Qazi Abdul Qadir Khamosh. It is composed of the breakaway groups of Markazi Jamiat Ahl-e Hadith. Khamosh's points of disagreement with Professor Sajid Mir were the same as mentioned above, i.e. embezzlement of funds and using the organisation for personal ends. Qazi Abdul Qadir Khamosh declared his separation from all Ahl-e Hadith formations and formed Jamiat

Ulema Ahl-e Hadith whose objective was to unite all Ahl-e Hadith ulema on one platform regarding questions of sharia. Its central office is located at Acchahra Shopping Centre, Ferozepur Road.

Jamat Al-Dawa Ilal-Quran O Sunnah, Afghanistan

The founder of this organisation was Shaikh Jamilur Rahman, and it was founded at the time of Zaheer Shah. It had established 'rule of sharia' in the Kandahar province at the time the Russians were still in Afghanistan but a few provinces were under the control of Mujahideen. This organisation is not confined to Afghanistan, but has its network in Pakistan as well.

According to Maulana Abu Ataullah Taj Muhammad, secretary, external affairs, Jamat Al-Dawa Ilal-Quran O Sunnah:

> Shaikh Jamilur Rahman has done quite a bit of work in Pakistan. When Afghan refugees flooded Pakistan, he set up madrasas for their religious education. Thus, our offices were established in Islamabad, Karachi, Quetta and other places. All Ahl-e Hadith organisations in Pakistan got in touch with us. Our wish is that all Ahl-e Hadith organisations in Pakistan should come together.

Sirat Al-Mustaqeem, June 1995

The Ahl-e Hadith mujahideen of Pakistan took part in the war in Afghanistan from the platform of Jamat Al-Dawa Ilal-Quran O Sunnah. Its centres in Pakistan are located in Der and Bajora Agency areas where several of its madrasas are working. Its amir is Shaikh Samiullah, and Shaikh Abdur Rob is the deputy amir. It is also a part of Majlis Amal Ahl-e Hadith, Pakistan.

Tahaffuz (Protection) Harmain Sharifain Movement

The founder of Tahaffuz Harmain Sharifain Movement was Maulana Muhammad Madni who was the principal of Jamia Asariya in Jhelum. Its basic objective was the protection of sacred places in Saudi Arabia and creating favourable conditions for the Saudi government in Pakistan. It was founded in 1985. Among its patrons are Muhammad bin Abdullah, imam, Ka'ba, and Professor Al-Shaikh Abdul Qadir Habibullah Al-Sindhi, Madina University.

This organisation was formed at the time when the Shia pilgrims had demonstrated at Ka'ba against the Saudi government. It tried to negate any Shia influence in Pakistan. It acted on behalf of Ahl-e Sunnat Barelvi groups to support the movement for restoration of tombs of Prophet's Companions destroyed in Jannatul Baqi (Madina). It receives support from Al-Haramain Foundation, Saudi Arabia, and other government institutions of that country.

Majlis Amal, Ahl-e Hadith

This is a united front of Ahl-e Hadith organisations. It was founded on 10 October 2001, at the Muttahida Jamiat Ahl-e Hadith centre, Multan Road, Lahore. Its objective is to try for consensus among Ahl-e Hadith organisations on different issues in the changed situation after 11 September 2001. Its convenor is Professor Sajid Mir. The following organisations are represented in it:

Organisation	Representative
1. Markazi Jamiat Ahl-e Hadith	Professor Sajid Mir
2. Jamiat Ghurba Ahl-e Hadith	Maulana Muhammad Idris Hashmi
3. Jamat Al-Dawa	Hafiz Abdus Salam Bhatwi
4. Jamat Al-Mujahideen	Dr Muhammad Irshad Randhawa
5. Muttahida Jamiat Ahl-e Hadith	Maulana Ziaullah Shah Bukhari
6. Jamat Ahl-e Hadith	Maulana Muhammad Husain Shekhupuri
7. Tahreekul Mujahideen	Commander Owais Sajjad
8. Jamat Al-Dawa Ilal-Quran O Sunnah	Shaikh Samiullah

Majlis Amal Ahl-e Hadith has taken a common stand in the changed circumstances on madrasas. So far it has organised three meetings to arrive at a consensus on different issues. The common agenda agreed upon in the first meeting is as follows:

> Ahl-e Hadith Majlis Amal does not consider Parvez Musharraf as the spokesman of Islam and Pakistan but that of America and its allied countries. We consider that his recent steps are against the interest of Islam and Muslims and condemn them strongly. We demand that he should not spoil the relationship

between the army and the people in his pursuit for power and save the peaceful internal situation from deteriorating further. He should stop making statements against mujahideen. America and its allied countries only understand the language of power. They will not engage in any meaningful dialogue till the Muslim community hit them hard through guerril la war as they did the Russians (in Afghanistan).

Sahifa Ahl-e Hadith, monthly, Karachi,
November 2001

Chapter XI
BARELVI ORGANISATIONS AND GROUPS

In Pakistan, the largest number of organisations is of Barelvi persuasion. There are forty-three big organisations having large networks; of them six are political, twenty-one are religious-cum-sectarian, and six are jihadi. Two organisations are *tablighi* and another two are working in the field of education. They may be classified as follows:

Religious and Political Organisations

1. Jamiat Ulema Pakistan (Noorani Group)
2. Jamiat Ulema Pakistan (Niazi Group)
3. Jamiat Ulema Pakistan (Nifaz Shariat Group)
4. Jamiat Ulema Pakistan (Fazal Karim Group)
5. Pakistan Awami Tahreek
6. Jamiat al-Mashaikh

Organisations for Promotion/Protection of Sects (Non-political)

1. Jamat Ahl-e Sunnat
2. Markazi Jamiat Ahl-e Sunnat
3. Alami Tanzeem Ahl-e Sunnat
4. Tahreek Minhaz al-Quran

5. Alami Dawat Islamia
6. Ulema Council
7. Tahreek Tahaffuz Khatm Nabuwat
8. Muttahida Ulema Council
9. Ittihad Ulema Pakistan
10. Amir Millat Foundation
11. Mustafai Tahreek
12. Majlis al-Dawa Islamia
13. Ittihad al-Mashaikh
14. Jamat Riza-e Mustafa
15. Sunni Ulema Council
16. Sawad Ahl-e Sunnat
17. Ulema Mashaikh Council
18. Caravan-e Islam

Organisations Involved in Sectarian Clashes

1. Sunni Tahreek
2. Anjuman Naojawanan-e Islam (Tariq Mahboob Group)
3. Anjuman Naojawanan-e Islam
4. Anjuman Tulaba Islam
5. Sipah Mustafa

Jihadi Organisations

1. Islamic Front (Lashkar-e Islam)
2. Tahreek Jihad
3. Sunni Jihad Council
4. Mujahideen Lashkar Ababeel
5. Tanzeemul Arifin
6. Shiran Islam
7. Lashkar Mustafa

8. Lashkar Ahl-e Sunnat
9. Ansar al-Islam
10. Jamiat Ansar al-mujahideen Alami

The Barelvi organisations and groups were born from the wombs of Jamat Ahl-e Sunnat and Jamiat Ulema Pakistan. All the organisations are related, some way or other, to these two organisations. In the two chapters related to these organisations, I have dealt with the history and background of the organisations of Barelvi persuasion. Summary information of these organisations and groups are listed in Table XIV followed by their descriptive details.

Jamiat Ulema Pakistan

Jamiat Ulema Pakistan is a representative political organisation of Barelvi persuasion which is now composed of four breakaway groups. The largest group is JUP (Noorani), and the second largest is JUP (Fazl Karim).

BACKGROUND

Jamiat Ulema Pakistan was founded in March 1948. It was the changed name for All India Sunni Conference which was founded in April 1946 in Varanasi, and its chief secretary was Maulana Syed Muhammad Naimuddin Muradabadi. All India Sunni Conference had supported the establishment of Pakistan and that is why it was renamed Jamiat Ulema Pakistan.

Jamiat Ulema Pakistan was founded in Madrasa Arabia Anwarul Uloom, Multan, because of the efforts of Allama Syed Ahmad Kazmi. Its first president was Allama Abul Hasnat Syed Muhammad Ahmad Qadri

Gateway to Terrorism

Table XIV: *Hanfi-Barelvi Organisations in Pakistan*

Sr. No.	Organisation	Central amir/ secretary/patron	Founded	Nature	Central Office
1.	Jamiat Ulema, Pakistan (N)	Maulana Shah Ahmad Noorani	1951	Political	Karachi
2.	do (Nifaz Shariat Group)	Engineer Salimullah	1998	do	Noori Masjid, Opp. Railway Station, Lahore
3.	do (Fazal Karim Group)	Sahibzada Fazal Karim	1999	do	Bashir Mansion, 1, Turner Road, Lahore
4.	Tahreek Minhajul Quran	Allama Tahir Qadri	1989	Sectarian	Model Town, Lahore
5.	Pakistan Awami Tahreek	Do	1990	Political	Do
6.	Jamiat Al-Mashaikh	Peer Fazal Haq		do	Sikkim Morh, Allama Iqbal Town, Multan
7.	Sunni Tahreek	Mohammad Abbas Qadri	1990	Sectarian	27 A, Muin Plaza, 1 Floor, Baba-e Urdu Road, Karachi
8.	Jamat Ahl-e Sunnat	Syed Riaz Husain Shah	1953	do	Nizam Building, Opp. Lady Wellington Hospital, Azadi Chowk, Lahore
9.	Alami Jamat Ahl-e Sunnat	Pir Afzal Qadri	1998	do	Nek Abad, Gujrat
10.	Alami Dawat Islamia	Sahibzada Fayazul Hasan Qadri	1998	Tablighi	Haq Bahu House, Judicial Colony, Thokar Niaz Beg, Lahore
11.	Ulema Council	Sahibzada Said Ahmad Shah Gujrati	1998	Ulema unity	180, Madina Masjid, Ravi Road, Lahore

380

Sr. No.	Organisation	Central amir/ secretary/patron	Founded	Nature	Central Office
12.	Tahreek Tahaffuz Khatm Nabuwat	Sardar Mohammad Khan Al-Ghari	1998	*Khatm Nabuwat*	do
13.	Muttahida Ulema Council	Maulana Abdur Rauf Malik	1998	Sectarian	Lahore
14.	Ittihad Ulema Pakistan	Pir Syed Asif Ali Gilani	1998	Nationalist	
15.	Amir Millat Foundation		1998	Tablighi/ trust	Jahanzeb Block, Allama Iqbal, Lahore
16.	Anjuman Naojawanan-e Islam	Tariq boob	1998	Sectarian	Karachi
17.	Mustafai Tahreek	Ghulam Murtaza Saidi	1996	do	Union Press, Circular Road, Opp. Mochi Darwaza, Lahore
18.	Majlis al-Dawa Islamia	Sahibzada Hamiduddin		Tablighi	Sayal Sharif, Mauza Sahiwal, District Sargodha
19.	Ittihadul Mashaikh (Q)	Sultan Riazul Hasan Qadri		Sectarian	Haq Bahu House, Shahdara Station, Lahore
20.	Ittihad al-Mashaikh (Z)	Dr Khalid Raza Kohri	1953	Do	Zakori Sharif, Dera Ismail Khan
21.	Tanzimul Madaris	Mufti Abdul Qayoom Hazarwi		Educational	Jamia Nizamiya Rizviya, Lohari Gate, Lahore
22.	Tanzeem Mashaikh Azzam	Masood Ahmad Siddiqui	2001	Sectarian	Faisalabad
23.	Jamat Raza-e Mustafa	Abu Daud Haji Md. Siddique, MNA		Sectarian	Zeenatul Masjid, Chowk Darussalam, Gujranwala
24.	Sunni Ulema Council	Nazakat Husain		Sectarian	Lahore

Gateway to Terrorism

Sr. No.	Organisation	Central amir/ secretary/patron	Founded	Nature	Central Office
25.	Sawad Azam Ahl-e Sunnat	Maulana Kaukab Nurani	2001	Nationalist	Okara
26.	Ulema Mashaikh Council	Maulana Ayaz Zaheer Hashmi	2001	United	Lahore
27.	Dawat-e Islami	Maulana Ilyas Qadri	1984	Tablighi	Karachi
28.	Mujahid Lashkar Ababil	Jawed Mujaddidi	1998	Jihadi	Jama Masjid Madina, Ravi Road, Lahore
29.	Sunni Jihad Council	Allama Said Ahmad	1997	do	Gujranwala
30.	Tahreek Jihad Jammu Kashmir	Major Tariq Zul-Qarnain	1997	do	Chehla Bandi, Muzaffarabad
31.	Tanzeemul Arifin	Shujat Ali Majahid	1991	do	Township, Lahore
32.	Sipah Mustafa	Allama Allahbakhsh Nayyar	1989	Sectarian	Jama Masjid, Old Idgah, Jhang Sadar
33.	Caravan-e Islam	Mufti Mohammad Khan Qadri		do	Jamia Islamia, 1, Fasih Road, Islamia Park, Lahore
34.	Harkat-e Inqilab Islami	Khalid Mahmood Qadri	1998	Jihadi	Numania Building, Taksali Gate, Neat Bhati Police station, Lahore
35.	Shizan Islam	Shujat Ali Mujahid		do	Naqsh Lasani Nagar, Shakar Garh, District Narewal
36.	Lashkar Islam (Islamic Front)	Allama Liaqat Azhari	1996	do	368 D, Satellite Town, Jamia Razuia, Ziaul Uloom, Rawalpindi
37.	Lashkar Mustafa	Major (Retd) Yaqoob Saifi		do	

Sr. No.	Organisation	Central amir/ secretary/patron	Founded	Nature	Central Office
38.	Lashkar Ahl-e Sunnat	Qadri Ghulam Farid Usmani		do	Nak Abad Maradiya Sharif, Bypass Road, Gujrat
39.	Ansarul Islam		1995	do	Mirpur
40.	Jamiat Ansarul Mujahidin Alami	Abdurrahman Kashmiri	1994	do	Do
41.	Anjuman Tulaba Islam		1994	Students wing	Lahore
42.	Minhajul Quran Students Mag	Nazir Lohani	1994	do	Model Town, Lahore
43.	Alami Idarah Tanzeemul Islam	Allama Said Mujahidi	1999	Sectarian	Gujranwala
44.	Nizam-e Mustafa Party	Haji Hanif Tayyab	2002	Political	Multan

and the chief secretary was Syed Kazmi. A separate branch, Jamiat al-Mashaikh, was established for mystics and teachers of Hadith which was a part of Jamiat Ulema Pakistan. Jamiat Ulema Pakistan first demonstrated its presence by organising a 'Shariat Day' in the entire Pakistan on 7 May 1948. It also played a vital role in Khatm Nabuwat movement in 1953. The Majlis-e Amal established by Shia, Sunni, Deobandi, and Ahl-e Hadith organisations in 1953 had Allama Syed Qadri as its president. During the movement, his son Maulana Khalil Ahmad Qadri was sentenced to death by hanging. After the death of Syed Muhammad Qadri in 1961, Jamiat Ulema Pakistan remained dormant till 1968. In 1968, a conference was organised in Jamia Naimia, Gharo Shahu, Lahore, in which Allama Abdul Ghafoor Hazarwi was made the president. In the 1970 elections, Jamiat Ulema Pakistan had bagged the largest number of votes in West Pakistan, among all the religious organisations. It also played an important role in the Nizam-e Mustafa Movement in 1977.

CHARTER

The following are the salient features of the charter of Jamiat Ulema Pakistan:

1. Full implementation of the Quran and Sunnah in Pakistan
2. Equal rights for all citizens
3. Administration of equal justice to all
4. Administration of laws of sharia by courts
5. Women's rights – social, economic, and political – should be protected according to sharia

6. The policy of external affairs should be free from all pressures; proximity with Muslim countries
7. Providing all assistance for the people of Jammu and Kashmir in their struggle for freedom
8. Zakat and *Ashra* (tithe) should be implemented in Pakistan, eliminating bank interest

Groupism in Jamiat Ulema Pakistan

Dissensions cropped up in Jamiat Ulema Pakistan in the general elections of 1988, when Maulana Noorani decided to support Pakistan Awami Ittihad and Maulana Abdul Sattar Niazi decided to support the Muslim League and Islami Jamhoori Ittihad. Now, JUP has four breakaway groups.

JAMIAT ULEMA PAKISTAN (NOORANI GROUP)

This is the largest group and its leader is Maulana Shah Ahmad Noorani. Its branches can be found in all the four provinces.

JAMIAT ULEMA PAKISTAN (FAZL KARIM GROUP)

This group came into existence when Sahibzada Fazl Karim became a minister in Punjab province, and Maulana Niazi had some disagreements with him and he was turned out from the organisation. Fazl Karim formed his own group which is now the second largest group of Jamiat Ulema Pakistan.

JAMIAT ULEMA PAKISTAN (NIAZI GROUP)

During 1988 general elections, there was disagreement between Maulana Abdul Sattar Niazi and Maulana Ahmad Shah Noorani on the question of joining

Awami Jamhoori Ittihad. As a result, Jamiat Ulema Pakistan was divided into two groups. After the death of Maulana Niazi, Maulana Syed Hasnain has become the leader of his group.

JAMIAT ULEMA PAKISTAN (NIFAZ SHARIAT GROUP)

The leader of this group is Engineer Salimullah. JUP sources say that Maulana Niazi had turned Maulana Fazl Karim out of the organisation at his instance, but later Maulana Niazi had differences with him as well and he was turned out. Engineer Salimullah formed his own group, Nifaz Shariat, which does not have much of a presence.

Jamat Ahl-e Sunnat Pakistan

Jamat Ahl-e Sunnat was founded in Karachi in 1956. Its first amir was Maulana Muhammad Shafi Okarwi. In the beginning, it worked as a *tablighi jamat* and published missionary literature. During the tenure as amir of Allma Syed Sa'dat Ali it extended its network and branches were established in different parts of the country. In 1966, Jamat Ahl-e Sunnat had 200 offices in Karachi alone and it had fifty madrasas located in different mosques for the study of the Holy Koran. In the 1970 elections, it had participated from the platform of Jamiat Ulema Pakistan. In June 1986, the officiating president, Mufti Mukhtar Ahmad Naimi had dismissed all central and state-level office bearers. This led to the division of Jamat Ahl-e Sunnat into two groups. Sahibzada Fazl Karim declared his group to be a political one and announced his intention to take part in active politics. During the Zia regime when all political parties were being registered, he got his group registered as a political formation, and Sahibzada Jamaluddin Qadri became the president. After the death of Mufti Mukhtar Ahmad Naimi, the second group had Dewan Al Saidi Muini as its president and Sahibzada Syed Hamid Kazmi as the head of the management. Up to 1994, both the groups worked separately but were not much active. In 1994, they came together and formed Sunni Supreme Council under the leadership of Pir Muhammad Karamshah. Sunni Supreme Council resolved differences among the groups and reorganised Jamat Ahl-e Sunnat. It declared Sahibzada Syed Mazhar Kazmi as the central amir of Muttahida Jamat Ahl-e Sunnat, and Pir Muhammad Afzal Qadri as the chief secretary (central). In June 1998, Maulana Pir Afzal resigned from Jamat Ahl-e Sunnat and Syed Riaz Husain Shah, *khateeb* of Ittifaq masjid, Model Town, was made the chief secretary.

CHARTER

On 2 April 2000, International Sunni Conference was held in Multan in which the following objectives were included in its charter:

1. To take stock of what has been gained and lost in this century, and to decide the course of action for the next
2. To awaken consciousness about Ahl-e Sunnat
3. To organise Ahl-e Sunnat on the religious plane
4. To work for reformation of faith and to implement faith in practical life
5. To reform the society and promote pure religious

values
6. To protect and propagate the concept of Pakistan
7. To protect the rights of Ahl-e Sunnat
8. To establish links with scholars and Ahl-e Sunnat groups of the world
9. To assist oppressed Muslims of the world, particularly those in Kashmir

ORGANISATIONAL STRUCTURE

The Sunni Supreme Council looks over all the affairs of the Jamat Ahl-e Sunnat. Its leader is Mufti Abdul Qayoom Hazarwi. In the elections of Jamat Ahl-e Sunnat in 1999, Sahibzada Syed Mazhar Kazmi was made the central amir for the third time, and Syed Riaz Husain Shah was made the chief secretary (central). The provincial branches are responsible for work at the divisional and district levels.

SUNNI SECRETARIAT

A twelve-acre plot has been bought by Jamat Ahl-e Sunnat for one crore rupees on GT Road near Lahore, to build the Sunni secretariat on the style of Mansoora and Oeaisa Housing Society. According to *Akhbar Ahl-e Sunnat*, Jamat Ahl-e Sunnat's mouthpiece, the following departments will be working there:

Sunni Parliament
A world institute that would recommend educational, spiritual, social, economic, and other programmes for the progress of Ahl-e Sunnat sect.

Idarah Tahqiqat (Research) Ahl-e Sunnat
A research institute to conduct research on different aspects of Ahl-e Sunnat movement.

Markaz Khidmat Khalq (Centre for Social Service)
An institute to provide spiritual and practical service to humanity according to religious guidelines.

Sunni Institute of Policy Studies
A rare institute of its kind where experienced (retired) generals, journalists, intellectuals, ulema, and technocrats will discuss issues and recommend measures whereby Ahl-e Sunnat will be able to determine its policies according to the demands of the time.

Baitul Ehsan Wal-Hikmat
Jamat Ahl-e Sunnat feels that it has got Muslims of different ways of faith (Naqshbandi, Qadri, Chishti, Suhrawardy) in its fold. That is why the international secretariat is establishing Baitul Ehsan Wal-Hikmat for the spiritual and practical development of people of all ways of faith.

Guest House
There will be a guest house for advanced students and visitors.

Library
A world-status library with residential facilities will be established.

World Teachers' Training for Ulema
Sunni secretariat will have an academy for the training of students who have acquired degrees. Here the ulema will be familiarised with the requirements of today and trained to use their knowledge to optimal effect.

Sunni Institute of Modern Languages
Learning of languages is intrinsic to all scholarship, cultural exchanges, and political dialogues. That is why Sunni Institute of Modern Languages will foster

learning of different languages of the world.

Rabeta Alam Ahl-e Sunnat

Thousands of Ahl-e Sunnat organisations, madrasas, schools, colleges are working in the world. This office will establish links and coordinate the activities of the above institutions.

Sunni Mosques

Ahl-e Sunnat mosques will number thousands if not lakhs in the whole of Pakistan. Jamat Ahl-e Sunnat wishes to compile a record of their workings and their management committees, and then make arrangements for their protection from encroachments by people of misguided ways of faith.

Institute for Legal Help

With help of known advocates, an institute will be established where lawyers and the ulema will jointly seek solutions for emerging problems.

Online Islamic University

Jamat Ahl-e Sunnat has decided to start a university on the Internet. Students will be able to study Islamic philosophy and other subjects up to MA and MPhil levels on the Internet. It will be the first university of its kind in the world.

Sunni Education Board

It will establish an education board to prepare syllabi for schools, colleges, and universities, and formulate educational policies.

Women's Institute

The secretariat will have a department to promote women's education according to Islamic principles.

Consultative Board for Islamic Trade and Industry
There will be joint consultative board of the ulema and economists who will provide guidance to traders and industrialists.

Bank al-Khair (Islamic Bank)
No bank seems to exist in the world which is based on Islamic principles although sincere efforts are being made at several places in this direction.

Institute for Orators and Debaters
There will be an institute to train orators and debaters who can speak forcefully in favour of the true ways of faith and defend them against false ways.

Institute for Higher Studies
An international-level institute of higher studies will be established where students passing out from different institutions will first be given foundation courses in the Holy Koran, Hadith, and Fiqh (Islamic Jurisprudence). Research degrees like PhD will be awarded by seeking affiliation with national and international universities.

Mass Communication
To disseminate and promote religious knowledge, a centre for mass communication will be established that will teach how to utilise the advantages of the print and the electronic media.

Sunni Publications
A publication house will be established to meet the requirements of printing books and other materials.

Darul Ifta Wal-Qaza
There will be a forum for muftis who would deliberate upon crucial and controversial issues, and courts will

be established to administer judgments.

Markazi Aiwan Na't

There will be a training academy for na't (singing the Prophet's eulogy). Jamat Ahl-e Sunnat feels that like the Prophet's life, this is also an appropriate subject for awarding degrees like MA.

Teacher Training School

Sunni secretariat proposes to establish a training school where teachers will undertake refresher courses.

Institute for Information Technology

There will be an institute for information technology that will familiarise teachers with the newest technology and arrange for instructions in computer courses.

Sunni Database Centre

A comprehensive database will be prepared that will give information about all Ahl-e Sunnat institutes and people all over the world.

Sunni Secretariat Residential Scheme

A residential complex of fifty houses has been conceived. If people show interest, it can gradually be converted into a 'Sunni City'.

Construction of a Historic Mosque

International secretariat, after all, embodies the management of a religious organisation. Its general scheme will remain incomplete without a mosque. It has been decided that a mosque will be established that will be grand and glorious in terms of architecture and design.

Construction of a Local Hospital

The secretariat will have its own staff to look after, in addition to the local population. Keeping this in mind, it has been decided to construct a middle-level hospital.

Model Schools and College

For the religious and modern education of children, separate model schools will be established for boys and girls. When they pass out from school, a college will also be established to meet their requirements.

Life Membership of the Secretariat

A budget estimate of forty crore rupees has been made for the construction of all the buildings. It may go even higher. Such a huge investment and a monthly expenditure of 10–15 lakh rupees call for an extraordinary mobilisation of resources, that would be possible only through the help of God and His Prophet. Friends may contribute 5,000 rupees to become life members, in addition to a monthly contribution.

Ordinary Membership

For ordinary membership one must pay 1,000 rupees, in addition to a monthly contribution which would be voluntary. This will be a way of keeping in touch with the secretariat on a permanent basis. (*Source*: *Akhbar Ahl-e Sunnat*, October 2001)

Markazi Jamat Ahl-e Sunnat (Noorani Group)

The leader of this group is Maulana Shah Ahmad Noorani.

BACKGROUND

Markazi Jamat Ahl-e Sunnat was founded in December 2001 in Karachi. Its background can be traced to the Sunni Conference organised by Jamat Ahl-e Sunnat in Multan in April 2000. Maulana Noorani was also invited to the conference but he declined to go saying that the conference had been kept a secret from him, and the last moment invitation was simply a ritual. He could not be persuaded to attend the conference and his supporters formed a new group.

CLASH WITH JAMAT AHL-E SUNNAT

As a reaction to the newly formed Markazi Jamat Ahl-e Sunnat, the monthly *Al-Said*, Multan, wrote an editorial in its January 2000 issue that added to the tension between the two groups. The editorial accused Maulana Noorani of being the agent of Jamat-e Islami and the Wahabis. Some excerpts from this editorial follows:

> Along with reading elegies on these Deobandis and Wahabis, we also regret the behaviour of those gentlemen whose predecessors had created Pakistan. They got full respect in Pakistan and enjoyed the leadership of Ahl-e Sunnat. The high and the low of Ahl-e Sunnat people made them the apple of their eye. They monopolised the leadership of Ahl-e Sunnat for a long time and did whatever they liked.

But eventually they have decided to act as the agents of Deobandis and the Wahabis rather than working for their own religion and sect.

Some office bearers of Jamat Ahl-e Sunnat have helped Maulana Noorani in his evil designs. They were holding positions in Jamat Ahl-e Sunnat and had sworn loyalty to it. But forgetting all this, they devoted themselves to fulfilling the wishes of Maulana Noorani. There were a lot of complaints against them for their negative activities – rebelling against the central authority of the Jamat, violating the charter, involvement in conspiracies, incendiary written statements, misusing the name of Ahl-e Sunnat, and so on and so forth. There is a long list of crimes in their accounts. But the central leadership ignored all this and did not take any action against them thinking that such actions will increase bitterness and harm the Jamat and the sect. Finally the time for new elections came. In the election for constitutional democracy they were cold-shouldered, and then, at the time of the new elections, they were dismissed. It was a terrible blow for them. Faced with such consequences, a meeting was called in Karachi on 27 December 2001 with Maulana Noorani in the chair, and the founding of a rival Jamat Ahl-e Sunnat was announced.

Nida-e Ahl-e Sunnat, the mouthpiece of Markazi Jamat Ahl-e Sunnat, gave a spirited reply to the above in its April 2002 issue. The whole volume of the journal was devoted to the defence of Markazi Jamat Ahl-e Sunnat against the charges levelled against it in the above editorial. It was pointed out that the real objective of Sunni Conference, 2000, was to highlight

Sunni-Wahabi differences, and this plan was made during the Nawaz Sharif regime. The current leader of Jamat Ahl-e Sunnat, Allama Riaz Husain, was the *khateeb* of Ittifaq Mosque (the mosque of Sharif family in Model Town). Nawaz Sharif used him and gave resources for the 'Ya Rasool Allah' rally in Rawalpindi. According to the writer of the article:

> After the Ya Rasool Allah rally in Islamabad, all the leaders were accorded a reception by the then Home Minister Shujat Husain. The leaders are still alive, so is Shujat Husain. If these ulema have anything called conscience, let them say on oath that resources for the Ya Rasool Allah rally were not given by the government. I would like to say further, with your permission, that the objective of this rally was to incite Sunni-Wahabi clashes in the country. The Nawaz Sharif government wanted to promote Ahl-e Sunnat against Lashkar-e Tayyaba, and did not want to challenge it directly. Earlier, Shahbaz Sharif had approached Maulana Noorani with this proposal. But the leader of Ahl-e Sunnat declined to do any such thing as that would amount to leading the country towards chaos and disorder. But some sacred beards had already become prey to this conspiracy of the government.

> The Multan Sunni Conference, 2000 was a part of this conspiracy. It had been announced a year earlier, at the bidding of the Nawaz Sharif government. The chief editor was the central figure of this conference. Despite attending the Majlis-e Shura of Jamiat Ulema Pakistan on 17 January 2000, he did not invite the members to the conference or even mention it in their presence, even though the conference was to be

held on 1 April 2000.

In this meeting of the Shura, i.e. 17 January 2000, the leader of the Ahl-e Sunnat had resigned from presidentship; at this the chief editor had requested him to withdraw his resignation. On 25 January 2000, in the meeting of the workers, the chief editor kept mum about the Sunni conference. He wanted to announce his resignation from the presidentsh ip of Jamiat, Punjab. I and other friends dissuaded him. On the same day, after the *asar namaz*, he went to the house of the Ahl-e Sunnat leader to request him to withdraw his resignation. He did not say a word about the conference there too. This is becaus e he had a special agenda for the Sunni conference. If they had gone to invite him they would have been compelled to speak about this (that it was being organised at the instance of Nawaz Sharif) to him which they did not dare. On 12 October 1999, Nawaz Sharif, who had promised to make him a leader of Maulana Noorani's stature, was thrown into jail. Now these gentlemen realised that they must invite Maulana Noorani because the original patron was not there. After knowing the objective of the conference, there was no need to attend it.

There is considerable bitterness between Jamat Ahl-e Sunnat and Markazi Jamiat Ahl-e Sunnat now. According to an important leader of Jamat Ahl-e Sunnat in Rawalpindi, 'Actually Maulana Noorani is not able to stomach the idea of the Sunni secretariat.' According to Muhammad Nawaz Kharal, secretary, press and publications, Jamat Ahl-e Sunnat, Punjab: 'One evidence of their (Markazi Jamat Ahl-e Sunnat) hypocrisy is that Maulana Noorani opposed the referendum of President Musharraf from the platform of Jamiat Ulema Pakistan, even though his own Markazi Jamat Ahl-e Sunnat was at the vanguard of the propaganda in favour of the referendum. They want to reap benefit either way.'

ORGANISATIONAL STRUCTURE AND NETWORK

Markazi Jamat Ahl-e Sunnat has a well-knit organisation with a wide network. It has organised assemblies and rallies with great efficiency, and demonstrated its strength. Its network is spread through all the four provinces of Pakistan. However, Karachi and Hyderabad in Sindh, and Rawalpindi, Lahore, and Multan in Punjab are the most important centres of Markazi Jamat Ahl-e Sunnat.

Alami Tanzeem Ahl-e Sunnat

Pir Muhammad Afzal Qadri was the chief secretary (central), Jamat Ahl-e Sunnat. But he had disagreement with the way it worked and resigned from it on 30 May 1998, forming his own group with the name, Alami Tanzeem Ahl-e Sunnat. Its main objective was to exert pressure on the government for Nizam-e Mustafa. For this, he organised protests in Rawalpindi on 12 October 1999 and was arrested. Similarly, he organised a demonstration at the GHQ, Rawalpindi, and was imprisoned for four months. Pir Muhammad Afzal represents an extreme form of Barelvi persuasion.

One of the points included in the programme of Alami Tanzeem Ahl-e Sunnat is that every Friday at 9.30 a.m. members must demonstrate silently, holding

placards with the statement: 'Oh Rulers! Impose
Nizam-e Mustafa on Yourselves and Pakistan.' But
these demonstrations were not organised properly at
many places. Its attitude is hostile towards other
organisations, as indicated by its printed charter. The
preamble to this charter reads as follows:

> Some organisations, pretending to be Sunni
> formations, curry favour with people of false beliefs
> and cause incalculable harm to Ahl-e Sunnat. Thus it
> has become important to unite those who are firm in
> their Ahl-e Sunnat belief throughout the world, and
> further instruct them on matters of belief and
> practical life.

CHARTER

1. To preach Islam and deal with the forces inimical to
   it.
2. To implement Islamic 'dos' and 'don'ts', and
   persuade the government of Islamic countries to
   implement Nizam-e Mustafa.
3. To promote intellectual, cultural, and practical
   values among Muslims in the light of Ahl-e Sunnat
   persuasion and forge unity among them.
4. To establish an international core fund to fulfil the
   religious, social, and welfare requirements of the
   Muslims of the world.

NETWORK

The network Alami Tanzeem Ahl-e Sunnat in Pakistan
is confined to Punjab province, and to Karachi and
Hyderabad in Sindh. Its important centres are there in
Gujrat, Lahore, Gujranwala, and Rawalpindi. Its

central office is located in Gujrat where one madrasa is also working.

ORGANISATIONAL STRUCTURE

The organisational structure of Alami Tanzeem Ahl-e Sunnat is not very well knit or strong. Among its intended programmes are Islamic fund, Sunni Parliament, Ulema board, organising classes for the Holy Koran translation and Fiqh, fifteen-day mobile training camp, preparing scholars in foreign languages, world Sunni secretariat, and so on. But not a single programme has got off the ground yet.

LASHKAR AHL-E SUNNAT

Lashkar Ahl-e Sunnat works under the aegis of Alami Tanzeem Ahl-e Sunnat. Its convener is Qari Ghulam Farid Khan Usmani. Its central office is in Gujrat. Its objective is to fight in the way of God and establish Islamic order.

Lashkar Ahl-e Sunnat's main job is to raise funds for some Barelvi jihadi organisations. Now, the mujahideen of Lashkar Ahl-e Sunnat receive training in the training camp at Kotli in Jammu and Kashmir. All in all, Lashkar Ahl-e Sunnat is not much active in the jihadi front.

RESOURCES

Alami Tanzeem Ahl-e Sunnat raises funds from the people of Pakistan as well as from Pakistani expatriates. Some sources say that a major part of its funds comes from an important officer of the income tax department who provides funds for different programmes.

Dawat-e Islami

Dawat-e Islami is the *tablighi jamat* of Barelvi persuasion. It was created as a reaction to Deobandi Tablighi Jamat. Both have the same style. Maulana Zakaria's book, *Fuzail al-a'mal* has a seminal status in Tablighi Jamat. Maulana Ilyas Qadri's book *Faizan-e Sunnat* has a similar status for Dawat-e Islami. The lessons that Tablighi Jamat teach after *maghrib namaz* (sunset prayer) from *Fuzail al-a'mal* are taught by Dawat-e Islami from *Faizan-e Sunnat*. The system of mobile preaching, the Friday assembly, and the annual assembly are common to both. The only difference is that of turban. Members of Dawat-e Islami take special care to wear green turbans.

Maulana Ilyas Qadri had founded Dawat-e Islami in Karachi in 1984, to save Barelvis from the influence of the Deobandi Tablighi Jamat, and to preach the teachings of Imam Raza Ahmad Khan Barelvi. At the time of its founding, the Deobandi and Ahl-e Hadith organisations were consolidating themselves in Pakistan. Because of the war in Afghanistan, the impact of these organisations had begun to be felt substantially. The Tablighi Jamat had already spread to different countries of the world. The Shias were greatly encouraged by the Iranian revolution and they looked up to Ayatullah Khomeini for spiritual leadership. In this rat race, the Barelvis had been left behind. Dawat-e Islami filled this gap, paving the way for Barelvi revival. Later, Sunni Tahreek and other Barelvi organisations were born from its womb.

Dawat-e Islami is a non-political organisation that

concentrates totally on the life and teachings of its founder, Maulana Ilyas Qadri who claimed to have brought about a spiritual revolution in the life of his disciples. For the disciples, it is obligatory to keep green turban, *miswak* (wooden tooth brush), and comb with them all the time to ensure cleanliness. It is also desirable to keep a mirror, needle and thread, and oil. They cannot wear trousers or any other 'English' dress. They do not wear black shoes. They can sleep on the floor, or use mat or durrie. The life of Maulana Qadri is a model for his disciples and they try to live their lives according to the teachings of the Prophet just as their mentor did.

Every member of Dawat-e Islami is a disciple of Maulana Qadri for whom seventy-two commandments are obligatory to become a true Muslim. For women, the number of commandments is sixty-three. Of them, forty-five commandments are to be carried out daily, ten are to be carried out in a week, four in a month, and one in a year. Besides them, there are twelve commandments that are to be carried out during the entire span of one's life. It is necessary to write down in 'Madni Diary' the roster of one's activities everyday, to see how many commandments have been carried out. The majority of these commandments are about religion though a lesser number is about organisational practices. For example, five times *namaz* a day is obligatory for everyone; so is the reading of the Holy Koran and its translation. But the translated version should be the one by Imam Reza Ahmad Khan Barelvi. Similarly, the disciples must read *Faizan-e Sunnat* everyday. The disciples are advised not to laugh too much because that deadens the heart.

Maulana Ilyas Qadri said that those who carry out the commandments throughout their lives would automatically go to heaven. But his disciples feel that only Maulana Qadri could fulfil that requirement. Even the most committed disciples can carry out only 30–35 commandments a day. This list of commandments is similar to the six points devised by Tablighi Jamat. Tablighi Jamat also claims that someone who can obtain the six points will automatically enter heaven.

Dawat-e Islami has an edge over Tablighi Jamat in the sense that the former has an organisational network throughout Pakistan and it is also establishing madrasas. In Karachi alone, it has more than 200 madrasas. This number will touch 800 if one takes into account its madrasas all over the country. In Karachi, the biggest of its madrasas is Jamia Madina, which also works as its secretariat.

Sunni Tahreek

Sunni Tahreek is a sectarian organisation of Barelvi persuasion that resorts to violence. The government has put it under surveillance on 12 January 2002.

BACKGROUND

Sunni Tahreek was founded in 1990 by Muhammad Salim Qadri. He was from Saidabad, Karachi. After his matriculation examination he started driving an autorickshaw for livelihood. When Dawat-e Islami was founded in 1980, he became its leader in the Saidabad Municipality. His rise began from here. His incendiary speeches soon ensured a place for himself in Dawat-e Islami and Jamiat Ulema Pakistan. In Karachi, he became known as Salim Saidabadi. In the 1988 general elections, Jamiat Ulema Pakistan nominated him as its candidate for Sector 75 in the Sindh Assembly. But he was defeated. After the elections, Salim Qadri left autodriving and started a cloth business and a poultry farm. In 1990, he broke away from Dawat-e Islami and formed Sunni Tahreek.

Sunni Tahreek came into being as a reaction to the growing influence of Ahl-e Hadith and Deobandi organisations. He received support from Jamat Ahl-e Sunnat, Anjuman Naojawanan-e Islam and the leaders of Jamiat Ulema Pakistan. Akram Qadri, an active member of Sunni Tahreek in Jacob Lane, Karachi, told me that Sunni Tahreek was funded by the Barkati Foundation to safeguard the rights of Ahl-e Sunnat people.

CHARTER

Sunni Tahreek declares itself as a non-political organisation and concentrates on a four-point programme:

1. To safeguard the interests of the Ahl-e Sunnat people.
2. To protect Ahl-e Sunnat mosques.
3. To protect common people from false beliefs.
4. Handing over of the Ahl-e Sunnat mosques and graveyards by the administration to the Barelvis.

Sunni Tahreek complains that the Deobandi and Ahl-e Hadith people have monopoly over the administration, government posts, and religious and government institutes. The representation of the Barelvi sect is minimal. It asserts that Ahl-e Sunnat cannot achieve their rights till they have adopted the ways of Ahl-e Hadith and Deobandi organisations.

It is to be noted here that Sunni Tahreek has adopted a conciliatory approach to MQM. Several important MQM workers are also members of Sunni Tahreek. According to Akram Qadri, 'Several Shias are also there in Sunni Tahreek which is proof of its being a non-sectarian formation.'

SUNNI TAHREEK AND SECTARIANISM

Right after its inception, Sunni Tahreek styled itself as a violent sectarian organisation and began to target Sipah Sahaba and Lashkar-e Tayyaba. It had a number of clashes with these two groups in Karachi, Hyderabad, Sahiwal (Punjab), and Nawab Shah in which seventeen Sunni Tahreek workers were killed. The total toll in these clashes was forty-seven. Sunni Tahreek's main targets were Ahl-e Hadith and Deobandi mosques. They maintain that earlier these were Ahl-e Sunnat mosques that were encroached upon.

OCCUPATION OF MOSQUES

Sunni Tahreek made its first show of strength on 18 December 1992 when it organised a rally at M A Jinnah Road in Karachi. The objective of this rally was to put pressure on the administration to hand over Masjid Noor (Ranchorh Line) to it. Soon the rally turned violent and cars were put to flame. Dozens of people were injured, and thirty-four Tahreek workers were arrested. After this incident, the Tahreek caught public attention, though earlier it had already demonstrated against Salahuddin, the editor of the weekly *Takbeer* (Karachi). After the rally, the Tahreek's movement for forceful occupation of Deobandi and Ahl-e Hadith mosques began in right earnest. It maintained that earlier all these mosques were under the supervision of Barelvi ulema. About Masjid Noor, its *khateeb*, Maulana Muhammad Amin said, 'This masjid was built by Maulana Shabbir Ahmad Usmani in 1948. Since then it has been a Deobandi mosque. Members of Sunni Tahreek have raided it several times, injuring more than thirty of our students. Several of our students were also kidnapped.'

After three months of the incident at Noor Masjid, members of Sunni Tahreek attacked Ibrahim Reza mosque in Burma Colony, Karachi. They claimed that it was a Barelvi mosque, though the imam of the mosque maintained that it had been a Deobandi mosque from its very inception. On 21 March 1992, members of Sunni Tahreek tried to occupy it forcefully. That led to a bloody clash in which Abdussalam, Sunni Tahreek's veteran member for sixteen years, was killed. Violent clashes spread in the area and the administration sealed the mosque.

After these two incidents, Sunni Tahreek increased the frequency of attacks on Deobandi and Ahl-e Hadith mosques in Punjab and Sindh. Aslam Qadri claims to have 'dethroned Maulanas of false beliefs from sixty-two mosques in ten years'.

ASSASSINATION OF SALIM QADRI

Salim Qadri was killed along with five others on 18 May

2001. Among the five were his nephew Hafiz Muhammad Anis, his sister's husband Altaf Husain, his driver Muhammad Abid Baloch, and the police guard Hafiz Raza. After this incident, sectarian clashes broke out in Karachi. Sipah Sahaba was blamed for this and Deobandi and Ahl-e Hadith madrasas and mosques were attacked. One of the killers of Salim Qadri was killed on the spot in the return fire and he was a member of the Sipah Sahaba. The Sunni Tahreek demanded of Home Minister Muinuddin Haider, to arrest the killers and started agitation throughout the country. When the killers were not arrested Sunni Tahreek declared that it would take revenge on its own. After a few days, terrorists killed the home minister's brother, Dr Ehtasham. In the beginning, Hizb Azeemat that had links with leaders of Sunni Tahreek accepted responsibility, but after investigations it was found that Lashkar-e Jhangvi was involved in the murder.

After the murder of Salim Qadri, Sunni Tahreek, rather than weakening, grew in strength in Karachi. Rigorous attempts are being made to spread its organisational network. According to Ibn Aas, columnist of the daily *Ummat*: 'The Tahreek has got a martyr now who will lead it from strength to strength.' The current amir of Sunni Tahreek said in an interview with *Zarb-e Islam* on 15 January 2002:

> The government stands between us and the killers (of Salim Qadri). Our government is totally ineffectual. It talks of eliminating terrorism but patronises these very forces. If the government had dealt with

terrorism strictly, the Home Minister would not have lost his brother.

ORGANISATIONAL STRUCTURE

The current amir of Sunni Tahreek is Maulana Abbas Qadri. Among its central leaders are Maulana Akram Qadri, Iftikhar Ahmad Bhati, Sarwat Ejaz, Qari Allama Khalilur Rahman, Maulana Ismail, Qari Riaz Said, and Maulana Abbas Reza al-Barui. Sunni Tahreek has no provincial structure. There are central leaders and there are divisional conveners who report directly to the central amir. The total number of divisional centres in Sindh, Baluchistan, and Punjab is fourteen. The central amir and other leaders look after the central secretariat.

THE AHL-E SUNNAT SECRETARIAT

The central secretariat of Sunni Tahreek is located in a massive building at the Baba-e Urdu Road in Karachi. This houses the offices of the central amir and other leaders. There is also the office of Ahl-e Sunnat Khidmat Committee which is engaged in building new mosques and madrasas in Karachi, Hyderabad, and Sindh. This committee has also established a hospital on a 2000 yards plot in Saidabad, Karachi. Several departments like ambulance centre, computer institute, students' assistance, jahez (dowry) fund, and food distribution programme are under the supervision of this committee. There is a mosque and a madrasa attached to the secretariat.

After the changed situation in Afghanistan, Abbas Qadri, leader of Sunni Tahreek, has begun collecting funds with *kashkool* (begging bowl) for assisting the Afghan people, that aroused the curiosity of the inhabitants of Karachi. The leaders have been able to collect funds worth more than one crore rupees through this method.

FINANCE

Barkati Foundation is the main source of funding for Sunni Tahreek. The Ahl-e Sunnat secretariat and Saidabad Hospital were funded by the Barkati Foundation. Apart from the monthly contribution from members, Milad Fund, Jahez Fund, and Tahaffuz Ahl-e Sunnat Fund contribute more than two crore rupees to the Sunni Tahreek coffers.

NETWORK

The network of Sunni Tahreek is spread out in fourteen divisions and districts of the country. However, Karachi is its nerve centre. After Karachi, it has important centres in Hyderabad, Sukkur, Nawab Shah, Multan, Bahawalpur, Lahore, Sahiwal, Mian Chunno, Sialkot, Rawalpindi, Gujrat, Quetta, and Jafarabad. Details of the network of Sunni Tahreek are given in Table XV.

MQM AND SUNNI TAHREEK

The English daily *The News* published a report on religious violence on 1 January 2002. According to this report, there is mutual cooperation between Sunni Tahreek and MQM (Muttahida Qaumi Movement). This cooperation began when, during Benazir Bhutto regime, Nasirullah Babar had started operation against MQM. To save themselves from being rounded up, a large number of MQM activists joined Sunni Tahreek. As for Sunni Tahreek, swelling of its ranks helped it mount attacks on Deobandis and Wahabis and occupy their mosques.

While working in Karachi, this fact was evident to me. I had the opportunity of meeting several Sunni Tahreek workers who were earlier associated with the MQM. They also accepted the fact that they joined Sunni Tahreek for fear of being arrested. Several of them are joint members of both Sunni Tahreek and MQM. They argue that MQM is a platform for political rights whereas Sunni Tahreek provides a platform for religious rights.

DISSENSIONS IN SUNNI TAHREEK

After the death of Salim Qadri, groupism has started in Sunni Tahreek. The reasons for dissension are as follows:

1. Forceful steps were not being taken for the arrest of Salim Qadri's killers.
2. Embezzlement of funds.
3. The leadership is monopolised by a caucus.

Saiful Islam

Several members of Tariq Road and Jacob Line broke away from Sunni Tahreek and formed this group in December 2001. Its leader is Maulana Aslam.

Sunni Ekjahti Forum

Several members of Sunni Tahreek from Thatha, Hyderabad and Karachi have formed this group.

Hizb Azeemat

This is an underground group. Who are there in this

group? No one knows for sure. However, the religious circles in Karachi maintain that it had links with Sunni Tahreek leaders.

Maulana Azhar Mushtaq, *khateeb* of a mosque in Karachi and a leader of Sunni Tahreek gave the following perspective on the issue of dissensions: 'Now, agencies (secret) have been given the task of weakening Sunni Tahreek. It is being divided into small groups to dilute its strength. But no such efforts will succeed, because those who are breaking away are of no importance. They got importance because of their attachment to the Tahreek. They are wrong if they think that each of them will become a Salim Qadri. Actually, they are the agents of MQM and Deobandis who had infiltrated into the Tahreek. Their departure will purify it.'

Table XV: *Sunni Tahreek's Network in Pakistan*

Sr. No.	District/Tehsil	Amir/Convener	Centre/Office
1.	Lahore	Abdul Sattar Qadri	Near Samanabad Road, Multan Road, Lahore
2.	Gujranwala	Hafiz Muhammad Qasim Zia	
3.	Gujrat	Muhammad Wasim Qadri	
4.	Faisalabad	Shadab Raza Mustafai	People's Colony, Faisalabad
5.	Multan	Choudhury Muhammad Khan Qadri	Jamia Islamia Khairil Ma'd, Qasim Fort, Multan
6.	Rawalpindi	Muhammad Sajjad Qadri	Near Jama Masjid, Lal Karni, Rawalpindi
7.	Qasoor	Dr Hafiz Muhammad Shahid Husain	

Sr. No.	District/Tehsil	Amir/Convener	Centre/Office
8.	Rahim Yar Khan	Hafiz Shafi Saidi	
9.	Attock	Dr Syed Wakil Ali Shah	
10.	Gujarkhan	Abdul Mannan	
11.	Toba tek Singh	Maulana Hamiduddin Rizvi	Noor Park, Toba tek Singh
12.	Lala Moosa	Allama Maqsood Zia Sialawi	
13.	Peshawar	Muhammad Inamullah Qadri	Jamia Imamia, Peshawar
14.	Dera Ismail Khan	Bilal Arish	
15.	Karachi		Baba-e Urdu Road, Karachi
16.	Hyderabad	Muhammad Khalid Qadri	Jamia Anwar Qadiriya, Hyderabad
17.	Nawab Shah	Abdur Rahim Qadri	Jamia Darul Uloom Ghausiya, Nawab Shah
18.	Sukkur	Maulana Noor Ahmad Qasmi	Jamia Ghausiya, Sukkur
19.	Larkana	Muhammad Nawaz Qasmi	
20.	Meerpur Khas	Muhammad Shahid	
21.	Thath	Manzoor Ahmad Qadri	
22.	Sakrand	Muhammad Tahir Qadri	
23.	Quetta	Sa'dullah Baruzai	

Pakistan Awami Tahreek

Pakistan Awami Tahreek has turned into a big political formation of Barelvi persuasion. Its chairman is Allama Tahir Qadri. It was born from Tahreek Minhajul Quran in 1993, and it remains a source of strength for Pakistan Awami Tahreek.

Tahreek Minhajul Quran

Tahreek Minhajul Quran was formed on 17 October 1981, with the following aims and objectives:

1. Reform of the Muslim community
2. Unity among Muslims
3. Revival of religion
4. Forums for preaching
5. Welfare of the common people
6. Spread of education and awareness
7. Implementation of Islam (in daily life)
8. Establishment of an Islamic Commonwealth

ORGANISATIONAL STRUCTURE

Tahreek Minhajul Quran is managed by an Executive Council whose chairman is Tahir Qadri. The following departments are working under it:

Preaching and Training

This department provides human resource to *tablighi* activities and the Tahreek.

Education

This is the most effective department of Tahreek Minhajul Quran. More than 1,000 schools in the country are being run by it. A madrasa, Jamia Islamia Minhajul Quran, has been established in Model Town, Lahore. It has 1,400 students. There is also a plan to establish a university there.

Press and Publication

It publishes the writings and speeches of Allama Tahir Qadri and sells them. It also deals with the media.

Construction
This department looks after the construction of Minhajul Quran schools throughout Pakistan. In Lahore it has several other construction projects.

Assemblies
This department organises assemblies that are addressed by Tahir Qadri.

Finance
This department looks after the funds collected from within the country and from abroad.

MINHAJUL QURAN SECRETARIAT

Minhajul Quran Secretariat has been built on 16 *kanals** of land that houses the offices of different departments. A sum of five-and-a-half crore rupees has already been spent on the construction of the secretariat.

MINHAJ CITY

Minhaj city has been established in Lahore on the style of Mansoora. It is managed by Minhajul Quran Housing Cooperative.

Pakistan Awami Tahreek is a political organisation that is going to take part in the October 2002, elections.

Lashkar-e Islam (Islamic Front)

Lashkar-e Islam has been merged with Islamic Front, an important jihadi organisation in Kashmir. Lashkar-e Islam was a known jihadi organisation of Barelvi persuasion that had begun to work very methodically. It was the only one among the Barelvi organisations to

---

* Measure of land like bigha, acre etc

have its own camp and organisational structure. Its amir is Allama Liaqat Azhari who had laid the foundation of Lashkar-e Islam in 1996, with support from Muhammad Amin Barkati, leading businessman of Karachi, Salim Qadri of Sunni Tahreek, Maulana Shah Ahmad Noorani of Jamiat Ulema Pakistan, and Maulana Ilyas Qadri of Dawat-e Islami.

Before formally announcing the formation of the organisation, its camp was established in Sohna in Azad Kashmir and its centre in Kotli. The famed spiritual figure of Kotli, Sahibzada Zahid Sadeeq agreed to become the patron. He stressed on the spiritual training of mujahideen to keep them on the right path. When the management was constituted, Liaqat Azhari became the amir of the organisation and Moosa Khan Lodhi became the supreme commander.

Islamic Front was founded in 1994. Earlier, it was known as Ikhwanul Muslimeen. A group of students had formed this after breaking away from JKLF. Its leader is Hilal Ahmad Beg who had already taken part in militant missions in Occupied Kashmir under the pseudonym, 'Kokapari'. Hilal Ahmad Beg is the brother of Farida Apa, a well-known leader and former parliamentarian of Occupied Kashmir. Islamic Front had claimed responsibility for an attack on a temple in Srinagar. Ikhwanul Muslimeen was also known for such activities.

ORGANISATIONAL STRUCTURE

In February 2000, the leadership of both Lashkar-e Islam and Islamic Front had a joint meeting in Kotli where they decided to merge. This meeting went on for two weeks. According to Lashkar-e Islam sources, the officers of ISI also took part in it. Some sessions were also held in Muzaffarabad and Islamabad. After mutual consultation, Allama Liaqat Azhari was appointed the chief secretary, and Hilal Ahmad Beg was appointed supreme commander. It was decided that the organisation will be called Islamic Front and it will be structured on military lines. Allama Liaqat Azhari was made the secretary of communication in Pakistan with the responsibility of building a set-up for raising material and human resources, whereas the Islamic Front (with the earlier management) will further strengthen its network in Occupied Kashmir.

NETWORK

Lashkar-e Islam, which will be now called Islamic Front, has its network in Azad Kashmir, particularly in Kotli, Khuiratta, Meerpur, and Bhambar. Its central liaison office is in Rawalpindi. In the beginning, it was decided that the branches would be opened throughout the country. However, in April 2001, all other units except those in Karachi and Rawalpindi were closed, so that it could be projected as a jihadi organisation of Kashmiris. But several Pakistani youths from Sunni Tahreek and ATI have already received training from the camp of Lashkar-e Islam, and the trend is still continuing.

SOHNA CAMP

The camp of Lashkar-e Islam (now, Islamic Front) is located in Sohna, Azad Kashmir. Islamic Front had a base camp in Keel Sector. In other words, it has two camps now. Shahid, a twenty-year old youth from

Hyderabad, Sindh, told me in Sohna that he had arrived there for military training and he was associated with Dawat-e Islami. He said that he had studied up to the middle school, and worked in a tailoring shop in Hyderabad. He was drawn towards jihad because of a jihadi assembly that was held there. 'When it was announced that those who wanted to join jihad might give in their names, I offered myself. I have two more brothers and a sister. My father, who is an experienced tailor, did not create much fuss in giving me permission. I had promised him that after jihadi training I would return home. But the atmosphere here is such that I don't feel like returning (home).' About the atmosphere in the camp, he said that it was very cordial, that everyone helped one another, and if anyone committed any wrong, he was immediately punished.

IMPORTANT LEADERS

Muhammad Amin Barkati (patron)
The famous businessman, and the chairman of Barkati Foundation, Muhammad Amin Barkati, is among the richest men in Pakistan. Barkati Foundation provides substantial funds to Barelvi organisations like Dawat-e Islami, Sunni Tahreek, and Jamiat Ulema Pakistan (Noorani). He is the patron of Islamic Front (erstwhile Lashkar-e Islam), and has funded the camp in Sohna.

Allama Liaqat Azhari
Allama Liaqat Husain Azhari is now the chief secretary of Islamic Front and the deputy chairman, Muttahida Jihad Council. He belongs to Shahpur village, Poonch, in Occupied Kashmir. After the incidents in 1989, his family migrated to Pakistan and settled down in

Karachi. Allama Liaqat Azhari had taken initiation (spiritual) from the hands of Dawat-e Islam's Maulana Ilyas Qadri, and established Lashkar-e Islam on his advice. Azhari claims that he and his organisation are non-sectarian; he is accorded honour by Deobandi Ahl-e Hadith jihadi organisations too.

Hilal Ahmad Beg

Hilal Ahmad Beg is from a well-known political family of Srinagar. His sister, Farida Apa, is working for Dukhtaran-e Millat. Hilal Ahmad is known for his militant activities.

Sunni Jihad Council (Al-Barq)

Sunni Jihad Council is regarded as a representative jihadi organisation of Barelvi persuasion. In Kashmir, it has merged with Al-Barq. But in Pakistan, Sunni Jihad Council will continue to work to gain support for its jihadi stand.

BACKGROUND

Sunni Jihad Council was founded by Pir Muhammad Said Ahmad Mujaddidi in 1997 in Jamat Al-Dawa. Its objective was the participation of Barelvi sect in the jihad in Kashmir and diluting the strength of Deobandi and Ahl-e Hadith jihadi organisations working there. According to Said Ali Reza, Supreme Commander of the organisation:

> It is regrettable that some people have tried to spread their false beliefs on the pretext of jihad in Kashmir. They have even torched shrines and tried to occupy mosques. This is a conspiracy against Muslims. We know how to defend territorial as well as religious

borders. God willing, Kashmir will be freed by Sunni Jihad Council, because it is a representative platform for the majority of Muslims.

Dawat Tanzeem Islam, monthly, March 1999

ORGANISATIONAL STRUCTURE

Pir Mujaddidi is the central secretary of Sunni Jihad Council. The central amir is Sahibzada Pir Muhammad Atiqur Rahman. After its merger into Al-Barq in Kashmir, Nazim Farooq Quraishi will be the secretary of the militant wing. Other office bearers are as follows:

Deputy Amir   Allama Mufti Muhammad Arif Naqshbandi (Kotli)
Secretary, Finance Allama Talib Husain Mujaddidi
Secretary, Jihad   Allama Tahir Reza Qadri
Chief Commander   Sahibzada Syed Ali Reza Bukhari

Another institute called Alami Idarah Tanzeemul Islam is affiliated to Sunni Jihad Council that helps it in its management.

Merger of Mujahideen Lashkar Mustafa

Mujahideen Lashkar Mustafa which was a small jihadi formation merged in Sunni Jihad Council in June 1999. The central leaders of Lashkar Mustafa, under the leadership of Allama Nasir Reza Qadri, declared its merger in Sunni Jihad Council in Meerpur. This merger strengthened Sunni Jihad Council and the news was published prominently, though a small group of Lashkar Mustafa stayed away from the merger.

Madrasas of Sunni Jihad Council

Sunni Jihad Council has established madrasas in different refugee camps in Azad Kashmir. Its madrasas at Gulpur and Sohalnan have already started working. They have provisions for the study of the Holy Koran and elementary education. The expenses are borne by Sunni Hurriyat Council, UK.

NETWORK

Sunni Jihad Council has greater control over the management of organisation than on militant programmes. It has opened its branches throughout Punjab, particularly in the districts of Gujranwala, Sialkot, Gujrat, Bahawalpur, and Bhawalnagar that provide human resource to the council. In Sindh, its units are there in Hyderabad and Karachi, but they are not very active. The details of the network of Sunni Jihad Council are presented in Table XVI.

Affiliation with Al-Barq

Sunni Jihad Council borrowed military expertise from Al-Barq and entrusted to it the responsibility of launching its mujahideen in Occupied Kashmir on payment basis. Al-Barq is the jihadi wing of the political party, People's League in Occupied Kashmir. Sunni Jihad Council also declared Al-Barq to be its jihadi wing, while Al-Barq treated the Council as one of its supporting organisations.

However, a time came when this mutual relationship soured. The reason for this is the following incident which was recounted by an important member of the

Sunni Jihad Council in Lahore: Sunni Jihad Council made a contract with a commander of Al-Barq to train its mujahideen in Gujranwala (rather than in the camp) and arrange for their launching so that the council could take part directly in militant missions in Occupied Kashmir. The commander charged four and a half lakh rupees, and the entire amount was to be paid in advance. The money was duly paid. After a month, the council received complaints from some young mujahideen against the commander. Rather than replying to the complaints, the commander ran away along with a number of mujahideen. He reappeared on the scene after a year. The leadership of Al-Barq refused to accept responsibility on the plea that Sunni Jihad Council had not taken them into confidence when they had made the contract with the commander. After this, Sunni Jihad Council began to make efforts to start its own camp.

The two formations came together again in 2000, and in February 2002 they had a mutual contract for military activities.

Sohna Camp, Azad Kashmir

Sunni Jihad Council established its own training camp in Sohna in August 2000. However, it does not look like a training camp. The *khateeb* of Sohna Jama Masjid, Allama Hafiz Muhammad Shafi Siddiqi is the patron of this camp. The mujahideen of Sunni Jihad Council are receiving training from an Al-Barq commander. The Islamic Front also helps in the training of these mujahideen.

FINANCE

The main source of funding for Sunni Jihad Council is the Hurriyat Council, UK, whose chief secretary is Maulana Muhammad Sadiq Zia. He is from Kotli. His brother Maqbool Husain Zia, and his siter's husband Choudhury Shah Muhammad were killed in a violent incident in July 2000. A Deobandi jihadi organisation was blamed for this. It used to exert pressure on the two gentlemen for funds from Sunni Hurriyat Council. This incident happened after they refused funds. The daily *Nawa-e Waqt*, Lahore, published a press release on this incident on 25 July 2000. The following is the text of this press release:

> All Jammu and Kashmir Sunni Jihad Council organised a condolence meeting under the chairmanship of Allama Sahibzada Muhammad Hamid Raza (Sialkot). In the meeting, *fateha* was read for Maqbool Husain Reza, brother of Allama Sadiq Zia, Sunni Hurriyat Council, UK, and for a close relative Choudhury Shah Muhammad. They had been killed by a group of terrorists in the Muthrani village, Kotli, and their corpses were thrown into water. The people present in the meeting expressed their anger and sorrow at this gruesome incident. They said that some well-known terrorists who are the agents of RAW, are spreading violence in the guise of mujahideen. They are doing it to defame the real mujahideen and stall the process of independence in Kashmir. The people present in the meeting made a strong plea with the governments of Azad Kashmir and Pakistan to institute an independent inquiry into the incident so that the criminals are arrested and given exemplary punishment.

Sunni Hurriyat Council raises funds from UK and other European countries for Sunni Jihad Council. Sunni Jihad Council's own department of finance is also quite active in raising funds. A sum of about forty lakh rupees is raised every year for the jihad fund.

Table XVI: *Sunni Jihad Council*

Lahore	Muhammad Umar Qureshi	Swami Nagar, St 6, Tezab Ahata, Lahore
Sialkot	Sahibzada Muhammad Hamid Raza	Jamia Hanfiya, Do Darwaza, Sialkot
Gujrat	Allama Qadri Liaqat Ali	Darul Uloom Ziaul Quran, Bokan Sharif, Gujrat
Daska	Mufti Husaniuddin Naqshbandi	
Haroonabad	Faryad Ali	
Khariyan	Syed Zainul Abedin Shah	
Rawalpindi	Sahibzada Muhammad Ali Raza	Idarah Talimat Islamia, Sector 3, Khayaban Sir Syed, Rawalpindi
Multan	Maulana Muhammad Sadiq Sairabi	Jamia Islamia Khairul Muad, Fort Kuhna Qasim, Multan
Bahawalpur	Sardar Aftab Ahmad Khan	Jama Masjid Sairani, Bahawalpur
Karachi	Allama Asif Husain Ziai (provincial amir)	Jamia Naimiya, Federal B area, Karachi
Hyderabad	Dr Muhammad Zubair Mujaddidi	Markazi Jama Masjid, Hyderabad
Muzaffarabad	Khwaja Muhammad Dar	Upper Chattar, Muzaffarabad
Meerpur	Allama Muhammad Bashir Ahmad Mustafwi	Near Al-Jabeer Hotel, Meerpur
Rawlakot	Commander Shahid Khan	Near Lorry Adda, Rawlakot
Kotli	Allama Qari Mahmood Ahmad Tabassum	Near Shaeed Chowk, Kotli
Gujranwala	Allama Talib Husain Mujaddidi	Markazi Jama Masjid Naqshbandiya, B Block, Model Town, Gujranwala

Tahreek Jihad, Jammu and Kashmir

The name Tahreek Jihad Jammu and Kashmir was first heard during the Kargil war. Thirty of Tahreek Jihad's mujahideen died in the Kargil front. It was born in 1997 out of the merger of Ansar al-Islam and Al-Barq. Al-Barq, however, maintained its separate identity, whereas many members of Ansar al-Islam (a big organisation of Barelvi persuasion) joined Tahreek Jihad.

Tahreek Jihad has its affiliation with Abdul Ghani Bhat's party, Muslim Conference, the majority of whose members are of Barelvi persuasion. Tahreek Jihad also styles itself as a Barelvi organisation and raises funds and human resource on this basis.

ORGANISATIONAL STRUCTURE

The organisational structure of Tahreek Jihad, Jammu and Kashmir is not strong. Only two of its departments are active: military department that looks after the camp at Dongi in Kotli district; and the department of management that looks after finance, press and publication, jihadi preaching, and gathering human resource.

Major (Retd) Tariq Zul-Qarnain is the central amir. It is said that he had been associated with ISI, and looks after the management of the organisation. Ashfaq Ahmad Bharwal is the supreme commander and is in charge of Kotli camp. Tahreek Jihad, Jammu and Kashmir calls itself 111 Brigade. Its responsibility is to carry out missions in the tehsils of Surankot, Mendhar, Naoshehra, and Badhal.

NETWORK

The network of Tahreek Jihad is not very wide (see

Table XVII). It has its branches in Kotli and Meerpur districts in Azad Kashmir, as also in Gujrat and Khanewal in Punjab. It raises its manpower from these areas. Small Barelvi jihadi formations like Tanzeemul Arifin and Shiran-e Islam also contribute human and material resources to it. The mujahideen of these two organisations receive their training from Tahreek Jihad's camp and then get launched in Occupied Kashmir.

MILITARY STRENGTH

According to Tahreek Jihad's mouthpiece, *Al-Khatim* (October 2001), the number of its martyrs in Occupied Kashmir has gone beyond a thousand, though the facts are to the contrary. The total number of martyrs of its parent organisations, Al-Barq and Ansar al-Islam, does not add up to this number. According to Commander Sajid, a member of Tahreek Jihad in Meerpur, fifteen of Tahreek Jihad mujahideen were killed in Occupied Kashmir in 2000 and twenty-five in 2001.

Apart from its role in the Kargil War, Tahreek Jihad had also led missions on Indian army posts in Poonch and Surankot.

Table XVII: *Tahreek Jihad, Jammu and Kashmir*

Muzaffarabad	Tariq Zul-Qarnain	Chahla Bandi, Muzaffarabad, Azad Kashmir
Kotli	Ashfaq Ahmad Bharwal	Gali, Kotli
Nakyal		Commander Taimur Shaheed Markaz, Badawa Chowk, Sector Nakyal
Dongi (camp)	Subedar Ahmad Ilmuddin Ghazi	Zulfiqar Haider Mansooh camp, Near Dongi, District Kotli
Meerpur	Muhammad Shakil Mujahid	Chungi No. 4, Meerpur, Ph: 33579

Gujrat	Ajmal Bhat Qadri	i. Milad Chowk, Kotla Arbab Ali Khan, Gujrat, Ph: 57695
Gujrat		ii. Khalil Qadri Shaheed, Markaz Awan Sharif, Gujrat
Gujrat		iii. Kadia Nawala, Gujrat, Ph: 585125
Gujrat		iv. Ghulam Mustafa Attari Shaheed Markaz Kashmir Nagar Jadalior, Gujrat
Gujranwala	Ehsanullah	Zafar Iqbal, near Markaz Naoshehra Darkan, Gujranwala
Khanewal		Commander Syed Safdar Ali Markaz, Behind Mirror Factory, Khanewal Town
Mian Chunno		Bahar Madina Masjid, Mahalla Masoodabad, Mian Chunno
Tandowala Yar	Muhammad Iqbal Tahri	Nagori Plot, Tandowala Yar (Sindh)
Hyderabad		Shahi Bazar, Hyderabad, Ph: 860811

Harkat-e Inqilab Islami

Harkat-e Inqilab Islami is a small jihadi organisation of Barelvi persuasion whose activities in Occupied Kashmir are very limited. Its main leader is Khalid Mahmood Qadri from Alipur Chatt, Gujranwala district. He has established a few branches of Harkat-e Inqilab Islami in some districts of Punjab.

Qadri had formed this organisation in 1998. In 2001, Harkat-e Inqilab Islami built its central office in Muzaffarabad. But the government of Azad Kashmir is trying to do away with small organisations, Harkat-e Inqilab Islami being one of them. Its office in Muzaffarabad was sealed on 17 January 2002. But Qadri is not ready for merger with any other organisation.

Harkat-e Inqilab Islami has set up Al-Raza (trust) to raise funds. Its central office is located in Kabir Street, Urdu bazar, Lahore. In 2000, Al-Raza raised twenty-five lakh rupees for its jihadi fund. Different branches of Harkat-e Inqilab Islami are listed in Table XVIII.

Table XVIII: *Harkat-e Inqilab Islami Branches*

District/Tehsil	Secretary/Convener	Centre/Office
Lahore	Khalid Mahood Qadri	Nomania Building, Texali Gate, Lahore
Gujranwala		Maktab al-ilm Wal-Irshad, Alipur Chatta, Gujranwala
Mianwali	Malik Muhammad Zubair	Jamia Akbariya, Mianwali
Chishtiyan	Nasir Mahmood Qadri	Chowk Urdu Bazar, Chashtiyan
Sadiqabad	Yusuf Chisti	Asthana Alia Chishtiya Nizamiya, Nizamabad, Sadiqabad
Multan	Maulana Muhammad Salim Chishti	Bazar Chaorhi Sarai Multan
Bhawalnagar	Maulana Meher Raza	
Muzaffarabad		Chehla Bandi, Muzaffarabad, Azad Kashmir
Bahawalpur	Salim Husain	

Ababeel Mujahideen Alami

This jihadi organisation was founded in Lahore in November 1998 by Choudhury Himayat Ali. Among other founder members were Muhammad Iqbal Mujaddidi, Nadeem Malik, and Ghulam Mustafa. They were the former office bearers of the Barelvi Students' organisation, Anjuman Tulaba Islam (ATI), and they supported Jamiat Ulema Pakistan (Noorani Group). The background of this organisation is said to be the growing influence of Deobandi and Ahl-e Hadith jihadi organisations in Occupied Kashmir that had led to sectarian clashes there. The founders of Ababeel Mujahideen Alami felt that since the majority of people in Occupied Kashmir are Barelvis, the leadership of jihad should be in the hands of this sect. To put his organisation on firm footing, Choudhury Himayat Ali made a close study of jihadi organisations and their methods. With this end in view, he participated in the assemblies of Lashkar-e Tayyaba and went to Afghanistan for training. After returning from there he laid the foundation of Ababeel Mujahideen Alami and began to send youths to Kashmir for jihad. For training and launching, Ababeel Mujahideen Alami has no front of its own. In the beginning, it had a contract with Al-Barq for training of its mujahideen. Later, it established links with Tahreek Jihad. Himayat Ali wanted to build a training camp for the mujahideen of Ababeel Mujahideen Alami because most of the training camps were under the control of different sectarian groups and they harassed Barelvi youths. On 31 August 1999, Himayat Ali entered Kashmir through Poonch sector along with four Pakistani and four Kashmiri youths. A couple of kilometres inside Kashmir they were all attacked and killed. According to newspaper reports, they had killed thirty-three Indian army personnel, but one of his close friends told me that other jihadi groups were alarmed by the growing strength of Ababeel Mujahideen and Himayat Ali was killed because of their betrayal.

Ababeel Mujahideen Alami also claims to have sent mujahideen to the Kargil front. December 1999 issue of the monthly, *Kanz al-Iman* records: 'According to the report of secret agencies, when the mujahideen returned from Kargil, the Ababeel mujahideen outnumbered all other groups. If some group had twenty members, others had fifteen or twenty-five.

But Ababeel mujahideen had seventy-five.'
Currently, the central chief secretary of Ababeel
Mujahideen Alami is Iqbal Mujaddidi. Its network is
present in Lahore, Multan, Gujranwala, Pakpatan, Okara,
and Muzaffarabad (see Table XIX). It does not have its
own means of training and launching the mujahideen.
The number of its martyrs has exceeded 100.

Table XIX: *Branches of Ababeel Mujahideen Alami*

Sr. No.	District/ Tehsil	Secretary	Office/Centre
1.	Lahore	Javed Iqbal Mustafa	Jama Masjid Madina, Ravi Road, Lahore
2.	Gujranwala	Ghulam Mustafa	
3.	Sialkot	Zahid Sulahri	Jamia Hanfiya, Darwaza Sialkot
4.	Qasoor	Tahir Javed Awan	
5.	Deepalpur	Maulana Munawwar Husain	
6.	Okara	Farid Owais	Jamia Islamia Ashraful Madaris, Okara
7.	Sahiwal	Ghulam Nabi Wad	Madrasa Anwar Faridiya, Sahiwal
8.	Pakpatan	Muhammad Said Chishti	Jamia Usmania Faridiya, Pakpatan
9.	Naoshehra Darkan	Ahsan Sethi	

Ansar al-Islam

Till 1995, Ansar al-Islam had been one of the
important jihadi organisations in Occupied Kashmir.
But gradually it faded out. It suffered the greatest blow
when Ashfaq Ahmad Bharwal joined Tahreek Jihad
with a majority of its members. It has a kind of
disjointed structure in Meerpur only.

Jamiat Ansar Mujahideen al-Alami

The chief commander of this formation is Abdur Rahman Kashmiri. It had participated in some missions along with other jihadi organisations in Jammu sector. But it did not receive any help from Pakistan and Azad Kashmir. Now it is confined to Meerpur, and provides guides to jihadi organisations.

Tanzeemul Arifin

Tanzeemul Arifin was established in 1991. Hazrat Sultan Bahu's disciples and other Barelvi youths have been its members. Its leader is Sahibzada Sultan Muhammad Ali.

Its role in Occupied Kashmir is minimal. Usually, it contributes material and human resources to other jihadi organisations. Its central office is located in Kotli. It had also strong presence in Jhang and Shorkot. Efforts are afoot to merge it in Al-Barq or Islamic Front.

Lashkar Mustafa

This is a small jihadi formation of Barelvi persuasion, a big chunk of which had already joined Sunni Jihad Council. Major (Retd) Yaqoob Saifi is its leader. It is facing extinction. The only way open to it is to join some bigger formation.

Sheeran-e Islam

This formation was founded in 1995. Shujat Ali Mujahid is its leader. It had no presence in Occupied Kashmir. Its network was limited to a few districts in Punjab. In practical terms, it has already been banned.

Alami Idarah Tanzeemul Islam

The founder of Alami Idarah Tanzeemul Islam was Muhammad Said Ahmad who was the *khateeb* of Markazi Jama Masjid Naqshbandiya at Gujranwala. He is also the chief secretary of Sunni Jihad Council. His son, Muhammad Rafiq Amjad Mujaddidi, is the amir of Tanzeemul Islam. The main objective of this organisation is to bring about a spiritual revolution through the ways of Ahl-e Sunnat, and establish links with Islamic movements in different parts of the world.

Jamia Tanzeemul Islam has been established at Gujranwala under the aegis of Alami Idarah Tanzeemul Islam. The offices of the organisation and those of Sunni Jihad Council will be shifted there. Its network is confined to Gujranwala, Gujrat, Khariyan, and Jhelum.

Sipah Mustafa, Pakistan

This organisation was formed in 1989 in Jhang. Its leader is Allama Allahbakhsh Nayyar. Its objective is to protect the rights of the Barelvi sect. When the clashes between Sipah Sahaba and Shia organisations were at its height, this organisation came on the scene to register the presence of Barelvi sect. Sipah Mustafa declared its alienation from Deobandi and Shia organisations. However, its intense hostility was reserved only for Sipah Sahaba.

Sipah Mustafa tried to establish its network in the towns of Punjab, but was not successful. It was further weakened after the formation of Sunni Tahreek. Now, it is confined to Faisalabad and Jhang.

Alami Dawat-e Islamia

This is a non-political formation that works only on the *tablighi* front. It establishes links among the disciples of Hazrat Sultan Bahu. Sahibzada Fayazul Hasan Qadri is its leader. Its central office is located in Thokar, Niaz Beg, Lahore.

This organisation has never endeavoured to establish a formal network at district or local levels, even though its members are spread throughout the country. However, Tanzeemul Arifin, its affiliated jihadi organisation has its branches in several districts of Punjab and Azad Kashmir.

Sunni Ulema Council

The amir of Sunni Ulema Council is Maulana Nazakat Husain. The aim of the council is to unite Sunni ulema on a single platform. However, it is not a very active organisation.

Jamiat Al-Mashaikh

The leader of Jamiat Al-Mashaikh is Pir Fazal Haq. It is active on the political front, but does not have enough clout to win elections. It plays a certain role in the formation of various united fronts involving religious and political organisations. Its presence is confined to a few areas of Mardan and Dera Ismail Khan.

Caravan-e Islam

The leader of this organisation is Mufti Muhammad Khan Qadri who is the former president of ATI. Its objectives are non-sectarian. Its central office is in Jamia Islamia, Islamia Park, Lahore.

Sawad Azam Ahl-e Sunnat

Its leader is Maulana Kaokab Noorani. There is also a Deobandi organisation bearing the same name which is more active than its Barelvi counterpart. The latter is active only in Karachi, Lahore, Okara, Sahiwal, and Checha Watani.

Ulema Mashaikh Council

Its leader is Maulana Ayaz Zaheer Hashmi. It is not an effective organisation.

Mustafai Tahreek

The objective of this organisation is to protect the mosques and graveyards of Barelvi sect. Its leader is Ghulam Murtaza Saidi. Its central office is located in Mochi Gate, Lahore.

Jamat Riza Mustafa

It is a small organisation whose patrons are Maulana Abu Dawood and Haji Muhammad Said. Its central office is in Gujranwala.

Anjuman Fidayan-e Mustafa, Pakistan

Anjuman Fidayan-e Mustafa is a religious organisation of Barelvi youths. Its central president is Allama Syed Saleh Hashmi. According to its brochure, its objectives are promotion of Ahl-e Sunnat school of thought and establishment of Barelvi madrasas and libraries in the country. It is a non-political organisation which has its presence in the mosques in Punjab. It organises religious events and rituals throughout the year. Its organisational details are given in Table XX:

Table XX: *Organisational Details of Anjuman Fidayan-e Mustafa*

Position	Name	Address
Chief Patron	Sahibzada Saidul Hasan Shah	Zeb Asthana Alia Chiraghia, Walton, Lahore
Patron and Chairman, General Assembly	Dr Syed Mufti Najib Ahmad Hashmi	Sialkot
Central Chairman	Allama Syed Saleh Muhammad Shah Hashmi	Zeb Asthana Alia, Targ Sharif, Mianwali District
Senior Deputy Chairman	Hafiz Muhammad Ashiq Chishti	Shekhupura District
Deputy Chairman	Sahibzada Fayaz Ahmad Owaisi	Bahawalpur
Founder and Secretary General	Hafiz Muhammad Akbar Jatoi	District Muzaffargarh
Joint Secretary	Master Syed Abdul Ghafoor Shah	Bahawalpur
Joint Secretary	Syed Pir Baharshah Bukhari	Sargodha
Finance Secretary	Muhammad Ilyas Qadri	Khariyan, District Gujrat
Secretary, Communications	Syed Mahmoodul Hasan Shah	Arif Wal-Azlah, Pakpatan
Editor (Tarjuman Fidayan Mustafa)	Hafiz Muhammad Ashraf Raza	Rahwali, District Gujranwala

Anjuman Tulaba Islam

It is a representative organisation of Barelvi students, whose network is spread out among a number of educational institutions. However, dissensions in Jamiat Ulema Islam have led to groupism in this organisation too. The largest group supports Maulana Shah Ahmad Noorani. Its centre is Islamia University, Bahawalpur.

Anjuman Naojawanan-e Islam

This is an organisation for those active members who have grown out of Anjuman Tulaba Islam and are now entering their profession. In other words, it is linked with ATI. It has also split into two groups. The group led by Tariq Mahboob is more active and supports Maulana Shah Ahmad Noorani.

Tahreek Tahaffuz Khatm Nabuwat

Tahreek Tahaffuz Khatm Nabuwat is a Barelvi organisation formed to oppose the Qadianis. Its patron is Ahmad Shah Noorani, and the chairman is Sardar Muhammad Khan al-Ghari. Its central office is located at Jamia Jalaliya Mazhar Islam, Siraj Park, Lahore. It is not a very effective organisation.

Tanzeemul Mashaikh Ahl-e Sunnat

Tanzeemul Mashaikh Ahl-e Sunnat is a big organisation of the spiritual figures and *Pirs* of Ahl-e Sunnat persuasion. Its main centre is in Frontier Province while its branches exist in all the provinces of Pakistan.

This organisation has also split into two. The bigger group is led by Dr Khalid Reza Zakori. The second group is led by Riazul Hasan Qadri who has the support of Sultan Bahu's disciples. The activities of this group are confined to Jhang, Sharkot, and Lahore.

Tanzeem Mashaikh Azzam, Pakistan

This organisation was formed in 2000 in Faisalabad by Masood Ahmad Siddiqi. Its mouthpiece, *La-sani Inqilab* (November 2001) claims that it has big networks in Karachi and Lahore, and the number of members has already exceeded 2000. Of them, more than 200 are saints and *Pirs* of different spiritual ways.

Aims and Objectives

The above journal also describes the aims and objectives of the organisation:

> The foremost objective of Tanzeem Mashaikh Azzam, Pakistan, is to promote spiritualism and Islam, and remove difficulties that might come in the way. The aim of this world organisation is to free people from narrow, sectarian thoughts link them to the true bond of Islam and bring about a spiritual revolution. Through such efforts people will be aware of the true teachings of Islam and realise that in this epoch of political, religious and linguistic chauvinism, this organisation brings the message of peace and harmony.

Chapter XII
SHIA ORGANISATIONS AND GROUPS

In Pakistan, a total of twenty-three Shia organisations and groups are working. Of them, three take part in politics and elections, ten have been involved in sectarian clashes, and two are *tablighi* in nature. There are three jihadi and one educational organisations as well.

Tahreek-e Ja'fariya is regarded as the representative Shia organisation which has already split into several groups. Four organisations are exclusively composed of Shia ulema and they address their concerns. There are innumerable groups for *zikr* and mourning, but they are beyond the purview of our study. The background to the growth of Shia organisations in Pakistan is as follows:

The first All-Pakistan Shia Convention was held in 1953 under the aegis of Idarah Tahaffuz Huqooq Shia. It had made a charter of demands for protecting the rights of Shias. After Shia-Sunni clashes broke out in 1963, the All-Pakistan Shia Ulema Conference was held in 1964 and these demands were reiterated. A Shia Demands Committee led by Syed Muhammad Dehlawi was formed. During the Bhutto regime, this committee remained very active. Topping the list of demands were introduction of separate courses of Islamic Studies for Shia students and Shia Wakf laws, etc. This was the period of Iranian revolution. The

Shia youths of Pakistan were influenced by this and they established links with it. Several Shia organisations were formed in colleges and universities. All of them came together on the platform of Imamia Students Organisation (ISO) on 22 May 1972. Besides being the representative Shia students' organisation, ISO slowly came to be regarded as one of the most powerful organisations of the Shias in Pakistan.

Meanwhile, several other Shia organisations had come on the scene, but their impact was limited. According to Tasleem Reza Khan, an ex-leader of ISO:

> At that time there were three Shia organisations on the scene – All-Pakistan Shia Conference, Idarah Tahaffuz Huqooq Shia, and Shia Political Party. Muzaffar Khan Qazalbash was the leader of All-Pakistan Shia Conference who acted according to the wishes of the government of the time and some ulema made fun of him because of this. Similarly, Idarah Tahaffuz Huqooq Shia (Forum for Protection of the Rights of the Shias) was alluded to as 'Tahaffuz Huqooq Shikam' (Protection of Rights of Belly). They spread the propaganda that there was a youth organisation whose lifespan wouldn't be more than that of a dewdrop.
>
> *Safeer Inqilab* by Tasleem Raza Khan

ISO worked along with Shia Demands Committee, but these demands were not fulfilled. On 6 July 1977, General Ziaul Haq imposed martial law, and declared implementation of Nizam-e Mustafa on the demands of Qaumi Ittihad. The Shia position on this issue is articulated as follows:

As all the religious organisations which were a part of Qaumi Ittihad pertained to 'Fiqh Hanfi', Ziaul Haq structured Nizam-e Mustafa on it. It was not acceptable to us. The Shias had no objection to Nizam-e Mustafa; rather, it was their long-standing wish. But they did not want their *Fiqh* (jurisprudence) replaced by some other system. The Shias had demanded that after the imposition of Islamic system in the country, every group should be governed by its own *Fiqh*.

Safeer Inqilab

At that time, the famous scholar, Mufti Jafar Husain was the member of Islami Nazariyati Council. He resigned from the council on this issue, and started a movement against the government from the platform of Wafaq Ulema Shia, Pakistan. To take a clear stand on the issue All-Pakistan Shia Convention was held in Bhakkar on 13 April 1979, where the foundation of Tahreek Nifaz Fiqh Jafariya was laid and Mufti Jafar Husain was made its leader. Meanwhile, Ziaul Haq announced the *Zakah O Ashar* ordinance and the Tahreek Nifaz Fiqh Jafariya announced a convention in Islamabad on 5 July 1989, to oppose it. As a consequence of this convention, the government and Tahreek Nifaz Fiqh Jafariya made the 'Islamabad Pact' according to which the Shias were exempted from the purview of the ordinance.

Tahreek Nifaz Fiqh Jafariya became the representative organisation of the Shias. All the Shia organisations that appeared later were born from the womb of Tahreek Nifaz Fiqh Jafariya or ISO. Table XXI lists all the Shia organisations in Pakistan.

Table XXI: *Shia Organisations in Pakistan*

Sr. No.	Organisation/ Group	Amir/Secretary/ President	Founded	Nature	Central Office
1.	Tahreek-e Ja'fariya (banned)	Allama Sajid Naqvi	1979	Political/ sectarian	Jamia-Al-Muntazir, H Block, Model Town, Lahore
2.	Tahreek Nifaz Fiqh Jafriya	Allama Hamid Mausoodi	1984	Political/ sectarian	Ali Masjid, Satellite Town, Rawalpindi
3.	Pasban-e-Islam		1989	Sectarian (Underground activities)	
4.	Shuba Political Party	Peer Nau Bahar Shah	do	Political	Lahore
5.	Tahreek Tahaffuz Haqooq Shia	Hafiz Riyaz Hussain		Sectarian	Jamia-Al-Muntazir, H Block, Model Town, Lahore
6.	Tahreek-e-Haqooq-e-Ja'fariya	Mushtaq Hussain Jafri	1990	Do	740, Q Block Flats, Model Town, Lahore
7.	Hizbul Jihad	Agha Murtaza Poya	do	Political	Merged in Pakistan Awami Tahreek
8.	Alami Majlis Ahl-e-Bait	Mohsin Ali Najafi	do		Post Box No. 1613, Islamabad
9.	Sipah Muhammad	Allama Rai Jafar Raza	1990	Sectarian	Thokar Niaz Beg, Lahore
10.	Majlis Tanzeem-ul-Islam	Maulana Syed Abul Hasan Naqvi		*Tablighi/* social	27-B, Buoy Shah Road, Near Sabri Masjid, Sandakalan, Lahore

Sr. No.	Organisation/ Group	Amir/Secretary/ President	Founded	Nature	Central Office
11.	Tanzeem Ghulaman Al-e-Imran	Al-Haj Muhammad Iqbal Hira		Sectarian/ reformist	Lahore
12.	Tahreek Ikhwat Islami	Allama Inayat Ali Shakir		Ittihad Bainul Muslimeen	Lahore
13.	Majlis Amal Ulema Shia	Allama Muhammad Hasnain Al-Sabqi		Ittihad Bainul Muslameen	Lake Road, Anarkali, Lahore
14.	Hizbul Mumineen		1991	Jihadi	Muzaffarabad
15.	Ali Tigers		1991	Jihadi	Muzaffarabad
16.	Khomeini Tigers		1991	Jihadi	Muzaffarabad
17.	Azadaari Council	Syed Ali Raza Gardeezi	1991		Multan
18.	Imamiya Students Organisation	Agha Hasan Qazalbash	1972	Sectarian	5/A, Muslim Town Morh, Lahore
19.	Jamiat Tulaba-e-Jafriya		1972	do	
20.	Shia Supreme Council	Ghazi Abdullah Jin	1972	do	Dera Ismail Khan
21.	Imamiya Organisation		1976	do	36, Haider Road, Islamic Centre Islampura, Lahore
22.	Imammeens		1999	do	Lahore
23.	Anjuman-e-Wazeefa Sadaat Momineen	Syed Iftikhar Hussain Jafri	1999	do	Lahore
24.	Tahreek Wehdat Milli	Syed Abbas Raza Moosavi	1999	United front	11, Fan Road, Lahore

441

Sr. No.	Organisation/ Group	Amir/Secretary/ President	Founded	Nature	Central Office
25.	Mukhtar Force	Allama Hamid Moosavi	1999	do	Satellite Town, Rawalpindi

Tahreek-e Ja'fariya (Banned)

Tahreek-e Ja'fariya was banned in Pakistan on 12 January 2002. But it is still active due to its effective network. It has been renamed Millat Jafariya, a nomenclature that has not yet caught public attention.

BACKGROUND

Tahreek Nifaz Fiqh Jafariya was founded on 13 April 1974, in Bhakkar. The famous scholar, Mufti Jafar Husain was instrumental in establishing this organisation. He was a member of Islami Nazariyati Council, but came into conflict with Ziaul Haq who wanted to impose Hanfi Islam on Pakistan. He resigned from the Council on this issue, and started a movement against the government from the platform of Wafaq Ulema Shia, Pakistan. To take a clear stand on the issue All-Pakistan Shia Convention was held in Bhakkar on 13 April 1979, where the foundation of the Tahreek was laid. Mufti Jafar Husain and Allama Mirza Yusuf Husain Lucknowi were candidates for amir. However, the overwhelming support of ISO led to Mufti Jafar Husain's victory, and ISO began to wield a big clout in Tahreek's affairs. This was opposed by many Shia ulema, which led to dissensions. There is no doubt about the fact that ISO remained the main lever of power in Tahreek-e Ja'fariya for a period. It formed the 'constitutional structure' of the organisation. In 1980, when Ziaul Haq announced *Zakat O Ashar* ordinance, Tahreek-e Ja'fariya announced its convention on 5 July 1980 in Islamabad. It was ISO that raised manpower for this convention, and laid a siege of the central secretariat. As a result, the 'Islamabad Pact' was made and the government agreed to introduce separate courses for Shia students on Islamic studies and keep the Shias outside the purview of *Zakat O Ashar* ordinance. Imam Khomeini had played an important role in this pact; he got an assurance from Ziaul Haq about the above measures. A message from the Imam was also read out in the convention in which he had exhorted the Shias to keep their morale high.

After this convention, Tahreek-e Ja'fariya came to be regarded as the representative Shia organisation on the national scene. It also received support from the government of Iran. When Mufti Jafar Husain died on 29 August 1983, Tahreek-e Ja'fariya was thrown into confusion. Maulana Hamid Ali Moosavi put himself forward as the candidate for amir and he was elected in an assembly of Shia ulema in the Ali Masjid of Rawalpindi. After this, people in Pakistan began to take initiation from him.

However, one group of members who were not satisfied with the new developments called a conference on 10 February 1984 in Bhakkar and elected Allama Syed Ariful Husaini as the chairman. The leaders of Wafaq Ulema Shia, ISO, Asghariya Organisation, and Asghariya Students Organisation (the last two organisations are very effective in Sindh and have been involved in sectarian clashes) were present in this conference. Later, efforts to unite the two groups began and a convention was held near Rawalpindi. But Hamid Ali Moosavi did not participate in it as he, allegedly, had entered into a 'deal' with the government whereby the government recognised his group as the representative Shia organisation. Thus, Tahreek-e Ja'fariya was split into two, and sometimes they came close to clashes. Both the groups reached Iran to prove the authenticity of their leadership. Eventually, Ariful Husaini got the support of Imam Khomeini and he was appointed as the Imam's representative in Pakistan.

Tenure of Allama Ariful Husaini

After receiving the endorsement from Imam Khomeini, Ariful Husaini Group emerged as the representative Shia organisation in the country and it spread its network everywhere. Allama Ariful Husaini had the support of ISO whereas Maulana Moosavi had the support of the majority of Shia ulema. ISO played a seminal role to project Ariful Husaini as the representative Shia leader and started a movement throughout the country. Ariful Husaini was also opposed by another group of Shia ulema, known as Wafaq Ulema Shia, who had become active once again. Further, he and Tahreek-e Ja'fariya were also opposed by Shia *zakirs*. But the incident that gave a new fillip to his support is known as the 'Quetta Incident'.

The 'Islamabad Pact' between Ziaul Haq and Tahreek-e Ja'fariya under Mufti Jafar Husain had not been implemented fully till 1985. To exert pressure on the government, it was decided to observe 6 July 1985, as a 'Special Day'. Protest assemblies were held in Lahore, Peshawar, and Quetta. The assemblies in Lahore and Peshawar were peaceful, but the demonstrators in Quetta turned violent. The police resorted to firing in which twenty demonstrators died, and dozens of participants were arrested. Alamdar Road was blocked. It should be mentioned here that Tahreek-e Ja'fariya's big madrasa, Jamia Imam al-Sadiq, is located on this road. The office of the Tahreck was also located there. After this incident the Shia youths entered the madrasa and began to manhandle the people present there. They had the view that Tahreek-e Ja'fariya was getting the Shia youths eliminated. Tahreek-e Ja'fariya's view on this incident is that these people belonged to the rival group and were sent by the secret agencies. Ariful Husaini announced a long march on 1 May 1996 to get those arrested on 6 July 1985 released. But the government released them before that date. Ariful Husaini himself welcomed those who were released; as a result of this agitation, the majority of the Shia community began to support him.

Allama Ariful Husaini had stayed in Najaf with Imam Khomeini who had appointed him his representative in Pakistan. He also had links with Hizbullah in Lebanon, and to build the ISO on the lines of Hizbullah, he had sent several Pakistani youths there.

Allama Ariful Husaini was assassinated on 5 August 1988 in Peshawar. Fazal Haq, former Governor General, Frontier Province, was blamed for his murder. Tahreek-e Ja'fariya not only mentioned him

in the FIR, but also accused him in its statements in
newspapers and assemblies.

Dissensions in Tahreek-e Ja'fariya

After the death of Ariful Husaini, dissensions spread in
Tahreek-e Ja'fariya. Allama Sajid Naqvi was made the
chairman, but a big group did not agree upon his
name, though they had to abide by the decision of the
Shura. The same group later opposed several decisions
of Sajid Naqvi, and groupism began to affect the
functioning of Tahreek-e Ja'fariya.

Dr Muhammad Ali Naqvi's Opposition

Tahreek-e Ja'fariya participated in all the elections of
1990 from the platform of PDA. Dr Muhammad Ali
Naqvi who was the secretary, press and publication,
Tahreek-e Ja'fariya and had also considerable clout
within ISO had serious disagreements with Sajid
Naqvi on the distribution of tickets. This disagreement
was so serious that ISO severed its links with Tahreek-e
Ja'fariya. Thus, Tahreek-e Ja'fariya was divided into
two groups. However, till 1992 this disagreement and
division was limited to the management only. What
was the nature of this disagreement? Qaisar Naqvi, an
ex-member of ISO, says: 'There were two reasons for
this. Allama Sajid Naqvi wanted to make the Tahreek a
political formation, but Dr Naqvi insisted that it
should remain a Shia organisation and should work
like Jamat-e Islami. Then, the candidates who were
selected by Tahreek-e Ja'fariya had no links with it, but
had entered it through money power. If they had won,

they would have changed their political loyalties. ISO had differences with Sajid Naqvi as he had embezzled its funds that had come from Iran. Actually, Allama Sajid Naqvi was ready to sacrifice Shia interests for money, and he was straying from the revolutionary path of Imam Khomeini.' To bring about a change in the leadership of Tahreek-e Ja'fariya, Dr Muhammad Ali Naqvi formed a separate group and through his efforts Allama Fazal Moosvi was elected its leader. Allama Fazal Moosvi was in America and he was elected in absentia. That is why this group could not be very active. After this failure, Dr Naqvi resigned from Tahreek-e Ja'fariya.

Founding of Pasbaan-e Islam

After leaving Tahreek-e Ja'fariya, Dr Muhammad Ali Naqvi remained inactive for two years. In 1994 he founded an organisation named Pasbaan-e Islam, that mainly participated in underground activities. He received the support of those ISO youths who were unhappy with Allama Sajid Naqvi. Police records reveal Pasbaan-e Islam to be a violent organisation whose objective was to fight Sipah Sahaba. According to one report, dozens of its youths had received military training in Hizbul Mumineen's camps at Parachinar and Muzaffarabad. The activities of Pasbaan-e Islam began to come to light after the death of Dr Muhammad Ali Naqvi. He had organised it according to modern methods, but after his death the organisation was divided into two groups. One group accepted the leadership of Sajid Naqvi; the second group is led by Rashid Abbas Naqvi, ex-president of ISO, who committed himself and his group to promoting Dr Naqvi's mission. Pasbaan-e Islam got a severe jolt when Hamad Raza, one of its important members, was arrested by the police in Sahiwal in January 1996 along with a heavy cache of arms. He was charged with several crimes of robbery. However, Pasbaan-e Islam announced that it had expelled him a year earlier as he was involved in activities outside the purview of the charter. During interrogation, he supplied the police with information about the organisation's network and about its active members who were involved in incidents of violence.

From the clues supplied by him the police conducted raids and three leaders of the organisation were arrested. Their names are Faiz Haideri, Shabbir Jafri, and Tauqeer Husain alias Bawa. Faiz Hyderi died in police violence in the Nawakot police station. The police tried to pass it off as suicide but were not successful. Buckling under pressure, they released the other two leaders who, the police had claimed, were involved in several incidents of terrorism. Hamad Raza was released for cooperating with the police, but he was killed under mysterious circumstances in 1997.

After this both the groups spent their time in a war of attrition in which one tried to prove the other a terrorist group. They informed the police about each other's group and a number of leaders were arrested, and cases were filed against them. Several cases were filed against Rashid Abbas, leader of Dr Naqvi group, and Imran Choudhury, leader of Allama Naqvi group. Both of them absconded. In 1996–97, Allama Sajid

SHIA ORGANISATIONS AND GROUPS

Naqvi declared disbanding of his group. Pasbaan-e Islam has lost all power now.

Disagreement about changing name

In March 1993, during the Faisalabad convention the name 'Tahreek Nifaz Fiqh Jafariya' was changed to 'Tahreek-e Ja'fariya, Pakistan' and it was decided to launch it as a political party. This decision was not unanimous. Some argued that the organisation was shedding its religious identity in pursuit of power. This decision had sown the seeds of Sipah Muhammad in Tahreek-e Ja'fariya. Allama Murid Abbas had said this in a press conference in Rawalpindi: 'We were terribly upset by the violence let loose by Sipah Sahaba and its propaganda against the Shias. One of our delegations that included members of ISO and IO met Allama Sajid Naqvi and requested him to announce the fatwa of "kufr" (apostasy) against Azam Tariq, amir of Sipah Sahaba, and we would kill him. Allama Sajid Naqvi not only declined the request but gave us a sharp reprimand.'

When the name was changed from Tahreek Nifaz Fiqh Jafariya to Tahreek-e Ja'fariya, Pakistan, it was argued that, 'the word "nifaz" (promulgation) indicates that we want to promulgate our Fiqh in Pakistan. But the removal of this word has changed this impression and the Pakistani Shias have got a social and political platform.'

Allama Sajid Naqvi's Marriage with a Model and Disagreements with ISO

The leader of Tahreek-e Ja'fariya, Sajid Naqvi secretly

449

married a model girl, Shazia Qurban, in 1994. The marriage was kept a secret for a year, but Tahreek-e Ja'fariya leadership got wind of it. Sajid Naqvi was a married man but when he met this girl he liked her and married her in accordance with the rules of sharia. Tahreek-e Ja'fariya leadership had serious reservations about this marriage for several reasons: first, Shazia Qurban was a model and so her reputation was not good; second, some leaders felt that she was close to some secret agencies and had relations with some important figures; third, she was known in a particular circle. The leadership exerted pressure on him to get separated from her quietly. Sajid Naqvi rejected any such suggestion and shifted her to I 10, Islamabad. He kept on saying that the bungalow belonged to one of his friends, but later it was known that he had bought it for forty-five lakh rupees for his new wife. On 20 December 1995, he had a son by his new wife. In July 1996 the leaders of Tahreek-e Ja'fariya, after extensive consultation, met Sajid Naqvi and asked him to either divorce Shazia Qurban or to send her abroad. Sajid Naqvi once again refused to oblige. ISO's central president also met him with a delegation reiterating the same demands, but in vain. At this, ISO dismissed him from its central leadership and rejected his status to act as its representative in future.

Later, ISO also alleged that he embezzled the funds for ISO that came from Iran and bought the bungalow for his wife with the money. ISO also tried to expel him from his office forcefully, but was not successful.

Establishment of Ja'fariya Students Organisation

The supporters of Sajid Naqvi in Tahreek-e Ja'fariya opposed the actions of ISO and formed a rival students organisation named Jafariya Students Organisation.

Besides the second marriage of Sajid Naqvi, another incident that rocked Tahreek-e Ja'fariya was the hanging of Mahram Ali, an accused in the bomb explosion in the session court, Lahore, in January 1997. Maulana Ziaur Rahman Faruqi, the leader of Sipah Sahaba, and nineteen police personnel were killed in this incident. Various Shia organisations demanded that Sajid Naqvi should come out in support of Mahram Ali as he was innocent and not involved in the incident. But Sajid Naqvi declined to do this. After this incident there was terrorist violence in Muminpura on 11 January 1998, in which twenty-five Shias were killed. Sajid Naqvi was not allowed to take part in their funeral rites. Mahram Ali had also written in his will before his hanging that Sajid Naqvi and the current leaders of the Tahreek should not be allowed to take part in his funeral prayer.

Founding of Shura Wahdat Islami

In September 1999, a number of Shia ulema had a meeting in Islamabad. Led by the known leaders of Tahreek-e Ja'fariya, Allama Javed Hadi and Allama Abid Husain Husaini the meeting decided to dissolve the Shura. In the light of Sajid Naqvi's second marriage and his other behaviours that had hurt the community, and in the light of the growing oppression on the Shia community, the committee decided that a new leadership should assume office. For this purpose, a preliminary search committee with fourteen members was formed that was to choose the new leadership on October 31. However, before that day came, Sajid Naqvi was removed from office and Allama Fazal Moosvi was made the new leader. The new group was named Shura Wahdat Islami. Now, both the groups claim that they are real successors of Tahreek-e Ja'fariya.

ORGANISATIONAL STRUCTURE AND NETWORK

Tahreek-e Ja'fariya is the only Shia organisation in Pakistan that has its network throughout the country. It is managed by a supreme council led by the president who is elected by members. Allama Sajid Naqvi is the current president.

Tahreek-e Ja'fariya has seven affiliated departments and forums. They are as follows:

1. Jamiat Tulaba Ja'fariya (organisation of Shia madrasa students)
2. Imamiya Doctors
3. Imamiya Engineers
4. Imamiya Teachers
5. Imamiya Lawyers
6. Imamiya Peasants
7. Islamic Employees Welfare Organisation

Madrasas and Centres of Tahreek-e Ja'fariya

The following madrasas are centres of Tahreek-e Ja'fariya and centres of sectarian activities as well. A list of important centres of the Tahreek is presented in Table XXII.

1. Jamia Al-Manzar, Model Town, Lahore
2. Jamia Imam Al-Sadiq, Alamdar Road, Quetta
3. Madrasa Jamia Imam Husain, Khanqah Dogra, Shekhupura
4. Qasr Zainab, Bhakkar
5. Jamia Al-Saqlain, Multan
6. Jamia Imam Sadiq, Karachi
7. Jamia Ma'riful Islamia, Peshawar
8. Madrasa Khomeini, Malhuwali, Attock
9. Madinatul Uloom, Gulshan-e Iqbal, Karachi
10. Jamia Al-Shia, Kot Ado
11. Jamia Imaiya Sajjadiya, Rahim Yar Khan
12. Markaz Tahqeeqat Islamia, Sargodha
13. Jamia Al-Jafariya, Rahim Yar Khan
14. Jamia Ahl-e Bait, Islamabad
15. Madrasa Dars Al-Muhammad, Faisalabad
16. Madrasa Ayatul Hukm, Rawalpindi

DEMANDS OF TAHREEK-E JA'FARIYA AND ITS CURRENT STATUS

On 20 August 2000, a delegation of Tahreek-e Ja'fariya in Punjab under the leadership of Sibtain Kazmi met the governor of Punjab and placed before him the following demands:

1. General permission to Shia ulema for address on TV
2. In the new allotments for housing societies, land should be allocated for Shia mosques
3. A representative from the Shia community should be included in the syllabus committee of the

department of education. Authentic Shia books should be purchased for libraries

4. Ban on mourning assemblies in some areas should be lifted. Ban on the use of loudspeakers in programmes of mourning should be lifted.

5. Families affected by sectarian violence should be given aid by the government.

6. Lashkar-e Jhangvi camps in Afghanistan should be closed. Its close links with Jaish-e Muhammad should be investigated.

Till today, Tahreek-e Ja'fariya sticks to these demands. According to an important member of Tahreek-e Ja'fariya: 'We will not change our stand whatever restrictions are imposed on us.' The ban imposed on Tahreek-e Ja'fariya on 12 January 2002, has been challenged in the High Court. Despite the ban, however, it is still working as before. It is part of Muttahida Majlis Amal (MMA) (United Action Committee) and intends to take part in the elections in October.

Table XXII: *Important Centres of Tahreek-e Ja'fariya (Banned)*

Sr. No.	District/ Tehsil	President	Office/Centre
1.	Lahore	Zulfiqar Haider	Jamia Almuntazir, H Block, Model Town, Lahore
2.	Multan	Shaffaqat Bhatta	Jamia Saqlain, Multan
3.	Faisalabad	Yavar Husain Shamsi	Madrasa Al-e-Muhammad, Faisalabad
4.	Jhelum	Babar Shah	
5.	Jhang		Near Hasnina High School, Jhang
6.	Gujrat	Asgher Ali Yazdani	

Sr. No.	District/ Tehsil	President	Office/Centre
7.	Sargodha	Shabir Bukhari	Centre Tehqeeqat-e-Islamia, Sargodha
8.	Jacobabad	Syed Nazeer Abbas	
9.	Peshawar	Bakhtiyar Razi/ Imdad Hussain	
10.	Dera Ismail Khan	Ghazi Abdullah/ Najmul Hasan	
11.	Lucki Maroot	Murtaza Hussain	
12.	Karachi		Jamia Imam Sadiq, Karachi
13.	Quetta		Muridabad, Quetta
14.	Meerpur Khas	Hafiz Muhammad Akbar Rashid/ Muhammad Ayyub Shaikh	Madina Masjid, Shahi Bazar, Meerpur Khas,
15.	Kohat		Jamia Ulooviah, Chakarkot, Kohat

Sipah Muhammad (Banned)

In 1993, a group within Tahreek-e Ja'fariya emerged that held the view that the Tahreek should not change its name, and that Allama Sajid Naqvi should have formed a jihadi wing of the organisation to confront Sipah Sahaba. ISO supported this view. Responding to the demands of this group, the president of Tahreek-e Ja'fariya in Jhang district, Ghulam Reza Naqvi, declared the formation of Sipah Muhammad in 1993. Many youths from ISO and IO joined it immediately. Another view about the formation of Sipah Muhammad is that in 1992 when Sipah Sahaba had threatened to kill Asif Zardari, he formed Sipah Muhammad to confront it and supplied it not only with money but arms as well. Sipah Muhammad held its first general meeting in Mochi Gate, Lahore, in which about 2,000 people participated, most of whom were armed. Dr Muhammad Ali Naqvi, the leader of the disgruntled group of Tahreek-e Ja'fariya and leader of Pasbaan-e Islam, had also participated in it. After the meeting, the leaders of Sipah Muhammad called a press conference in which they said publicly, 'We are weary of carrying corpses. God willing, we will settle all the scores now. We will wipe out the name of Sipah Sahaba from history.'

In the beginning, the leadership of Sipah Sahaba and the law-enforcing agencies did not take any notice of this new group. It came to notice when it claimed responsibility of the attack on Azam Tariq in Sargodha. By 1994, it had already established its strong centre at Thokar Niaz Beg, Lahore.

Violence by Sipah Muhammad

From 1993 to 2001, Sipah Muhammad has been involved in 250 incidents of violence. This is the only organisation that forced newspapers to publicise its stand. For example, in December 1994, its members mounted an attack on the office of the daily *The Pakistan Observer* on the plea that it did not give them sufficient coverage, that its owner had close links with the leadership of Sipah Sahaba, and that Sipah Sahaba published its anti-Shia literature from its press. The management of the newspaper entered into a dialogue with its leadership, but some disgruntled workers (of Sipah Muhammad) began to fire and broke some furniture in the office. After this incident, its leader

Murid Abbas Yazdani came to apologise to the editor of the newspaper, saying that it was the handiwork of a few impulsive youth. During his trip to Islamabad, he was arrested from outside the Rawalpindi Press Club. This arrest was in consequence of the FIR lodged against him after the murderous attack on the Sipah Sahaba leaders, Ziaur Rahman Faruqi and Azam Tariq. The following day the Rawalpindi police arrested dozens of Sipah Muhammad members. Sipah Muhammad's attacks on newspapers were not confined to Islamabad. Immediately after this incident, some leaders addressed a conference at Press Club, Quetta, and threatened: 'The newspapers that do not give us sufficient coverage will have their offices gutted.'

Six terrorists belonging to Sipah Muhammad are still wanted by the police.

Dissensions in Sipah Muhammad

By 1994, Sipah Muhammad had established a strong centre in Lahore. In December 1994, the police raid on its headquarters to round up its leaders resulted in a bloody clash in which the police came under fire and five of their cars were gutted. After this the police made an elaborate plan to eliminate Sipah Muhammad.

By the end of 1995, Sipah Muhammad was divided into two groups. The cause of this break-up was Ghulam Reza Naqvi's active role in Milli Ekjahti Council and his consent to its programme of ending sectarian violence. Allama Murid Abbas Yazdani accused Ghulam Reza of compromising with Sipah

Sahaba and straying away from his religious beliefs. After a few months both the groups came together, but the internal dissensions continued. Finally, Sipah Muhammad pulled out of Milli Ekjahti Council.

The decline of Sipah Muhammad can be traced from August 1996 when Murid Abbas Yazdani was killed in Rawalpindi. Police investigations revealed that this was the result of his disagreement with Ghulam Reza Naqvi who was behind this murder. The police arrested the killer who admitted to his crime openly. The people of Thokar Niaz Beg who gave refuge to Sipah Muhammad leadership turned against it and they began to expel the members of Sipah Muhammad. The police took advantage of the situation, raided the place and arrested Ghulam Reza Naqvi and dozens of Sipah Muhammad members.

On 14 August 2001, when Sipah Muhammad was banned, it was a very different organisation than it had been in 1996. It strength had waned substantially. The Punjab Police regard it as one of their greatest achievements. Those Sipah Muhammad members who acted as informers of the police are still free and can be seen frequently in police stations and offices. About the dissensions in Sipah Muhammad, Tahreek-e Ja'fariya has the following stand (based on an interview with Syed Wajid Ali Naqvi, president of the Punjab unit, as published in *Zindagi*, 24–31 January 1998):

Q: There were differences among them (members of Sipah Muhammad). Can you tell us whether his own people had not got Allama Murid Abbas Yazdani killed?

A: In Milli Ekjahti Council charter there was a particular section – section no. 4 that was about the code of conduct to which Murid Abbas Yazdani was a signatory. In this section, respect for the Prophet, Prophet's Companions, their wives and Ahl-e Bait (the Prophet's extended family) was declared to be part of one's faith. This was not liked by quite a few people in his party because of which disagreement grew. I cannot say definitively whether members of his own organisations have killed him, but one certainly heard such things.

Present Leaders of Sipah Muhammad

President	Allama Rabeta Alam-e Islami Jafar Raza
Senior vice-president	Malik Hasan Ali
General secretary	Agha Abbas Qazalbash
Important leaders	Syed Husain Abbas, Jamil Husain, Asaf Ali, Muhammad Riaz Haider, Ashfaq Ali Nana, Syed Bashir Hasan, Tasdeeq Husain, Bashir Husain, and Shabir Hussain. (They are from Lahore, Khanqah Dogran and Jhang.)

Imamiya Students Organisation

Imamiya Students Organisation (ISO) is a countrywide organisation of Shia students. Besides being active in educational institutions, it plays a vital role in the politics of Shia community and in sectarian clashes. It is taken to be the real strength of the Shia community.

BACKGROUND

The first Shia students organisation was formed in 1966 under the name of Shia Students Association by Dr Syed Haider Husain Shamsi who was a student of King Edward Medical College, Lahore. But this association was confined to King Edward Medical College. This association inspired formation of other students' organisations among whom Jamiat Tulaba Asna Ashariya, Shia Students Organisation, and Ja'fariya Students Organisation were important. However, the networks of these associations were also limited to a couple of local colleges. In 1967, these associations had a general meeting in which all of them came together to form Shia Students Association (SSA). In 1969, the second annual conference of SSA was held in Lahore. It was presided over by Syed Mubarak Mahmud Ali Gilani and the chief guest was Madame Maryam Bahnam, director general, Khana Farhang Iran. The conference decided upon a three-point programme:

1. To unite Shia students on one platform
2. To help them in education
3. To inspire them to follow the ways of Prophet Muhammad and Ahl-e bait

Till 1972, this organisation was not too active, divided as it was into different groups. In that year, Ali Reza Naqvi and Niaz Naqvi, students of Engineering University, Babar Naqvi of King Edward Medical

College, and Dr Syed Majid Naoroz Abidi, the founder member of SSA called a meeting of all Shia students' organisations in the Engineering University. Once again, Shia Students Association was formed. On 11 June 1972, the management of the association had a meeting at the residence of Naoroz Abidi, which was also attended by three Shia ulema – Maulana Syed Sadiq Ali Najafi, Maulana Syed Murtaza Husain, and Maulana Agha Ali Moosavi. In consultation with the three ulema, the association was named Imamiya Students Organisation and its cabinet was announced. Syed Marghoob Zaidi was appointed the president (central), Khair Muhammad Budh was vice-president, Shaikh Nawazish Ali was general secretary, and Ali Raza Naqvi was the joint secretary. ISO's first programme, Husain Day was organised in Punjab University, Lahore. Hanif Rai (state minister, treasury), Maulana Mufti Jafar Husain, Maulana Syed Murtaza Husain, and Maulana Syed Sadiq Ali Najafi attended the programme which was hugely publicised. This event spread ISO's fame and its network throughout the country. Its first national conference was held in Jamiatul Mantazar in 1975.

ISO and Iranian Revolution

At the time when ISO was established the revolutionary movement in Iran was going on. ISO was the only Shia organisation in Pakistan that first came out in support of the movement and provided it with human resource from Pakistan. When the Shia ulema supporting Khomeini were violently suppressed in Iraq, ISO initiated a protest movement in Pakistan and printed posters with the statement: 'There was a bloodbath there, and we were silent here.'

In 1978, when Pakistan invited the Shah of Iran to visit the country, ISO printed posters with the statement, 'We do not welcome the Killer Shah.' In that year ISO established direct links with Khomeini in Paris, and wrote a letter to him supporting his movement. Imam Khomeini replied: 'I had expected this from sons of Muslims; I appreciate your feelings, and hope that you will also root out the vestiges of colonialism from your country.'

After this, ISO began a protest movement in Pakistan, supporting Khomeini and opposing Shah. When the Iranian revolution became a success, ISO declared that they must imitate Imam Khomeini. During the Iran-Iraq war too, ISO continued to support the revolutionary government in Iran. It sent several doctors from Pakistan to Iran. Its delegations continued to visit that country. In 1982, when Imam Khomeini sent message to the Shias of the world to join the front, several delegations of ISO reached Iran.

ORGANISATIONAL STRUCTURE AND NETWORK

The current president (central) of ISO is Farhan Haider Zaidi. A Majlis-e Shura looks after its management. The president is elected every year. ISO has an efficient organisation having the following departments:

Department of Training
This department organises assemblies for training throughout the year. The centre for training is Madrasa Hasnain, Jhamra.

Department of Preaching (tabligh)
This department sends *tablighi* delegations to Shia areas.

Department of Press and Publication
The central office of this department is at Muslim Town, Lahore.

Department of Management
This department looks after organisational management in entire Pakistan. Its central office is at Muslim Town, Lahore.

Department of Education
This department helps poor students of ISO.

Department of Finance
Its head office is in Lahore.

Department of Muhbeen
This department looks after the needs of students up to the matriculation level.

The network of ISO is spread throughout Pakistan. However, its branches are strong in Rahim Yar Khan, Dera Ismail Khan, Northern Areas, and Karachi. In Sindh, Asghariya Students Organisation supports it. The managements of the two organisations are different, but they have the same objective and follow the same method. ISO's central office is in Lahore. Shia madrasas and mosques also work as its offices.

Imamiya Scout

One department of ISO goes by the name of Imamiya Scout. The chief scout is Nasir Shirazi. The objective of founding this department is to train the ISO youth in such a way that they can handle tricky situations.

The scouts also exhibit their skill in the mourning assemblies during Muharram.

Imamiya Organisation

Imamiya Organisation was set up in December 1974. Its objective was to keep the ISO youth in touch with the organisation after they leave ISO and enter professional and practical life, so that they should continue to provide conceptual, spiritual, and material support to the ISO.

Till 1984, IO was not very active. After that it began to admit non-ISO members as well, and charted a different course than Tahreek Nifaz Fiqh Ja'fariya. One reason for this was IO's disagreement with Allama Ariful Husaini. When IO began to work as an independent organisation, its ex-president (central), Dr Muhammad Ali Naqvi, resigned from its membership on the plea that it was moving away from Tahreek-e Ja'fariya. After his resignation, IO's relation with ISO came to an end.

Founding of Imameens

Dr Muhammad Ali Naqvi founded Imameens in place of IO, that acted as a parent organisation for ISO. In an interview with the monthly *Al-Arif* in 1989, Dr Naqvi said:

> As long as IO acted according to its basic aims (patronage to ISO) I remained connected with it. But when I saw that people outside the organisation were joining it and substantial changes are taking place in its aims and objectives, I thought it advisable to leave

it. Imameens is not another name for IO, but an inheritor of its original objectives.

Safeer Inqilab by Tasleem Raza Khan, p.116

Majlis-e Amal Ulema Shia, Pakistan

This is an important non-political organisation of the Shia ulema whose leader is Allama Muhammad Hasnain. Its general secretary is Maulana Ali Ghazanfar who is also the deputy amir of Majlis-e Amal Tahaffuz Khatm Nabuwat. The objective of this organisation is to protect the Shia belief system and to unite Shia ulema on one platform and to promote understanding among other communities. Its network is limited to Punjab. According to one Shia leader, this organisation has the support of a powerful Iranian lobby. It has differences with the policies of Tahreek-e Ja'fariya.

Alami Majlis Ahl-e Bait, Pakistan

This is a non-political Shia organisation that works for the development of the community. Its patron is Mohsin Ali Najafi and its president is Syed Ghulam Hasan Naqvi. Its central office is located in Jamia Ahl-e Bait, Nazimuddin Road, Islamabad. It has an educational trust, Jabar bin Hayan, which establishes schools and madrasas in different parts of the country. It has already established nine educational institutions.

Alami Majlis Ahl-e Bait, Pakistan gets funding from the government of Iran and from rich Shias in Europe and America. It publishes missionary literature and distributes it freely. It also brings out its mouthpiece

Al-Saqlain which publishes scholarly articles on Shia system of beliefs and the imams. A study of these articles indicates that the objective of this organisation is to make the environment conducive for the reappearance of Imam Mahdi. It is paying special attention to educational programmes in Sakardo. Apart from Islamabad and Sakardo, its network is also present in Chakwal, Rawalpindi, and Lahore.

Alami Majlis Ahl-e Bait, Pakistan, supports the political ideology of Tahreek-e Ja'fariya.

Tahreek Tahaffuz Huqooq Shia

This is among the first organisations to be established by the Shia community. Venerable figures like Allama Safdar Husain Najafi and Mufti Jafar Husain had been among its patrons and presidents. Tahreek Nifaz Fiqh Jafariya was one of its offshoots. The objective of this organisation is the protection of the right of Shias in Pakistan. It also establishes madrasas in different parts of the country.

The centre of its activities is Jamiatul Mantazar, Model Town, Lahore. The principal of this institute, Hafiz Syed Riaz Husain, is the president and the general secretary is Syed Mahboob Ali Shamsi. It has the support of the ulema from different parts of the country, but it does not have a good organisational network.

Tahreek Huqooq Jafariya, Pakistan

This organisation is limited to Lahore and the adjoining districts. It intends to bring an end to sectarian clashes, and arranges International Imam Husain Peace Conference in Lahore every year during Muharram. Except for this event, it has very few other programmes. Its leader is Mushtaq Husain Jafri.

Majlis Tanzeemul Islam

This is a socio-religious organisation of the Shias that endeavours to solve the social problems of the community. Allama Syed Alu Al-Hasan Naqvi is its patron. Its area is limited to Lahore and its central office is at Sandakalan. This organisation is known for its sufficient material resources.

Tanzeem Ghulaman Aal Imran, Lahore

The objective of this organisation is to establish Shia mosques and madrasas. Its president is Alhaj Muhammad Iqbal Heera. It has established several mosques so far, spending seventy lakh rupees. Its central office is in Lahore. It does not have a good network.

Tahreek Ikhwat Islami

The leader of this organisation is Allama Inayat Ali Shakir. It was founded in 1980. Its objective is to forge unity and harmony among Muslims.

Anjuman Wazifa Sadat Mumineen

It is a non-political organisation founded in 1912. It provides educational loans to Shia students throughout the country. Its current president is Syed Iftikhar

Husain Jafri (Quetta), and the general secretary is Syed Hasan Mehdi (Lahore). Its central office is in Lahore.

Tahreek Wahdat Milli

The objective of this organisation is to unite Shia ulema of different views on one platform. Its chairman is Syed Abbas Reza Moosavi. It is not an important organisation.

Islami Islahi Trust

This trust was founded in 1990 by the Iranian scholar, Mirza Ahsan Al-Hairi Al-Haqqani. The president of the trust was Allama Muhammad Hasnain Sabqi. Mirza Ahsan Al-Hairi established Shia mosques, madrasas, and *imambargahs* in Lebanon, Syria, India, and Africa and earmarked grants for them. In Pakistan, his trust has established thirty-three Shia madrasas and thirty mosques and *imambargahs*. The central office of this trust is located in Darul Tabligh Al-Jafariya, Islamabad. This trust provides fund to different Shia political and sectarian organisations.

Shia Jihadi Organisations

Seven Shia jihadi organisations are working in Occupied Kashmir. They are:

1. Hizbul Mumineen
2. Ali Tigers
3. Khomeini Tigers
4. Abbas Tigers
5. Alamdar Kashmir Tigers

6. Lashkar Ali
7. Zarb-e Haider

Apart from the first one, the rest of the organisations are not so active. Ali Tigers has its links in Pakistan. Some of its small units are working in Para Chinar and the Northern Areas, but they are not very active.

Hizbul Mumineen

Hizbul Mumineen is a representative Shia organisation that was founded in Srinagar in 1991. In Occupied Kashmir, its activities are limited to Srinagar, Baramula, and Bagam. It had begun its activities with the name 'Pasban' but soon changed it to the current name. The thirty-five-year old Shuja Abbas is the amir of Hizbul Mumineen. Its management is looked after by a six-member 'Shura Khadimeen' whose work is supervised by a three-member higher Shura, 'Shura Alia Shura Khadimeen'. The amir or anyone else does not have the right to take any decision single-handedly, without consulting the Shura.

Hizbul Mumineen has a twelve-tyre organisational structure. The tehsil and district level commanders are responsible for actions in their areas. The district commander is accountable to the supreme commander. The platoons and camps are named after Shia imams or Prophet's family, for example, Lashkar Haiderkar, Hazrat Hamzah Company, Zaid Ibn Ali Company, etc.

Hizbul Mumineen's network is spread out in Azad Kashmir and Pakistan. ISO supports it wholeheartedly. It has its base camp and training camp in Muzaffarabad where 300 mujahideen can be accommodated and trained at a time. So far, Hizbul Mumineen has trained 2,500 mujahideen. More than 100 of its mujahideen have been killed in Kashmir; of them, more than 50 per cent come from Azad Kashmir, Frontier Province, and Punjab.

Chapter XIII

ORGANISATIONS AND GROUPS ALIGNED TO JAMAT-E ISLAMI IDEOLOGY

Jamat-e Islami is the largest religious organisation in Pakistan. It works on a non-sectarian basis, trying to rise above differences of views among various religious groups. Several other allied organisations have also been influenced by the ideology of its founder, Maulana Abul A'la Maududi, while some groups broke away from Jamat-e Islami and formed smaller organisations. Their total number is fourteen; of them two are political, four are jihadi, four are students and youth-related, and one is for the ulema. The details regarding these organisations are given separately along with brief accounts of allied/affiliated organisations.

Jamat-e Islami

Jamat-e Islami is a well-knit religious and political organisation of Pakistan. Besides Pakistan, it is also working in India, Bangladesh, and Occupied Kashmir. However, the managements of the organisation in these countries and Occupied Kashmir are different, whereas its branches in Arab counties, America, and Europe work under the aegis of the Pakistani branch.

BACKGROUND

Jamat-e Islami was founded on 26 August 1941, by Abul Ala Moududi. It grew after the establishment of Pakistan. It participated actively in the Khatm Nabuwat movement of 1953, and against Ayub Khan. It could not make much gain in the 1970 elections. In 1977 Jamat-e Islami organised the movement for Nizam-e Mustafa. Moulana Moududi had been the amir of Jamat-e Islami till his death. In 1972, Mian Tufail Muhammad was appointed the amir and he remained amir till 1987. During his tenure, Jamat-e Islami took part in Ziaul Haq's Majlis-e Shura and participated in the Afghan War. On 6 November 1987, the current amir of Jamat-e Islami, Qazi Husain Ahmad, assumed office and gave the organisation a popular face. He played a vital role in forming Islami Jamhoori Ittihad (the united election forum against the People's Party) and in 1990, this Ittihad was a part of the government. The 1993 elections were fought from the platform of Pakistan Islamic Front. Pasban, the youth wing of Jamat-e Islami, played a significant role in that election. But Jamat-e Islami was defeated in the elections. It did not take part in the elections in 1997.

In addition to its political role, Jamat-e Islami also has wide range of religious, *tablighi*, and jihadi activities.

ORGANISATIONAL STRUCTURE

Jamat-e Islami has 15,824 members. Among them 1,295 are women. The candidates for membership are 2,844. It has 56,455 workers of whom 9,381 are women.

In Pakistan, Jamat-e Islami has 1,932 branches and 1,317 offices. They organise *tablighi*, jihadi, and political programmes throughout the year, and send their reports to the centre at Mansoora.

The power to formulate policies and take decision about the management vests in Majlis-e Shura. Majlis-e Shura appoints an amir who takes practical steps to implement policies. He is helped in this by six deputy amirs and the four state amirs. The amir cannot take any decision on his own, but has to take the permission of the Majlis-e Shura. Several departments work under the amirs. The names of the current amirs are:

Deputy Amirs, Pakistan

1. Maulana Jan Muhammad Abbasi
2. Choudhury Rahmat Ilahi
3. Professor Abdul Ghafoor
4. Professor Khurshid Ahmad
5. Choudhury Muhammad Aslam Salimi
6. Liaqat Balooch Qeem (general secretary)

Syed Munawwar Husain, Deputy

1. Khalid Rahman
2. Muhammad Ashraf Malik
3. Farid Ahmad Pracha

Department of Management
The function of this department is to keep in touch with all the branches in the country, organise central programmes, and to keep in touch with other religious and political organisations. Rashhed Ahmad is the

secretary of this department.

Department of Religious Learning
This department organises *tablighi* assemblies and readings of the Holy Koran and compiles reports of such programmes at different places.

Training Department
This department organises programmes and camps for workers and members for their ideological indoctrination. Maulana Muhammad Sultan is the secretary of this department.

Department of Common Affairs
This has been divided into seven branches: (i) Management, (ii) Security, (iii) Transport, (iv) Hospitality, (v) Cleaning, (vi) Horticulture, (vii) Building and Construction, including water, electricity, and gas. This department is under the supervision of Muhammad Nawaz Tareen.

Department of Press and publications
This department keeps links with the media, publicises the programmes, organise press conferences, and issues press releases. The secretary of this department is Amir Al-Azeem.

Department of Public Relations
This department establishes links with other religious and political organisations and their leaders. The secretary of this department is Safdar Ali Choudhury.

Election Cell
An election cell has been established with Choudhury Mushtaq Ahmad as its supervisor. It compiles survey reports of all central and state electoral constituencies.

The following institutes/forums are working under the aegis of Jamat-e Islami, Pakistan:

Department of Social Service

The patron of this department is Qazi Husain Ahmad, and Ahsanullah Waqas is the general secretary. According to the annual report of Jamat-e Islami, Pakistan, in 2001, it spent a sum of Rs 4,24,06,795 on various plans as per details given below:[*]

Sr. No	Details	Amount (Rs)
1.	Aid for 125 students and 2115 helpless widows	3,46,94,230
2.	Hides of sacrificed animals (from Madrasas)	14,59,049
3.	Fitrana, through allied organisations	49,24,462
4.	Iftar and Ramzan	15,86,677
5.	Qurbani fund (through madrasas and allied organisations)	2,32,23,867
6.	Mansoora dispensary	2,60,656
7.	Sixteen destitutes	1,98,300
8.	Natural calamity	19,97,000
9.	Madrasa Uloom, Hyderabad	50,000
10.	Afghan fund	13,65,190
11.	Drought fund (through allied organisations)	12,38,500
12.	Chechnya fund	20,87,715
13.	Middle East fund	5,37,849
14.	Bangladeshi prisoners	8,110

Mosque-Maktab Scheme

The main objective of this scheme is to organise elementary education in the mosque, and provide

---

[*] Translator's Note: It is not clear in case of all the above heads whether they are on the debit or credit side. This might create confusion.

special assistance to poor children and adults. Last year, sixty-two mosque-*maktabs* were opened under this scheme. Professor Muhammad Saaid is the head of this scheme.

Geographical Information Centre
This centre is located in Peshawar. It has produced new maps of Pakistan, the Islamic world, and the whole world. It also runs a human rights network, which compiles the record of oppression against Muslims in different parts of the world.

Islamic Publication Limited
This institute is located in Lower Mall, Lahore, and publishes hundreds of books on Jamat-e Islami and religious topics. In 2001, it published 204 books, of whom 197 were in Urdu and seven were in English.

Kisan Supplies Services
This is a profit-making concern that produces pesticides; a fertiliser unit is also being established. Its director is Hasan Saheeb Murad. In 2001–02, its sale proceeds from pesticides and seeds were twenty-three crore rupees.

Allied Organisations of Jamat-e Islami

Fifteen organisations work under the aegis of Jamat-e Islami:

Jamiat Ittihad Ulema
This organisation works to bring unity among different religious groups. It played a central role in establishing Milli Ekjahti Council and Afghan Defence Council. Its president is Maulana Abdul Malik, and its central office is located at Mansoora, Lahore.

Hizbul Mujahideen

This is the jihadi wing of Jamat-e Islami. Its chief secretary in Pakistan is Muhammad Usman.

Islami Jamiat Tulaba

Islami Jamiat Tulaba has been founded to work in colleges and universities. It also takes part in jihadi activities. In Pakistan, the total number of its members is 1,155, and candidate members are 1,430. Friends of the Jamiat Tulaba run into 13,000.

Jamiat Tulaba Arabiya

This organisation works in madrasas. The total number of its members is 218, and candidates members are 108. Friends of Tulaba Arabiya run into 1,400. It has 105 offices in the country. Ziaur Rahman Faruqi is the head of this organisation.

Islami Jamiat Talibat

This is the women students wing of Jamat-e Islami. The total number of its members is 175, and candidates members are sixty-seven. Friends of Talibat number 863.

Kisan Board

This board looks after the problems of peasants. It is a powerful organisation. Its membership runs into 35,000 and its network is spread out in seventy-four districts. Sadiq Khakwani is its president, and its central office is located at 106, Kamran Block, Allama Iqbal Town.

National Labour Federation

NLF is the central trade union of Jamat-e Islami. It has 311 unions in its fold. Its central office is located behind MAO College, Sanda Road, Lahore. Its president is

Muhammad Islam and general secretary is Muhammad Zafar Khan.

Pakistan Islamic Medical Association

This forum works among doctors. Its membership runs into 2,226, of whom 170 are women. It organises medical relief camps in different Islamic countries. It has also established Paima Pharmaceuticals that will begin work soon. Its president is Dr Hafizur Rahman and its central office is located in Islamabad.

Islamic Homoeopathic Medical Association

This association is working in thirty-one districts. Four clinics have been constructed by it. Its president is Dr Abdur Razzaq.

Pakistan Business Forum

It works in different chambers of commerce in Pakistan and tries to encourage trade among Muslim countries. Its president is Shaikh Tanvir Ahmad Maggon.

Shabab Milli

Shabab Milli is the new name for 'Pasban'. This works among illiterate youths and school dropouts. Its membership runs into 85,000.

Tahreek Mehnat Pakistan

This forum works among labourers, particularly those who work in brick kilns. It has its network in thirty-two districts, with a membership of 764. Its president is Nazir Ahmad.

Islami Nizamat Ta'lim

This organisation looks after the schools established by Jamat-e Islami, prepares syllabi, and sets up new schools. Last year, eighteen new schools were added, taking the total number of schools to 1,245. The chairman of this organisation is Professor Ghafoor Ahmad, and the director is Hasan Suhaib Murad.

FOF and Women's University
This foundation deals with the foreign students, and is now setting up a women's university for which the building has already been bought. The general secretary of this foundation is Tayyab Gulzar.

Funds and Finances of Jamat-e Islami
Jamat-e Islami has established a number of funds for different schemes and management of expenses. In addition to members' obligatory contribution, money is raised for all the funds throughout the year. Some important funds are as follows:

1. Kashmir Fund
2. Kashmir Security Fund
3. Bosnia Fund
4. Security Fund
5. Chechnya Fund
6. Kosovo Fund
7. Baitul Maqaddas (Jerusalem) Fund
8. Ethiopia Fund
9. Drought Relief Fund
10. Cordoba Fund
11. Flood Relief Fund
12. Aid Foundation
13. Martyrs of Islam Fund
14. Ghazali Fund

The allied organisations also raise funds on their own for their expenses.

Mansoora

Mansoora is the headquarters of Jamat-e Islami. It is located in Multan Road, Lahore. The central secretariat of Jamat-e Islami and the Punjab secretariat are located here. Apart from schools, a hospital, guest house, etc., it has a residential sector as well. The residential sector is in two parts; the amirs of Jamat-e Islami and other staff members live in one part, and those who have bought properties here live in another part. Jamat-e Islami's external affairs department is also located here. It is very active and keeps in touch with jihadi organisations and activities throughout the world. Aziz Ghaffar is the director of this department. Different allied organisations have also their offices in Mansoora. Facing Mansoora is Mansoora Phase II, which is basically a residential colony. Adjoining this is the building of Ulema Academy.

Cordoba Madinatul Uloom

Jamat-e Islami is setting up a township in the Chakri Town, which is 35 km away from Rawalpindi. An area measuring 20,000 kanals of land is being bought for this purpose (15,000 kanals have already been bought). This township has been given the name Cordoba. The land has cost more than twenty crore rupees. There is a plan to shift the central offices to Cordoba.

Organisations Close to Jamat-e Islami Ideology

There are some organisations and groups having ideological affinity with Jamat-e Islami. A list of such organisations and groups are presented in Table XXIII.

Table XXIII: *Organisations and Groups Close to Jamat-e Islami Ideology*

Sr. No.	Name of Organisation/ Group	Leader/Amir	Nature	Centre
1.	Jamat-e Islami, Pakistan	Qazi Husain Ahmad	Political/ Religious	Multan Road, Mansoora, Lahore
2.	Tanjeem Islami	Dr Israr Ahmad	Political/ Religious	Model Town, Lahore
3.	Markaz, Anjuman Khuddam-ul-Quran	Dr Israr Ahmad	*Tablighi*	Model Town, Lahore
4.	Tahreek-e-Islami	Maulana Naim Siddiqui	Political	Waris Colony, Behind Mansoora, Lahore
5.	Jamiat Ittihad-ul-Ulema	Maulana Abdul Malik	Ulema wing	Multan Road, Mansoora, Lahore
6.	Pasbaan	Altaf Shakoor	Youth organisation	Hasan Square, Karachi
7.	Shabab Milli	Shafiq Bhat	Youth wing	Multan Road, Mansoora, Lahore
8.	Hizbul Mujahideen	Syed Salahuddin	Jihadi	G-9–3, Islamabad
9.	Al-Badr Mujahideen	Bakht Zamin	Jihadi	368, D Block, Satellite Town, Rawalpindi
10.	Hizb-e-Islami	Commander Sarfaraz Masood	Jihadi	Nakyal Sector, Kotli
11.	Jamiatul Mujahideen	General Abdullah	Jihadi	Lower Plate, Muzaffarabad
12.	Islami Jamiat-e-Tulaba		Students Organisation	36-A, Zaildar Park, Achchra, Lahore
13.	Jamiat Tulaba Arabia	Ziaur Rahman Farooqi	Organisation of madrasa students	36-A, Zaildar Park, Achchra, Lahore
14.	Tanzeem Rabta Al-Madaris	Maulana Abdul Malik	Education board	Mansoora, Lahore

Tahreek-e Islami Pakistan

Tahreek-e Islami was born in 1993 when a group within Jamat-e Islami broke away from it. This group was led by Maulana Naim Siddiqui, Maulana Mukhtar Gul (amir), Hafizur Rahman Ahsan, and Kamal Salar. The reason for their breaking away from the parent organisation was their disagreement with the leadership about the electoral alliances in the 1993 elections in which Jamat-e Islami had decided to fight alone from the platform of Islamic Front. This group had taken the stand that the Jamat-e Islami should form an alliance with Muslim League, or else the People's Party could come to power once again. Moreover, they also objected to Jamat-e Islami's close links with Pasban and said that the leadership of Jamat-e Islami was playing in the hands of Pasban youths. Jamat-e Islami was of the view that Tahreek-e Islami Pakistan has been formed by Muslim League (N) by spending a lot of money, and that this group consisted of poets and writers who had no following among the common people. This group had the support of Mian Tufail, ex-amir, Jamat-e Islami. This group resigned from Jamat-e Islami as a protest, founded Tahreek-e Islami, and supported Muslim League in the elections.

Maulana Naim Siddiqui was appointed the first amir of Tahreek-e Islami. Soon dissensions began and it was divided into two groups barely six months after its birth. One group was led by Maulana Naim Siddiqui and the other group by Maulana Mukhtar Gul. Now, Tahreek-e Islami does not have any sizeable following and its presence is limited to Rawalpindi only.

Markazi Anjuman Khuddamul Quran, Lahore

The founder and leader of this organisation is Dr Israr Ahmad. It was founded on 21 July 1972 by seven different individuals. It was decided that those who wanted to join it as its founders could do so by paying Rs 5,000 in cash, and their names would be included in the Founders' Assembly.

OBJECTIVES

Among the organisation's basic objectives are to promote understanding of the Holy Koran and to pave the way for the restoration of Khilafat. For promoting understanding of the Holy Koran, it has set up Jamiul Quran, the Quran Academy, and Quran College in Lahore that conducts correspondence courses throughout the country. Its management is organised on the pattern of the management of Jamat-e Islami. There are four different ways in which one can be associated with the Anjuman:

Founders

Those who paid Rs 5,000 at its inception, and paid Rs 50 per month. The monthly contribution has been subsequently increased in stages to Rs 100, Rs 200, and now, Rs 400.

Admirers

Those who paid Rs 10,000 upfront sometime after the founding of the Anjuman and have been paying Rs 400 per month are covered under the category of admirers.

Permanent Members

Those who paid Rs 5,000 upfront and have been paying Rs 200 per month fall in this category.

Ordinary Members
Ordinary members are required to pay only Rs 100 per month.

From the above, it appears that the participation in the Anjuman is based on one's financial capability. But the Anjuman holds the view that 'the rules and regulations of the Anjuman keep sufficient scope for individuals who cannot pay anything directly, but can contribute their time, energy, and skill. Moreover, the nature of the Anjuman is not of an organisation but that of an institute.' Dr Israr Ahmad is the lifelong president of the Anjuman.

Tanzeem Islami

Along with Markazi Anjuman Khuddamul Quran, Dr Israr Ahmad also founded a political formation known as Tanzeem Islami whose objective is to restore the legacy of the Four Caliphs (Khilafat-e Rasheda). It declares that when it will have one lakh trained youths, it will begin the Khilafat movement. Tanzeem Islami does not take part in electoral politics.

PASBAN

Qazi Husain Ahmad, Jamat-e Islami's amir, had laid the foundation of the youth organisation, Pasban, with the motto, 'Against Oppression'. Its main objective was to draw those youths who were outside the folds of other youth outfits of Jamat-e Islami. Pasban came to public attention very soon. It played a crucial role in conducting the elections of Islamic Front in the general elections of 1993, and in giving Jamat-e Islami a popular face. But the older members of Jamat-e Islami had differences with it and it was disbanded. But its president, Muhammad Ali Durrani, tried to preserve it and severed relationship with Jamat-e Islami. When Faruq Al-Ghari laid the foundation of Millat Party in 1998, Muhammad Ali Durrani declared Pasban's merger with it. But the president of the Karachi branch of Pasban, Altaf Shakoor, preserved a separate identity for Pasban. It is now confined to Karachi and Rawalpindi, but it has lost its impact.

Hizbul Mujahideen

Hizbul Mujahideen is the biggest jihadi organisation in Kashmir. After the ban on Jaish-e Muhammad and Lashkar-e Tayyaba in Pakistan, it is now the most powerful jihadi organisation in Pakistan also. It is an allied organisation of Jamat-e Islami and functions according to its principles and decisions.

INCEPTION

Hizbul Mujahideen was officially declared to be formed on 1 November 1989. However, youths associated with Jamat-e Islami had already started jihadi activities in Occupied Kashmir. Syed Salim Gurdezi said, 'These jihadi activities were part of a plan and not chaotic. Actually, in the elections for the state assembly of Occupied Kashmir in 1987, Muslim United Front (Muslim Muttahida Mahaz) was defeated by fraud. This led the youth to think that the time had become ripe for armed struggle. Jamat-e Islami had been working on this plan for quite sometime. In 1983, Maulana Saduddin, the amir of

Jamat-e Islami in Occupied Kashmir had gone for haj. On his return journey he made a stopover in Pakistan precisely for this reason. Here, the blueprint of Tahreek Jihad was being prepared. Apart from meeting the leaders of Islamic movements, the Maulana met General Ziaul Haq and had a detailed discussion with him about starting armed struggle in Occupied Kashmir and the strategies that were to be adopted for it. That was the defining moment for the starting of jihad in Kashmir.' Syed Salim Gurdezi is the amir of Jamat-e Islami in the district of Bagh in Azad Kashmir. It is the same constituency from where Abdur Rashid Turabi, amir of Jamat-e Islami in Azad Kashmir, was elected to the legislative assembly. Gurdezi has spent a long period of time in Azad Kashmir and is intimately acquainted with the functioning of Hizbul Mujahideen. While discussing about its background, he said that when the blueprint of jihad in Kashmir was prepared, scores of Jamat-e Islami youths went to Afghanistan for training. That was the beginning of a trend that continued for years. In 1984, a two-member delegation led by Ghulam Hasan Lone came to Azad Kashmir for training, and then went to Afghanistan. In 1987, Muhammad Ashraf, a youth associated with Jamat-e Islami, founded a group called 'Zia Tigers' and its units were formed in Badgam, Baramula, and Kupwara. Two youths, Ghulam Ahmad Azad and Manzoorul Islam received jihadi training and then began to organise other youths. In 1988, the youths of Jamat-e Islami formed another group known as Al-Hamza Group with its centre in Sopore. Its leader was Maqbool Alai. On 28 June 1988, three mujahideen were rounded up in an Indian army raid and an American-style pistol and silencer were recovered from them. On 31 August, the armed struggle was started officially, according to a preconceived plan. After this, Jamat-e Islami started making efforts to set up a united jihadi front, and Hizbul Mujahideen was founded on 1 November 1989. According to a printed brochure of Hizbul Mujahideen, the name 'Hizbul Mujahideen' was arrived at by combining Syed Ahmad Shaheed's Tahreekul Mujahideen and Gulbuddin Hikmatyar's Hizb-e Islami. Among the commanders whose names were announced at the time were Muhammad Maqbool Alai, Muhammad Ashraf Dar, Muhammad Abdullah Bangroo, Muhammad Ayyub Bangroo, Muhammad Ilyas, Shaikh Ghulam Nabi, Farooq Ahmad Ganai, Ghulam Qadir Khan, Muzaffar Ahmad Meer, Badar Munir, and Tahir Asif. All of them have been killed in one mission or the other.

Two months after Hizbul Mujahideen was founded, a meeting was held in which a twenty-member council was formed, and a five-member Shura was constituted to formulate policies. In this meeting, Hilal Ahmad Mir al-Maroof Nasirul Islam was appointed amir of the management while Muhammad Ahsan Dar was appointed chief commander for jihadi activities.

CONSTITUTION

The constitution of Hizbul Mujahideen was approved on 10 June 1990. According to it, the central management of Hizbul Mujahideen would vest in chief patron, amir, and chief commander. The allied/affiliated organisations would be looked after by district and local commanders. There would be a Majlis-e Shura at the central level represented by two members from each district. Jamat-e Islami, Jammu and Kashmir, had the right to appoint anyone as chief patron, and the chief patron had the right to appoint anyone, in consultation with the Majlis-e Shura, as the amir of Hizbul Mujahideen. The amir of Hizbul Mujahideen, in consultation with Majlis-e Shura, could appoint commanders and the chief commander. But it had to be approved by the chief patron. However, contrary to this constitution, all decisions were taken by the Majlis-e Shura of Jamat-e Islami, Pakistan. It kept on appointing individuals of its choice at different levels of Hizbul Mujahideen. This interference became a source of major controversy in Hizbul Mujahideen later.

MANAGEMENT AS PER CONSTITUTION

In June 1990 the new Majlis-e Shura was constituted. Jamat-e Islami appointed its amir of the Srinagar branch, Syed Salahuddin, as the chief patron of Hizbul Mujahideen. Syed Salahuddin kept Nasirul Islam as the amir in the new set-up also, and appointed Muhammad Ahsan Dar as the chief commander.

MERGER OF JIHADI ORGANISATIONS IN HIZBUL MUJAHIDEEN

Hizbul Mujahideen was born out of the merger of Zia Tigers, Al-Hamza, Maududi Squad, and Ansarul Islam in it. Later, Tahreek Jihad Islami, Al-Badr, and Allah Tigers also merged in it.

Al-Badr was active in the areas of Islamabad and

Pulwama. Abdul Hamid Fayaz, secretary of Tahreek Tulaba, Jammu and Kashmir, was its chief patron. Tahreek Jihad Islami was active in Sopore and it was led by Commander Abdul Majeed Dar. Allah Tigers was a powerful group. It had played a significant part in destroying the cinema halls and radio stations in Srinagar and other areas. Its commander was Ghazi Ilyas.

In 1990, Syed Salim Gurdezi and Masood Sarfaraz from Jamat-e Islami, Azad Kashmir, crossed the Line of Control and entered Occupied Kashmir. (Currently, Salim Gurdezi is the amir of Jamat-e Islami in the Bagh district and Masood Sarfaraz has formed his own jihadi group, Hizb-e Islami.) These two have been looking after the training of those coming from Occupied Kashmir to Azad Kashmir, and those Pakistani mujahideen going to Afghanistan for training, and then launching all of them in Occupied Kashmir. That is why they had close links with the three organisations mentioned above. They had been sent to Occupied Kashmir to facilitate the merger of these three organisations/groups in Hizbul Mujahideen. They persuaded the leadership of the three organisations to merge in Hizbul Mujahideen. In mid-October 1990, in a secret hideout at Gandharbal where Ghulam Nabi Naoshahri, the officiating amir of Jamat-e Islami, Jammu and Kashmir, was staying along with Syed Salahuddin, Commander Shamsul Haq, Al-Badr's chief patron Abdul Hamid Fayaz, Saifullah Khalid and Allah Tigers' Ghazi Ilyas, these two gentlemen conducted the merger of these two groups (Al-Badr and Allah Tigers) in Hizbul Mujahideen.

Later, in the last week of October, in a similar meeting, Abdul Majeed Dar of Tahreek Jihad Islami also agreed to the merger of his group to Hizbul Mujahideen. In the same meeting Syed Salahuddin appointed Abdul Majeed Dar as the general secretary of Hizbul Mujahideen. Syed Salim Gurdezi and Muhammad Masood Sarfaraz returned after accomplishing their mission.

HIZBUL MUJAHIDEEN'S POLICY

The policies of Hizbul Mujahideen, according to its brochure, are as follows:

- Hizbul Mujahideen shall have regards for all individuals of the Muslim world, groups and rulers who consider jihad obligatory (for Muslims), and cooperate with them. But no one shall be allowed to use jihad and mujahideen for their own interests.
- Hizbul Mujahideen shall use its manpower and weaponry only against enemies and their agents.

AIMS AND OBJECTIVES

In the same brochure, the following aims and objectives are listed:

- To create awareness about jihad among Muslims and prepare them to assist the mujahideen in Kashmir and Muslims in general.
- Physical, psychological, and ideological grooming of youths and organising their participation in the jihad in Kashmir.
- To raise resources for the mujahideen involved in jihadi activities and help the refugees and all those who are affected (by jihad in Kashmir).

- To make the youths involved in jihadi activities an instrument of Islamic renaissance.

CONDITIONS FOR JOINING HIZBUL MUJAHIDEEN

The following are the conditions for joining Hizbul Mujahideen:

All those who want to free Kashmir from the forceful occupation of India can join Hizbul Mujahideen, provided that:

1. They understand the beliefs and aims of the organisation and are ready to embrace martyrdom, which is the chief objective.
2. They must observe the obligatory part of sharia and avoid committing great sins.

MILITARY ORGANISATION

Among all the jihadi organisations operating in Pakistan and Kashmir, Hizbul Mujahideen has the most well knit military structure. The decision to reorganise Hizbul Mujahideen on modern military methods was taken on 3 November 1991. In the light of this decision its earlier structure was changed substantially. The positions of patron, amir, and general secretary in Occupied Kashmir were done away with. However, in Pakistan these positions were kept at the central, provincial, divisional, and district levels. The position of supreme commander was retained at the central level. A supreme council was constituted to replace Majlis-e Shura. Different department were founded under different commanders to carry out different activities. For example, launching department, intelligence department, press and publications, department of education and training, logistics department, finance department, and department of communications. Syed Salahuddin was appointed the supreme commander and Abdul Majeed Dar was appointed advisor general to the supreme commander.

The Hizbul Mujahideen's military structure was constituted as follows: The central command council consists of seven members, including the chief commander, operations. There are three or four battalions in each district led by the battalion commander. Every battalion has three companies led by platoon commanders. Every platoon has three sections led by section commanders. Each section has eleven mujahideen, each platoon has thirty-three, each company has ninety-nine, and a battalion has 313 mujahideen.

Hizbul Mujahideen has named the sections, platoons, companies, and battalions after the names of Prophet's Companions, saints, famed personalities, and military generals. Following are the names of some battalions, companies, and platoons of Hizbul Mujahideen:

Important Companies
1. Hazrat Abu Bakr Company, Aarizal Berwa
2. Hazrat Umar Faruq Company
3. Hazrat Usman Company
4. Hazrat Ali Company
5. Hazrat Bilal Habshi Company, Pahalgam
6. Hazrat Salman Farsi Company
7. Hazrat Abu Huraira Company, Srinagar
8. Hazrat Abu Ubaidullah Company
9. Hazrat Imam Husain Company, Srinagar
10. Ibn Haider Company, Sansbal

11. Hazrat Mauz Company, Islamabad
12. Hazrat Hamza Company
13. Ma'z bin Jabal Company
14. Hazrat Abbas Company
15. Hazrat Jafar Company, Pampura
16. Tariq bin Ziyad Company, Chadwara
17. Syed Abul Ala Moududi Company
18. Dr Nazir Shaheed Company
19. Liaqat Ali Khan Company
20. Shaheed Ziaul Haq Company

Battalions

1. Al-Mudassir Battalion
2. Al-Muzammil Battalion
3. Al-Fajr Battalion
4. Hazrat Siddiq Akbar Battalion
5. Hazrat Umar Faruq Battalion
6. Faruq Azam Battalion
7. Hazrat Ali Battalion
8. Hazrat Abu Huraira Battalion
9. Al-Badr Battalion

Platoons

1. Hasan Al-Banna Shaheed Platoon, Baramula
2. Syed Qutb Shaheed Platoon
3. Syed Jamaluddin Afghani Platoon, Bhadarwah
4. Baba Hanifuddin Quraishi Platoon, Banihal
5. Sultan Arifeen Platoon, Kokarnag
6. Shaikh Hamza Platoon, Kashtwar
7. Syed Abul Ala Moududi Platoon, Kolgam
8. Mian Tufail Muhammad Platoon, Pulwama
9. Naim Siddiqui Platoon, Taral
10. Dr Nazir Shaheed Platoon, Avantipura

11. Qazi Husain Ahmad Platoon, Shangsnogam
12. Qaid-e Azam Platoon, Udhampur
13. Allama Iqbal Platoon, Khoum
14. Shaheed Liaqat Ali Khan Platoon
15. Abdur Rashid Turabi Platoon
16. Hamid Gul Platoon, Islamabad
17. Maulana Saduddin Platoon, Baramula
18. Maulana Ghulam Ahmad Ahrar Platoon, Shopiyan
19. Qari Saifuddin Platoon, Chadwara
20. Syed Ali Shah Gilani Platoon
21. Shaheed Abid Sultan Platoon
22. Shaheed Abdullah Platoon, Kolgam
23. Shaheed Nisar Platoon, Deri Nag
24. Azad Platoon
25. Shaheed Aejaz Dar Platoon, Srinagar
26. Ashraf Shirazi Platoon, Magam
27. Professor Abdul Ahad Platoon, Langat
28. Shaheed Gul Muhammad Platoon, Kupwara
29. Firdaus Platoon, Lolab
30. Shaheed Umar Platoon, Naogam
31. Shaikh Dawood Platoon, Badgam
32. Tanveer Platoon
33. Shabbir Sultan Platoon
34. Asadullah Platoon, Kharam
35. Shaheed Abdur Rahman Platoon, Srinagar Gafwarah
36. Abdullah Shaheed Platoon, Mohenjo-Daro
37. Shaheed Mushtaq Platoon, Qazigund
38. Shabbir Shaheed Platoon, Larkipura
39. Husain Ahmad Shaheed Platoon
40. Shaheed Abdus Sattar Platoon, Kangan
41. Professor Nazir Ahmad Shaheed Platoon, Sopora
42. Shaheed Javed Platoon, Fatehpura

43. Shaheed Rafiq Platoon
44. Shaheed Ghulam Husain Platoon
45. Shaheed Basharat Platoon
46. Shaheed Khalid Kausar Platoon, Akangam
47. Shah Ashrafuddin Platoon
48. Shaheed Gul Platoon, Doda
49. Shaheed Ashraf Dar Platoon, Lal Chowk, Srinagar
50. Shaheed Jihad Kashmir Platoon, Sanora Kalipura
51. (a) Shaheed Ziaul Haq Platoon, Srinagar
    (b) Shaheed Akhtar Abdur Rahman Platoon, Civil Lines, Srinagar
52. (a) Ashraf Shirazi Platoon
    (b) Shaeed Muhammad Rafiq Abangar Platoon, Kolgam

IMPORTANT MISSIONS OF HIZBUL MUJAHIDEEN

According to the brochure published by Hizbul Mujahideen on Kashmir, it claims to have carried out ten big missions so far. Their details, as published in the brochure, are as follows:

Wular Barrage

In February 1990, Hizbul Mujahideen bombed the Wular Barrage on Jhelum river that was under construction. On the pretext of controlling the water of the Jhelum river, India wanted to destroy the agricultural and industrial development of Pakistan by building this barrage. India could not resume work on it in the last eleven years.

Eliminating Three Generals

In the three wars that India fought with Pakistan, no officer above the rank of brigadier was killed. Hizbul Mujahideen claims to have killed three Major

Generals. Major General Inder Kumar Verma was killed in Rafiabad (Baramula district) and Major General Chena was killed in Doda (Jammu) by the militants of Hizbul Mujahideen. Apart from three Major Generals Hizbul Mujahideen also killed the Director General of CRPF, K M Singh. In addition to these, five brigadiers, dozens of colonels, majors, and captains were killed by them.

Destruction of Communication System
In 1993, Hizbul Mujahideen attacked with rockets the micro system installation near Banihal Tunnel on the Jammu–Srinagar highway and destroyed it.

Attack on Maulana Azad Stadium
On 24 January 1995, Hizbul Mujahideen exploded three bombs at Maulana Azad Stadium at the time when the governor of the state, General K V Krishna Rao was delivering his speech. Eighteen people died on the spot and more than a hundred were injured. Among the dead were the two bodyguards of General Krishna Rao, two police officers, and an army project operator, Anchan Singh. Among the injured were Krishna Rao himself, his advisor, Mr Goswami, and Dhanraj Malhotra.

Ambush on Jammu–Srinagar Highway
In 1991, Hizbul Mujahideen mounted an ambush near Qazigund on a convoy of 350 vehicles of the Indian army. Twenty-five vehicles were totally destroyed in the attack, killing about 200 army personnel and injuring about 500. Among the dead were Major George, Major Sidhu, and Major Gill. This ambush has added considerable glamour to the Hizbul Mujahideen lore.

Breaking of Jammu Jail

Three fighters of Hizbul Mujahideen under the leadership of Commander Irfan Ahmad broke the Kot Balwal Jail in Jammu amidst tight Indian security and reached Pakistan. This convinced the world about the efficacy of Hizbul Mujahideen's military training.

Operation Victory

On 23 and 24 April, Hizbul Mujahideen carried out missions under 'Operation Victory'. The areas from Orhi to Udhampur, and from Kupwara to Kashtwar reverberated with explosions and gunfire. The Srinagar correspondent of BBC reported that Hizbul Mujahideen carried out twenty-four missions in these two days, including ten landmine explosions. The Indian newspapers published it prominently.

Attack in Delhi

On 9 May 2001, fighters of Hizbul Mujahideen carried out two explosions – one in the defence ministry and another near the army headquarters. These explosions took place in South Block and Sena Bhavan that were under tight security. Sena Bhavan houses the main office of the army and South Block that of the defence ministry.

Attack on RAW office

On the night between 20 and 21 May 2001, Hizbul Mujahideen mounted an attack on CGO Complex on Lodhi Road. This complex houses BSF's headquarters, and the offices of CRPF, Indian secret agency RAW, and other agencies. The BSF's Gurbachan Jagat confirmed that grenades were hurled at the building. The weapons used in this attack were the same as those used in the attack on Srinagar secretariat by

Kashmiri mujahideen. *Hindustan Times*, one of the foremost Indian dailies, reported the attack and opined that the security arrangement of the Indian secret agencies was of no use at all.

Mission Near Sangrama Bridge
On May 29 Hizbul Mujahideen attacked a vehicle of the Indian army with landmines near Sangrama Bridge, when it was going from Baramula to Srinagar. The sound of the explosion was heard from 5 km away. Among the dead were Major Sikka, Major Nayyar, Havildar Bhushan Singh, and Constables Rana Singh and Jasvinder Singh.

IMPORTANT MARTYRS OF HIZBUL MUJAHIDEEN
According to Hizbul Mujahideen records, the following of its commanders have been killed so far:

1. Ashraf Dar, who was among the founder leaders of Hizbul Mujahideen. He was killed on 22 October 1992 in Sanora, Kalipura in Badgam district.
2. Shamsul Haq, whose real name was Ghulam Muhammad. He was the amir of Hizbul Mujahideen. He was killed along with two of his companions on 12 December 1993 in Badgam district.
3. Burhanuddin Hijazi (real name Ali Muhammad Dar). He was the first amir of Jihad Council and deputy supreme commander of Hizbul Mujahideen. He was killed on 9 August 1998.
4. Commander Ahmad Hasan, who was the deputy supreme commander of Hizbul Mujahideen. He was killed in Jammu in 1997.
5. Maqbool Alai, who was an inhabitant of Shaheed

Manjwa, Badgam, and the divisional commander of Hizbul Mujahideen. He was killed in a mosque in Badgam on 9 April 1993.

6. Commander Abdur Rashid Islahi (Saifullah Khalid Shaheed), who was the chief commander at Jammu.

7. Ghazi Nasibuddin Shaheed, who was the deputy supreme commander of Hizbul Mujahideen.

8. Commander Masood Tantrey (Abdul Hamid), who was the deputy commander of Hizbul Mujahideen and its chief spokesman. He was killed in Sanganpura on 24 July 2001.

9. Basharat Shaheen was from Beol Qasba near Gujar Khan.

10. Commander Arshad Ayyub (Abdul Rasheed) was the district administrator of Hizbul Mujahideen in Kupwara. He was killed on 27 October 1992 at Warpura in Kupwara.

11. Commander Umar Sarfaraz, who trained mujahideen for a number of years. He was killed on 22 October 1992 in Sanora, Kalipura, along with Commander Ashraf Dar.

12. Commander Mamoon Rasheed, who was the chief of intelligence in Hizbul Mujahideen.

13. Maqbool Alai, who was among the founders of Hizbul Mujahideen.

Zarbul mujahideen, Hizbul Mujahideen's mouthpiece, reports in its October 2001 issue: 'In Occupied Kashmir, Hizbul Mujahideen has so far killed three major generals, six brigadiers, 451 majors, 1,170 captains, and 27,000 soldiers of the Indian army. As for its own losses, so far 12,000 of its fighters and about

15,000 of its sympathisers have achieved martyrdom.'

NETWORK

The network of Hizbul Mujahideen is spread out in Occupied Kashmir, Azad Kashmir, and Pakistan. It had its training camp in Khost province of Afghanistan, which was later occupied by Al-Badr. The former Taliban government supported Al-Badr against Hizbul Mujahideen. Henceforth, Hizbul Mujahideen's relation with Afghanistan was limited to getting mujahideen from there. The district-wise divisions of Hizbul Mujahideen are listed in Table XXIV.

Occupied Kashmir

According to Salim Gurdezi, Hizbul Mujahideen's network is spread throughout Occupied Kashmir. Several other jihadi organisations also use its network. But a *mujahid* of Jaish-e Muhammad from Rawlakot, Abu Nasr (who had been to Occupied Kashmir a couple of times) claimed that Hizbul Mujahideen's presence is limited to Islamabad, Sopore, Kupwara, Gandharbal, and Baramula. The current secretary of Hizbul Mujahideen in Occupied Kashmir is Saiful Islam.

Azad Kashmir

Hizbul Mujahideen's network is present in all the districts of Azad Kashmir. Its headquarters is in Muzaffarabad. It has seven district-level and nineteen tehsil-level units in Azad Kashmir. Several allied units work under the tehsil unit. Hizbul Mujahideen had three jihadi camps in Azad Kashmir; two of them were near Muzaffarabad. The third was in Ankyal sector, which has later been taken over by Commander

Masood Sarfaraz.

Pakistan

In Pakistan, Hizbul Mujahideen has twenty-seven district-level and 207 tehsil-level units. The local and ward-level units number 1,540. Most of its camps in Pakistan are located in Frontier Province, which are five in number. Two jihadi camps are in Boniar, one in Thanda Pani (Abbottabad), one in Balakot, and one in Chatral. Hizbul Mujahideen's offices are still working in Pakistan. According to Rao Suroor, Hizbul Mujahideen's secretary in Dera Ghazi Khan: 'After the ban on some jihadi organisations, other organisations have also closed their offices and left. Except for Hizbul Mujahideen, all others have been advised to shift their offices to Azad Kashmir. We are working freely.' As opposed to the claims of Rao Suroor, in the town of Dera Ghazi Khan the offices of Harkatul Mujahideen, Jaish-e Muhammad (defunct), and Lashkar-e Tayyaba (defunct) were not only open but also functioning on 13 February 2002.

According to its annual report, Hizbul Mujahideen opened thirty-two new offices in Pakistan in 2001. Through the year, 2,692 members received training. The active members number 2,558, whereas the total number of mujahideen is 12,987.

Foreign Countries

Hizbul Mujahideen units are working in some Arab states and in the UK. But, according to Muhammad Fayyaz, one office secretary of Hizbul Mujahideen in Lahore, these units are not very active.

Forums that Provide Human Resource

The allied organisations of Jamat-e Islami in Pakistan play a significant role in providing human resource to Hizbul Mujahideen.

Islami Jamiat Tulaba

The most effective source of manpower for Hizbul Mujahideen is Islami Jamiat Tulaba. Students in various colleges and universities reach Hizbul Mujahideen through the jihad department of Jamiat Tulaba. Till 2001, more than 500 members and workers of Jamiat Tulaba had crossed over to Occupied Kashmir. Last year, thirty-nine of these were killed there. Currently, about 1,000 members of Jamiat Tulaba are either in the camps of Hizbul Mujahideen, or in Kashmir or in touch with Hizb. Besides helping with human resource, the Jamiat Tulaba also contributes funds to Hizbul Mujahideen.

Jamiat Tulaba Arabiya

Jamiat Tulaba Arabiya works as Jamat-e Islami's allied organisation in madrasas. It has jihadi links with Hizbul Mujahideen. The number of Jamiat Tulaba Arabiya members killed in Occupied Kashmir is 2000. It raises substantial funds for Hizbul Mujahideen. Ten of its members were martyred in 2001.

Jamat-e Islami

Jamat-e Islami has 2,000 trained jihadi members and workers in Pakistan. They have fought in the fronts in Afghanistan and Occupied Kashmir. Jamat-e Islami plays a significant role in providing human resource to Hizbul Mujahideen. Last year, twenty-two of Jamat-e Islami members were killed in Occupied Kashmir.

Other Forums

Among other forums, there are National Labour Federation and Shabab Milli that provide human resource to Hizbul Mujahideen. Many of their office bearers are also the office bearers of Hizbul Mujahideen.

Forums Providing Material Resource

Hizbul Mujahideen's annual report for the year 2001 records that 7,200 collection boxes were kept at different places throughout the country. The amount collected from these boxes were 2,37,680 rupees which was just one third of the collection of the previous year. In the same year 24,000 animal hides were collected. Six new motorcycles and three double-cabin cars were bought in that year. Apart from its own resources, Hizbul Mujahideen receives a big share of its funding from Jamat-e Islami which has set up several allied forums precisely for this.

Kashmir Fund

This is the most effective forum for raising funds. The leader of this forum is Abdur Rasheed Turabi who is the amir of Jamat-e Islami in Azad Kashmir. Apart from the collection in Azad Kashmir, a sum of 2,12,34,147 rupees were collected from Pakistan in Kashmir Fund in 2001. The total sum collected was 5,56,76,762 rupees. This is as per the report of Jamat-e Islami.

Kashmir Security Fund

This fund has been set up to help families of martyrs

and fighters. In 2001, the amount collected under this head was 5,67,929 rupees.

Al-Khidmat Foundation
Al-Khidmat Foundation has contributed 7,99,004 rupees in that year.

Martyrs of Islam Foundation
This forum has also been set up to help the families of martyrs. Besides the martyrs belonging to Hizbul Mujahideen, this also helps the families of those killed in Afghanistan and Chechnya. Last year, this foundation has spent 1,24,202 rupees.

Islamic Mission, UK.
This is the biggest source of funding from foreign countries for Hizbul Mujahideen. Its president is Syed Tufail Husain Shah. It collects funds from the UK and other European countries for Jamat-e Islami, Hizbul Mujahideen, and its allied departments.

Dissensions in Hizbul Mujahideen

Dissensions in Hizbul Mujahideen began much earlier when Nasirul Islam had disagreement with the policies of Hizbul Mujahideen and left it just after a few months of joining. Later, the breaking away of Al-Badr dealt it a severe blow. Among the recent instances of dissensions are the rebellion of Masood Sarfaraz and Majid Dar's declaration of ceasefire, that affected the overall functioning of the organisation. According to a media spokesman of Jamat-e Islami in Lahore, 'Behind all these dissensions are the hands of "agencies" which are afraid of the growing strength of Hizbul Mujahideen and follow the policy of "divide and rule" to keep it under control.' Following is a brief account of the dissensions in Hizbul Mujahideen.

Resignation of Nasirul Islam

Before joining Hizbul Mujahideen, Nasirul Islam was the leader of the jihadi group, Ansarul Islam. After a few months of his joining, he had differences with the commander-in-chief. At that time Nasirul Islam was the amir of Hizbul Mujahideen. He was an orthodox adherent of the Deobandi school of thought and began to oppose Hizbul Mujahideen's proximity with Jamat-e Islami. His second grouse was that Ahsan Dar, the commander-in-chief, monopolised all power. A Kashmiri *mujahid* of Jamiatul Mujahideen, Shakilur Rahman (code name) who now lives in the Bagh district said that Nasirul Islam was unhappy because he was kept ignorant of major affairs, and the funds collected under the heads of jihad and the Kashmiris were not utilised properly. Ahsan Dar's stand was that Hizbul Mujahideen was the jihadi wing of Jamat-e Islami and since most of the mujahideen are adolescent young men, they sometimes get impulsive and go out of control as they have guns in their hands. Hence it was necessary that Hizbul Mujahideen should operate under the guidance of Jamat-e Islami. He expressed this view in a conference. After this conference, the disagreement between Nasirul Islam and Ahsan Dar grew in intensity. The Majlis-e Shura of Hizbul Mujahideen supported Ahsan Dar's stand and Nasirul Islam left Hizbul Mujahideen along with Ghulam Rasool Shah, Manzoor Ahmad Shah, and dozens of other mujahideen. He formed a separate group, Hizbul Mujahideen Nasirul Islam Group which was later renamed Jamiatul Mujahideen.

Muhammad Ahsan Dar's Resignation
Before joining Hizbul Mujahideen, Ahsan Dar was the leader of the jihadi group, Zia Tigers. He was appointed commander-in-chief of Hizbul Mujahideen. But slowly the influence of the chief patron, Syed Salahuddin, grew and he had the same complaint against Syed Salahuddin as Nasirul Islam had against him. Ahsan Dar resigned from Hizbul Mujahideen on health grounds and the leadership of Jamat-e Islami appointed Syed Salahuddin as the commander-in-chief.

Breaking Away of Al-Badr
Al-Badr was an important jihadi group that merged in Hizbul Mujahideen in 1990. But in 1998, its disagreement with the leadership of Hizbul Mujahideen came out in the open. Al-Badr complained that Hizbul Mujahideen is unduly influenced by Jamat-e Islami, a fact that has antagonised a lot of mujahideen. Bakht Zamin, the leader of Al-Badr also complained that Syed Salahuddin monopolised all powers in Hizbul Mujahideen. He also alleged irregularities in the use of Hizbul Mujahideen funds. Eventually, the Majlis-e Shura of Hizbul Mujahideen expelled Bakht Zamin and his supporters, after which Bakht Zamin formed Al-Badr Mujahideen in 1998 and forcefully occupied the Aogi training camp.

Majid Dar's Disagreements
Majid Dar was the commander-in-chief of Hizbul Mujahideen who relinquished his position in November 2001 and Saiful Islam was appointed in his

place. Hizbul Mujahideen sources strongly contradicted the view that Majid Dar resigned because of any disagreement. They insisted that he resigned on health grounds. However, his disagreement with the top leadership of Hizbul Mujahideen and Jamat-e Islami had already begun in the month of July last year, when he had declared ceasefire with India in Kashmir without taking Jamat-e Islami into confidence.

On 24 July 2001, Majid Dar called a press conference and declared ceasefire in Kashmir for three months. It was a shock to other leaders of Hizbul Mujahideen and Jamat-e Islami. According to a member of Jamat-e Islami in Muzaffarabad, Muhammad Tariq, 'It was a blow that has pushed us eleven years behind.' The stand of Qazi Husain Ahmad, amir of Jamat-e Islami in Pakistan was that, 'This declaration indicates the stand of a few individuals. You cannot blame the entire Jamat-e Islami for this. Our stand is that Hizbul Mujahideen will keep on its fight against India. The people who made the declaration are the victims of some conspiracy. They will regret their decision' (*Source: Jasarat*, daily, 8 July 2000). A more surprising fact was that Syed Salahuddin confirmed the declaration with the modification that the ceasefire would remain valid for fifteen days. A commander of Hizbul Mujahideen who is known for his passion for tea at Sangam Hotel said that the situation was so complex that Jamat-e Islami was even ready to remove Syed Salahuddin. But the mujahideen insisted that Syed Salahuddin must remain the supreme commander. Abdur Rashid Turabi had to abide by this decision. The second demand was that he should disassociate Jamat-e Islami from the declaration of Majid Dar. This was not possible, because Majid Dar was counted among widely respected jihadi leaders. His Tahreek Jihad Islami had strengthened Hizbul Mujahideen substantially when it had merged in it. He was also held in high esteem by the mujahideen in Occupied Kashmir and his removal could have engendered discontent among them. When I asked who could be behind this, he said, 'The needle of suspicion points towards secret agencies. They could have influenced Majid Dar. He was not so naïve to take such a stand without valid reasons.'

After fifteen days, Syed Salahuddin declared the end of the ceasefire. Majid Dar sent in his resignation to the leadership of Hizbul Mujahideen, but it was not accepted and he was asked to complete his term. However, the leadership of Jamat-e Islami and Hizbul Mujahideen kept a tight grip on things for fear of any unforeseen developments. In practical terms, it made Saiful Islam the chief commander of Hizbul Mujahideen in Occupied Kashmir. He was launched in Occupied Kashmir through Nepal in December 2001.

After relinquishing charge, Majid Dar began to participate in political activities. According to a report, he met the ex-chief of RAW on 24 April 2002, in which he declared his intention to participate in the October elections. After this declaration, Hizbul Mujahideen began a mission, called 'Take Care of Traitors', to wrest charges from Dar's supporters in Occupied Kashmir and to appoint new commanders in their places. After this, the district commanders declared their disassociation with Majid Dar. According to Hizbul Mujahideen sources, the command council had called Dar's divisional commanders, Zafar Abdul Fattah and Asad Yazdani, to the base camp from Occupied Kashmir on 8 August 2000. But as the commanders refused to come, it was decided that they should be expelled from the organisation. After this, the operation 'Take Care of Traitors' began and it was completed in May 2002. The Hizb sources claim that this operation was carried out without any opposition and the commanders close to Majid Dar were made totally ineffective. One commander, Asghar Rahman, who was expelled along with Dar for anti-party activities, got in touch with Sher Ilahi, the commander of Kupwara district and expressed his willingness to abide by the decisions of the organisation. Others like Mumtaz Husain, Commander Abdullah, Adil Mushtaq, Malik Asad, and Majid Ghani have also expressed their allegiance to the organisation.

Revolt by Commander Masood Sarfaraz

In October 2000, Hizbul Mujahideen met another roadblock when the commander of the Peer Panjal regiment, Masood Sarfaraz, revolted against it. Masood Sarfaraz had a political background, as he was the nephew of Sikandar Hayat, prime minister of Azad Kashmir.

Masood Sarfaraz was the commander of the Peer Panjal regiment, Kotli. The regiment was named after the Peer Panjal Mountain in the Jammu region. The responsibility of this regiment was to train the Hizbul Mujahideen members. When Majid Dar had declared the three-month ceasefire in Occupied Kashmir, Masood Sarfaraz had opposed it and declared that he would continue jihadi activities there. Their disagreement began from there, which soon took the form of clashes. To take control of Jamat-e Islami offices and base camps, Abdur Rasheed Turabi (amir of Jamat-e Islami in Azad Kashmir) reached Kotli with 500 armed mujahideen. He was accompanied by Commander Shamsher Khan who had replaced Masood Sarfaraz. As the news reached Masood Sarfaraz, he also advanced along with his armed supporters. Both the groups began to exchange fire. This encounter continued for twenty hours without any interference from the central management. Masood Sarfaraz won this war of attrition and he occupied the offices and camp at Kotli. As many as twelve mujahideen were killed and dozens of them were injured in this encounter. This bloody clash was not limited to Kotli but spread to the areas of Sohna, Samahni, Khuiratta, and Nakyal. The common people of these areas not only saw it with their own eyes, but also could not escape its consequences as bullets and rockets fell on their houses too.

Jamat-e Islami held Al-Badr and its amir, Bakht Zamin responsible for this violence. The fortnightly mouthpiece of Hizbul Mujahideen, *Jihad Kashmir*, published an article 'Kotli Incident – Real Facts' in its October 2000 issue, in which all responsibility for the incident was laid at the door of Al-Badr. The article was written by Dr Muhammad Mushtaq, Jamat-e

Islami's general secretary in Azad Kashmir. The following is an excerpt from this article:

> The mujahideen in Jamat-e Islami participate in jihad through Hizbul Mujahideen. Each departmental secretary is a member of the central command council, including the deputy amir. The amir of Jamat-e Islami, Azad Kashmir, has the power to appoint or dismiss him. The amir had appointed Masood Sarfaraz too.

For sometime now, the following complaints have been received from mujahideen, commanders, and from other sources in Pakistan and Azad Kashmir:

1. At every level, responsibilities are given not on the basis of merit and efficiency but on personal loyalty. Many competent people who refused to toe the line have been expelled from the set-up and made ineffective. Commander Shamsher Khan who has played a crucial role in consolidating jihad in the valley and Jammu, has been made ineffective in the organisation, along with a host of sincere commanders and mujahideen.

2. The advisory system has not been fully implemented. The instructions from the central management were not carried out. All decisions have been taken arbitrarily or through the 'Kitchen Cabinet'.

3. Competent and sincere people were sidelined and criminals were given responsibilities. As a result, the cause of jihad, the organisation, and Pakistan were all maligned.

4. Rather than imparting training to mujahideen with sympathy and warmth, they have been

subjected to beating and torture in the camps. Even after attention was drawn to this fact, corrective measures were not taken.

5. The mujahideen who were under training or in the front were told fictitious stories to turn them against Islamic movement.

6. It is a rule that jihad funds can be collected only on the receipts of Jamat-e Islami or Hizbul Mujahideen. Fake receipt books were printed in the name of regiments without the permission of the management.

7. Funds were spent arbitrarily on personal likes and dislikes rather than on approved heads.

8. Such incidents have also been brought to the notice of the management where individuals were targeted merely on the basis of suspicion.

Committees were constituted to look into all these allegations, but investigations could not be conducted because of lack of cooperation from Masood Sarfaraz, and corrective measures could not be taken. Later, he resigned from the Shura and even the primary membership so that he did not have to answer for any of these irregularities. The Majlis-e Shura instituted committees and the management made all efforts, but his unhelpful attitude continued. When all possibilities of correction were lost, the central Majlis-e Shura and the amir of Hizbul Mujahideen, Syed Salahuddin, removed him from his responsibilities and appointed the immensely capable commander, Shamsher Khan, in his place. To implement the decision, a team of office bearers reached different camps on 1 October. When the decisions were announced to the mujahideen, they accepted them without demur. There was some protest at one or two places, but on the whole, the mujahideen accepted the management's decisions with equanimity. Later, the amir of Jamat-e Islami also visited some centres and explained the situations that called for these changes. Brother Masood Sarfaraz also accepted the decision and sent instructions to mujahideen at one place to handover everything to the management. He also expressed similar wishes to some other office bearers on phone. Allah be praised that the orders were implemented in such a peaceful manner. However, on the night of 1 October, Al-Badr's Bakht Zamin suspended his visit to Chakwal and reached Kotli with his troops and made his office the centre of a new operation. Brother Masood Sarfaraz also took shelter there. Incitement by Al-Badr and some other groups and manipulation by some invisible hands made him sabotage the earlier decision. On 2 October, at 4 a.m., the Kotli centre was surrounded from all sides and intensely fired upon. When ambulances tried to take the injured mujahideen to hospital, their tyres were punctured. The road was blocked and the driver was attacked. The area turned into a battle front. The injured remained there for two hours. The management remained a helpless witness to all this. This encounter continued for fourteen hours. The mujahideen associated with the management had made strategic plans to attack the lumpens, but the thought that any loss of life would ultimately be the loss of the movement dissuaded them. The management decided to shift offices from Kotli. The arbitrators stood guarantee to the fact that if the offices were vacated, the rival group would not re sort to firing anymore and all matters would be sorted out through discussions. But the following morning,

three different camps were attacked. In all this, Bakht
Zamin Sahib and Al-Badr were at the vanguard. Al-
Badr also made contacts with the media and the press.
Journalists were called to its office for briefing and
the jihad and its leaders were maligned. As a result of
this mischief, lives were lost in different incidents and
the cause of the jihad and Islamic Movement was
harmed. Those on whom the Islamic Movement and
the mujahideen had placed unshakeable confidence
became the cause of their ruin. After this incident it
became apparent that Bakht Zamin and Masood
Sarfaraz were linked by some invisible thread and
they have come together to ruin the organisation.
The way these leaders of jihad have killed innocents,
insulted the management, and tried to harm the fifty-
year old organisation deserves a moment for
reflection for all of us. These elements are not meant
for jihad but for decimating it. It is a measure of their
egotism and evil intentions that they stooped to such
a level; or there may be some other hidden hands
manipulating them. It may be both. But despite their
machinations to sabotage the management's
decisions, the mujahideen are with the Hizb, and by
the grace of Allah, all responsibilities will remain with
the true management. It is necessary now to be
vigilant so that these traitors find no place in the
organisation, and they be exposed on all fronts. Their
target is not India, but the Islamic Movement and its
leadership... May Allah save us from the mischief of
Devil and men. We pray to Allah to purify the caravan
of jihad from black sheep, so that the freedom of
Kashmir and completion of Pakistan may become a
reality.

After this, Masood Sarfaraz formed his separate jihadi

organisation, Peer Panjal Regiment which was later renamed 'Hizb-e Islami'. The local administration did not take any action on that bloody incident.

Current Situation

Hizbul Mujahideen is taken to be the greatest and the most representative organisation of the Kashmiris. After the ban on jihadi organisations on 13 January 2002, it has gained new prominence. The home ministry instructed all jihadi organisations except Hizbul Mujahideen to shift their offices to Azad Kashmir.

It has been given a prominent place in the new set-up of jihadi organisations. The chairmanship of Muttahida Jihad Council will stay with it permanently. Many small jihadi organisations have also merged in it.

Table XXIV: *Hizbul Mujahideen: District-wise Division*

Sr. No.	District/Tehsil	Secretary	Centre/Office
1.	Lahore	Ayaz Geelani	Office Jamat-e Islami, Laton Road, Lahore
2.	Wahari	Muhammad Tariq Javed Bhatti	Jinnah Road, Wahari
3.	Mianwali	Anwar Mahmood Anwar	Hamas Street, Mohalla Islampura, Mooch, Mianwali
4.	Chakwal	Ahmad Gulfam	Office Jamat-e Islami, Chakwal
5.	Jhang	Commander Mohammad Yusuf	Jhang Sadar
6.	Mandi Bahauddin	Khalid Muhammad Gujjar	Chowk Alvi Hospital, Mandi Bahauddin
7.	Khanewal	Raja Mohammad Rasheed Khyal	
8.	Sargodha		Bait-ul-Akram, Fazil Town, Sargodha

Sr. No.	District/Tehsil	Secretary	Centre/Office
9.	Dera Ghazi Khan	Rao Suroor	Office, Jamat-e Islami, Block No. 13, Dera Ghazi Khan
10.	Rawalpindi	Shamsur Rahman Sawati	Baitul-Akram, Al-Ikraam Building, Mureed, Rawalpindi
11.	Mianwali	Osama Farooq	Main Bazar, Mianwali
12.	Multan	Hammad Rasheed Ziaee	Office, Jamat-e Islami, Multan
13.	Bhakkar	Naved Zafar Gilani	Baitul-Akram, Near Punjab Public High School, Mandi Town, Bhakkar
14.	Bahawalpur	Tariq Hashmi	
15.	Gujranwala	Muhammad Akbar Mujahid	
16.	Bhawalnagar	Riyaz Ahmad Ayaz	
17.	Toba Tek Singh	Maulana Abdur Rahman	Baitul-Akram, Garden Town, Toba Tek Singh
18.	Faisalabad	Abdul Haq Shah	Jama Masjid, Kachehri Bazar, Faisalabad
19.	Kamaliya	Haq Nawaz Haidri	Delhi Chowk, Kamaliya
20.	Texla	Syed Aqeel Haider	Texla
21.	Peshawar	Fazlo Wadood	Jamat-e Islami Office, Peshawar
22.	Der	Hazrat Ahmad Bhai	Jamat-e Islami Office, Der
23.	Chitral	Suroor Khan Suroor	Huzoor, Chitral
24.	Hazara Division	Khalid Kaka Khel	Khalabat, Township
25.	District Haripur	Muhammad Ashfaq Awan	
26.	Karam Agency	Noorullah Gul	Karam Agency
27.	Muzaffarabad		Baitul-Akram, Bela Noor Shah, General Bus Stand, Muzaffarabad
28.	Rawlakot	Abdur Rahman Ghazi	Near Lorry Adda, Rawlakot
29.	Bagh		Bagh
30.	Meerpur	Muhammad Raheel Dar	Meerpur

Sr. No.	District/Tehsil	Secretary	Centre/Office
31.	Kotli		Roli Gali, Kotli
32.	Palandri	Muhammad Bashir Khan	Near Bismillah Book Shop, Palandri

Al-Badr Mujahideen

Al-Badr is considered to be a reasonably big jihadi formation that is engaged in militant activities in Occupied Kashmir. Bakht Zamin is its amir. It is aligned to the thinking of Jamat-e Islami, and it has organisational links with Tahreek-e Islami and Pasban.

BACKGROUND

Al-Badr Mujahideen traces its beginnings from Al-Badr of East Pakistan (now Bangladesh) in the seventies of the twentieth century. It had been formed by the youths of Jamat-e Islami and Islami Jamiat Tulaba. This organisation had also taken part in the war in Afghanistan. According to a brochure of Al-Badr:

> In 1979, when Russia descended on Afghanistan with all its aggressive vanity, the youths of Al-Badr joined our Afghan brothers to fight a superpower like Russia from the very first day. They began a holy jihad and defeated the Russian colonialists at every place. With their own blood they wrote the glorious and immortal history of Afghanistan's freedom and Russia's defeat. Al-Badr mujahideen took prominent part, especially in the victory of Kabul, Logar, Gardez, Khost, and Jalalabad.

When armed struggle began in Occupied Kashmir, the

517

youths of Jamat-e Islami in Srinagar formed a group called Al-Badr. They had received training in Al-Badr's training camps in Afghanistan. It began militant activities in Occupied Kashmir in 1989.

Merger with Hizbul Mujahideen

Hizbul Mujahideen was a united front of the jihadi organisations of Jamat-e Islami school of thought. Seven big formations came together and began to work under one management. Al-Badr was a big formation among them in terms of its human and military strength. Abdul Hamid Fayaz was its chief patron. Al-Badr was active in Anantnag (Islamabad) and Pulwama.

In the middle of October 1990, Abdul Hamid Fayaz and Commander Saifullah Khalid declared Al-Badr's merger in Hizbul Mujahideen. Salim Gurdezi and Masood Sarfaraz played an important role in bringing about this merger. Al-Badr leaders were given high positions in Hizbul Mujahideen. In Pakistan, however, Al-Badr kept its separate identity and it was known to be allied to Zarbul Mujahideen. It is important to note here that before the Hizb established its own camps, its mujahideen received training in Al-Badr jihadi camps in Afghanistan, Kashmir, and Mansehra.

Separation from Hizbul Mujahideen

Al-Badr Mujahideen broke away from Hizbul Mujahideen a couple of years later. A *mujahid* of Al-Badr in Kotli states the reason for this separation as follows:

Our foremost grouse against them was that Hizbul Mujahideen had been penetrated by such elements as believed in negotiating with the Indian government. Rather than discouraging them, Jamat-e Islami and Hizbul Mujahideen chose to ignore it. The mujahideen were demoralised by the behaviour of these Indian agents, and there was a slow-down in jihadi activities. Hizbul Mujahideen worked under the tight leash of Jamat-e Islami and was not ready to act on its own. They made a hero of Mast Gul (of Charar Sharif incident fame) in Pakistan, though the mujahideen in Occupied Kashmir knew what his real character was.

According to this *mujahid*, there were also differences on financial matters. The funds were managed by Jamat-e Islami and the leadership of Hizbul Mujahideen was getting corrupted. Answering a question, this *mujahid* leader said hesitatingly that after separation, they had bitter clashes at several places over assets. Hizbul Mujahideen wanted to grab everything. The incidents that took place in Muzaffarabad in 1997 (in which five persons were killed) were over the distribution of arms. Another leader of Al-Badr told me the following:

Al-Badr used to provide Hizbul Mujahideen with funds. In Occupied Kashmir also, the real work was done by Al-Badr. Jamat-e Islami wanted to control it, but we wanted to remain free from its pressure. That is why it formed Hizbul Mujahideen. But we were in key management positions there. The training and launching of Pakistani and Kashmiri mujahideen were our responsibility. But Jamat-e Islami's attitude towards Al-Badr was extremely unfavourable. The bulk of jihad fund was given to Hizbul Mujahideen, and Al-Badr was ignored. We raised our own jihad fund, but Jamat-e Islami demanded to see the accounts. The dissensions began when the non-jihadi leaders of Jamat-e Islami started casting aspersions on the character of Al-Badr and levelled charges of embezzlement on Bakht Zamin Bhai. There was no basis for such charges; I myself have seen him crying when these charges were hurled against him. Once he told the leaders of Jamat-e Islami to go to his home and see how the son of his martyred brother could not have enough rags to cover his body. These non-jihadi leaders visited the camps and expected treatment of five-star hotels. How could one manage that in military camps? In brief, Jamat-e Islami kept on tightening the pressure on Al-Badr and put Professor Abdullah of Rawalpindi in-charge of all the camps. After reaching the camps, his first demand was to have a toilet with commode for himself. We kept on catering to their whims and fancies, but finally our cup of patience brimmed over when the Jamat-e Islami asked Bakht Zamin to resign. Bakht Bhai was ready to resign but the mujahideen did not want him to. On the insistence of mujahideen he declined to resign and Al-Badr charted its separate way. It is clear that it is they who suffered damage because of this. We began jihadi activities in a better way.

ORGANISATIONAL STRUCTURE

Al-Badr has a strong and well-knit structure. Its management is structured on the lines of Hizbul Mujahideen. The management and jihadi wings have been kept separate. The central amir is Bakht Zamin,

Advocate, and the commander-in-chief is Nasir Ahmad Mujahid. Bakht Zamin is from the district of Der in Frontier Province. He is a law graduate. During the days of the Afghan War, he was in charge of Al-Badr camps. The list of office bearers is as follows:

Central Amir	Bakht Zamin
Patron	Professor Fazal Wahid
Central Deputy Amir	Ahmad Hamza
General Secretary	Qari Ajaz Ali
Finance Secretary	Nasiruddin
Secretary, Press and Publications	Habib Sa'd Siddiqi
Secretary, Jihad and Preaching	Professor Fazal Wahid
Amir, Training Camps	Commander Qari Ajaz Ahmad
Launching Commander	Abdul Hai Jawar
Secretary, Indoctrination	Umar Faruq Jadon

For organisational purposes, Al-Badr Mujahideen has divided Pakistan into several divisions:

1. Hazara Division
2. Malakand Division
3. Peshawar Division
4. Kohat Division (This includes Dera Ghazi Khan, Leh, Bhakkar, and Muzaffargarh)
5. Jammu Division
6. Middle Punjab Division
7. Karachi Division (including Sindh)

NETWORK

Al-Badr's network is present in the provinces of

Punjab, Sindh, and Frontier Province. Its network and offices function in Faisalabad, Sargodha, Rawalpindi, Lahore, and Gujranwala in the Punjab province, Mansehra, Dera, and Mardan in Frontier Province, and Karachi in Sindh. District-wise details of its network are presented in Table XXV.

Al-Badr Mujahideen receives support from Tahreek-e Islami and Pasban, especially Pasban whose cooperation strengthened its network substantially.

In the first phase of the Taliban government in Afghanistan, Al-Badr had three camps there. Bakht Zamin had founded the camp at Khost. But the Taliban expelled Al-Badr from Afghanistan on the assumption that it was supporting Gulbuddin Hikmatyar, and its camps were occupied by Harkatul Mujahideen. Right in front of the Khost camp was Osama bin Laden's camp where Arab mujahideen received training. When Harkatul Mujahideen occupied Al-Badr's camp at the instance of Taliban, Amir Hamza, Al-Badr's commander, met Osama and on his intervention Al-Badr was allowed to shift its arms from there. This was the same Harkatul Mujahideen camp that America attacked with cruise missiles in 1999. According to a leader of Al-Badr, Osama was near the camp at the time of the missile attack.

CAMP AND CENTRE

Al-Badr's centre is under construction near Sawan River on the road from Rawalpindi to Islamabad. The plan has a mosque, madrasa, Islamic school, hostel for mujahideen, hospital, and library. The head of this centre is Mazhar Mahmoud Choudhury.

Aogi Camp

Al-Badr's camp is located in the jungles of Kolsh valley, on the east of Pakkal valley, which is three hours' journey from Mansehra. The manager of the camp is Umar Faruq Jadon. The central training institute was held every two months. This camp has been closed temporarily since February 2002, and the training infrastructure has been shifted to Azad Kashmir. But till April 2002, the jihadi training had not resumed.

Finance

Al-Badr Mujahideen devised new means of collecting funds for jihad. Jihadi Mushaira, military exhibition, demonstrations, etc., were introduced by Al-Badr Mujahideen for the first time. These means were immensely successful. In 1999, it took the 'Caravan Kashmir' to different parts of the country with the help of Pasban, along with a trailer carrying the model of a fifty foot Islamic atom bomb. This caravan was accompanied by mujahideen and the parents of Al-Badr martyrs who addressed audiences at different places. It started from Karachi on 5 February and reached Muzaffarabad on 13 February. Al-Badr sources reported that a sum of ninety lakh rupees was raised in those ten days.

Al-Badr also receives funds from several big industrialist groups of Karachi. It raised nine lakh rupees from the hides of sacrificed animals in 2001. Al-Badr has its central account with one of the banks of Rawalpindi: Zamiruddin, Account No. 1803, National Bank, Satellite Town, Rawalpindi. It has an account in

Muzaffarabad as well, where funds from abroad are directly deposited.

Human Resource

Al-Badr had to face difficulties about recruiting cadres. They adopted two ways to get round this problem. They got in touch with Deobandi madrasas and propagated jihad in them. Delegations were sent to schools and colleges too. Similarly, supporting organisations and agencies were also contacted. According to a *mujahid* of Al-Badr in Kotli, lack of manpower is no longer a problem for the group. On the contrary, it cannot provide training to the vast numbers that are coming, and all those who have been trained cannot be launched. He said that the madrasas of Deobandi and Jamat-e Islami schools of thought are important sources of manpower for Al-Badr. Madrasa Tafheemul Quran in Mardan is an important centre of Al-Badr.

Relation with Al-Qaida

On 6 August 1999, Reuters published the news that the commander-in-chief of Al-Badr, Nasirullah Mujahid (Almaroof Al Hamza) met Osama bin Laden near Jalalabad (Afghanistan) and assured him of support in case of any American attack on him. The meeting was said to have taken place in 'Daranta'. Nasir Ahmad Mujahid said that the Arab fighters had made full preparations to repulse any attack. 'We will fight till the end, our final goal is martyrdom. We are not afraid of arrest or death.' Nasir Ahmad Mujahid further stated, 'America cannot destroy us. If any such effort is made, our hands can reach Bill Clinton's (former president of America) neck.' Amir Hamza declared that all Muslims of the world consider Osama bin Laden as their leader. Two days after the publication of this news the Al-Badr spokesman denied any such meeting. It further clarified that although Al-Badr considered Osama a Muslim hero, Amir Hamza made no such statement to the effect that all Muslims of the world should accept him as their leader.

When we talked to Al-Badr Mujahideen sources about this, we were told that the meeting indeed took place and Osama bin Laden had assured Al-Badr of help to alleviate the difficulties it was facing in Afghanistan. 'In those days we were receiving feelers from the Taliban government that it was going to close down our training camps in Afghanistan. His intervention eased matters for us.'

Rift with Jamat-e Islami and Hizbul Mujahideen

After breaking away from Hizbul Mujahideen, Al-Badr was regarded as its rival group. There have been clashes between the two groups at several places in Azad Kashmir. In 1997, when Al-Badr broke away from Hizbul Mujahideen, there was a bloody fight between the two groups in the valley of Neelam in Muzaffarabad. Newspapers first reported it as firing by the Indian army, but KPI (Jamat-e Islami's news agency) reported on the following day that it was a fight between Al-Badr and Hizbul Mujahideen over the distribution of arms.

Hizbul Mujahideen has always had the full support of Jamat-e Islami. To break this nexus, Al-Badr aligned with Tahreek-e Islami, a breakaway group from Jamat-e Islami, in the 1993 elections. Side by side, it had also enlisted the support of Gulbuddin Hikmatyar's Hizb-e Islami. In Pakistan it also tried to enlist the patronage of Muslim League (N), though this effort did not succeed. Pasban which was earlier a part of Jamat-e Islami management, was a supporter of Al-Badr Mujahideen from the start. Apart from this, it improved its relationship with Taliban in Afghanistan and supported it against its fight with the Northern Alliance.

Military Activities

From 1991 to 2002, Al-Badr Mujahideen's 760 fighters have been killed in Occupied Kashmir. From the following break-up of these fighters from different places, one can gauge the level of support for the group in those places:

1. Faisalabad   40
2. Sargodha   20
3. Lahore   24
4. Gujrat   9
5. Gujranwala   14
6. Mardan   13
7. Mansehra   21
8. Der   18
9. Karachi   19
10. Quetta   2

Al-Badr Mujahideen has fighters from Arab and other countries. So far, eighteen of its Arab mujahideen have been killed in Occupied Kashmir. They were from Sudan, Saudi Arabia, Yemen, Algeria, and Egypt. There were also eleven mujahideen from Afghanistan and two from Turkey. According to a report published in a brochure, the activities of Al-Badr Mujahideen from September 2000 to 2001, were as follows:

> Al-Badr Mujahideen, true to its tradition established in the earlier years, has conducted powerful missions against various Indian army units this year also, from September 2000 to September 2001. It mounted more than 300 attacks on them, killing 2,469 soldiers and twenty-three commissioned officers. Army camps and dozens of army vehicles were destroyed. The Indian army has openly confessed that, 'It is not within our power to stop these youths filled with the flame of martyrdom.' In these fierce attacks against the Indian army, about eighty-six of our youths have sacrificed their lives in the path of righteousness.

The January 2002 issue of the monthly Al-Badr claimed that in 2001 Al-Badr Mujahideen conducted 158 attacks on army camps in which 3,221 Indian soldiers were killed. The details of these and other attacks, according to the journal, are as follows:

1. Attacks on army camps   158
2. Ambush   77
3. Attacks on task force   32
4. Attacks for victory or martyrdom 48
5. Anti-ambush attacks   27
6. Anti-crackdown   82

Indian Army Casualties
1. Soldiers killed 3,221
2. Brigadier 01
3. Colonels 05
4. Majors 19
5. Captains 34
6. Lieutenants 17
7. JCOs 23
8. Black Cat commandos 82
9. Soldiers wounded 2,403
10. Task force soldiers killed 98
11. Special Police Officers (SPO) 32
12. Task Force soldiers wounded 19

Material Loss Suffered by the Indian Army
1. Ventine vehicles 28
2. Gypsy 32
3. Oil depots destroyed 11
4. Jeeps 25
5. Arms depots destroyed 19
6. Camp buildings destroyed 23

Current Situation

In the beginning, Al-Badr Mujahideen was the organisation of youths in Occupied Kashmir. Slowly it was swamped by Pakistani mujahideen, so much so that now it is one of the big formations of Pakistani mujahideen. Youths from Azad Kashmir are also there. In the new jihadi organisational set-up, it has been asked to join the Muttahida Jihad Council (so far, Al-Badr was not a part of it, and the prime reason for this is said to be the chairmanship of Syed Salahuddin) and give primacy to the mujahideen from Occupied Kashmir for the jihadi activities there.

Table XXV: *Al-Badr Mujahideen: District-wise Division*

Sr. No.	District/Tehsil	Secretary	Centre/Office
1.	Lahore	Janisar Ahmad Zahid	94, Habib Park, Near Jamia Tanvirul-Quran, Multan Road, Lahore
2.	Faisalabad	Ejaz Qadir Ghazi	Aminpur Bazar, Faisalabad
3.	Okara	Sajid Inqilabi	5, Kachehri Road, Okara
4.	Toba tek Singh	Ali Hasan Badri	Shorkot Road, Toba tek Singh
5.	Muzaffargarh	Muhammad Yasir Bhai	Near Municipality Office, Muzaffargarh
6.	Multan	Muhammad Farooq	Hazoori Bagh Road, Multan
7.	Tehsil Jaranwala	Dr Riyaz Usman	Inside Ghalla Mandi, Jaranwala
8.	Tehsil Chatyana	Ikramul Haq	Chatyana, District Faisalabad
9.	Tehsil Gojrah	Mohammad Abdullah Cheema	Gojrah, District Faisalabad
10.	Tehsil Kamalia	Alamgir Mujahid	Kamalia, District Faisalabad
11.	Tehsil Tilla Gang	Aasif Mujahid	Tilla Gang, District Chakwal
12.	Tehsil Texla	Umar Farooq	
13.	Sargodha	Abdur Rahim	Rahmat Park, College Road, Sargodha
14.	Bhawalnagar	Mohammad Shahid Qamar	
15.	Karachi	Khalid Raza	Railway Housing Society, Gulshan Iqbal, Karachi
16.	Malakand	Amir Farhad	
17.	Peshawar	Gauhar Rahman	Alam Zeb Markaz Shaheed, Peshawar
18.	Mansehra	Naim Khan	
19.	Der	Ziaur Rahman	Main Chowk Der Bazar, Der
20.	Abbottabad	Muhammad Kalim Abbasi	Idgah Road, Abbottabad
21.	Charsadda	Zahid Farooq	
22.	Kotli		Shaheed Chowk, Kotli

Sr. No.	District/Tehsil	Secretary	Centre/Office
23.	Bagh	Farhad Ali	Kachehri Road, Bagh
24.	Chham Sector	Commander Mohammad Shafiq Afghani	
25.	Haripur	Habibullah Hazbi	Baitul Akram Hizbul Mujahideen, Haripur
26.	Karam Agency	Nurrullah Gul	Karam Agency

Jamiat Al-Mujahideen

Jamiat Al-Mujahideen is a jihadi organisation of the mujahideen from Occupied Kashmir. As opposed to other jihadi organisations, Jamiat Al-Mujahideen had this policy from the beginning that it would have only Kashmiri youths as its members. This is a breakaway group of Hizbul Mujahideen.

BACKGROUND

Jamiat Al-Mujahideen was founded in 1991. Its first leader was Nasirul Islam who had earlier founded Ansarul Islam. When Ansarul Islam had merged in Hizbul Mujahideen, Nasirul Islam was made the amir of Hizbul Mujahideen. But just after a few months of the merger he had differences with Ahsan Dar, commander-in-chief of Hizbul Mujahideen. The cause for these differences was the hold of Jamat-e Islami on Hizbul Mujahideen. As matters came to a head, he broke away from Hizbul Mujahideen along with other leaders like Ghulam Rasool Shah and Manzoor Ahmad Shah and formed the Hizbul Mujahideen Nasirul Islam Group, which was renamed Jamiat Al-Mujahideen in 1991.

Jamiat Al-Mujahideen is a purely jihadi organisation without links with any political party in Occupied Kashmir or Azad Kashmir. It is opposed to All-Party Hurriyat Conference and considers it a stumbling block in the way of the mujahideen and their struggle. It thinks that after the freedom of Kashmir, All-Party Hurriyat Conference would put hurdle in the way of establishing an Islamic state there.

ORGANISATIONAL STRUCTURE

Jamiat Al-Mujahideen has been structured on the same jihadi lines as Hizbul Mujahideen. There is an amir who looks after the political affairs and the management of the organisation. The military wing is headed by the commander-in-chief. Every vice commander-in-chief supervises over four divisional commanders. The divisional commander is the boss of district commanders. The area commanders work under the district commander. The current office bearers of Jamiat Al-Mujahideen are as follows:

Amir	Abdul Rafey
Patron	General Abdullah
Commander-in-Chief	General Abdus Salam
Deputy Amir	Muhammad Saleh
Secretary, Azad Kashmir	Sadullah
Secretary, Camps and Launching Commander	Commander Sajjadul Haq
Secretary, Press and Publications	Abdullah Haroon

When it began militant activities in Occupied Kashmir, Jamiat Al-Mujahideen was quite successful in its missions. But after 1996 when several of its commanders were killed, there was a considerable slow-down in its activities. However, in terms of its strength it is still considered to be a powerful jihadi organisation with network in different towns of Occupied Kashmir. In February 2000, its leader Ghulam Rasool Shah who is generally known as 'General Abdullah' broke the Indian jail and reached Azad Kashmir. After this, there has been a resurgence in Jamiat Al-Mujahideen activities.

Jamiat Al-Mujahideen receives the bulk of its funding from expatriate Kashmiris. It also receives funds from Kashmiris and Pakistanis in Azad Kashmir, Rawalpindi, and Islamabad.

The base camp of Jamiat Al-Mujahideen is located in Muzaffarabad, but its real roots are in Occupied Kashmir. It has been given special prominence and several small organisations of Kashmiri muhajirs have merged in it. It is different from Jamiatul Mujahideen of Deobandi school of thought; in fact its greatest fear is that people might take it to be a sectarian organisation. When efforts were made to align it with some Deobandi jihadi organisations, it declined on the plea that such a nexus would dilute its impact. It even threatened to close its base camp in Azad Kashmir if it is pressurised to toe this line.

Hizb-e Islami

Masood Sarfaraz is the supreme commander and amir of Hizb-e Islami. It was founded in July 2000. Commander Masood Sarfaraz is the nephew of Sir

Sikandar Hayat, prime minister of Azad Kashmir. He was among the founder members of Hizbul Mujahideen. Hizb-e Islami was born from the womb of Hizbul Mujahideen. Masood Sarfaraz was the amir of Hizbul Mujahideen in the Peer Panjal Regiment in Kotli. But he had had differences with Syed Salahuddin, the supreme commander of Hizbul Mujahideen and the leadership of Jamat-e Islami, and financial assistance to this regiment was stopped. These differences came out in the open when Hizbul Mujahideen declared ceasefire in Occupied Kashmir and Masood Sarfaraz refused to accept it. As a result, there was a bloody clash that has earlier been recounted.

After separating from Hizbul Mujahideen Masood Sarfaraz retained the name 'Peer Panjal Regiment' but later, it was changed at the instance of Majlis-e Shura. About the name 'Hizb-e Islami' it is said that Masood Sarfaraz had earlier fought along with Gulbuddin Hikmatyar's Hizb-e Islami and his permission was taken before naming this organisation. Hizb-e Islami has now become an important jihadi organisation and it has reorganised its units at Kotli, Bagh, Meerpur, Bajera, Muzaffarabad, and Rawlakot.

Chapter XIV
MISCELLANEOUS GROUPS

There are some groups and organisations working in Pakistan that do not have any alignment with the earlier groups. Among them Hizbul Tahreer, Al-Muhajiroon, Jamatul Muslimeen, and Al-Murid are important names. Moreover, some individuals and trusts having specific commitments are also working. Among them, Idarah Tulu' Islam is quite prominent, which works for promoting the teachings of Allama Parvez. His rather liberal outlook is not liked by many sectarian groups.

Al-Muhajiroon (Harkatul Khilafat)

The name Al-Muhajiroon was heard for the first time in 1999, when big posters and signboards with the message 'Return of Khilafat' were seen at different places in Lahore. It is a non-registered organisation whose objective is the revival of Islamic Caliphate. Some of its programmes were held in Lahore, Rawalpindi, and Islamabad. But it could not establish a wide network. Its main emphasis is on distributing literature in the form of pamphlets, etc.

However, it is not an unfamiliar name outside Pakistan. It has its network in Egypt, Syria, Morocco, and Yemen. Umar Bakri, arrested in the Daniel Pearl case, is its patron. Among its leaders in Pakistan are Adeel Shahid and Jameel Shahid (Abu Ibrahim). They are real brothers and claim that Shaikh Umar has entrusted them with the responsibility of managing the affairs of Al-Muhajiroon, Pakistan. Forty-five youths have already become its members.

Adeel Shahid is a young man of twenty-eight who had done FSc from Lahore and then went to the UK to do BSc in computer science where he got in touch with Shaikh Umar. His younger brother has completed his engineering degree from the UK. Khalid Mahmud Shahid, Adil Shahid's father, has been living in Holland for the last forty years. The brothers claim that Al-Muhajiroon is preparing the conceptual framework for the system of Khilafat.

In Pakistan, it has its office only in Lahore, at the following address:

101, O Block
Garden Town, Lahore
Ph: 0300–9448745, 5883154

Al-Murid (Danish Sara)

Al-Murid is not a proper organisation. It is a *tablighi* trust founded by Allama Javed Ahmad. It is also known as 'Danish Sara'. Its aims and objectives are as follows:

> What is Danish Sara? This is a way of thought and a world fraternity that endeavours to rise above all sectarian and orthodox considerations and understand Islam purely on the basis of the Holy Koran and the Sunnah. Members of this fraternity explain this ideal to others and help one another in fulfilling the

demands of faith. It has been established to carry out the responsibility that vests in the ulema through the Holy Koran after they have acquired scholarship about religion. What we want to achieve in this regards is this: First, to make Muslims aware of the accountability on the Day of Judgment through a study of the Holy Koran. Second, the message of religion should be conveyed to people with the help of modern means of communication. Third, for the religious education of Muslims, courses should be organised that will not only impart religious learning, but also teach them how to lead their individual and collective lives without being corrupted by worldly evils. They should be taught to honour the Prophet and help the religion, which is the demand of their faith. Their lives in this world should be dedicated to Allah and they should have the courage to die for Him.

The True Concept of Religion, a brochure

The central secretariat of Danish Sara is located in Garden Town, Lahore. Its twelve branches are working in different parts of the country.

Jamatul Muslimeen

Jamatul Muslimeen claims that all religious and sectarian organisations are false. Only it represents true religion sanctified by the Holy Koran and Sunnah.

Its amir was Masood Ahmad who was member of Jamiat Ghurba Ahl-e Hadith, Karachi. When he had differences with Maulana Abdur Rahman Salafi he left it and formed his own group. Masood Ahmad claimed that the Shias, the Sunnis, Ahl-e Hadith, the Wahabis are all misguided; only he could show the path of salvation.

Jamatul Muslimeen has got a good hold in Karachi. It has also established its network in Peshawar. Most of its members are from Ahl-e Hadith sect.

Hizbul Tahreer

Hizbul Tahreer is a world group for the revival of the Caliphate. It began to work in Pakistan in 2000 and established its centres in Karachi, Islamabad, and Lahore. In Pakistan, its spokesman is Naved Ahmad. Before 11 September 2001, its members used to gather at the Pak Tea House for their weekly meeting. It has also organised a few big programmes. It lays greater emphasis on distribution of literature. Naved Ahmad claims that Hizbul Tahreer is trying to bring about a revolution through peaceful means. But after 11 September 2001, the secret agencies of the government are harassing it.

Chapter XV

UNITED FRONTS OF RELIGIOUS AND JIHADI ORGANISATIONS

Currently, five united fronts of political and jihadi groups are working in the country. Their aims and objectives are widely different from one another. They are as follows:

1. Afghan Defence Council
2. Muttahida Majlis-e Amal
3. Milli Ekjahti Council
4. Muttahida Jihad Council
5. Jammu Jihad Council

Organisations and groups of different persuasions are members of these united fronts. There is one united front composed of only sectarian groups. It has already been dealt with in the foregoing chapters.

Afghan Defence Council

Afghan Defence Council was founded on 10 January 2001. It is composed of twenty-eight political and religious groups. Its leader is Maulana Samiul Haq.

BACKGROUND

In the beginning of 2001 when the Security Council slapped economic sanctions on Afghanistan, the leader of Jamiat Ulema Islam (S), Maulana Samiul Haq organised a conference of religious and political organisations at Jamia Haqqania, Kora Khatak, so that a strategy might be worked out to save the Taliban and Osama bin Laden. As many as twenty-eight religious and political organisations took part in it to form the Afghan Defence Council, and Maulana Samiul Haq was unanimously elected as the chairman. According to the published brochure of the Afghan Defence Council, the following resolutions were passed in the conference:

Boycott of American Goods

'This conference warns America, European Community, and India to change their attitude towards the Muslim world, Pakistan, and Afghanistan. Otherwise, a movement will be initiated to make the people of Pakistan boycott goods produced in these countries. This conference demands of the NGOs operating here to persuade America, India, and their stooges to desist from violation of fundamental rights and human rights of the people of Afghanistan. Otherwise, it will be understood that they are also involved in it. In that case, they will have to pack up their baggage and no one will guarantee their security in Pakistan.'

Palestine

'This conference regards the struggle of Arab mujahideen for the freedom of Palestine as a sacred crusade and invites the whole of the Muslim world to take part in it.'

Osama bin Laden, Crusader of Islam

'This conference regards Osama bin Laden as the

greatest crusader of Islam. His struggle is a struggle for freedom, not terrorism. The protection of Osama bin Laden is not simply the duty of Taliban or Afghanistan but the duty of the whole Muslim world. The hostile and repressive attitude of America and other evil powers have turned him into a hero of the Muslim world.'

The Kashmir Problem
'This conference offers full support to the struggle of the Kashmiris and regards it as holy jihad. It appeals to the honourable tribes living on the north-western borders of Pakistan to remain alert.'

Copies of the fatwa issued by Shaikh Abdullah bin Abdur Rahman al-Jabareen, a religious scholar of Riyadh, Saudi Arabia, were also distributed, whereby any business with America or such companies that help the Israelis was declared 'haram' (impermissible). In the light of this fatwa, an elaborate list of goods to be boycotted was also prepared, with the caption 'If you cannot buy a bullet for the mujahideen, then do not pay for the bullets of the Jews.'

The second meeting of Afghan Defence Council was held in Islamabad and its management was constituted. Liaqat Balooch of Jamat-e Islam was made the coordinator. An intelligence cell was also constituted to oversee whether America was using Pakistani land in its attack on Afghanistan.

The real character of Afghan Defence Council emerged after 11 September 2001 when America declared war against Afghanistan. Afghan Defence Council organised demonstrations throughout the country, but on the whole it failed to draw common people on the road. Thirty-two religious and political organisations are included in Afghan Defence Council. Their names are as follows:

Organisation/Group	Sect/Persuasion
1. Jamiat Ulema Islam (F)	Deobandi
2. Jamiat Ulema Islam (S)	Deobandi
3. Jamiat Ulema Pakistan	Barelvi
4. Jamat-e Islami	
5. Markazi Jamiat Ahl-e Hadith	Ahl-e Hadith
6. Sipah Sahaba (defunct)	Deobandi
7. Tahreek Ittihad Pakistan (General Hamid Gul – president)	
8. Tanzeemul Ikhwan	Deobandi
9. Tanzeem Islami	
10. Harkatul Mujahideen	Deobandi
11. Jaish-e Muhammad	Deobandi
12. Lashkar-e Tayyaba	Ahl-e Hadith
13. Harkat-al Jihad Islami	Deobandi
14. Al-Badr Mujahideen	Deobandi
15. Pakistan Shariat Council	Deobandi
16. Tahreek Taliban Afghanistan	Deobandi
17. Majlis Ulema Council	Deobandi
18. International Khatm Nabuwat	Deobandi
19. Jamiat Mashaikh Pakistan (z)	Deobandi
20. Jamiat Isha't Tauheed Al-Sunnah	Deobandi
21. Sawad Azam Ahl-e Sunnat	Deobandi
22. Muslim League (Kabir Wasti)	
23. Pakistan Ulema Council	Deobandi
24. Motamar Al-Muhajiroon	Deobandi
25. Hizbul Mujahideen	Jamat-e Islami

26. Mashaikh Pakistan	Deobandi
27. Muttahida Ulema Forum	Barelvi
28. Banian-e Pakistan	
29. Jamiat Ittihadul Ulema	Jamat-e Islami
30. PPI Pakistan	Jamat-e Islami
31. NPP	Jamat-e Islami
32. Jamiat Ulema Islam (Azad Kashmir)	Deobandi

Muttahida Majlis-e Amal

Muttahida Majlis-e Amal is a union of six religious organisations. It was founded in January 2002, and at that time its objective was articulated as follows: 'The borders of the country are at risk now. To resist external pressure, we must forge internal unity.' In the beginning, its agenda was to get religious leaders like Qazi Hasan Ahmad and Maulana Fazlur Rahman released. But now it has transformed as an election alliance and will take part in the coming general elections. The following organisations are its members:

1. Jamat-e Islami
2. Jamiat Ulema Islam (F)
3. Jamiat Ulema Islam (S)
4. Jamiat Ulema Pakistan (N)
5. Tahreek-e Ja'fariya
6. Markazi Jamiat Ahl-e Hadith

Milli Ekjahti Council

Milli Ekjahti Council was founded in March 1995. Maulana Samiul Haq played an important role in its formation. Its first regular meeting was held on 19 April 1995 in Karachi where a twenty-two-point programme was chalked out to remove sectarian clashes. Twenty-three organisations took part in it and thirty-three ulema of different persuasions signed the document. These twenty-three organisations included Sipah Sahaba, Sipah Muhammad, Tahreek-e Ja'fariya, Jamat-e Islami, Jamiat Ulema Islam (both groups), Markazi Jamiat Ahl-e Hadith, and JUP (both groups). The second meeting was held on 23 April 1995 in Lahore. It was hosted by Tahreek-e Ja'fariya and a seventeen-point code of conduct was devised. There were serious differences among some organisations at the stage of the approval of the code of conduct, so much so that Tahreek-e Ja'fariya and Sipah Sahaba threatened to walk out of the meeting. But they were persuaded to stay on and after seven-hour-long discussions and debates, the code of conduct was finally approved.

However, this code of conduct could never be implemented, and Sipah Muhammad broke away from the Council. Tahreek-e Ja'fariya and Sipah Sahaba also did not show much respect for the code of conduct, which diluted the power of Milli Ekjahti Council. Its political exploitation has also reduced its efficacy. Milli Ekjahti Council has now become practically defunct.

Muttahida Jihad Council

Muttahida Jihad Council was formed in 1999. It had seven members at the time of its formation and its leader was from Tahreekul Mujahideen. Now the membership has increased to seventeen, and the current chairman is Syed Salahuddin, the supreme commander of Hizbul Mujahideen. Shaikh Jamilur Rahman of Tahreekul Mujahideen is the general secretary and Liaqat Ali Azhari, the secretary of Lashkar-e Islam (Islamic Front) is the deputy chairman. The following are the names of organisations which are members of the Muttahida Jihad Council and office bearers representing such organisations:

1. Muslim Janbaz Force — Muhammad Usman (amir)
2. Hizbul Mujahideen — Syed Salahuddin (supreme commander)
3. Tahreekul Mujahideen — Shaikh Jamilur Rahman (base commander)
4. Jamiatul Mujahideen — Muhammad Abdul Rafey (amir)
5. Harkatul Mujahideen — Muhammad Ashfaq (amir, Azad Kashmir)
6. Al-Barq Mujahideen — Malik Hilal Rahi (amir)
7. Tahreek Jihad — Major Tariq Zul-Qarnain (supreme commander)
8. Al-Umar Mujahideen — Naimul Haq (amir, base camp)
9. Islamic Front — Hilal Ahmad Beg (president)
10. Al-Fatah Force — Khaki Nasrullah, (amir, Azad Kashmir)
11. Harkatul Jihad Islami — Jan Muhammad (amir, Azad Kashmir)
12. Hizbullah — Ishtiaq Ahmad (president)
13. Al-jihad — Zamir Khan (supreme

commander)
14. Hizbul Mumineen Shuja Abbas (amir)
15. Liberation Front Salim Haroon (president)
16. Lashkar-e Islam Allama Liaqat Azhari

OBJECTIVES
1. To unite jihadi organisations on one platform
2. To work out a collective military strategy
3. To remove mutual differences among jihadi organisations
4. To work out a common stand on national and international issues

SYED SALAHUDDIN'S DISMISSAL

Muttahida Jihad Council could never implement the above objectives. It suffered a severe blow when Hizbul Mujahideen declared ceasefire in Occupied Kashmir. Muttahida Jihad Council unanimously dismissed Syed Salahuddin from its leadership, and appointed Muhammad Usman, the leader of Muslim Janbaz Force as the officiating chairman. However, after the so-called ceasefire ended, Syed Salahuddin was appointed chairman once again.

WAR STRATEGIC PLAN

In the new jihadi set-up, Muttahida Jihad Council was made very active and it was made obligatory for all jihadi organisational members to obey its instructions. The Council made a plan in the context of the tension on borders, that was called 'War Strategic Plan'. In a secret meeting it was decided that all the jihadi organisations would handover to a committee the maps and other battle plans that they had managed to wrest from Indian army camps. This committee would formulate the strategy in response to Indian planning and then instruct different organisations about their missions. In the event of Indian army's advance towards the Line of Control, the War Strategic Committee asked the details of the fidayeen squads of the jihadi organisations to mount attacks on the army from the rear. According to the Lahore daily *Khabrein* of 20 May 2002, Tahreekul Mujahideen gave the names of ten squads, Jamiatul Mujahideen gave the names of seven squads, and Hizbul Mujahideen gave the names of more than eighteen squads. Other organisations are also trying to form similar squads.

Jammu Jihadi Council

Jammu Jihad Council is a united front of five big jihadi formations in Kotli, Khuiratta, and Nakyal. The objective is to forge a common strategy in the event of any emergency. The following formations are its members:

1. Harkatul Jihad Islami 313 Brigade
2. Lashkar-e Tayyaba
3. Al-Badr Mujahideen
4. Harkatul Mujahideen
5. Tahreekul Mujahideen

The leader of this council is Ilyas Kashmiri, the chief commander of Harkatul Jihad.

Chapter XVI
RELIGIOUS AND JIHADI ORGANISATIONS OF AZAD KASHMIR

Religious Organisations

About a dozen religious organisations are working in Azad Kashmir. The networks of organisations operating in Pakistan are also present here. Most of the religious organisations do not take part in electoral politics of Azad Kashmir. The basic reason for this is that they do not have much of a following here. Only six groups take part in politics and make alliance with purely political organisations. A brief account of these organisations follows:

JAMAT-E ISLAMI, AZAD JAMMU AND KASHMIR

Jamat-e Islami was founded in Azad Kashmir in 1973. Its first amir was Colonel (Retd) Muhammad Rasheed Abbas. After his death, Rasheed Turabi has taken over. So far, it does not have much of a political impact. Turabi had once been elected member of the Azad Kashmir assembly. His constituency was in the Bagh district. Islami Jamiat Tulaba, aligned to Jamat-e Islami, has considerable impact in this area. After this comes Hizbul Mujahideen, its jihadi wing.

According to Turabi, the management of Jamat-e Islami in Azad Kashmir has nothing to do with Jamat-e

Islami, Pakistan. However, it follows the same policies and programmes pursued by Jamat-e Islami in Pakistan. The motto of Jamat-e Islami in Azad Kashmir is 'Kashmir will be an Islamic state'. It also claims that it is committed to the freedom of Occupied Kashmir and accession to Pakistan. Jamat-e Islami is also working in Occupied Kashmir. At the popular level, its leader is Syed Ali Shah Gilani. Its headquarters is in Srinagar; however, its real strength is evident in places like Sopore, Baramula, Shopiyan, Kolgam, and Bandipura. About a dozen organisations are working in the social and educational fields in these places under the aegis of Jamat-e Islami.

AZAD JAMMU AND KASHMIR JAMIAT ULEMA ISLAM

This is the representative organisation of Deobandi school of thought in Azad Kashmir. Maulana Muhammad Yusuf Khan of Pulandri is its chairman. Ideologically, it is aligned to Jamiat Ulema Islam, Pakistan. Its impact is limited to Pulandri, Bhambar, Bagh, Kotli, and Muzaffarabad. Its membership is huge for which it is considered a force to reckon with in electoral politics. Five jihadi organisations of Deobandi persuasion are working in Azad Kashmir.

JAMMU AND KASHMIR JAMIAT ULEMA PAKISTAN

This is an organisation of Barelvi persuasion operating in Azad Kashmir, and is aligned to Jamiat Ulema Pakistan. Its current amir is Maulana Atiqur Rahman from Meerpur. There are many Barelvi shrines and mosques in Azad Kashmir. However, its political presence is minimal.

AZAD KASHMIR JAMIAT AHL-E HADITH

This is a religious organisation of Ahl-e Hadith persuasion in Azad Kashmir. Maulana Muhammad Yunus Asari of Muzaffarabad is its leader. On the political plane, it pursues the policies of Muslim Conference. Maulana Asari is also a member of the Muslim Conference's management. It supports the jihadi group Tahreekul Mujahideen.

AZAD KASHMIR JAMIAT AL-MASHAIKH

Among the religious and political organisations in Azad Kashmir, this one represents the 'Mashaikhs', i.e. grand teachers. On the political plane, it is aligned to Muslim Conference. Its amir is Syed Sadiq Husain Adil. Its impact is limited to the Barelvi ulema.

AZAD KASHMIR TAHREEK NIZAM-E MUSTAFA

This is a group of Barelvi school of thought. Its leader and president is the Pir Sahib of Niriyan Sharif, Poonch district. It supports Tahreek-e Amal Party. It does not have much of a presence.

Gateway to Terrorism

Table XXVI: Division of Jihadi and Militant Organisations in Azad Kashmir

Sr. No.	Organisation	Secretary/ Amir	Persuasion/ Affiliation	Centre/Office
1.	Hizbul Mujahideen	Syed Salahuddin	Jamat-e-Islami	Baitul Akram, Bela Noor Shah General Bus Stand, Muzaffarabad
2.	Al-Badr	Bakht Zamin	Deoband	Shaheed Chowk, Kotli
3.	Lashkar-e-Tayyaba	Abdul Aziz Alvi	Ahl-e Hadith	Chehla Bandi, Muzaffarabad
4.	Jaish-e-Mohammad	Maulana Asmat-ullah	Deoband	Neelam Road, Near Petrol Pump, Chehla Bandi, Muzaffarabad
5.	Harkatul-Mujahideen	Amiruddin Mughal	Deoband	Upper Chatar, Muzaffarabad
6.	Jamiatul Mujahideen Alami	Mualana Habibur Rahman	Deoband	Chehla Pul, Muzaffarabad
7.	Harkatul Jihad Islami	Commander Muzaffar Hussain Kashmiri	Deoband	Near District Hospital, Kotli
8.	Jamiatul Mujahideen	General Abdullah	Jamat-e-Islami	Lower Plate, Muzaffarabad
9.	Tehrik-ul-Mujahideen	Maulana Rafiq Akhtar	Ahl-e Hadith	Darul Hujra, Bajgiran, Shaheed Makki Road, Muzaffarabad
10.	Tehrik-e-Jihad	Abdul Majeed	Deoband	Near Lorry Adda, Kotli
11.	Al-Barq Mujahideen	Farooq Qureshi	Barelvi	Haider Khan Street, Near Kashmir Law College, Muzaffarabad

Sr. No.	Organisation	Secretary/Amir	Persuasion/ Affiliation	Centre/Office
12.	Tehrik Jihad Jammu and Kashmir	Tariq Zul-Qarnain	Barelvi	Chehla Bandi, Muzaffarabad
13.	Sunni Jihad Council		Barelvi	Muzaffarabad
14.	Zarb-e-Islamia	Aslam Wani	Barelvi	Merging in Jammu and Kashmir Liberation Army
15.	Karwan-e-Kahlid		Barelvi	Merging in Jammu and Kashmir Liberation Army
16.	Zarb-e-Momin		Barelvi	Merging in Hizbul Mujahideen
17.	Zarb-e-Islami	Commander Masood Sarfaraz	Jamat-e-Islami	Nakyal Sector, Kotli
18.	Tanzeemul Arifin	Shujat Ali Mujahid	Barelvi	Muzaffarabad
19.	Sheran-e-Islami		Barelvi	Muzaffarabad
20.	Harkat-e Inqilab Islami	Khalid Mahmood Qadri	Barelvi	Upper Chatar, Muzaffarabad
21.	Ababeel Mujahideen Alami	Javed Iqbal	Barelvi	Muzaffarabad
22.	Lashkar-e-Mustafa	Major (Retd) Yaqoob Saifi	Barelvi	Merged in Al-Barq
23.	Lashkar Ahl-e Sunnat	Ghulam Fareed Usmani	Barelvi	Is being folded up
24.	Mujahideen Jammu and Kashmir	Zahoor Bhatt	Barelvi	Chehla Bandi, Muzaffarabad
25.	Islamic Front	Moosa Khan Lodhi	Barelvi	Aaghar, Kotli
26.	Muslim Janbaz Force	Mohammad Usman	Barelvi	Chehla, Muzaffarabad
27.	Al-Jihaad	Sameer Khan	Barelvi	Upper Chattar, Muzaffarabad

Gateway to Terrorism

Sr. No.	Organisation	Secretary/ Amir	Persuasion/ Affiliation	Centre/Office
28.	Hizbullah	Mushtaq Ahmad	Muslim League	Upper Chattar, Muzaffarabad
29.	Al-Umar Mujahideen	Mushtaq Zargar	Muslim League	Kail Sector, Azad Kashmir
30.	Alfateh Force	Zainul Abideen		Muzaffarabad
31.	JKLF (Amanullah Group)		Non-Religious	Muzaffarabad
32.	JKLF (Yaseen Malik Group)			
33.	Dastageer Tigers			
34.	Hizbul-Momineen	Shuja Abbas	Shia	Chehla, Muzaffarabad
35.	Khomeini Tigers		Shia	
36.	Ali Tigers		Shia	
37.	Alamdar Kashmir Tigers		Shia	
38.	Abbas Tigers		Shia	
39.	Lashkar Zarb-e-Momin		Shia	
40.	Lashkar-e-Ali		Shia	
41.	Zarb-e-Haider		Shia	
42.	Al-Mujahid		Shia	
43.	Allama Iqbal Tigers			
44.	Qaid-e-Azam Tigers			

552

Sr. No.	Organisation	Secretary/ Amir	Persuasion/ Affiliation	Centre/Office
45.	Jihad Tigers			
46.	Islamic Students League			
47.	Liberation Students League			
48.	Balakot Operation	Azam Inqilabi		Muzaffarabad
49.	Al-Maqbool			
50.	Shabbir Shah Tigers			
51.	Pak Tigers			
52.	Azad Tigers			
53.	Kashmir Freedom Movement			
54.	Shah Hamdan Tigers			
55.	Sultan Badshah Tigers			
56.	Shahabuddin Tigers			
57.	Jamiat Ansar Al-mujahideen Alami	Commander Abdur Rahman Kashmiri	Barelvi	Meerpur
58.	Aljihad Federation Movement	Habibur Rahman Farooqi	Barelvi	Muzaffarabad
59.	Jammu and Kashmir Liberation Army	Commander Sajid Siddique	Barelvi	Kotli

Gateway to Terrorism

Sr. No.	Organisation	Secretary/Amir	Persuasion/ Affiliation	Centre/Office
60.	Kashmir Freedom Movement		Barelvi	
61.	Mahaaz Azadi	Azam Inqilabi	Barelvi	
62.	Mahaaz Islami			
63.	Hizb-e-Tauheed	Mubashir Fahad		Muzaffarabad

Jihadi Organisations

As many as 104 jihadi organisations have been formed in Azad Kashmir till now. Of them fifty-five are active ones. Twenty-five organisations have their networks in Pakistan also. The number of organisations that are active in Occupied Kashmir and have their offices or branches in Azad Kashmir is twenty-five.

There are two main centres of jihadi organisations in Azad Kashmir – Muzaffarabad and Kotli. Their central offices are located in these two big cities. The greatest number of organisations (thirteen) is of Barelvi persuasion. However, organisations of Deobandi and Ahl-e Hadith persuasions are more well-knit and active. The number of jihadi organisations aligned to Deobandi persuasion is five and that of Ahl-e Hadith is three. Shia jihadi organisations number seven. Jihadi organisations aligned to political parties in Occupied Kashmir, Azad Kashmir, and Pakistan are twenty-one; of them nineteen are purely religious groups, though the sectarian aspect is not overlooked. But because they are aligned to political formations, ordinarily they are not considered to be sectarian organisations.

Most of the jihadi organisations/groups have been discussed in the earlier chapters. The following organisations are operative only in Occupied Kashmir and Azad Kashmir and are regarded as important jihadi formations to reckon with. Some jihadi groups are confined to a small town or city; often they break up as easily as they are formed. Some details of the jihadi and militant organisations in Azad Kashmir are listed in Table XXVI.

MUSLIM JANBAZ FORCE

This is an important organisation of Kashmiri mujahideen and is aligned to People's Democratic Forum (erstwhile People's League). Its leader is the well-known Kashmiri leader Shabbir Ahmad Shah.

This organisation was founded in 1990 in Srinagar. Its first amir was Baba Badar who later left it because of disagreement with Shabbir Shah. In 1996, when the Indian government invited leaders of four organisations for discussion, Baba Badar was among them.

Muslim Janbaz Force remained very active in Occupied Kashmir till 1997. From 1990 to 1997, it carried out as many as 300 missions in which more than 300 of its mujahideen lost their lives. In 1997 when Shabbir Shah declared temporary ceasefire for the first time and agreed to participate in a dialogue with the Indian government, its activities reduced substantially. The commander of Muslim Janbaz Force refused to abide by this decision. Later Shabbir Shah reached an understanding with Muslim Janbaz Force.

Muslim Janbaz Force is also a member of the Muttahida Jihad Council. It has its base camp in Azad Kashmir while its central office is in Muzaffarabad. Muhammad Usman is the amir of Muslim Janbaz Force in Azad Kashmir. He had also been the temporary chairman of Muttahida Jihad Council. Most of the mujahideen in Muslim Janbaz Force are from Occupied Kashmir, even though Mujahideen are also recruited from Azad Kashmir and Pakistan. It has the support of several organisations of Barelvi persuasion from Pakistan and Azad Kashmir. In the new jihadi dispensation, several Barelvi jihadi groups from Pakistan have merged in it.

OPERATION BALAKOT (MAHAZ-E AZADI)

Operation Balakot is among the early jihadi organisations of Occupied Kashmir. Its leader is Azam Inqilabi. He has renamed the erstwhile Mahaz-e Azadi as Operation Balakot. Its objective was to provide a united front to jihadi organisations and fight together for freedom. This organisation was formed in 1990, the period when Hizbul Mujahideen and JKLF were at their peak. But there was no consensus among different organisations. Operation Balakot emerged as an independent formation. Earlier, its links with Azad Kashmir were not very effective. Azam Inqilabi forged links and founded a base camp there for training mujahideen, and he himself shifted to Muzaffarabad. However, in 1995 he returned to Srinagar and declared that henceforth he would struggle for freedom through the political process.

Azam Inqilabi reactivated Mahaz-e Azadi, but the activities of Operation Balakot also continued though he is stated to have disassociated himself from it. Now, Mahaz-e Azadi is active in Occupied Kashmir, but its branches in Azad Kashmir have lost their impact.

HIZBULLAH

Hizbullah, which was founded in 1990 in Srinagar is the jihadi wing of Muslim League. Its leader is Mushtaqul Islam. It has the support of Muslim Conference in Azad Kashmir, and that of Muslim

League in Pakistan.

Hizbullah is not a big jihadi formation. Its activities in Occupied Kashmir are limited to Srinagar. It received special treatment in Azad Kashmir during the presidentship of Sardar Abdul Qayyum. Its base camp is located in Muzaffarabad in Azad Kashmir. It is part of Muttahida Jihad Council. The amir of Azad Kashmir and Pakistan is Ishtiyaq Hameed. The youths of Muslim Students Federation (MSF), Azad Kashmir and Pakistan, are members of Hizbullah. Muslim League had asked MSF to cooperate with it. The Muzaffarabad office of Hizbullah claimed that seventeen of its Pakistani members have been killed in Occupied Kashmir. Mushtaqul Islam has been in Indian jail for the last nine years.

Al-Jihad

Before 1995, Al-Jihad was a part of Al-Fatah. In 1995 when Muhammad Aslam Wani had differences with Kashmir People's League, he separated from it and formed his own group. He felt the need of a jihadi wing and founded Al-Jihad and made Muhammad Nazeer its chief commander.

Al-Jihad has its impact in Kewara and Baramula areas. Its base camp is located in Azad Kashmir. Its organisational network can be found in several districts of Azad Kashmir. Its president in Azad Kashmir is Zamir Khan. Though it is regarded as an organisation composed of Kashmiri youths, Al-Jihad recruits members from Azad Kashmir also. It is a member of Muttahida Jihad Council and it has got a prominent place in the new jihadi dispensation. Henceforth, Jaish-e Muhammad and Lashkar-e Tayyaba will operate in Occupied Kashmir under its name and will be under the management of Al-Jihad. Abdul Aziz, the Supreme Commander of Al-Jihad, will be the head of this management.

JAMMU AND KASHMIR LIBERATION FRONT

The freedom struggle in Occupied Kashmir was first started by Jammu and Kashmir Liberation Front when in 1965 Maqbool Bhat and Amanullah Khan had founded a guerrilla group, NLF, with the help of Mir Abdul Qayoom, Major Amanullah Khan, and G M Lone. In June 1966, Jammu and Kashmir Liberation Front had begun militant activities. In 1989 when jihad began in Occupied Kashmir, JKLF was given the central role. JKLF calls it freedom struggle and not jihad. JKLF advocates an autonomous united Kashmir.

JKLF cannot be called a religious-jihadi organisation, though the Yasin Malik Group characterises their struggle as jihad. But it is opposed to any interference by religious groups. JKLF's militant struggle is not within the purview of this research work. Its differences with Hizbul Mujahideen and its consequent decline have already been alluded to.

AL-UMAR MUJAHIDEEN

Al-Umar Mujahideen is a small jihadi organisation. In Occupied Kashmir, its activities are limited to Srinagar and its surrounding areas. Its offices are located in Muzaffarabad and Kotli in Azad Kashmir, while its main centre is Keel Sector. It is successful among the refugee Kashmiri youths in Azad Kashmir. They idealise its leader Mushtaq Zargar.

According to Mushtaq Zargar, Al-Umar Mujahideen was founded in 1988, but it came out in public only in 1990. Before the founding of Al-Umar Mujahideen, Mushtaq Zargar was in JKLF. In 1989, he had differences with Yasin Malik and he formed his own group. He aligned with Maulana Umar Faruq's Awami Action Committee for gaining political mileage. It is said about Mushtaq Zargar that he has close links with ISI. Between 1988 and 1990 he visited Pakistan a couple of times. Not only did he acquire military training here, but trained mujahideen also. In October 1992, he was arrested in Saharanpur in police raid and remained in different jails in Occupied Kashmir till January 2000. During his imprisonment Latiful Haq was the leader of Al-Umar. He said that it was on Yasin Malik's information that the police had conducted the raid.

In December 1999, the hijacking of the Indian plane led to the release of Mushtaq Zargar along with Masood Azhar and Umar Sayeed. Since then he has been living in Azad Kashmir. When Jaish-e Muhammad was formed he was often seen with Masood Azhar in public meetings. Despite Maulana Masood Azhar's request he has not joined Jaish-e Muhammad. An interview with Mushtaq Zargar was published in the fortnightly *Jihad-e Kashmir* on 21 January where he articulated the stand of Al-Umar in the following words:

> The stand taken by our organisation is corroborated by the Koran and the Sunnah. We stand by jihad that can never be subordinated to the conventional

politics. We will obtain Occupied Kashmir through jihad, and then it will be annexed to Pakistan.

Al-Umar Mujahideen also conducts fidayeen attacks in Occupied Kashmir. *Al-Dawa*, Lashkar-e Tayyaba's mouthpiece, published an interview with Mushtaq Zargar in its April 2001 issue where he has admitted this fact:

> Lashkar-e Tayyaba and Al-Umar mujahideen carried out many courageous missions including fidayeen missions. The people of Kashmir are very happy at this, because India had led the propaganda that it was Lashkar-e Tayyaba that was carrying out fidayeen missions. Now, Al-Umar Mujahideen is also working hand in hand with Lashkar-e Tayyaba.

Al-Umar Mujahideen raises manpower from Occupied Kashmir and Azad Kashmir. But its training infrastructure is located only in Keel Sector in Azad Kashmir.

ZARB-E ISLAMI JAMMU AND KASHMIR

This is the organisation of Kashmir refugee youths. It demands freedom from India and the right of self-determination, i.e. the choice to remain an independent state or become a part of Pakistan. According to Zarb-e Islami, this decision should be left to the people of Kashmir. It does not support any religious or political organisation, and abides by the decisions of the All-Party Conference.

Zrab-e Islami's president is Aslam Wani who is an educated young man from Srinagar. The vice-president, Nasim Wani is also from Srinagar. It is not a big jihadi organisation. About fifty young men from Muzaffarabad, Kotli, and Rawlakot constitute its membership. It does not have a good network; its importance lies in facilitating the launching of mujahideen from other organisations. It has links with students' organisations across the border. On 19 February 2001, the government of Azad Kashmir had banned Zarb-e Islami, but this ban was not strictly implemented. Its office at Chahlabandi, Muzaffarabad, is still working. Zarb-e Islami says that this ban was the result of disinformation by those organisations that were sowing the seeds of sectarianism in Occupied Kashmir. 'We are opposed to this (sectarianism), but these organisations are powerful and they have the support of the government of Azad Kashmir.'

Nasim Wani is an intelligent young man who has been living in Muzaffarabad for the last five years. When I asked him why Zarb-e Islami was banned he said: 'There are some sectarian jihadi organisations here whose mujahideen in Occupied Kashmir are more interested in correcting the faith of the people than jihad. This often leads to a very complex situation there resulting in bloody clashes. The security network is so pervasive there that the forces immediately get to know of it and raid the hideouts. When caught, these mujahideen promptly admit that they are from Pakistan and have gone there to do jihad. The local people who give them shelter become the target of the security forces. We had appealed to the leaders of jihad here to send only Kashmiri mujahideen to Occupied Kashmir with the instruction that they should not interfere with the religious faith of the local people. Probably they did not like our suggestion.' I asked him who were the leaders of jihad? He replied, 'The leaders of jihadi organisations.' He did not want to amplify this theme. I changed track and asked him, 'What is the overall role of jihadi organisations in the struggle for freedom?' Nasim Wani replied, 'Kashmir has remained a flashpoint because of them, and that role is enough. The remaining responsibility vests in the political parties, to take advantage of the situation and carry out further the process of dialogue. The Kashmiris must be included in the dialogue because it is, after all, their destiny that is to be decided.' Nasim Wani said that he wanted to extend Zarb-e Islami to Pakistan, but has suspended this programme because of the ban on jihadi organisations. He did not say anything about procuring of funds and finance.

AL-FATAH JAMMU AND KASHMIR

Al-Fatah Force is an organisation of Kashmiri youths, and is aligned to Faruq Rahmani's political party, Kashmir People's League. It was formed in 1994 by the breakaway groups of Jihad Force and Al-Jihad. Its first leader was Zainal Abedin who had taken part in the state general elections in Occupied Kashmir in 1997. Aejaz Rahman from Srinagar is its current leader.

It does not have any network in Azad Kashmir and Pakistan. It has one office in Muzaffarabad and another at Islamabad. Most of the mujahideen of Al-Fatah Force are from Occupied Kashmir; however, some Barelvi organisations from Azad Kashmir and Pakistan help it with funds and manpower.

In a meeting in Islamabad, Janab Faruq Rahmani, the leader of People's League and patron of Al-Fatah Force, said: 'Al-Fatah Force is confined to Occupied Kashmir, and Kashmiri youths are operating it. Its mujahideen believe more in action than in words.' I asked him whether he would call it, armed struggle for freedom or jihad? He replied, 'Our struggle is for freedom. But this is also jihad; we consider it as such and are acting accordingly.'

'In strict religious terms?' I asked.

'Yes, in strict religious terms. We are Muslims and our actions in this context fall within the purview of jihad. However, Al-Fatah's view of jihad differs from those of other sectarian jihadi organisations. We have resorted to jihad only for our freedom struggle.'

In the context of the sectarian jihadi organisations Faruq Rahmani said, 'I had said in a programme of Lashkar-e Tayyaba that if they had limited jihad only to the freedom struggle they would not have been in a mess. There would be no ban on them. But they chose to publicise the fact that their mujahideen are Pakistani.' He further said, 'Al-Fatah Force is free from all sectarian feelings. Some jihadi organisations have already been identified as sectarian and communal. But Al-Fatah's struggle is purely for the freedom of Kashmir.'

MUJAHIDEEN JAMMU AND KASHMIR

This is a small jihadi formation whose leader is Zahoor Ahmad Bhat. Its presence is limited to Muzaffarabad, Kohala, and Dhirkot. Its activities are not yet too apparent in Occupied Kashmir. Its offices in

Muzaffarabad were closed by the government of Azad Kashmir on 19 February 2001. The reason cited for this was that it was extracting contribution from people forcefully. But Zahoor Ahmad Bhat refuted this and said, 'We are mujahideen, we cannot stop jihad. Neither shall we close our offices.'

In the new jihadi dispensation, Mujahideen Jammu and Kashmir has not been accorded any prominent status. It has been asked to align itself with JKLF (Yasin Malik Group). It has not accepted this suggestion and has declared to retain its individual identity.

Chapter XVII
RELIGIOUS WELFARE ORGANISATIONS

In Pakistan, seven big religious welfare organisations are operating. They are as follows:

Al-Akhtar Trust International

This an important forum that assists mujahideen. Its central office is located in Khanqah Imdadiya Ashrafiya, Karachi. Maulana Shah Hakim Muhammad Akhtar is its patron. Al-Akhtar International is working in the following areas:

1. Economic assistance to mujahideen (of Kashmir, Afghanistan, and Arakan)
2. Construction and Extension of madrasas and mosques
3. Digging deep wells in the drought-prone areas of the Thar desert
4. Flood relief
5. Ambulance and mobile hearse

Constructing a hospital in Karachi and a medical centre in Thar are among its programmes. However, its most active department is publishing, which publishes religious books in different languages. It helps organisations of Deobandi school of thought with substantial funds. It has closer proximity with

Harkat al-Jihad Islami and Harkatul Mujahideen. In the Thar areas it has got several welfare schemes. About twenty wells have already been dug up there. It had mounted a special drive for collecting funds for the Taliban and Afghan mujahideen. According to Muhammad Haris, a student of Jamia Ashraful Madaris, Karachi, fifteen students from this madrasa had been sent to Afghanistan; of them five are still missing. No one knows whether they died in Afghanistan or they are alive.

The network of Al-Akhtar Trust is not very wide. Twenty-two of its offices are working in Karachi and inside Sindh. In Punjab, it has its offices in Lahore, Bhawalnagar, and Pak Patan. Outside the country, its offices are working in the UK, Burma, and Bangladesh.

The following are the details of its offices:

Central office: Secretary – Maulana Hakim Muhammad Mazhar,
Khanqah Imdadiya Ashrafiya and Jamia Ashraful Madaris,
Gulshan Al-Madaris, Gulshan-e Iqbal 2, Karachi
Ph: 4981 958-4975 758–4975 658

Details of branches if Al-Akhtar Trust within the country are given in Table XXVII.

Table XXVII: *Branches of Al-Akhtar Trust in the Country*

City	Office Secretary	Address
Karachi		Ashraf Sindh Baloch Society, Gulistan Jauhar Block 12, Karachi Masjid, Hafsa Soorti Muslim Cooperative Society, Model Colony Maleer Karachi Asharfi Masjid, Near Clifton Play Land, Karachi

City	Office Secretary	Address
Karachi	Maulana Abdur Rahman	Jamia Masjid Rawal Pul Park, Block No. 6, Karachi. Ph: 4521460
Karachi	Sufi Shamim Ahmad	New Shamim Ahmad Jewellers, Shop No. 10, Ali Centre, Tariq Road, Karachi, Ph: 4532367
Karachi	Feroz Abdullah Memon	Mari Food Industry, Export Processing Zone, Landhi Karachi, Shafiq Sons, Shop No. 101, Bohri Bazar, Sadar Karachi
Karachi	Hafiz Mohammad Saud	House No. 10/15-C11, Nazimabad No. 2, Karachi, Ph: 6688080
Meerpur Khas	Qari Ashraf	Masjid Baitul Mukarram, Aziz Abad, Meerpur Khas
Meerpur Khas	Naseer Ahmad	Madrasa Baitul Uloom, Tandoo Jan Mohammad, District Meerpur Khas, Ph: 68441
Meerpur Khas (Jhaddoo)		Darul-Uloom Islamia, Jhaddoo.
Meerpur Khas (Mathi)		Madrasa Noorul Huda, Mathi
Lahore	Sufi Abdul Muqeem	Yadgar Khanqah-10, Imdaya Asharfiah, Jama Masjid Qudsia, Qaid-e-Azam Main Road, Lahore
Pak Patan	Hafiz Abdul Nasir	House No. 100, Near Masjid Noor, College Road, Mohalla Samadh Nawala, Pak Patan
Bhawalnagar	Maulana Jalil Ahmad Ikhwan	Madrasa Jamia-al-Uloom, Idgah Bhawalnagar, Ph: 72378-74100

Al-Rasheed Trust International

Al-Rasheed Trust is a welfare organisation of Deobandi ulema who are associated with the Taliban, Jaish-e Muhammad, and Sipah Sahaba. The government of Pakistan has banned it and frozen all its accounts. Among its main objectives are: economic assistance to the ex-government of Taliban in Afghanistan, economic assistance to jihadi organisations, welfare schemes in different areas, construction of madrasas and mosques, distribution of religious literature, etc. Al-Rasheed Trust has forty branches in Pakistan, and despite the ban they are working freely.

The founder of the trust was Maulana Mufti Rasheed Ahmad. He is counted among the great Deobandi scholars. He had enunciated more than 50,000 fatwas in his sixty-two-year-long life. He died on 3 March 2002. He founded the trust on 19 February 1996. Its basic objective at the time was to run welfare schemes in Pakistan. However, it has been providing funds to the Taliban for a long time. Before the end of the Taliban regime, more than one thousand employees of the trust were working in Afghanistan. Its greatest scheme was the production of bread. It had 500 production units for bread and five big centres for disbursing food. The expenses of running one bread production unit were twenty-one lakh sixty thousand rupees. The expenses of all the 500 units were one crore seventy-five lakh rupees. Three lakh people were the beneficiaries of this scheme. The trust constructed twelve mosques in Afghanistan. After Edhi Foundation, it is the most resourceful trust (in Pakistan). Despite the ban, it has raised twenty-five crore rupees from Pakistan between 1 January to 31 March 2002. On the occasion of Eid al-Azha this year, it sacrificed one crore four thousand animals.

The welfare schemes of Al-Rasheed Trust are not confined to Afghanistan, but extend to Chechnya,

Kosovo, and Arakan (Burma). In 2001, its accounts were audited by Sharif Kogan & Co., an audit farm of Karachi, that raised questions about different heads of expenditure. In 1999–2000, the trust received 14.6 crore rupees as contribution and spent 13.6 crore rupees. A sum of 750,000 dollars was sent to Chechnya about which sources say that the amount never reached the Chechnyan Muslims. Al-Rasheed Trust says that this amount was given to a religious leader, Shaikh Umar bin Ismail and Zelam Khan (ex-president of Chechnya). In the same year, the trust had given twenty crore rupees to the Taliban in cash. This was in addition to the welfare projects in Afghanistan. A sum of twenty-one lakh rupees was sent to the Muslims of Kosovo. Another sum of twenty-five lakh rupees were distributed among the flood-affected people of Rawalpindi.

After the end of the Taliban regime, the trust has got permission from Hamid Karzai to operate in Afghanistan. Its schemes are still running there.

OFFICES OF AL-RASHEED TRUST
1. Central Office Near Darul Iftah Walarshad, Nazimabad, Karachi Ph: 6683301
2. Islamabad 37A, City Plaza, Ph: 2870197, Fax: 2870196
3. Lahore Room 7, 3rd Floor, Sadiq Plaza, Opp. Masjid, Shahdamal Road, Lahore
4. Peshawar Madina Restaurant, 1st Floor, Opp. Government Higher Secondary School No. 1, GT Road, Peshawar

5. Quetta — Upper Storey, Shafiq Sons, Shari' Iqbal, Kandahari Bazar, Quetta
6. Sukkur — Al-Farooq Masjid, Barrage Road, Sukkur
7. Multan — Upper Storey, Wahid Jwellers, Kachehri Road, Near Chowk Clock Tower, Multan
8. Chatral — Shahi Bazar, Chatral, Ph: 09933-301901
9. Mengora — Upper Storey, Akbar Khan Plaza, Sohrab Khan Chowk, Mengora, Sawat
10. Abbottabad — 2nd Floor, Zarbat Hotel, The Mall, Abbottabad
11. Mansehra — Behind Ravi Road, Mansehra, Ph: 0987-301901
12. Hyderabad — Office Number 90–91, Al-Rahim Centre, Phase 2, Hyderabad
13. Rahim Yar Khan — Upper Storey, Aziz Medicine, Shahi Road, Rahim Yar Khan
14. Dera Ghazi Khan — Makki Manzil, Block Number: 9, Near Al-Ghari Machinery Store, Dera Ghazi Khan
15. Bahawalpur — Opp. Masjid Ahl-e Hadith, Model Town, Ghalla Mandi Road, Bahawalpur
16. Faisalabad — Govindpura, St No. 3, Near Ara Road, Faisalabad
17. Rawalpindi — Room 7, 1st Floor, Moti Plaza, Mari Road, Rawalpindi
18. Sahiwal — Room 17, Al-Safa Building, Pasha

	Street, Sahiwal
19.Mari	Upper Storey, Al-Habib Restaurant, Near GPO, Mari
20.Gujranwala	Thanewala Bazar, Near Batala Bakery, Gujranwala
21.Sargodha	Upper Storey, Khaja Durrie Store, Jama Masjid, Gol Chowk, Sargodha
22.Sialkot	Opp. Habib Bank, Paris Road, Sialkot
23.Dera Murad Jamali	Behind Jama Masjid Madrasa Miftahul Uloom, Bus Adda, Dera Murad Jamali
24.Kohistan District	Opp. Andes Hotel, Old Bus Adda, Bazar Kamila Dasu, Kohistan District
25.Gilgit	Opp. Tablighi Markaz, Kundas Town, Gilgit

Martyrs of Islam Foundation

This foundation works under the aegis of Jamat-e Islami. Its patron is Qazi Husain Ahmad and Hafiz Muhammad Idris is the chairman. Its main objective is to help the families of martyrs killed in Afghanistan and Kashmir. It works for the release of mujahideen in enemy prisons and helps their families.

Al-Khidmat Trust, Pakistan

This trust is also working under the aegis of Jamat-e Islami. Besides collecting funds for mujahideen, it also raises funds for constructing mosques and madrasas.

This trust runs ten schools and industrial homes for girls. It has its centres in Lahore, Karachi, and Faisalabad.

Barkati Foundation

The head of this foundation is Amin Barkati who is a leading industrialist of Karachi. It provides funds to jihadi and sectarian organisations of Barelvi persuasion.

Rabeta Trust

This trust was established by the Saudi Welfare Organisation, Rabeta Alam-e Islami, in 1988 with the cooperation of Pakistan government. This is one of the trusts banned by America in October 2001. The objective of this trust was to fetch the Pakistanis trapped in Bangladesh. Rabeta Alam-e Islami is working in ninety countries of the world. Its affiliated organisation, International Islamic Relief Organisation, helps Muslims in welfare activities. It is totally funded by the government of Saudi Arabia.

The weekly *Ahl-e Hadith* of Lahore published an interview with its director in Pakistan and Afghanistan, Rahmatullah Nazeer Khan, in its issue of 2 November 2001, where he said:

> We concentrate on mosques, health, education, and other welfare activities. We spend two crore rupees (every two months) on Muslim orphans. There are four orphanages – one each in Peshawar, Jalalabad, Mansehra and Gilgit – where about 1,500 orphans have been given shelter. There are a further eight thousand orphans who live with their relatives, but

we look after their needs. The department of health H H Health spends about thirty lakh rupees per month. There are small and big hospitals in Peshawar, Jalalabad, and Quetta. Similarly, the trust helps Muslim students in different countries, and arranges for tent and food for homeless people. It installs tube wells and digs deep wells in drought-prone areas. It has constructed about 600 mosques in Pakistan, Kashmir, and Afghanistan. The biggest project of Rabeta Alam-e Islami in these parts is the proposed rehabilitation of Pakistani families trapped in Bangladesh. In this regard, Rabeta Alam-e Islami has been in dialogue with the governments of Pakistan and Bangladesh for the last four years, and has established a trust called 'Rabeta Trust'. In 1988, a contract was signed by the government and Rabeta Alam-e Islami, whereby the Government of Pakistan contributed an initial twenty-five crore rupees to the trust and Rabeta Alam-e Islami contributed five crore rupees to it. Rabeta Trust intends to build 40,000 residential units for those families. Besides health and hygiene, this scheme includes construction of mosques and educational institutions. An estimate of twenty-five crore dollars has been worked out for all the schemes.

The Nawaz Sharif government had constituted a sixteen-member board to look after the affairs of the trust. Its details are as follows:

1. Ex-officio chairman Prime Minister Nawaz Sharif
2. Chairman   Shahzada Talal bin Abdul Aziz
3. Vice chairman   Dr Salih Abid, Secretary
                      General, Rabeta Alam-e Islami
4. Vice chairman   Sartaj Aziz, central minister.

5. Director General and Secretary General of Trust	Syed Amin Ajil Attas
6. Deputy Secretary General of Trust	Mian Tayyab Husain (Cabinet secretary)
7. Member of Trust	Choudhury Shuja't Husain
8. Member of Trust	Syed Yusuf Jasimul Hajji
9. Member	Dr Abdullah Umar Naseef
10. Member	Shaikh Hamad Azamil
11. Member	Dr Adnan Khalil Pasha
12. Member of Trust	Shaikh Abdul Malik Yusuf Al-Hamad (Abu Zahibi)
13. Member of Trust	Engineer Abdul Mohsin Muhammad Idris
14. Member	Shamshad Ahmad Khan (foreign secretary)
15. Member	Mian Shahbaz Sharif
16. Member	Janab Majid Nizami

In 1992, this 'Board of Rabeta Trust' constituted various committees to speed up work. There was a committee of census as well. This committee visited Bangladesh and conducted a survey of 41,000 families and issued them cards. The Board also constituted a housing committee that has already obtained a ninety-six-acre plot of land in the district of Mian Chunno in Punjab. This was donated by the Government of Pakistan. In 1993, one thousand residential units were constructed. Only sixty-three families had been rehabilitated when the Nawaz Sharif government fell (first time). In 1993, Nawaz Sharif assumed power once again and the work resumed. Towards the end of

1997, it was decided in a meeting that 937 families would be brought over and rehabilitated in the already constructed residential units. An additional set of 10,000 units would be constructed. The cost of one residential unit is 6,000 dollars.

By virtue of being the prime minister, Nawaz Sharif was the chairman of Rabeta Trust. Whoever becomes the Prime Minister will be its chairman. Dr Salihul Abid, the Trust's first vice chairman at the time, was the Secretary General of Rabeta Alam-e Islami. Now, he has been replaced by Dr Abdullah Abdul Mohsin al-Turky as the Secretary General. Similarly, one of the members of the board, Dr Adnan Khalil Pasha is currently the Secretary General of International Islamic Relief Organisation.

Dr Salih Abid and Sartaj Aziz had issued an appeal for financial help in this good work on behalf of the board. In this appeal people were requested to contribute liberally to the trust for the rehabilitation of these Pakistani families left behind in Bangladesh. The following two bank accounts were also declared in which contribution was to be deposited:

1. For Pakistani Currency
   Habib Bank Limited, Secretariat Block, Islamabad.
   Account No.: 9536–3
2. For Foreign Currency
   Habib Bank Limited, Civic Centre Branch, Islamabad.
   Account No.: 97073–1

It was instructed that cheques should be sent in the name of 'Secretary General of Rabeta Trust'. Now the ex-officio chairman of Rabeta Trust is General Parvez

Musharraf.

After the ban on Rabeta Trust, the government spokesman told journalists on 14 October 2001, that when General Parvez Musharraf took over as chief executive, he automatically became the chairman of the trust. But he had not attended any of its meetings. Now, the president of Pakistan has ordered for the audit of all accounts of Rabeta Trust. The secretary of the Cabinet division has been made the chairman of Rabeta Trust.

Chapter XVIII

MADRASAS IN PAKISTAN

The number of madrasas in Pakistan has gone up to 6,761. In 1947, when Pakistan was established, there were only 245 madrasas in Pakistan. In 1988 the number reached 2,861. Between 1988 and 2000 this number increased by 136 per cent. At present there are 3,135 madrasas in the state of Punjab, 1,281 in the Frontier Province, 905 in Sindh, ninety-six in Baluchistan, 151 in Azad Kashmir, and 194 in Islamabad. This is according to a recent study conducted by the Institute of Policy Studies, Islamabad. However, according to the report of the ministry of education and the ministry of religious affairs published in 2000, the madrasas are 6,678 in number.

If the madrasas are divided on sectarian basis, we find that 64 per cent are of Deobandi, 25 per cent are of Barelvi, 6 per cent of Ahl-e Hadith, and 3 per cent are of Shia persuasion. The total number of students in the madrasas is close to thirteen lakh. In the last twelve years Shia madrasas have shown the highest increase, going up by 773 per cent. Ahl-e Hadith madrasas showed an increase of 131 per cent. In 1988, there were 785 madrasas of Deobandi persuasion. Madrasas of Barelvi persuasions were eighty. However, according to the report of the ministry of education and the ministry of religious affairs published in 2000, currently madrasas of Deobandi persuasion number 6761 (Translator's Note: There seems to be some discrepancy here; earlier it was said that the total number of madrasas is 6,761), of Barelvi persuasion 1,363, of Ahl-e Hadith 310, and of Shia sect 297. Institutions that are not affiliated to any board or any particular persuasion number 2,761. According to a survey, the number of madrasas committed to the ideology of some sect or the other is 4,108. Madrasas apparently not aligned to any ideology number 2,701. However, in practical terms, even these madrasas are close to some ideology or the other. For example, madrasas affiliated to Minhajul Quran represent Barelvi school of thought. Similarly, madrasas affiliated to Jamat Al-Dawa represent Ahl-e Hadith school of thought.

As far as the students in these madrasas are concerned, there are nine lakh thirty-three thousand boys (men) and four lakh thirty-nine thousand girls (women) studying in the 6,761 madrasas. According to Maulana Muhammad Salimullah Khan, president of Wafaqul Madaris Al-Arabiya, about sixty-two thousand students took examinations in 2001; this number was about sixty thousand in the year 2000. This accounts for the number of students appearing in examinations under one board only. Taken in totality, there were 4,54,000 students studying in madrasas in 1988. Of them there were 3,74,000 boys and 82,000 girls. Madrasas for girls number 448; 70.3 per cent of them are in Punjab. The Frontier Province accounts for 8.5 per cent, Sindh 9.1 per cent, and Baluchistan 4.4 per cent. Of them 175 madrasas are of Deobandi persuasion.

A large number of foreign students flock to the madrasas in Pakistan. They account for 15 per cent of the total number. Foreign students are 37 per cent in the madrasas of Baluchistan, 20 per cent in the madrasas of Frontier Province, 10 per cent in the madrasas of Sindh, and 2 per cent in the madrasas of Punjab.

The per capita expenditure on students in madrasas is 1,200 rupees per month. According to the census of 1988, 32.6 per cent madrasas received grant-in-aid from the Ministry of Zakat O Ashar. Now, the total number of teachers in madrasas is 30,125; of them 28,623 are exclusively meant for religious education and 1,502 are for conventional education. As opposed to this, in 1988 the number of teachers was 12,544. Thus, during the last twelve years the number of teachers in madrasas has also increased by 128 per cent.

This is the general picture of madrasas in Pakistan. They do not include madrasas that teach only the Holy Koran through different modes. If they are also included, the total number of madrasas will exceed fifty thousand. Currently, five big education boards are there to supervise the working of madrasas and organise examinations. Examinations are organised in the madrasas on the following lines:

1. Shahada Tahfeezul Quran al-Kareem: This examination is conducted after five years of primary instructions. It is based on memorising the Holy Koran and prayers, etc.

2. Shahada Al-Mutawassita (Middle): This examination is conducted after post-primary instructions for three years.
3. Shahada Al-Sanawiya al-Amma: This is equal to the matriculation level examination.
4. Shahada Al-Sanawaiya al-Khassa: This is a two-year course equal to FA.
5. Shahada Al-Aliya: This is a two-year course equal to BA.
6. Shahada Al-Alamiya: this is a two-year course equal to MA.
7. Shahada Al-Tauheed: This is a postgraduate diploma for one year.

All the madrasa students do not go through all these stages. In Alamiya stage, every year fifty students pass from Tanzeemul Madaris though more than 500 students take the examination. Most of the students drop out after the first two or three stages.

The above survey makes it clear that after 1988, there was a steep increase in the number of madrasas. Several causes, including the promulgation of *Zakat O Ashar* ordinance encouraged the growth of madrasas. Now, there are 2,500 madrasas in Punjab only that receive grants to the tune of eighty-five crore rupees per year from the Government Zakat Fund.

The question is: is the educational standard in these madrasas satisfactory? Most of the ulema think that madrasas are providing the best of religious education. The following is the view of Maulana Amjad Thanawi:

> All the madrasas of Pakistan, belonging to whichever ideology, are running a thousand times better than

schools and colleges. According to one survey, there are more than seven lakh students studying in the madrasas of Pakistan. Among them three thousand are studying the Holy koran 'by sight' (*nazera*). Ninety-eight thousand are engaged in memorising the Holy Koran. Fifty-three thousand are studying '*qirat*' (recitation of the Holy Koran) to become *Qaris*. More than twenty-six thousand are studying *Dars-e Nizami* (a special syllabus). About fifty-eight thousand female students are also pursuing their studies in different madrasas. Several thousand students are studying courses on fatwa.

Al-Banooriya, Monthly, Karachi, April–May, 2001

But another group of ulema is not happy with the standard of education in madrasas. For example, Maulana Wahid Khan says the following in this regard:

Thousands of students are passing out of madrasas each year, but they are not competent enough to shoulder the responsibility of *dawat* entrusted on them by Islam. The reason for this is that our entire madrasa education is based on the system of dialogue. Consequently, they read books well enough but they are not very competent in *dawat* (preaching). They can be good debaters but not good preachers.

Though Maulana Wahid Khan is from India, his remarks contain some element of truth. Some Pakistani ulema also support this viewpoint. Maulana Muhammad Hasan Shekhupuri, the amir of Jamat Ahl-e Hadith, Pakistan says:

The educational standard in madrasas is going down because students do not stick to one madrasa and the teachers are constantly engaged in drawing students from other madrasas. They are more interested in politics and raising funds than in study.

Siratul Mustaqeem, Monthly, Karachi, June 1995

NDFC is a non-governmental organisation in Peshawar. It is conducting a study on the syllabi of madrasas. Meera Khan, one of its directors, told me, 'We are trying to harmonise the syllabi with the demands of modern time. We invite ulema of all hues to our seminars. They recognise such a need, but are not serious about changing their syllabi.'

Pakistan Shariat Council is trying to bring about changes in the syllabi. It has also the view that the current syllabi are not fulfilling modern needs. Because of weaknesses in the syllabi and weaknesses in the management, the madrasas are promoting sectarianism.

Madrasas and Sectarianism

One weakness in the syllabus of madrasas of all sects is that rather than grooming scholars of learning, it grooms debaters. Moreover, there are such books in the syllabus that claim only a particular sect to be true followers of faith and all other systems of belief false. As for students, they seem more interested in degrees than covering the entire syllabus. Without acquiring proficiency in any branch of learning they pass out from madrasas and get employment in the education department or in some madrasas. Or they become *khateebs* in mosques. Their half-baked education becomes a breeding ground for sectarianism.

It is also a fact that there is a visible tendency in the students and teachers of madrasas towards sectarian groups. Maulana Abdur Rahman, the principal of a madrasa in Sargodha said in this context: 'The era of debate has come to an end. Earlier, the Maulanas engaged in debates and the issues would be resolved. This platform is no longer available to the students passing out from madrasas. That is why they join some sectarian group and vitiate the mind of people with their ill-digested knowledge. One advantage of debate was that it made the two contending parties study deeply to prepare for the debate. It may be a personal view, but no one can deny the fact that the members of Sipah Sahaba who have become victims of sectarian violence were from madrasas. This argument may not be valid about Tahreek-e Ja'fariya, because its members who were victims of sectarian violence were from colleges. However, even there, the number of students and teachers (who were victims of violence) from Shia madrasas was not negligible.'

Madrasas and Jihad

The majority of madrasas claim that their students do not have the permission to join jihad while they are still students, and that the madrasas do not groom students for jihad. If by jihadi grooming we mean military training, then it is true that 99 per cent of madrasas do not have any arrangement for such training. When I was working with the magazine section of a daily newspaper, I had conducted a survey for which I had prepared a questionnaire. One of the questions in it was: 'The number of students who have joined jihadi organisations?' Among fifteen madrasas under survey, the principal of only one madrasa reported that 500 of its students were related to jihadi organisations. But they did so on their own volition. However, there is no doubt about the fact that madrasas have played a crucial role in providing manpower to jihadi organisations and most of their office bearers are the former students of madrasas. For example, Masood Azhar, leader of Jaish-e Muhammad, Maulana Saifullah Akhtar, patron of Harkat al-Jihad al-Islami, Maulana Abdus Samad, amir of the same organisation are all ex-students of Jamia Banooriya Town, Karachi. Maulana Fazlur Rahman Khalil of Harkatul Mujahideen passed out from Madrasa Nomaniya, Dera Ismail Khan, the amir of Harkat al-Jihad al-Islami, Burma, passed out from Jamia Faruqiya, Karachi, and Maulana Junaidullah Akhtar, a leader of the same organisation, has passed out from Jamia Ashrafiya, Lahore. The same is true of other jihadi organisations as well.

Research is urgently needed on different aspects of madrasas and their students. My personal observations revealed that there are also other reasons, apart from jihadi motivation, for students of madrasas to join jihadi organisations. The foremost is the question of employment. They are not required to struggle for it (if they join some jihadi organisation). Second, during the Taliban regime, madrasa students got jobs in Afghanistan, and for that they had to join some jihadi organisation or the other. Different jihadi organisations also send these students to foreign countries and embassies for jihadi preaching and raising funds. For all these reasons the jihadi organisations have definitely drawn strength from these madrasas.

Important Madrasas Helping Jihad and Jihadi Organisations

The details of madrasas assisting jihadi formations of different persuasions are listed below:

DEOBANDI MADRASAS

In Pakistan, the number of Deobandi madrasas is 6,761. Of them 200 madrasas are of jihadi nature or provide practical help to jihadi organisations. A list of important Deobandis madrasas is presented in Table XXVIII–XXX. Some of them are discussed here.

Jamia Al-Uloom Al-Islamia, Banooriya Town, Karachi
This madrasa was founded in 1978 by Allama Yusuf Banooriya. Within a few years it became the biggest madrasa of Deobandi school of thought in Pakistan. There are 3,000 students, male and female, from inside and outside the country studying here. Apart from its twelve branches in Karachi, it has four centres for the religious education of children. One branch of this madrasa is also working in Fresh Meadow town of the New York state (USA). Important ulema of Deobandi persuasion come from Jamia Banooriya. Among them are Dr Mufti Nizamuddin Shamzai, Qari Abdul Halim, Maulana Fazal Muhammad, and Mufti Muhammad Naim who is its principal.

The central madrasa of Jamia Banooriya is located in a sprawling campus in the Site Area of Karachi. It has residential accommodation for 2,000 students. It has arrangement for education up to PhD for both male and female students. Its annual expenses are three crore seventy-seven lakh six thousand rupees. The following departments are working here:

1. Tajveedul Quran
2. Hifzul Quran (department of memorising the Holy Koran)
3. Shuba Kutb (calligraphy)
4. Shuba Takhsees
5. Darul Iftah
6. Department of computers
7. Shuba Musannifeen
8. Shuba Nashar O Isha't (press and publications)
9. Shuba Intezami (management)
10. Library
11. Madarsatul Banat (women's Madrasa)

It has also arrangements for learning English and modern sciences. These arrangements work through three branches:

1. Shuba Bairuni Tulaba (foreign students)
2. Shuba Maqami Tulaba (local students)
3. Shuba Madarsatul Banat (girl students)

The management board of Jamia Banooriya has bought six acres of land in the Site Area. There is plan for buying more land where the following institutes will be set up:

1. Banooriya Public School (Islamic school up to

matriculation)
2. Banooriya Medical Complex
3. Banooriya Medical College
4. Banooriya Computer Institute
5. Banooriya Technical Centre
6. Banooriya Degree College

Jamia Banooriya is the mainstay of many jihadi organisations. It played a special role in the formation of Jaish-e Muhammad. The late Maulana Abdur Rasheed, Late Maulana Yusuf Ludhianwi, and Mufti Nizamuddin Shamzai of this institution contributed substantially to its formation, though it was Maulana Masood Azhar who formally founded it. Earlier, Harkatul Mujahideen had the support of Jamia Banooriya; Sipah Sahaba also has its support. Its support for any organisation means the support of Deobandi sect throughout Pakistan. Thirty-five of its students were killed in the Afghan War (during 1979–87), and nineteen of its students have already been killed in Occupied Kashmir.

Jamia Yusufiya Banooriya, Karachi
This madrasa, located in Ashrafabad Society, Karachi, is an important madrasa of Deobandi school of thought. The number of students here is 800, of whom 350 are boarders. The number of teachers is thirty. There are four vehicles for ferrying across students. The principal of this madrasa is Hasanur Rahman Abdullah.

This is an important centre of Jaish-e Muhammad and Sipah Sahaba (both defunct). Most of the teachers are associated with either of these two organisations.

Darul Uloom Hanafiya, Aorangi Town, Karachi
The principal of this madrasa is Maulana Faizullah
Azad, who is the president of Jamiat Ulema Islam,
Sindh. He founded this madrasa in Aorangi Town in
1982. Now it has facilities for studying up to PhD.
There are 1,200 students from inside and outside the
country. For girls, there is Jamia Hanafiya Al-Banat
that imparts instruction up to the graduate level.

The principal. Maulana Faizullah, says, 'We do not
have the remotest link with jihad. What to speak of
arms and weapons, you wouldn't find even a knife
here.' About jihad he says, 'The responsibility for jihad
falls on the leader of the time. If the ruler is carrying
out jihad because of some extraordinary circumstances,
it is obligatory on each person, stage by stage. If a
smaller number of people are enough, let them carry
out the responsibility on everyone's behalf. If a greater
number of people are required, let them go
accordingly (*Source: Masihai*, monthly, Karachi).

However, Darul Uloom Hanafiya shows greater
sympathy for sectarian organisations like Sipah Sahaba
than purely jihadi organisations.

Madrasa Khalid bin Walid, Karachi
This madrasa is located in Korangi, Karachi. Its
principal is Maulana Abdur Rahman Mujahid. There
are about 500 students here, the majority of whom are
from Afghanistan, Burma, and Bangladesh. This is an
important centre of Harkatul Jihad Islami, Arakan
(Burma). It has facilities of training and
accommodation for mujahideen. It has close links with
Harkatul Jihad, Pakistan. Students from this madrasa
usually go to the training camps of Harkatul Jihad

Brigade 313. Apart from Afghanistan, they are also engaged in jihad in Occupied Kashmir.

This madrasa is affiliated to Wasaiqul Madaris and approved by Wafaqul Madaris Al-Arabiya. Fifty madrasas are working under this board in Karachi and Hyderabad. All these madrasas claim themselves to be jihadi madrasas, though there is very little jihadi activity in some of them. The list of these madrasas has been given separately.

Jamia Al-Rasheed, Ahsanabad, Karachi

This madrasa, located at Ahsanabad, is known as the main centre of Sipah Sahaba. It is approved by Wafaqul Madaris and has facilities for instruction up to PhD. There are about 1,500 students and forty teachers here. Its annual expenditure is forty lakh rupees. It has close links with Jamia Banooriya and Darul Uloom, Karachi. Most of the teachers are former students of these madrasas. Apart from Sipah Sahaba, there are many supporters of Jaish-e Muhammad and Harkat-al Jihad here. Forty-five students of this madrasa have already been killed in the fronts in Afghanistan, Chechnya, and Occupied Kashmir.

Jamia Husnul Uloom, Karachi

The principal of this madrasa is Maulana Zarooli Khan. Located in Gulshan-e Iqbal, this madrasa has facilities for instruction up to PhD. There are 1,200 students and forty teachers. There are separate arrangements for girl students. It does not receive any grant from the government. Its monthly expenditure is twenty lakh rupees. This madrasa is patronised by Sipah Sahaba and it has been the centre of its many activities. This madrasa treats all Deobandi organisations equally and the preachers and mujahideen of jihadi organisations have the permission to work here. However, Maulana Nazrooli Khan who is a leader of Jamiat Ulema Islam shows special favour to Jaish-e Muhammad.

Jamia Ehteshamiya, Karachi
The founder of Jamia Ehteshamiya in Jacob Line, Karachi, was Maulana Ehtasham-ul Haq Thanawi. Now his son Maulana Tanvirul Haq is the principal. It has facilities for instruction up to graduation level. There are about 500 students here, including foreign students. Its monthly expenditure is about fifteen lakh rupees.

Students in this madrasa do not have permission to join any jihadi organisation. Despite this, many students have joined these organisations and no action has been taken against them. Though all jihadi organisations have permission to work here, most of the teachers are associated with Harkat-al Jihad. The office of the journal of Harkat-al Jihad, Burma, *Al-Rabat*, is also located here. Its editor, Maulana Sadeeq is from Arakan and a teacher of this madrasa.

Jamia Hamadiya, Shah Faisal Colony, Karachi
Jamia Hamadiya, located in Shah Faisal Colony No. 2, Karachi, is an important institution of Deobandi school of thought. It is built on a beautiful and wide campus. Its principal is Maulana Abdus Samad Haljui. He is assisted by Maulana Abdul Wahid and Maulana Ghulam Muhammad. It has facilities for education up to PhD. It has also a department of computers. It is

affiliated to Wafaqul Madaris Al-Arabiya. There are about 1,000 students, including 200 foreigners. There is a separate building for girl students. Its annual outlay is fifty lakh rupees.

Jaish-e Muhammad is given importance here and the students have permission to attend its jihadi classes. However, the atmosphere here is more favourable to sectarian organisations and Sipah Sahaba is the most favourite among students and teachers.

Jamia Ashraful Madaris, Karachi
This madrasa is located in Nazimabad. It is aligned to the well-known Deobandi shrine, 'Khanqah Imdadiya Ashrafiya'. Its principal is Maulana Hakim Muhammad Mazhar, son of Maulana Hakim Muhammad Akhtar. It has facilities for instructions up to PhD. It has about 1,500 students, male and female, including foreign students. There are ninety teachers. The annual outlay is sixty-five lakh rupees. Al-Akhtar Trust, the religious welfare organisation, has its offices here. One branch of the madrasa is located in Sindh-Baloch Housing Society. This is the examination centre of Wafaqul Madaris. It has also facilities for computer education.

The relationship of Jamia Ashraful Madaris with jihadi organisations is limited to economic assistance only. Several teachers are associated with Jaish-e Muhammad, but the students are not allowed to have any association with jihadi organisations.

Jamia Darul Uloom, Karachi
Located in Aorangi Town, this is considered to be the latest Deobandi madrasa. Its principal is Maulana Justice Muhammad Taqi Usmani. His elder brother,

Maulana Muhammad Rafi Usmani, is the chairman of the madrasa. Several of its branches are working in Karachi. Its other big branch is working in Jama Masjid Baitul Mukarram, Gulshan-e Iqbal. Several Deobandi ulema are associated with this madrasa.

Jamia Darul Uloom has arrangements for imparting education in science, computers, and economics. It has facilities for instructions up to PhD in many subjects. It has also arrangements for Dars-e Nizami*. Its course of Darul Iftah** is rated higher than that of Jamia Banooriya. Students of economics passing out from this madrasa assisted the Taliban government substantially. Darul Iftah of Jamia Darul Uloom has declared Al-Barka Islamic Bank as an Islamic Bank. Maulana Taqi Usmani and Maulana Rafi Usmani are among the bank's board members.

The total strength of Jamia Darul Uloom is 45,000, including boys and girls. Its annual outlay exceeds one crore rupees. Jamia Darul Uloom is the mainstay of many jihadi organisations. Maulana Rafi Usmani and Maulana Taqi Usmani have practically helped in the formation of many of them. The mujahideen of these organisations have free access to the mosques and madrasas of Jamia Darul Uloom for offering discourses and raising funds. Students do not have permission to join jihadi organisations during study, though some may choose to drop out and fulfil this urge.

---

*   Translator's Note: 'Dars-e Nizami' is the oldest course for madrasa education devised in circa eleventh century. It is mainly composed of religious subjects, and has a minimal component of secular themes.

** A course that is studied to become a Mufti, i.e. someone who can give a fatwa (decree).

Jamia Faruqiya, Shah Faisal Colony, Karachi

Jamia Faruqiya, located in Shah Faisal Colony No. 2, has the status of the Central Board of Wafaqul Madaris Al-Arabiya. Its principal is Maulana Salimullah Khan who is the chairman of Wafaqul Madaris Al-Arabiya. The board arranges the examinations of its madrasas here. It has facilities for instructions up to PhD.

The total strength of students here is 2,600. Apart from Pakistan, students from Afghanistan, Iran, Bangladesh, Indonesia, Burma, and Arab and European countries also come here to study. The number of foreign students was 700, which declined in February–March 2002. Most of the Afghan students have been shifted to madrasas in Afghanistan. Its annual outlay (including the department of examinations) is seventy lakh rupees.

Jamia Faruqiya is a stronghold of both Sipah Sahaba and Jaish-e Muhammad. There have been two sectarian clashes here in the last two years, in which five teachers and three students of the madrasa were killed. According to Salimullah Khan, the principal: 'The students have no association with these organisations. We do not provide any kind of jihadi training to students here, nor do we draw them to sectarianism. We prepare scholars who spread the message of unity in the Muslim world' (*Source*: Interview with the weekly, *Zarb-e Momin*, Karachi, May 2001). As opposed to this statement, the students and teachers of the madrasa have been associated with these two organisations, and participated in the meetings and rallies organised by them. Moreover, the organisational meetings of Sipah Sahaba are also held here.

Jamia Anwarul Quran, Adam Town, Karachi
Jamia Anwarul Quran is one of the important
Deobandi madrasas of Karachi. It was founded by
Maulana Abdullah Darkhasti in 1980. Its principal is
Maulana Fidaur Rahman Darkhasti. It has a three-
storeyed building on a sprawling campus. It is
considered to be an important centre of Jamiat Ulema
Islam (S), Harkatul Mujahideen, and Sipah Sahaba.

The madrasa has facilities for instruction up to
postgraduate level. It also runs specialised courses
(three years) in several subjects, which are equivalent
to MPhil. It is affiliated to Wafaqul Madaris Al-
Arabiya. The total number of students here is 900.
Students from foreign countries like Iran, Afghanistan,
Indonesia, Thailand, Burma, and Bangladesh have
been studying here. But their number has reduced
from 300 to seventy-five after February 2002. There
are seventy teachers working here. It does not receive
any grant from the government. Its annual outlay is
twenty-five lakh rupees.

Darul Uloom Rahmaniya, Burmese Colony, Landhi, Karachi
This madrasa was founded in 1967. It is affiliated to
Wafaqul Madaris Al-Arabiya. It imparts education up
to the graduate level. Maulana Nazir Ahmad is the
principal of this madrasa. It is spread over a plot of land
measuring 15,000 square feet.

There are 500 students in the madrasa, majority of
whom are from Burma, Bangladesh, and Indonesia,
and they stay in the hostel. This is an important jihadi
madrasa and a prominent centre of Harkat-al Jihad
Islami, Pakistan, and Harkat-al Jihad Islami, Arakan.
The presence of a large number of foreign students is

due to the fact that they are from Burmese refugee
families that have settled in Pakistan or Bangladesh.
The annual outlay of the madrasa is seven lakh rupees.
It receives no grant from the government.

Jamia Miftahul Uloom, Hyderabad
This Deobandi madrasa is an important centre of
Sipah Sahaba. Its principal is Maulana Dad Shah. It has
facilities for education up to postgraduate level. The
total number of students is 400, most of whom come
from Sindh and southern Punjab. It has hostel facilities
for students. There is also arrangement for the
education of girls.

Madrasa Jaish-e Muhammad, Shikarpur
This madrasa was established in 2000 in the Jaish-e
Muhammad office at Shikarpur, at the instance of
Maulana Masood Azhar. Its principal is Master
Zulfiqar who is the local amir of Jaish-e Muhammad.
It imparts instructions in the study of the Holy Koran,
by sight and by memorising. However, its importance
lies in conducting courses in jihadi orientation that run
throughout the year.

Idarah Uloom Islami, Islamabad
Madrasa Kulliya Al-Darsat Al-Islamia (Idarah Uloom
Islami) is located on the Mari-Islamabad highway. It
was founded by Maulana Faizur Rahman Usmani in
September 1986. It has facilities for instruction up to
the postgraduate level.

Maulana Faizur Rahman Usmani is the chairman of
the madrasa. Among the members in the management
board are Qari Mahboob Ilahi, Maulana Iqbalullah,
Abdur Rauf Shah, and Maulana Abdul Ghafoor. There

are ten members in the education board, including Mufti Nizamuddin Shamzai and Dr Maqsood Alam Bukhari. There are 200 students and nineteen teachers in this madrasa. One of its branches, Madrasa Tahaffuz Al-Quran Al-Kareem, is working in Chatral, which has 110 students. Its monthly outlay is three lakh rupees. The madrasa abides by the decisions of Jamiat Ulema Islam (F), and extends cooperation to all Deobandi jihadi organisations. However, the founder of the madrasa is particularly well disposed towards Harkat-al Jihad al-Islami. It provides temporary accommodation to mujahideen.

Jamia Al-Uloom Al-Islamia Al-Faridiya, Islamabad
The principal of this madrasa is Maulana Abdul Aziz who is counted among important leaders of Harkat-al Jihad. It is approved by Wafaqul Madaris Al-Arabiya. Till March 2002, there were 350 students here including foreigners. After the Afghan students left, this number has come down to 305. It has facilities for instructions up to the postgraduate level.

This is counted among one of the important jihadi madrasas. The students are permitted to take part in jihadi activities and attend training camps during holidays. Several leaders of Harkat-al Jihad have been associated with this madrasa. Maulana Abdullah, one of the well-wishers of Sipah Sahaba, was from this madrasa. It was founded because of his efforts. He had become a victim of terrorism in this madrasa.

Jamia Makhzanul Uloom, Khanpur
The founder of this madrasa was Maulana Abdullah Darkhasti, the leader of Jamiat Ulema Islam. The

current principal is his son, Maulana Fazlur Rahman Darkhasti who is a well-wisher of Harkat-al Jihad. He had acquired jihadi training in this organisation. There are 500 students in this madrasa who are at different stages of Dars-e Nizami. Apart from Jaish-e Muhammad and Sipah Sahaba, it is also an important centre of Tahreek Tahaffuz Khatm Nabuwat. Twenty-four teachers and students of this madrasa have already been killed in Afghanistan, Chechnya, and Occupied Kashmir.

A law suit is currently going on in the Bahawalpur Bench of the High Court regarding its land. The lawyers who have constructed their chambers there claim that the madrasa has been built on government land. There have been several clashes between the two parties.

Jamia Islamia Baabool Uloom, Kehrorpacca
This madrasa has been used as the centre and office of Jaish-e Muhammad. Three students of this madrasa have died in Occupied Kashmir in September 2001. It is also a centre of activities of Sipah Sahaba.

Jamia Ashrafiya, Lahore
Jamia Ashrafiya was founded on 14 September 1947 by Mufti Muhammad Hasan Amritsari. He was the disciple and successor of Maulana Ashraf Ali Thanwi. When Mufti Muhammad Hasan died in 1961, his eldest son Maulana Ubaidullah took over as the principal. His younger brother, Maulana Abdur Rahman Ashrafi is the vice principal. Maulana Fazlur Rahim and Maulana Muhammad Akram Kashmiri help them as secretaries.

There are 1,500 students here, including 700 boarders. Before 13 January 2002, there were 200 foreign students here. This number has now dwindled to forty. It has facilities for instruction up to the graduate level. There are seven departments working here:

1. Dars-e Nizami
2. Hifz O Nazera (Study of the Holy Koran by sight and by memorising)
3. Department of Arabic
4. Department of English
5. Department of computers
6. Department of Iftah
7. Department of linguistics, research and publications

A new hospital has been established in the campus. For girl students, Madrasa Al-Faisal Al-Banat has been established in Model Town, Lahore, that has facilities for instructions up to the graduate level. There are 800 students in this madrasa, including foreigners. It has hostel facilities for 500 students.

The centre of the *tablighi* organisation, Siyanatul Muslimeen, is located in the madrasa. The students of the madrasa are not allowed to participate in jihadi activities while studying. Despite this rule, students not only acquire jihadi training but also take part in actions. Legally, these students are not allowed re-admission. The madrasa allows jihadi organisations to offer discourses and raise funds. However, many jihadi organisations are not happy with the attitude of the madrasa management and call it a 'government institute', as it receives grant from the government.

Several teachers of the madrasa are associated with sectarian organisations and are their active members.

Jamia Manzoorul Islamia, Lahore
The principal of this madrasa is Maulana Pir Saifullah Khalid who has been the leader of Jamiat Ulema Islam and Jaish-e Muhammad. Because of this, the madrasa is an important centre of jihadi organisations. The activities of Sipah Sahaba and Lashkar-e Jhangvi are an important feature of this madrasa. It makes special arrangement for providing hospitality to mujahideen and sectarian organisations.

There are 250 students in this madrasa. It has facilities for instructions up to the postgraduate level. There is no restriction on students in participating in jihadi activities. They can be members of any Deobandi jihadi organisation and Sipah Sahaba at the same time. Several students from this madrasa had gone to Afghanistan to help the Taliban after the US attacks; of them three are still missing.

Jamia Madina, Lahore
Mahmud Mian is the principal of this madrasa. It has two branches:

1. Jamia Madina, Karim Block, Ravi Road, Lahore.
2. Jamia Madina, Pajian Raiwind, Lahore

Both these madrasas have facilities for instructions up to the graduate level. The total number of students is 4,000. The annual outlay is close to six lakh rupees. The students are not allowed to take part in jihadi and sectarian activities. However, there is a jihadi environment in the madrasa, as it is one of the important centres of Sipah Sahaba and Jaish-e

Muhammad. It hosted important meetings at the time of reorganisation of Jaish-e Muhammad, Punjab.

Jamia Darul Uloom Al-Islamia
This madrasa was founded in 1948 by Qari Siraj Ahmad. It is affiliated to Wafaqul Madaris Al-Arabiya. Its principal is Maulana Musharraf Ali Thanawi, and the chief secretary is Qari Ahmad Mian Thanawi. Four of its branches are working in Lahore:

1. Markazi Madrasa, 291, Kamran Block, Allama Iqbal Town, Lahore
2. Jamia Darul Uloom Islamia, Old Anarkali, Church Road, Lahore
3. Jamia Darul Uloom Islamia, Darool Falah, Abbas Block, Mustafa Town, Lahore
4. Jamia Darul Uloom Islamia, Masjid Abu Bakr, Ravi Block, Allama Iqbal Town, Lahore

There are 865 Pakistani students in these madrasas. The number of foreign students now is forty. The monthly outlay is six lakh fifty thousand rupees. Every month, the Jamia publishes a booklet on religious instructions written by Maulana Ashraf Ali Thanawi and its copies are distributed freely. The madrasas do not receive any grant from the government.

Most of the teachers of these madrasas are associated with Jaish-e Muhammad, Harkatul Mujahideen, Harkat-al Jihad, and Sipah Sahaba. It is an important centre of Sipah Sahaba.

Al-Sharia Academy, Kangniwala, Gujranwala
This madrasa has been established to train teachers and ex-students of madrasas. It was founded in 1999 by Maulana Zahid Rashidi, general secretary of Pakistan

Shariat Council. It has been consistently trying to bring about changes in the syllabi. Apart from other courses, there are facilities for learning English language and computers here. Maulana Rushdie is also a leader of Jamiat Ulema Islam. He has close links with many Deobandi jihadi organisations.

Jamia Islamia, Kashmir Road, Rawalpindi
The principal of this madrasa is Qari Saidur Rahman, who is also the leader of Pakistan Shariat Council. There are 200 students in this madrasa, which has facilities for study up to the graduate level. Students are not allowed to take part in jihadi activities. However, several students from this madrasa have been associated with Jaish-e Muhammad and Harkatul Mujahideen. This madrasa is an important centre of Afghan Defence Council.

Jamia Umar Faruq Islamia, Samandari
This madrasa was founded by the former chairman of Sipah Sahaba, Maulana Ziaur Rahman Faruqi in 1988. Its principal is Maulana Rehan Mahmood Zia. It has facilities for instructions in all stages of Dars-e Nizami. There are 230 students and fourteen teachers here.

Besides being a centre of Sipah Sahaba this madrasa was a hideout for the terrorists of Lashkar-e Jhangvi. Some students of this madrasa had formed 'Haq Nawaz Jhangvi Tigers' that fizzled out on its own. Some of its office bearers had joined Lashkar-e Jhangvi.

Madrasa Jamiat Ulema Islam, Wahwa
This is an important jihadi madrasa of Dera Ismail Khan, which is being run by Jamiat Ulema Islam (F).

It has facilities for instructions up to the postgraduate level. It has 1,000 students, including many Afghan students. Students of this madrasa are allowed to acquire jihadi training during holidays.

Jamia Islamia, Dera Ghazi Khan

The principal of this madrasa is Maulana Abdus Sattar Rahmani who is the brother of Maulana Abdul Wahab, a known leader of Tablighi Jamat. It has facilities for instructions up to PhD. There are about 500 students here, including foreigners, and seventeen teachers. The monthly outlay is 85,000 rupees. Students are not allowed to take part in jihadi activities. However, the principal of the madrasa has close links with Maulana Abdus Samad Sayyal, the leader of Harkat-al Jihad Islami. Anwar Husain, a student of this madrasa said that Major General Mutasim Billah had helped greatly in setting up this madrasa. The amirs and mujahideen of Harkat-al Jihad are allowed to stay here and raise funds. The reason for this, according to Anwar Husain, is that the students and teachers of this madrasa have greater affinity with Tablighi Jamat, and Jamia Banooriya is against the Tablighi Jamat and supports Jaish-e Muhammad. That is why this madrasa patronises only Harkat-al Jihad. He further reported that a year ago when the madrasa had silver jubilee celebrations of the teaching of Bukhari Sharif, Maulana Abdus Samad Sayyal, chief patron of Harkat-al Jihad and Mufti Nizamuddin Shamzai had come to grace the occasion, and both of them bandied words regarding Jaish-e Muhammad and Harkat-al Jihad. He heard Maulana Abdus Samad telling Maulana Shamzai, 'You formed the Jamat for unity, but it became a cause for dissensions.'

Madrasa Khalidiya, Chechawatani, Sahiwal District
This madrasa was founded by Maulana Muhammad Masood Alvi who was killed in the Afghan War. He, along with Maulana Fazlur Rahman Khalil, had laid the foundation of Harkatul Mujahideen in the Paktian province of Afghanistan. Since then this madrasa has been providing manpower to Jamiatul Mujahideen Al-Alami. Nine of its students were killed in the Afghan War.

Jamia Khairul Madaris, Multan
This madrasa serves as the central secretariat of Wafaqul Madaris Al-Arabiya, one of the educational boards for madrasas. Its principal is Maulana Hanif Jalandhari. It has facilities for religious instructions up to PhD. It has also facilities for computer education. There are 2,000 students here, including female students.

Apart from Sipah Sahaba, Jamia Khairul Madaris extends help to other jihadi organisations also. The foundation of Jamiat Al-Mujahideen al-Alami, the first Deobandi jihadi organisation, was laid in this madrasa. Most of the teachers here have acquired jihadi training from different organisations. Before Jaish-e Muhammad emerged, it was an important centre of Harkatul Mujahideen.

Jamia Ashrafiya, Mankot, Multan
The founder and principal of this madrasa is Maulana Ashraf Shaad. It has facilities for instructions up to the postgraduate level. There are about 500 students here. The madrasa has facilities for PT and jihadi training for students, but they are not allowed to join jihad during

the course of study. Ten former students of this madrasa have been killed in Afghanistan and Occupied Kashmir. All Deobandi jihadi organisations are welcome here, but the teachers are closer to Harkat-al Jihad al-Islami.

Jamia Faruqiya, Shujaabad, Multan
The principal of this madrasa is Qari Zubair Ahmad. It has facilities up to the postgraduate level. There are 180 students here, including fifty-five foreigners. Abdur Rahman Shaheed, the well-known commander of Harkat-al Jihad al-Islami, was from this madrasa.

Jamia Usmania, Shorkot, Jhang District
This madrasa is an important centre of Sipah Sahaba and Jaish-e Muhammad. Maulana Masood Azhar had visited this madrasa when he had come to Shorkot. The students here are allowed to acquire jihadi training during the annual holidays. Its principal is Maulana Abdul Majeed.

Jamia Rahimiya Tarteelul Quran, Rahim Yar Khan
Qari Umar Faruq Abbasi is the principal of this madrasa, located in the Central Idgah of Rahim Yar Khan. It offers jihadi courses and discourses.

Jamia Furqania, Check Gate 47, Faisalabad
This is an important centre of Harkat-al Jihad. It was established in memory of Maulana Irshad Ahmad, the founder of Harkat-al Jihad. It offers, besides normal teaching, jihadi courses devised by Harkat-al Jihad. It is considered to be an important jihadi madrasa.

Madrasa Hanafiya Ashraful Uloom, Haranwali, Mianwali District
The founder and patron of this madrasa is Maulana

Qazi Mazhar Husain, who is the amir of Tahreek Khuddam Ahl-e Sunnat, Pakistan. His madrasa and his organisation work in opposition to the Shia aspirations. All Deobandi jihadi organisations are welcome here.

This madrasa has facilities up to the graduate courses. There are more than 200 students, including students from Afghanistan and Iran. There is no bar on students joining jihad. The principal of the madrasa is Maulana Muhammad Yaqoob.

Madrasa Darul Hadi, Bhakkar
This madrasa was set up with help from Maulana Khan Muhammad, a well-known Deobandi scholar. Currently, its principal is Muhammad Abdullah. It has facilities up to the graduate level. There are about 250 students here. Its annual outlay is two lakh rupees. It is an important centre of Sipah Sahaba and Alami Majlis Khatm Nabuwat. Besides, it also supports Jaish-e Muhammad. Earlier, the office of Jaish-e Muhammad was located here.

Darul Uloom Hanafiya, Chakwal
This madrasa is aligned to Khanqah Habibia Naqshbandiya, Chakwal. Its patron is Pir Abdur Rahim Naqshbandi. His son, Abdul Quddus Naqshbandi is the principal. It has facilities for study up to the postgraduate level. There are about 500 students here. It opposes the Shias and supports Sipah Sahaba. Students are not allowed to take part in jihad. Deobandi jihadi organisations are particularly welcome here.

Jamia Hanfiya Talimul Islam, Madani Mohalla, Jhelum
This madrasa was established in 1964 by Maulana Abdul Latif. Currently, its principal is Qari Habib

Ahmad Umar. It has facilities for instruction up to the graduate level. There are about 400 students here. This is an important centre of the anti-Shia organisation, Tahreek Khuddam Ahl-e Sunnat. Jaish-e Muhammad is accorded special welcome here.

Darul Uloom Haqqania, Akora Khatak, Naoshehra
Maulana Abdul Haq was the founder of Darul Uloom Haqqania, Akora Khatak. He was an important leader of Jamiat Ulema Islam. Currently, its principal is Maulana Samiul Haq, who is the leader of Jamiat Ulema Islam (S). Predictably, it is an important centre for the activities of Jamiat Ulema Islam. The foundation of Afghan Defence Council was also laid here and it serves as its headquarters.

Sprawled over an eight-acre piece of land, this madrasa has facilities for instructions up to PhD. There is also a high school attached to the madrasa that imparts general education. There are about 3,500 students and eighty teachers here. There is a special branch called Madrasa Ayesha Lil-Banat for girls, which has a strength of 200. There are separate hostels for boys and girls. Its annual outlay is more than one crore rupees.

Till January 2002, it had 1,000 foreign students, majority of whom were from Afghanistan and Iran. The number has now dwindled to 300. It is considered to be an important jihadi madrasa. Though no jihadi training is imparted to the students here, they are encouraged to acquire training. During the survey it came to light that 95 per cent students at the postgraduate level have already acquired military training. Harkatul Mujahideen and Harkat-al Jihad are given special importance here because the students from this madrasa acquire jihadi training from their camps. Many leaders of these organisations have also been associated with this madrasa.

Madrasa Haqqania, Dandekala Daryakhil, Miran Shah
The patron of this madrasa was Mulla Jalaluddin Haqqani, the ex-commander of the Taliban government. This madrasa has been closed.

Darul Uloom Islamia, Syed o Sharif, Sawat
The principal of this madrasa is Qari Abdul Ghafoor. It has facilities up to the postgraduate level. There are about 700 students here. This is considered to be an important centre of Jamiat Ulema Islam and Tahreek Nifaz Shariat Muhammadi.

Madrasa Abu Huraira, Khaliqabad, Naoshehra
The principal of this madrasa is Maulana Abdul Qayoom Haqqani, who is an important leader of Jamiat Ulema Islam. It offers courses up to postgraduate level. There are about 500 students, including 300 boarders. There are also facilities for girls here of whom 140 stay in the hostel. Several students of this madrasa occupied high position in the Taliban government in Afghanistan. Before the formation of Jaish-e Muhammad it was a prominent centre of Harkat-al Jihad. There are arrangements for jihadi training here. After America attacked Afghanistan, a fourteen-member delegation from this madrasa had gone to Afghanistan to take part in the war. On the whole, it is an important centre for jihadi activities. It also publishes a journal, *Al-Qasim*. It has been an important centre of Sipah Sahaba and Lashkar-e Jhangvi.

Darul Uloom Azakhil, Naoshehra
Maulana Rahimullah is the principal of this madrasa. It provides manpower to Harkat-al Jihad.

Darul Uloom Sayidia, Aogi, Mansehra
This is an extremely important madrasa of Frontier Province. Twenty-five of its branches are working at different places of the province. Among them are Madrasa Ayesha Lil-Banat, Darul Uloom Talimul Quran, and Jamia Bahrul Uloom. A total of 2,500 students, male and female, are studying in them. The principal is Maulana Saidur Rahman and the vice principal is Mufti Hafizur Rahman. It extends all cooperation to the Deobandi jihadi organisations, its best cooperation being reserved for Sipah Sahaba. It is the real strength of Sipah Sahaba in Sawat, Mansehra.

Madrasa Nizamul Uloom, Banno
The principal of this madrasa is Maulana Imdadullah Haqqani who is an important leader of Jamiat Ulema Islam (S). It offers courses up to the graduate level. There are about 500 students here. It is an important centre of Jamiat Ulema Islam and Sipah Sahaba.

Darul Uloom Islamia, Laki Maroot
This madrasa offers courses up to PhD Maulana Arifullah is the principal. There are 1,200 students here, including Afghan students. It is an important centre for Jaish-e Muhammad.

Darul Uloom Nomania, Atmanzai, Char Sidha
The principal of this madrasa is Maulana Ruhullah and his assistant is Muhammad Muslim Naqvi. It is approved by Wafaqul Madaris Al-Arabiya and it offers courses up to the graduate level. There are about 200

students here. The annual outlay is three lakh rupees. It receives grants from the government. The students are not allowed to take part in jihadi activities. Despite this rule, many of its students are associated with Harkatul Mujahideen. It also patronises Sufi Muhammad's Tahreek Nifaz Shariat.

Jamia Nomania Swatia, Dera Ismail Khan
Maulana Fazlur Rahman Khalil, the general secretary of Harkatul Mujahideen, is the alumnus of this madrasa. There are about 1,000 students here. It is a prominent centre for the activities of Jamiat Ulema Islam (F) and Harkatul Mujahideen.

Darul Uloom Khurwal, Durrah Adam Kheel
Maulana Hasan Jan is the principal of this madrasa in the tribal area. He was the first to invite Maulana Masood Azhar in the tribal area and assured him of all help. It offers courses up to the graduate level, and was the centre of Deobandi organisations during the Afghan War.

Madrasa Bunistan, Panchgor District, Baluchistan
This madrasa, located in Panchgor district of Baluchistan, has been an important jihadi centre since 1989. Its principal is Maulana Abdul Halim who is also an office bearer of Jaish-e Muhammad. It also offers Jaish-e Muhammad's jihadi courses and discourses.

Darul Uloom Islamia, Muzaffarabad
This madrasa in Muzaffarabad has been a jihadi centre since 1989. It has been a supporter of both Harkatul Mujahideen and Harkat-al Jihad. But when Maulana Masood Azhar announced the formation of Jaish-e Muhammad, the principal of the madrasa, Maulana

Qazi Mahmoodul Hasan Ashraf, invited him and
Mufti Nizamuddin Shamzai to Muzaffarabad and
dedicated the madrasa to Jaish-e Muhammad. It is now
an important centre of Jaish-e Muhammad.

*Madrasas Providing Human and Material Resources to
Harkat-al Jihad, Harkatul Mujahideen, and Jamiat Al-
Mujahideen Al-Alami*

1. Jamia Usmania, Tapoki Principal: Hafiz Masoodul
   Hasan Rashidi, (Jaish's
   local leader)
2. Jamia Haqqania, Principal: Maulana Abdul
   Qenchi Amar Sadoo, Shakur Haqqani (Jaish's
   Lahore local leader)
3. Jamia Usmania, Gol
   Chowk, Okara.
4. Jamia Madina, Okara Principal: Maulana Syed
   Amir Husain Gilani
   (Deputy amir of Jamiat
   Ulema Islam and patron of
   Jaish-e Muhammad)
5. Madrasa Owaisia, Principal: Maulana
   Block C, Dera Ghazi Muhammad Azam (Centre
   Khan of Jaish-e Muhammad)
6. Jamia Darul Uloom Principal: Maulana
   Kabirwala Muhammad Anwar
7. Jamia Hanfiya Principal: Maulana Nawaz
   Qadiriya, Multan
8. Jamia Abdullah bin (Centre of Jaish-e
   Masood, Khanpur Muhammad and Sipah
   Sahaba)
9. Madrasa Anwar Sahaba, (Centre of Jaish-e
   Allahabad, Rawalpindi Muhammad and Sipah

	Sahaba)
10. Darul Uloom Khulafa Rashideen, Jhandwala, Bhawalnagar	Mufti Abdul Qadir (Centre of Jaish-e Muhammad and Sipah Sahaba)
11. Ashraful Uloom, Shujaabad, Multan	Principal: Maulana Saifullah
12. Madrasa Ahraful Madaris, Jallowali Taonsa	Principal: Maulana Abdul Qayoom
13. Jamia Talimul Quran, Fatehpur, Leh	Maulana Abdul Sattar Taonsi
14. Madrasa Qasimul Uloom, Kot Amir, District Khairpur	Principal: Maulana Anwar Muhammad Jamali
15. Madrasa Darul Uloom, Kandhkot, Sukkur, Sindh	Principal: Maulana Abdul Aziz
16. Darul Uloom Al-Haseeb, Shahdadpur, Sangarh	Principal: Maulana Muhammad Yusuf (Jaish's local amir)
17. Jamia Islamia, Scout Colony, Karachi	Principal: Maulana Abdullah Khaki (leader, Jaish-e Muhammad)
18. Jamia Arabia Ishatul Quran, Huzro Atak	Principal: Maulana Abdus Salam (centre of Jaish-e Muhammad and Sipah Sahaba). Maulana Abdus Salam has met Osama bin Laden several times.
19. Jamia Faruqiya, Mengalabad, Quetta	Centre of Sipah Sahaba

Table XXVIII: *Important Deobandi Madrasas in Pakistan*

Sr. No.	Name of Madrasa/University	Level	Principal/ Headmaster	Total No. of Students	Annual Expenses (Rupees)	Address
1.	Darul-uloom Talimul Quran	Postgraduate		300		Bagh, Azad Kashmir
2.	Darul-uloom Talimul Quran	Postgraduate	Maulana Shaikh Mazhar Hussain	300	5 lakhs	Pilandri Poonch, Azad Kashmir
3.	Darul Uloom-al-Islamia	Postgraduate	Maulana Qazi Mahmood Alhasan	200	–	Chattar Do Meel Civil Secretariat, Muzaffarabad
4.	Jamiat-ul-Uloom Islamia	Postgraduate	Mufti Mohammad Owais Khan	300	–	Sector F-2, Meerpur, Azad Kashmir
5.	Jamia-al-Uloom Islamia al-Faridiya	Postgraduate	Maulana Abdul Aziz	305	–	Sector E-7, Islamabad
6.	Jamia Mohammadia	Postgraduate		400	–	F-4-6, China Chowk, Islamabad
7.	Madrasa Taleemul-Quran	Postgraduate		350	–	Jail Road, Zob
8.	Madrasa Miftahul Uloom	Postgraduate		400	–	Islamabad Colony, Zob
9.	Madrasa Furqaniah	Postgraduate		500	–	Ali Khel Khalaqai Qila Saifullah

613

Gateway to Terrorism

Sr. No.	Name of Madrasa/University	Level	Principal/ Headmaster	Total No. of Students	Annual Expenses (Rupees)	Address
10.	Darul-Uloom	Postgraduate		350	–	Hafizabad Colony, Sukkur Road, Tehsil Bori, Lor Allai
11.	Darul Quran	Postgraduate		450	–	Quetta Road, Lor Alai
12.	Madarsatul-Uloom-ul-Islamia	Postgraduate		300	–	Shahkareez Tehsil Road, Lor Allai
13.	Madarsatul-Uloom Al-Sharia	Postgraduate		200	–	Karkh Khazdar
14.	Madrasa Qasimul-Uloom	Postgraduate		500	–	Koshik Post Box No. 14, Khazdar
16.	Madrasa Arabia Kanzul-Uloom	Postgraduate	Maulana Amarullah	300	–	Yaroo, District Pasheen
17.	Jamia Miftahul uloom	Postgraduate		250	–	Yaroo Market Road, Pasheen
18.	Madrasa Ashraf-ul-Uloom	Postgraduate		300	–	Faizabad, Pasheen
19.	Madrasa Imdad-ul-Uloom	Postgraduate		400	–	Gali Karbala, Pasheen
20.	Jamia Islamia Behrul-Uloom	Postgraduate		500	–	Murda Kareez Chaman District Qila Abdullah
21.	Jamia Arabia Markazia Tajveedul-Uloom	Postgraduate		600	–	Near Saryab Custom, Quetta

Sr. No.	Name of Madrasa/University	Level	Principal/ Headmaster	Total No. of Students	Annual Expenses (Rupees)	Address
22.	Jamia Khairul-Madaris-Al-Arabia	Postgraduate		700	–	Sarki Road, Quetta
23.	Jamia Miftahul Uloom	Postgraduate	Maulana Hafizullah Deobandi	700	15 lakh	Bulochi Qila Sadiq Shaheed Road, Quetta
24.	Jamia Miftahul Uloom	Postgraduate		300	–	Sordo Panjgour
25.	Jamia Rasheedia	Postgraduate		600	–	Asiabad, Turbat
26.	Jamia Darul-Uloom	Postgraduate		600	–	Bhag Bolaan
27.	Jamia Khairul-Uloom	Postgraduate		800	–	Kherpur Mewali, Bahawalpur
28.	Darul-Uloom Madina	Postgraduate		1000	–	Model Town, B Block, Bahawalpur
29.	Jamia Darul Uloom	Postgraduate	Maulana Mohammad Hanif	700	–	Idgah, Bahawalpur
30.	Jamia Qadria	Postgraduate	Maulana Khalilullah	–	–	Markazi Jamia Masjid Rahim Yar Khan
31.	Jamia Mukhzan-al-Uloom	Postgraduate	Maulana Fazlur Rahman Darkhwani	500	–	Khanpur, Rahim Yar Khan
32.	Jamia Rasheedia Talimul Quran	Postgraduate		900	1 lakh monthly	Hospital Road, Sadiqabad

Gateway to Terrorism

Sr. No.	Name of Madrasa/University	Level	Principal/ Headmaster	Total No. of Students	Annual Expenses (Rupees)	Address
33.	Jamia Islamia	PhD	Maulana Abdus Sattar Rahmani	500	85,000 monthly	Rahmania Colony, Samina Road, Dera Ghazi Khan
34.	Madrasa Mairaj-ul-Uloom	Postgraduate		600	–	Tabi Qaisrani, Derah Ghazi Khan
35.	Jamia Qasmia Sharful Islam	Postgraduate		500	–	Chowk Saroor Shaheed, Muzaffargarh
36.	Muzahirul Uloom	Postgraduate		400	–	Kot Adoo, Muzaffargarh
37.	Madrasa Habibul Madaris	Postgraduate		350		Bakiwali Tehsil Alipur, Muzaffargarh
38.	Jamia Madina Sultan-ul-Uloom	Postgraduate		–		Kotla Rahim Yar Ali Shah, Muzaffargarh
39.	Jamia Arabia Ishaat-ul-Quran	Postgraduate		400	7 lakh	Hazar Watik
40.	Darul-Uloom Talimul-Quran	Postgraduate		350	–	Walsia, Attock
41.	Pracha Jamia Islamia	Postgraduate		400		Prachaabad No. 1 Tehsil Jund, District Attock
42.	Jamia Hanfia Talim-e-Islam	Postgraduate		300		Madni Muhalla, Jhelum

Sr. No.	Name of Madrasa/University	Level	Principal/ Headmaster	Total No. of Students	Annual Expenses (Rupees)	Address
43.	Darul Uloom Hanfia	Postgraduate	Sahibzada Abdul Qadees	500	–	Zia-ul Haq Shaheed Chowk, Chakwal
44.	Darul Uloom Talimul Quran	Postgraduate	Maulana Ashraf Ali	600	–	Raja Bazar, Rawalpindi
45.	Darul Uloom Farooqia	PhD		700	–	Dhamyal Camp, Qaid-e-Azam Colony, Rawalpindi
46.	Jamia Islamia	Postgraduate	Qari Saeedur Rahman	500	–	Kashmir Road, Rawalpindi
47.	Jamiatul-Uloom Al-Sharia	Postgraduate		900	–	Bakery Chowk, West Ridge No. 2, Rawalpindi
48.	Jamia Siddiqia	Postgraduate		700	–	Lala Rukh Wah Cant, Rawalpindi
49.	Jamia Qadria	Postgraduate	Maulana Muhammadullah	250	2 lakh monthly	Bhakkar, Rahimabad
50.	Madrasa Aizazul Uloom	Postgraduate		450	–	Dhandyanwala, Bhakkar
51.	Jamia Miftahul Uloom	Postgraduate	Maulana Mufti Shafaqqat Ali	600		Satellite Town, Sargodha
52.	Jamia Usmania	Postgraduate		500	–	Short Kot, Jhung
53.	Jamia Mehmoodia	Postgraduate	Maulana Manzoor Ahmad Faizan	500	12 lakhs	Cheneot Jhung

617

Gateway to Terrorism

Sr. No.	Name of Madrasa/University	Level	Principal/ Headmaster	Total No. of Students	Annual Expenses (Rupees)	Address
54.	Madrasa Fathul Uloom	Postgraduate			—	Cheneot
55.	Darul Uloom Rabbania	Postgraduate			—	Basti Riyazul Muslimeen, Phaloor, Toba Tek Singh
56.	Darul Uloom Ameenia	Postgraduate		500		Jaranwala, Faisalabad
57.	Jamia Islamia Imdadiya	Postgraduate	Maulana Nazeer Ahmad	700	15 lakhs	Satyana Road, Faisalabad
58.	Darul Uloom	Postgraduate		300	—	Peoples Party No. 2, Faisalabad
59.	Jamia Darul Uloom-ul-Quran	Postgraduate	Maulana Abdur Rahmad Zafar	—	—	Officers Colony, Faisalabad
60.	Jamia Islamia Arabia	Postgraduate		500		Madani Town Kariwalah Road, Near Ghulam Mohammadabad, Faisalabad
61.	Jamia Farooq-e-Azam	Postgraduate		1200		Jhung Road Mohalla, Rasheedabad
63.	Ashraful-Uloom	Postgraduate		900		Bhaghanpura, Gujranwala
64.	Madrasa Nusrat-ul-Uloom	Postgraduate	Mohammad Fayaz Khan Wati	700		Ghantaghar, Gujranwala
65.	Jamia Rahmania	Postgraduate		600		Allahabad, Thaing Mor, Chooniyan, District Qasoor

Sr. No.	Name of Madrasa/University	Level	Principal/ Headmaster	Total No. of Students	Annual Expenses (Rupees)	Address
66.	Jamia Asharfia	PhD	Maulana Obaidullah (PhD)	838	85 lakhs	Muslim Town, Ferozepur Road, Lahore
67.	Jamia Darul-uloom al-Islamia	Postgraduate	Qari Ahmad Miyan Thanvi	865	6.5 lakhs	Kamran Block, Allama Iqbal Town, Lahore
67.	Jamia Usmania	Postgraduate		500		Model Town, Lahore
68.	Jamiat-ul-Manzoor al-Islamia	Postgraduate	Maulana Saifullah Khalid	500	50 lakhs	Idgah Sadar, Lahore Cantt.
69.	Jamia Madinia	Postgraduate	Maulana Rashid Miyan	135	6 lakhs	Karim Park, Lahore
70.	Darul Uloom Islamia	Postgraduate		300	–	Central Jail, Lahore
71.	Jamia Mahmoodia	Postgraduate	Maulana Syed Amir Hussain Gilani	400	8 lakhs	Renalah Khurd, GT Road, Okara
72.	Jamia Darul Uloom	Postgraduate	Maulana Mohammad Anwar	500	–	Idgah Kabirwala, Khanewal
73.	Jamia Uloom Al-Sharia	Postgraduate	Maulana Nazeer Ahmad	300	–	Sahiwal
74.	Jamia Islamia Babul-Uloom	Postgraduate	Maulana Abdul Majeed	400	–	Kehror Paka, Lodhran
75.	Jamia Khairul Madaris	PhD	Maulana Haneef Jalandhari	1500	50 lakhs	Outer Delhi Gate, Multan

Gateway to Terrorism

Sr. No.	Name of Madrasa/University	Level	Principal/ Headmaster	Total No. of Students	Annual Expenses (Rupees)	Address
76	Jamia Siddique Akbar	Postgraduate		500	–	Abdali Masjid, Multan
77.	Jamia Qasim-ul-Uloom	PhD		700		Gulgasht Colony, Multan
78.	Jamia Mohammadia Arabia Hanfia	Postgraduate		500		Qasba Muzal, Multan
79.	Darul Uloom Rahimia	Postgraduate		400		Peer Colony, Multan
80.	Jamia Khalid Bin Walid	Postgraduate		600		Thengi Colony, Wahari
81.	Jamia Meraj-ul-Uloom	Postgraduate	Maulana Mohammad Azeem Khan/ Imdadullah Haqqani	500	–	Inside Lucky Gate, Banno
82.	Al-Markaz-ul-Islamia	Postgraduate	Maulana Qari Mohammad Abdullah	400	–	Sadat Hafiz Kheel, Banno
83.	Madrasa-e-Aliah Talimul-Islam	Postgraduate		350		Rai Nao-Rang, Laki Maroot
84.	Jamia Haleemiah	Postgraduate		400		Darrah Peezo, Laki Maroot
85.	Jamia Usmania	PhD		600		Near Addah Machan Kheel, Laki Maroot
86.	Darul Uloom al-Islamia	Postgraduate	Mufti Hameed Ullah Khan	700		Banoori Town, Laki Maroot

620

Sr. No.	Name of Madrasa/University	Level	Principal/ Headmaster	Total No. of Students	Annual Expenses (Rupees)	Address
87.	Jamia Darul Uloom-ul-Islamia	PhD	Maulana Hasan Khan	500		Durwesh Masjid, Peshawar
88.	Darul Uloom Talimul Quran	PhD		900		Bara Market, Peshawar
89.	Darul Uloom Usmania	Postgraduate	Maulana Mufti Ghulamur Rahman	700		Outer Asia Gate, Peshawar
90.	Markazi Darul Qura	Postgraduate	Qari Faizur Rahman Alvi	700	3 lakhs	Salt Factory, Peshawar
91.	Jamia Ashrafiya	Postgraduate	Ashraf Ali Qureshi	800	50 lakhs	Idgah Road, Peshawar
92.	Darul Uloom Islamia	Postgraduate	Maulana Hafiz Mohammad Jaan	500	–	Khar, Bajora Agency
93.	Madrasa Islamia Riyazul Uloom	Postgraduate		500	–	Barcheenia Gini Mamoonda Inayat Kilay, Bajora Agency
94.	Darul Uloom Islamia	Postgraduate	Maulana Idris	300	4 lakhs	Char Sadda
95.	Darul Uloom Nomania	Postgraduate	Maulana Roohullah	300	–	Atmaan Zai, Tangi Road, Char Sadda
96.	Darul Uloom Haqqania	PhD	Maulana Samiul Haq	2000	80 lakhs	Akora Khatak, Naoshera
97.	Madrasa Tahseenul Quran	Postgraduate	Qari Mohammad Umar	500	–	Hukam Abla, Naoshera

Gateway to Terrorism

Sr. No.	Name of Madrasa/University	Level	Principal/ Headmaster	Total No. of Students	Annual Expenses (Rupees)	Address
98.	Jamia Marif-ul-Sar'ia	Postgraduate	Maulana Qazi Abdul Halim	350	–	Banno Road, Dera Ismail Khan
99.	Darul-Uloom Nomania Al-Uloom	Postgraduate	Maulana Alauddin	500	7 lakhs	Inside Paivandgan, Dera Ismail Khan
100.	Madrasa Madinatul Uloom	Postgraduate		300		Warana Shaheedabad, Kurk
101.	Darul Uloom Islamia	Postgraduate	350			Babul Kheel, Tehsil Takht Nusrati, Kurk
102.	Madrasa Anjuman Talimul Quran	Postgraduate	Maulana Shehbaz Khan	–	–	Pracha Town, Pindi Road, Kohat
103.	Darul Uloom Sirajul Islam	Postgraduate		500	–	Kaahi, Kohat
104.	Darul Uloom Arabia	Postgraduate		400	–	Tal Kohat
105.	Darul Uloom Waana	Postgraduate	Maulana Taj Mohammad	300	–	South Waziristan
106.	Darul Uloom Talimul Quran	Postgraduate		500	–	Saidabad Colony, Der
107.	Jamia Maariful Uloom Al-Shariya	Postgraduate	Maulana Gul Naseeb Khan	400	16 lakhs	Taimer Girah, Der
108.	Darul Uloom Mazharul Islam	Postgraduate		500	–	Otch, Der

Sr. No.	Name of Madrasa/University	Level	Principal/ Headmaster	Total No. of Students	Annual Expenses (Rupees)	Address
109.	Darul Uloom Talimul Quran	Postgraduate		350	–	Shahpur Shaangla
110.	Jamia Islamia Talimul Quran	Postgraduate	Qari Abul Ghafoor	700	12 lakhs	Galkadeh No. 3, Seedu Sharif, Sawat
111.	Jamia Mazharul Uloom	Postgraduate		300	–	Mengora Green Chowk, Sawat
112.	Darul Uloom Islamia	Postgraduate	Maulana Rahimullah	500	–	Azakheel
113.	Jamia Usman Bin Affan	Postgraduate		400	–	Khwaza Kheela Sawat
114.	Darul Quran	Postgraduate		400	–	Rahimabad, Sawat
115.	Darul Uloom Islamia Arabia	Postgraduate		500	–	Shergarh, Mardan
116.	Darul Uloom Arabia	Postgraduate		370	–	Gujrat, Mardan
117.	Jamia Rasheediya	Postgraduate		450	–	Thandkoi, Sawabi
118.	Darul Uloom Sayidia	Postgraduate	Maulana Saeedur Rahman	500	30 lakhs	Aogi
119.	Darul Uloom Islamia Arabia	Postgraduate		390	–	Dalbori, Mansehra
120.	Jamia Talimul Quran	Postgraduate	Mufti Kifayatullah	300	–	Tirankari, Mansehra
121.	Jamia Arabia Sirajul Uloom	Postgraduate		300	–	Jabori, Mansehra

Gateway to Terrorism

Sr. No.	Name of Madrasa/University	Level	Principal/ Headmaster	Total No. of Students	Annual Expenses (Rupees)	Address
122.	Darul Uloom Mariful Quran	Postgraduate		350	–	Hanfia Markazi Jama Masjid, Mansehra
123.	Darul Uloom Ayyubia	Postgraduate		400	–	Tailoos Alai Tegraam
124.	Darul Uloom Islamia	Postgraduate		500	–	Central Jail, Haripur
125.	Jamia Aziziya	Postgraduate		400		Kehal Abbottabad
126.	Darul Uloom Isha Al-Tauheed Wa Al-Sana	Postgraduate		400	–	Pattan, Kohistan
127.	Jamia Talimul Quran	Postgraduate	Maulana Meer Afzal Khan	1000	15 lakhs	Village Hissar Dagar Boonez
128.	Jamia Islamia Nusratul Islam	Takhsees		280		Idgah Road, Gilgit
129.	Jamia Islamia	Postgraduate	Maulana Abdur Rahman	500		Satellite Town, Sakardo
130.	Jamia Arabia Siddiq Akbar	Postgraduate	Sahibzada Hifzur Rahman Shams	400		Tandowala Yar Akram Colony, Bakheroo, Hyderabad
131.	Jamia Miftahul Uloom	Postgraduate	Maulana Dard Shah	400	–	Site Area, Hyderabad
132.	Madrasa Anwarul Uloom	Postgraduate		290		Shikarpur Road, Sukkur
133.	Jamia Ashrafiya	Postgraduate	Mufti Mahfooz Ahmad	–	–	Walls Road, Sukkur

Sr. No.	Name of Madrasa/University	Level	Principal/ Headmaster	Total No. of Students	Annual Expenses (Rupees)	Address
134.	Jamia Anwarul Uloom	Postgraduate		250		Kundparo, Naushehra Firoz
135.	Darul Uloom Haseeniah	Postgraduate	Maulana Mohammad Yusuf	300	—	Shahdadpur, Sangarh
136.	Jamia Mahmoodiya Arabia	PhD		350		Latifabad No. 2, Golimaar, Nawabshah
137.	Jamia Darul Uloom	PhD (University)	Mufti Taqi Usmani	45000	1 crore	K Area Korangi, Karachi No. 14
138.	Jamiatul Uloom Al-Islamia	PhD (University)	Mufti Mohammad Naim	2000	3 crore	Allama Bandi Town, Karachi No. 5
139.	Madrasa Talimul Islam	Postgraduate		500	17 lakhs	Gulshan Umar Sohrab, Goth, Karachi
140.	Jamia Farooqia	Postgraduate	Maulana Saleemullah Khan	1000	35 lakhs	Shah Faisal Colony No. 4, Karachi No. 25
141.	Jamia Hamadiya	Postgraduate	Maulana Abdul Wahid	1000	50 lakhs	Shah Faisal Colony No. 4 Karachi No. 25
142.	Jamia Asharfia Haqania	PhD		700		Burmi Colony G 32, Landhi, Karachi
143.	Jamia Ahsanul Uloom	Postgraduate	Maulana Nadvi Khan	1200	20 lakhs	Gulshan Iqbal Block No. 2, Karachi

Gateway to Terrorism

Sr. No.	Name of Madrasa/University	Level	Principal/ Headmaster	Total No. of Students	Annual Expenses (Rupees)	Address
144.	Jamia Darul Uloom Hanfia	PhD	Maulana Faizullah Azad	600	12 lakhs	Sector 11-E, Aurangi Town, Karachi
145.	Darul Uloom Rahmania	Postgraduate		450	–	Buffer Zone, 15, A S North Karachi
146.	Jamia Anwarul Quran	Postgraduate	Maulana Fidaur Rahman Darkhasti	700	25 lakhs	11-E Adam Town, Karachi
147.	Jamia Usmania Ahya-ul-Uloom	Postgraduate		390	–	Municipal Town, Sector 9A, Karachi
148.	Jamia Usmania	Postgraduate		500	–	Sher Shah Colony C Block, Karachi
149.	Jamia Banooriya	Postgraduate		450	–	Adjacent Site Thana, Karachi
150.	Jamia Islamia Imdadul-Uloom	Postgraduate		500	–	Jama Masjid, Nazimabad No. 5, Karachi
151.	Madinatul Uloom	Postgraduate		500	–	Jama Masjid Block A, North Nazimabad, Karachi
152.	Madrasa Arabia Islamia	Postgraduate		600	–	Scout Colony, Commissioner Co-operative Housing Society, Karachi
153.	Madrasa Ashraful Madaris	Postgraduate	Maulana Hakim Mohammad Mazhar	1500	40 lakhs	Gulshan Iqbal town Block No. 2, Karachi

Sr. No.	Name of Madrasa/University	Level	Principal/ Headmaster	Total No. of Students	Annual Expenses (Rupees)	Address
154.	Jamia Islamia	Postgraduate	Maulana Abdullah Khani	700	10 lakhs	Scout Colony, Karachi
155.	Jamia Imam Abu Hanifa	Postgraduate		500		Mecca Masjid, Adamji Nagar, Mohammad Society, Karachi
156.	Jamia Islamia Tayyaba	Postgraduate		600		Shikarpur Colony, M A Jinnah Road, Karachi
157.	Madrasa Ashraful-Madaris Baitul Mukarram	Postgraduate		650		Korangi 3/1.2, Karachi
158.	Darul Uloom Saffa	Postgraduate		450		Municipal Town, Sector 3A, Karachi
159.	Mahadul Khail Al-Islami	Postgraduate		700		Bahadurabad, 445–3, Karachi
160.	Jamia Qartaba	Postgraduate		450		Shireen Jinnah Colony, Clifton, Karachi
161.	Jamia Yusufiya Banooriya	Postgraduate	Hasanur Rahman Abdullah	1500	30 lakhs	Sharafabad Society, Block No. 1, Karachi
162.	Jamia Islamia Makhzanul Uloom	Postgraduate		370		Banaras Colony, Karachi
163.	Jamia Al-Rasheed	Postgraduate		490		Ahsanabad, Karachi

Gateway to Terrorism

Sr. No.	Name of Madrasa/University	Level	Principal/ Headmaster	Total No. of Students	Annual Expenses (Rupees)	Address
164.	Darul Uloom Rahmaniya	Postgraduate	Maulana Nazeer Ahmad	500	15 lakhs	Burmese Colony 36 G, Landhi, Karachi
165.	Jamia Madina Islamia	Postgraduate	Maulana Abdul Kareem Abid	1200		Gulshan Iqbal, Karachi
166.	Jamia Qasmiya Hashmiya	Postgraduate	Maulana Faiz Mohammad Faiz	500		11-B North Karachi
167.	Darul Uloom Farooq Azam	Postgraduate	Maulana Mohammad Asif Qasmi	390	10 lakhs	4-ST Block, K North Nazimabad, Karachi
168.	Madrasa-e-Asharfiya Imdadiya	Postgraduate	Mufti Abdul Jabbar	500	10 lakhs	Karachi
169.	Idarah Uloom Islami	Postgraduate	Maulana Faizur Rahman Usmani	350	15 lakhs	Sattrah Jail, Near Toh Plaza, Islamabad
170.	Madrasa Tahaffuz-ul-Quran	Postgraduate	Maulana Mehboob Ilahi	129		Bambooriat, Chatral
171.	Jamia Islamia Khatm Nabuwat	Postgraduate		350	20 lakhs	Shahbazpur Road, Rahim Yar Khan
172.	Jamia Nizamiya Mairajul Uloom	Postgraduate	Mufti Nizamuddin	500	10 lakhs	Ittehad Town, Karachi No. 51

Sr. No.	Name of Madrasa/University	Level	Principal/ Headmaster	Total No. of Students	Annual Expenses (Rupees)	Address
173.	Jamia Ehteshamiya	Postgraduate	Maulana Tanveerul Haq Thanvi	350	12 lakhs	Adjacent Jama Masjid, Jacob Line, Karachi
174.	Jamia Al-arabia Ahsanul Uloom	Postgraduate	Maulana Mufti Zoudli Khan	1200	6 lakhs	Gulshan Iqbal No. 2, Karachi
175.	Madrasa Jama Al-Uloom	Postgraduate	Maulana Jalil Ahmad Akhwan	370	3 lakhs	Idgah, Bhawalnagar
176.	Madrasa Baitul Uloom	Postgraduate	Maulana Naseer Ahmad	300	3 lakhs	Tandoo Jan Mohammad, Meerpurkhas
177.	Darul Uloom Sadiqabad	Postgraduate	Maulana Peer Mohammad	500	4 lakhs	Aurangi Town No. 11.5, Karachi
178.	Madrasa Anwarul Quran	Postgraduate	Maulvi Hakim Mohammad Anwar	600	4 lakhs	Goth Haji Khuda Baksh, District Hyderabad
179.	Jamia Furqania	Postgraduate	Qari Mujeebur Rahman	400	3 lakhs	Bismillah Chowk, Hanjarpur, Sdiqabad
180.	Jamia Khulafa-e Rashideen	PhD	Maulana Khalid Mahmood	500	4 lakhs	Khyaban Suroor Block B, Dera Ghazi Khan
181.	Madrasa Haqqania	Postgraduate	Qari Saeed Ahmad	350	10 lakhs	Idgah Karampur, Kakar Hatta, Kabirwala
182.	Jamia Sorooriya	Postgraduate	Abdur Rahman Miyan	200	2 lakh	Wafati Colony, Lahore

Gateway to Terrorism

Sr. No.	Name of Madrasa/University	Level	Principal/ Headmaster	Total No. of Students	Annual Expenses (Rupees)	Address
183.	Darul Uloom Jamia Islamia	Postgraduate	Qari Mohammad Yusuf Haqqani	250	3 lakhs	Tajpur Road, Mughalpura, Lahore
184.	Jamia Anwarul Quran	Postgraduate	Mufti Mohammad Abdullah Baltastani	350	10 lakhs	Jama Masjid Ghafooria 111–2/G, Islamabad
185.	Madrasa Darul Quran	Postgraduate	Maulana Mohammad Faheem Sawati	400	4 lakhs	Tehsil Hatta, Shakheela Bara, Sawat
186.	Jamia Qasimul Uloom	Postgraduate	Mufti Lutfur Rahman	500	5 lakhs	Kashar Colony, Gilgit
187.	Almahad-ul-Islamia	Postgraduate	Maulana Kifayatullah Tassur	300	3 lakhs	Allama Chaghar Zai, Topi, District Boniar
188.	Jamia Talimul Quran	Postgraduate	Mufti Kifayatullah	350	3 lakhs	Tarangri, Mansehra
189.	Al-Jamia Al-Nomania	Postgraduate	Mufti Shahjahan	350	4 lakhs	Kohat Road, Budh, Bair Spain Jamat
190.	Madrasa Kanz al-Uloom	Postgraduate	Maulana Amrullah	400	4 lakhs	District Pasheen, Baru, Baluchistan
191.	Jamia Islamia Anwarus-Sahaba	Postgraduate	Maulana Abdur Rauf	600	6 lakhs	Gunar Farm, Tehsil Chedas District Diya Meer
192.	Jamia Darul Uloom Islamia	Postgraduate	Maulana Mohammad Yusuf	250	3 lakhs	Pilandri, Azad Kashmir
193.	Jamia Rahmania	Postgraduate	Maulana Inayatur Rahman	300	4 lakhs	Dargai

Sr. No.	Name of Madrasa/University	Level	Principal/ Headmaster	Total No. of Students	Annual Expenses (Rupees)	Address
194.	Madrasa Darul Uloom	Postgraduate	Kifayatullah	300	5 lakhs	Saidoo Sharif, Sawat
195.	Jamia Asharfia Jankot	Postgraduate		500	6 lakhs	Multan
196.	Darul Uloom Kabirwala	Postgraduate		400	–	Kabirwala
197.						
198.	Jamia Babul Uloom Kehrorpacca	Postgraduate		400	–	Kehrorpacca
199.	Jamia Islamia Amdabar	Postgraduate		300	–	Faisalabad
200.	Jamia Bilal	Postgraduate	Mohammad Ahmad Mujahid	150	–	Bilal Masjid, Sabzazar, Lahore
201.	Darul Uloom Farooq-e-Azam	Postgraduate	Qari Shafiqur Rahman	200	15 lakhs	Idgah Jia Moosa, Shahadra, Lahore
202.	Madrasa Nusratul Haq, Lahore	Postgraduate	Maulana Fazlur Rahman	100	2 lakh	9-A, Nisbat Road, Lahore
203.	Madrasa Jamia Rahmania	Postgraduate	Maulana Mohammad Ajmal Khan	500	15 lakhs	Abdul Karim Road, Lahore Cantt.
204.	Madrasa Tablighi Markaz	Postgraduate	Maulana Abdul Wahab	679	–	Rai Wind, Lahore
205.	Jamia Madina	Postgraduate	Maulana Muhibbun Nabi	261	2 lakh	Rasool Pak, Sabzazar, Lahore
206.	Jamia Hanifa, Faizul Uloom	Postgraduate	Mufti Sayed Muzammil Hussain	35	2 lakh	711, A Syedpur, Multan Road, Lahore

631

Gateway to Terrorism

Sr. No.	Name of Madrasa/University	Level	Principal/ Headmaster	Total No. of Students	Annual Expenses (Rupees)	Address
207.	Madrasa Mazharul Uloom	Postgraduate	Haji Mohammad Ishtiyaq	162	3 lakh	Idgah RA Bazar, Lahore
208.	Madrasa Mukhzaanul Quran	Postgraduate	Abdul Qadir	81	3 lakhs	Gali No. 21, Mughalpura, Lahore
209.	Madrasa Aliya Tajveedul Quran	Postgraduate	Maulana Mohammad Irshad	310	4 lakhs	Sheranwala Gate, Lahore
210.	Madrasa Abu Bakar Siddique	Postgraduate	Malik Khalil Ahmad	185	5 lakhs	Block No. 11 D/1, Green Town, Lahore
211.	Jamia Farooqia Shekhupura	Postgraduate	Maulana Mohammad Alam	150	3 lakhs	Sharqpur Road, Shekhupura
212.	Jamia Islamia	Postgraduate	Maulana Maqbool Ahmad	85	2 lakh	District Court, Shekhupura
213.	Madrasa Mubarak Darul Uloom	Third Level	Abdul Ghafoor	150	2 lakh	Sharqpur Road, Shekhupura
214.	Jamia Ziaul Uloom	Postgraduate	Qari Abdul Majeed	100	2 lakh	Saraya Salar Road, Manwala, District Shekhupura
215.	Madrasa Arabia Jamia Rashidiya	Third Level	Mohammad Latifullah	95	2 lakh	Manwala, District Shekhupura
216.	Jamia Mohammadiya	Postgraduate	Mohammad Irshad	82	2 lakh	Nankana Road, Shahkot, District Shekhupura

Sr. No.	Name of Madrasa/University	Level	Principal/ Headmaster	Total No. of Students	Annual Expenses (Rupees)	Address
217.	Madrasa Imdadul Uloom	Third Level	Maulana Mohammad Sharif	61	2 lakh	Shahkot, District Shekhupura
218.	Madrasa Darul Uloom Al-Arabia Hanifa	Third Level	Qari Mohammad Islmail	74	1.5 lakh	Narang, District Shekhupura
219.	Madrasa Farooq Azam	—	Choudhury Nasir Ahmad	60	2 lakh	Near Firdous Flour Mill, Muridke
220.	Madrasa Darul Uloom Usmania	—	Maulvi Mohammad Anwar	74	3 lakh	Near Factory Area, Muridke
221.	Madrasa Ishatul Quran	—	Qari Mohammad Ishaq	95	2 lakh	Sharqpur, District Shekhupura
222.	Madrasa Darus Safa al-Almiat	—	Miyan Noor Mohammad	123	2 lakh	Sharqpur, District Shekhupura
223.	Hazrat Nek Mohammad Madrasa Hifzul Quran	—	Qari Mohammad Yunus	119	2 lakh	Sharqpur, District Shekhupura
224.	Jamia Hazrat Miyan Saheb	Postgraduate	Qari Asghar Ali	110	4 lakhs	Sharqpur, District Shekhupura
225.	Madrasa Jamia Islamia Imdadiya	Postgraduate	Maulana Wajid Hussain	115	3 lakh	Aqsa Colony, Warbarton, District Shekhupura
226.	Jamia Arabia Islamia Hanfiya	Postgraduate	Choudhury Fazal Hussain	129	3 lakh	Circular Road, Qasoor

Gateway to Terrorism

Sr. No.	Name of Madrasa/University	Level	Principal/ Headmaster	Total No. of Students	Annual Expenses (Rupees)	Address
227.	Madrasa Jamia Usmania	Postgraduate	Qari Mohammad Sajawal	150	1.5 lakh	Raja Jung, Qasoor
228.	Darul Akramatul Quran	Postgraduate	Qari Mohammad Hussain	160	2 lakh	Mangoowala, Raiwind
229.	Madrasa Darul Uloom Mohammadiya	Postgraduate	Maulana Karim	139	3 lakh	Taragarh, District Qasoor
230.	Madrasa Mazharul Uloom	Postgraduate	Qari Wali Mohammad	153	3 lakh	Kanganpur, Qasoor
231.	Madrasa Faizul Quran	Postgraduate	Hafiz Mushtaq Ahmad	200	4 lakh	Chinyan City, Qasoor

Table XXIX: *Deobandi Madrasas (Under Wafaqul Madaris Al-Ahrar)*

Sr. No.	Madrasa	Class	Principal	No. of Students	Annaul Expenses (Rupees)	Address
1.	Madrasa Mamoora, Multan	Postgraduate	Syed Ataul Mubin Bukhari	500	15 lakh	Jama Masjid Khatam Nabuat Dar Nabi Hashim, Multan
2.	Madrasa Mamoora, Multan	Postgraduate	Syed Ataul Mubin Bukhari	400	–	Masjid Noor Tughlaq Road, Multan
3.	Madrasa Mamoora, Multan	Postgraduate	Syed Ataul Mubin Bukhari	400	–	Masjid Tooba, Wahari Road, Multan
4.	Jamia Maaz Multan	Postgraduate	Syed Mohammad Tufail Bukhari	300	–	Badahla Road, Multan
5.	Madrasa Talimul Quran	Middle	Syed Mohammad Tufail Bukhari	200	–	Makki Masjid, Chowk Haram Gate, Multan
6.	Madrasa Maamoorah, Lahore	Third Level		200	–	Hussain Street, Wehdut Road, New Muslim Town, Lahore
7.	Madrasa Khatm Nabuat	Middle		150	–	Masjid Ahrar, Rabooh, District Jhang
8.	Madrasa Khatm Nabuat	Middle		100	–	Masjid Basti, Lachyan, Rabooh
9.	Madrasa Farooq Azam	Postgraduate		250	–	Mauza Ashaba Chowk, Kali Hali, District Jhang

Gateway to Terrorism

Sr. No.	Madrasa	Class	Principal	No. of Students	Annaul Expenses (Rupees)	Address
10.	Madrasa Mahmoodiya Gujrat	Middle		150	–	Masjid Al-Mamoor Nagariyan, District Gujrat
11.	Darul Uloom Khatm Nabuat	Postgraduate		200	–	Jama Masjid, Chechawatani
12.	Darul Uloom Khatm Nabuat	Postgraduate		200		Masjid Usmania, Housing Scheme, Chechawatani
13.	Madrasa Muaviya	Third Level		200		Jhung Road, Toba Tek Singh
14.	Madrasa Abu Bakr Siddique	Middle		110		Jama Masjid Abu Bakr, Tilla Gung, District Chakwal
15.	Madrasa Ahrarul Islam	Third Level		100		Masjid Syyedna Ali, Chakrala, District Mianwali
16.	Madrasa Talimul Quran	Third Level		150		Jama Masjid, Shehli Gharabi (Behawalanger)
17.	Madrasa Al-Uloom Al-Islamia	Middle		100		Jama Masjid Garha Morh, Wahari
18.	Madrasa Khatam Nabooat Wahari	Foundation		110		Nawan Chowk, Garha Morh, Wahari
19.	Madrasa Khatm Nabuat	Foundation		150		Chak 76, Bhagwana Pura, Dist. Wahari

Sr. No.	Madrasa	Class	Principal	No. of Students	Annaul Expenses (Rupees)	Address
20.	Madrasa Khatm Nabuat Wahari	Foundation		200		Chak 88/AB Garha Morh, Wahari
21.	Madrasa Khatm Nabuat	Foundation		110		Green Town Rampur Road, Boreywalah
22.	Madrasa Maamoorah Khanewal	Foundation		105		Chak A-156, Jahanyan, District Khanewal
23.	Madrasa Ahrarul Islam	Postgraduate		100		Mustafabad, Karampur, Wahari
24.	Madrasa Arabia Mahmoodiya	Foundation		200		Chah Keekarwala, Mauza Bhatpur
25.	Madrasa Ahrarul Islam	Foundation		100		Chah Chareywala, Colorwali, Muzaffargarh
26.	Madrasa Mamoora, Muzaffargarh	Foundation		150		Masjid Muaviyah, Basti Meherpur, District Muzaffargarh
27.	Jamia Bustan Ayesha (Girls)	Postgraduate		300	–	Daar Bani Hashim, Multan
28.	Madrasa Al-Banat (Girls)	Founder		90	–	Garha Morh, Wahari

Table XXX: *Deobandi Madrasas (Under Wasaiqul Madaris)*

Sr. No.	Name of Madrasa/University	Level	Principal/ Headmaster	Total students	Annual Expenses (Rupees)	Address
1.	Jamia Aziziya		Maulana Abu Bakr Siddique			Aurangi Town, Karachi
2.	Jamia Madinatul Uloom		Maulana Abul Hussain			North Nazimabad, Karachi
3.	Jamia Darul Uloom Al-Islamia		Maulana Ahmad Hasan			Aurangi Town, Karachi
4.	Jamia Ashrafiya Haqqania		Maulana Rahmatullah			Burmi Colony, Karachi
5.	Jamia Islamia		Maulana Jafar			Burmi Colony, Karachi
6.	Madrasa Madinatul Uloom		Maulana Mohammad Sabir Ashrafi			Sau quarter, Karachi
7.	Jamia Khaleeliya		Maulana Idris Muzahiri			Moosa Colony, Karachi
8.	Jamia Usmania		Maulana Muhibbullah			Noorani Basti, Korangi
9.	Madrasa Rahmaniya		Maulana Hafiz Ahmad			Sau quarter, Karachi
10.	Madrasa Mohammad Bin Abdullah		Hafiz Hakim Sharif			Sau quarter, Karachi
11.	Madrasa Tajveedul Quran		Maulana Inamul Haq			Sau quarter, Karachi
12.	Jamia Hasneeniya		Maulana Zahid Hussain			Burmi Colony, Karachi
13.	Madrasa Khalid Bin Walid		Maulana Abdur Rahman Mujahid			50 C, Sau quarter, Karachi

Sr. No.	Name of Madrasa/University	Level	Principal/ Headmaster	Total students	Annual Expenses (Rupees)	Address
14.	Madrasa Moeenul Islam		Maulana Mohammad Sharif			Ilyas Goth, Chashma Goth, Karachi
15.	Sadiqiyah Tahfeezul Quran		Maulana Nabi Hussain			Sau quarter, Korangi, Karachi
16.	Ashraful Uloom		Maulana Mohammad Khalid Ashrafi			Sau quarter, Korangi, Karachi
17.	Madrasa Bilal Ibne Ribah		Maulana Abdul Kalam Nazamri			Sau quarter, Korangi, Karachi
18.	Madrasa Anas Bin Halik		Maulana Mohammad Ahsan			Sau quarter, Korangi Karachi
19.	Madrasa Riyazul Uloom		Maulana Zainul Haq			Sau quarter, Korangi Karachi
20.	Madrasa Imdadiya		Maulana Nurul Islam			Sau quarter, Korangi Karachi
21.	Madrasa Qasimul Uloom		Maulana Abdul Karim			Sau quarter, Korangi Karachi
22.	Madrasa Talimul Quran		Maulana Abdur Rahim			Peer Colony, Karachi
23.	Madrasa Siddiqiya		Maulana Wasiur Rahman			Masjid Firdous, Sau quarter, Karachi
24.	Madrasa Al-Hasan Islamia		Maulana Habibullah			Masjid Firdous, Sau quarter, Karachi

Madrasas of Ahl-e Hadith Persuasion

There are 500 Ahl-e Hadith madrasas of higher education in Pakistan. Of them 310 are affiliated to Wafaqul Madaris Salafiya and Madina University. One hundred of the madrasas are close to jihadi organisations. A list of these madrasas is provided in Table XXXI. The most important among them are as follows:

Jamia Al-Dawa Al-Islamia, Muridke

Jamat Al-Dawa has built its own network of madrasas. Its central madrasa, known as Jamia Al-Dawa Al-Islamia is located in the centre of Jamat Al-Dawa, Muridke. It has facilities for Dars-e Nizami in all stages. Its principal is Maulana Abdullah Salafi. There are 500 students and twenty-one teachers here. The main purpose of establishing these madrasas is to prepare manpower (staff) for the mosques and madrasas of Al-Dawa, and increase the number of madrasas that will propagate the view of Al-Dawa. There is a short cut to this as well: they have devised a twenty-one-day *tablighi* course, which consists of instructions for two weeks and actual preaching in public for one week.

Two madrasas of Jamat Al-Dawa are also working in Baluchistan, one in Quetta and the other in Turbat. These madrasas have a more important role in Baluchistan because they also double as centres of Jamat Al-Dawa and Lashkar-e Tayyaba. They also supply manpower to Lashkar-e Tayyaba.

Jamia Salafiya, Faisalabad

Jamia Salafiya in Haji Abad, Faisalabad, is an important institution of Ahl-e Hadith persuasion. Its patron is

Professor Sajid Mir, and the principal is Mian Naimur Rahman Tahir. This institution also houses the headquarters of Wafaqul Madaris Salafiya. According to this board, the madrasa has facilities for instructions up to PhD. There are about 3,000 students who are studying in different branches of the madrasa. For girls, there is 'Jamia Sadiqiya Lil-Banat'. It has an important department of *tabligh*, headed by Maulana Aminur Rahman Sajid.

Besides being a centre of *tablighi* activities, this centre is also a centre of jihadi activities. It provides human and material resources to Tahreekul Mujahideen, the Ahl-e Hadith jihadi organisation. Students and teachers from this madrasa have been visiting Tahreekul Mujahideen's Abdullah bin Mubarak Camp for military training. Last year, a caravan of forty had gone to Mansehra for this purpose.

Besides being a centre of political activities of Jamiat Ahl-e Hadith, Jamia Salafiya is also a centre of the sectarian activities of Ahl-e Hadith Youth Force, which works against both the Hanafis (Deobandi/Barelvi) and the Shias.

Madrasa Riazul Quran, Lahore
This madrasa approved by Wafaqul Madaris and working under the supervision of Markazi Jamiat Ahl-e Hadith, has facilities for instructions up to the postgraduate level. Its central secretary is Maulana Abdur Rasheed. There are 450 students, including foreigners who are also awarded scholarships.

Darool Hadith, Okara
This madrasa, spread over a plot of 5 *kanal*, is located

on the Sahiwal Road, Okara. It is run by Anjuman Ahl-e Hadith. It has 300 students pursuing different stages of Dars-e Nizami. English language is also taught here. Its secretary is Maulana Muhammad Ramzan. This madrasa helps Ahl-e Hadith jihadi organisations.

Abu Huraira Academy, Lahore
This academy was established by Mian Muhammad Jameel, the general secretary of Markazi Jamiat Ahl-e Hadith, in 1997. Apart from madrasa courses, it also imparts instruction up to BA (general education). This madrasa helps Ahl-e Hadith Youth Force and Tahreekul Mujahideen.

Jamia Lahore Al-Islamia (Rahmaniya), Lahore
The principal of this madrasa is Maulana Hafiz Abdur Rahman Madani. It has facilities for instructions up to the graduate level. There are about 1,000 students in this madrasa. Maulana Hafiz Abdur Rahman Madani was in the action committee of Markaz al-Dawa al-Irshad at the time of its formation. But he left it later because of differences over the concept of jihad.

Darul Hadith, Jamia Moaviya, Lahore
This madrasa, located in Shahdara, Lahore, is run by Jamat Ghurba Ahl-e Hadith. Its principal is Maulana Muhammad Idris Hashmi. This is a new madrasa that has come into prominence because of its activities. Efforts are being made to put it on the same footing as the Centre of Markazi Jamiat Ahl-e Hadith at 106, Ravi Road, Lahore. Despite differences, it prefers Jamat Al-Dawa and Lashkar-e Tayyaba to Tahreekul Mujahideen and Jamat Al-Mujahideen and extends

help to them.

Jamia Ahl-e Hadith, Lahore
Located at Chowk Dalgiran, Jamia Ahl-e Hadith is being run by Abdul Ghaffar Rupri. He is the son of Hafiz Abdullah Rupri, and amir of Jamat Ahl-e Hadith. This madrasa has been working since 1948 and has the following departments:

1. Tahfeezul Quran (Memorising the Holy Koran)
2. Dars-e Nizami
3. Wafaqul Madaris (Madrasa board)
4. Darul Iftah
5. Tasneef O Talif (Writings and publications)
6. Fann Manazera (Debate)
7. Dawat Wal-Irshad (Preaching)

There are about 400 students and sixteen teachers. The annual outlay is sixteen lakh rupees.

This madrasa is the centre of *tablighi* and political activities of Jamat Ahl-e Hadith. The debaters groomed here prepare booklets against the views of Barelvi, Deobandi, and Shia sects. It supports Jamat Al-Mujahideen.

Al-Jamia Al-Salafiya, Islamabad
Al-Jamia Al-Salafiya, Islamabad, is being run by Abdul Ghaffar Bukhari. It is affiliated to Madina University and Ummul Qura University, Saudi Arabia. There are about 1,000 students, including foreigners. It has facilities for madrasa instruction up to the postgraduate level, and general education up to BA level. The annual outlay is twenty lakh rupees.

Besides being a centre of sectarian *tablighi* work, it is also a centre of jihadi activities. It shows special favour to Tahreekul Mujahideen. Mujahideen are provided with accommodation and hospitality here.

Jamia Uloom Asariya, Jhelum
Spread over a vast tract of land, this madrasa was established by Maulana Muhammad Madani. After his death his son has taken over as the principal. Apart from Dars-e Nizami, it has facilities for instructions up to the PhD. It is affiliated to Wafaqul Madaris Salafiya and Madina University. Five alumni of Madina University are teaching here. Brilliant students of this madrasa are sent to Madina University and other universities of Saudi Arabia on scholarships. The founder of this madrasa is Muhammad bin Abdullah, Imam of Ka'ba. There are about 900 students here. The annual outlay exceeds one crore rupees.

The students and teachers of this madrasa are not allowed to take part in jihadi activities; however, it supports Jamat Al-Mujahideen and allows mujahideen to stay in the hostels.

Jamia Talimul Islam, Mamun Kanjan
This old madrasa in Mamun Kanjan, Faisalabad, was established in 1921 where a substantial number of foreign students have been studying. The founder of this madrasa was Maulana Fazl Ilahi who was the amir of Jamat Al-Mujahideen. Besides madrasa courses, it has also facilities for general education up to BA. This madrasa is also known because of its library, which is supposed to be the largest library of religious literature in Pakistan. The chief secretary of the madrasa is Abdur Rasheed Hejazi and the president is Abdul Qadir Nadvi.

This is a very important centre for the activities of Tahreekul Mujahideen and Jamat Al-Mujahideen. The students and teachers are allowed to take part in jihadi activities. Three of its students have been killed in Occupied Kashmir.

There are about 750 students here, including 550 boarders. Its annual outlay is seven lakh rupees. It does not accept any government grants, although it receives funds from Saudi Arabia.

Jamia Sania, Sahiwal

The principal of this madrasa is Maulana Abdur Rasheed Hazarwi. It has about 500 students. Besides Dars-e Nizami, it has facilities for general education as well.

Jamia Abi Huraira, Renalah Khurd

This madrasa is being run by Hafiz Shafiqur Rahman Lakhwi. It has facilities up to postgraduate level. There are about 300 students here.

Jamia Talimat Islamia, Faisalabad

The founder of this madrasa was Maulana Hakim Abdur Raheem Ashraf. Currently, Dr Zahid Ashraf is the secretary. This madrasa is an important centre of jihadi and sectarian activities.

Markaz Al-Darsat Al-Islamia, Faisalabad

This madrasa is being run by Hafiz Abdus Sattar, an alumnus of Madina University. It is a representative Ahl-e Hadith institution in Pakistan where courses taught in Madina University are followed. Its most important department is Idarah Khidmatul Kitab which is compiling the traditions (Hadith) in Arabic, English, and Urdu. For this, a fifty-member board of

645

ulema has been constituted, that includes ulema from Saudi Arabia and other Arab states. This madrasa supports Tahreekul Mujahideen.

Markaz Al-Tauheed Ahl-e Hadith, Dera Ghazi Khan
This madrasa, affiliated to Wafaqul Madaris Salafiya, is located at Chowk Chorahta in Dera Ghazi Khan. It has facilities for instructions up to the postgraduate level. It is an important centre for jihadi activities. Qari Abdur Rahim is the principal. There are about 500 students here. The monthly outlay is fifteen lakh rupees. Qari Abdul Jabbar, a member of the management board said, 'We have special arrangement for *tablighi* and jihadi activities. We extend our help to Tahreekul Mujahideen. All the Salafi madrasas between Rajanpur and Dera are connected through the offices located here. The madrasa runs special courses for jihadi training in which individuals other than students also take part.' Qari Abdul Jabbar said that most of the students of the madrasa have acquired jihadi training, but few of them could be launched. This is because Tahreekul Mujahideen picks up as many students as they require. The rest keep on waiting for their turn. Right in front of the madrasa is the office of Ahl-e Hadith Youth Force, which is a centre of *tablighi* and jihadi activities. There is also a medical dispensary attached to the madrasa.

Jamia Islamia, Rajanpur
This is the only residential Ahl-e Hadith madrasa in Rajanpur. There are 250 students, male and female, including foreigners, and six teachers. Its monthly expenses are thirty-five thousand rupees. The principal

Abdur Rahim Naim is an alumnus of Madina University. The following departments are working here:

1. Shuba Kutb (Dars-e Nizami up to postgraduate level)
2. Shuba Hifz O Nazera (Study of the Holy Koran)
3. Shuba Asri Taleem (Contemporary education, up to FA)
4. Department of social service
5. Department of jihad
6. Department of *tabligh*

The department of jihad is quite active. It organises training courses in which students from Dera Ghazi Khan to Rojhan and other members of the sect also take part.

Jamia Talimul Islam Muhammadia, Shekhupura
This madrasa, located in Faruqabad (district Shekhupura) is run by Markazi Jamiat Ahl-e Hadith. It has facilities for madrasa education up to postgraduate level and general education up to FA. For girls, there is Jamia Ayesha Siddiqa attached to the madrasa, which teaches a four-year Arabic course, Dars-e Nizami, and embroidery.

Dr Muhammad Amin Azhar, the principal, is also Markazi Jamiat Ahl-e Hadith's secretary of press and publications. There are 350 students here, including foreigners. The annual outlay is seven lakh rupees.

Darul Uloom Taqwiatul Islam, Samandari
This madrasa, located in Chowk No. 93 on G B Road is run by Markazi Jamiat Ahl-e Hadith. It has facilities up to postgraduate classes. It extends help to Ahl-e Hadith Youth Force and Tahreekul Mujahideen.

Jamia Muhammadia Ahl-e Hadith, Jampur
Jamia Muhammadia, Jampur, is being run by Idarah Tabligh Al-Islam, Jampur, in the district of Rajanpur. The principals are Maulana Muhammad Yasin and Muhammad Ismail. It has the support of Markazi Jamiat Ahl-e Hadith. There are about 300 students here. Idarah Tabligh Al-Islam publishes literature against Barelvi and Shia sects, and takes part in sectarian activities. Its students acquire training in the training camps of Tahreekul Mujahideen. It is a prominent centre for the activities of Ahl-e Hadith Youth Force.

Jamia Muhammadia Ahl-e Hadith, Fort Munro
Jamia Muhammadia Ahl-e Hadith, Fort Munro, is a centre for the activities of Jamat Al-Mujahideen, Tahreek Al-Mujahideen, Ahl-e Hadith Youth Force, and Markazi Jamiat Ahl-e Hadith. These groups organise their camps here from time to time. It is also regarded as the jihadi camp of Tahreekul Mujahideen.

Jamia Muhammadia Ahl-e Hadith, Khanpur
Jamia Muhammadia Ahl-e Hadith, Khanpur, located in the district of Rahim Yar Khan, is an important centre for sectarian jihadi activities. Its principal is Maulana Shamshad Salafi. Besides madrasa education up to the postgraduate level, it has also facilities for general education. There are about 350 students, including 255 foreign students in the madrasa. Its annual outlay is seven lakh rupees. The madrasa enjoys the patronage of Jamat Al-Mujahideen.

Jamia Darul Hadith Quddusiya, Kot Radha Kishan
This madrasa, located in Kot Radha Kishan, district

Qasoor, is an important Ahl-e Hadith institution. It has the following departments:

1. Department of Quranic studies
2. Department of Dars-e Nizami
3. Department of women's education
4. Schools department
5. Department of dawat and tabligh
6. Department of press, publications, and iftah

There are about 300 students here. The annual outlay of the madrasa is about eight lakh rupees. It is an important centre of Tahreekul Mujahideen.

Jamia Usmania, Sialkot
This madrasa, located in Camilla Road, Tariqpura, has Qari Muhammad Ayub as its founder and principal. He also supervises the working of the following madrasas:

1. Madrasa Hifzul Quran, Mohalla Khatikan, Sialkot
2. Madrasa Hifzul Quran, Marjal
3. Jamia Hajera Lil-Banat, Marjal
4. Madrasa Ta'limul Quran, Marjal

A total of 600 students, male and female, are studying in these madrasas. Jamia Usmania is affiliated to Wafaqul Madaris Salafiya, and it has facilities for instructions up to three stages of Dars-e Nizami. Its annual outlay is ten lakh rupees. It extends help to Ahl-e Hadith Youth Force and Jamat Al-Mujahideen.

Darul Hadith Jamia, Kamalia, Rajuwal, Okara
The managers of this madrasa are Dr Abdul Ghaffar Halim and Maulana Hafiz Hasan Mahmood, and its principal is Maulana Muhammad Yusuf. It has

facilities for instructions in all the stages of Dars-e Nizami. It has about 240 students. It is a centre of Jamat Ahl-e Hadith and Jamat Al-Mujahideen activities.

Jamia Al-Darasat Al-Salafiya

This madrasa was established in Siddo Sharif, Sawat, in 1994. Its founder was Shamsuddin Muhammad Ashraf who had also founded Jamia Asariya, Peshawar. It has facilities for all the stages of Dars-e Nizami Salafiya. A college for boys, a college for girls, and an orphanage are also being constructed here. There are about 400 students, including foreigners. The following are the stated objectives of this institution:

1. To spread the message of the Holy Koran and Sunnah according to Salafi ways.
2. Publication of Salafi ways of belief.
3. Efforts to remove accretions and innovations in religion, and other evils.
4. Reform of the individual and collective life of the society according to the Book and Sunnah.

This madrasa has been transformed into a centre of Tahreekul Mujahideen. After the government crackdown on jihadi organisations, the infrastructure of the Mansehra camp is being shifted here.

Jamia Salafiya Dawat Al-Haq

Jamia Salafiya Dawat Al-Haq, located in the Airport Road, Quetta, is the biggest madrasa of the Ahl-e Hadith sect in Baluchistan province. It was founded by Maulana Noor Muhammad Salafi in 1978. It has twenty-five branches in Baluchistan. When Maulana Noor Muhammad died in a sectarian incident,

Maulana Jebullah Salafi became Shaikhul Hadith (head teacher) and Maulana Niamatullah Muhid (son of Maulana Noor Muhammad Salafi) became the principal.

Jamia Salafiya Dawat Al-Haq is affiliated to Jamia Islamia, Madina. It is an entirely Arabic-medium madrasa. All the teachers of the department of sharia are the alumni of different universities in Saudi Arabia. There is also the Salafiya Public High School, which teaches courses up to matriculation. The principal of this school is Professor Muhammad Iqbal Qazi who is the former secretary of education, Baluchistan. It has about 700 residential students. The annual outlay is about 70 lakh rupees. This is the biggest centre of Tahreekul Mujahideen in the province, and it organises training camps here.

Jamia Muhammadia Ahl-e Hadith, Muzaffarabad
Jamia Muhammadia Ahl-e Hadith, located in Upper Chattar, Muzaffarabad is a prime educational institute of the Salafi sect. Three of its branches are working in Azad Kashmir. The principal of the madrasa is Maulana Muhammad Yunus Asari, who is also the amir of Markazi Jamiat Ahl-e Hadith in Azad Kashmir. There are 270 students here, and it has facilities for instructions up to the postgraduate level. The other thirty branches have facilities only up to the primary level. Its annual budget is thirteen lakh rupees. This is the biggest centre of Tahreekul Mujahideen and it has facilities for accommodation and jihadi training of mujahideen. According to Maulana Muhammad Yunus Asari, 'We have regards for the mujahideen of Tahreekul Mujahideen. We are always ready to help

them. God be praised, now the madrasa has become a centre of jihadi activities. We prefer Tahreekul Mujahideen to other organisations, because this organisation, besides fighting with infidels, is also working to consolidate the Faith in Occupied Kashmir.'

A new residential block has been built in Jamia Muhammadia Ahl-e Hadith at a cost of twenty lakh rupees. The local people said that this was due to the efforts of Muhammad Idris Mughal. He is a deputy registrar in a court in Azad Kashmir.

Table XXXI: *Ahl-e Hadith Madrasas*

Sr. No.	Madrasa	Principal/Headmaster	Class	No. of Students	Annual Expenses (Rupees)	Address
1.	Darul Hadith Mohammadiya	Maulana Rafiq Asri	Postgraduate	400	8 lakhs	Jalalpur Peerwala, Multan
2.	Jamia Salafiya Islamabad	Maulana Habibur Rahman Bukhari	Postgraduate	1000	25 lakhs	Sector I 10, Islamabad
3.	Jamia Salafiya	Miyan Naimur Rahman Zahir	University	900	–	Hajiabad, Faisalabad
4.	Al-Jamiatus-Sattariya Al-Islamia	Maulana Hafiz Abdur Rahman Salafi	Postgraduate	500	15 lakhs	Mohammadi Masjid, Street Mohammad Bin Qasim, Karachi
5.	Jamia Islamia	Syed Abdur Rahim Naeem	Postgraduate	500	15 lakhs	Rajanpur
6.	Madrasa Farooqul Islam	Maulana Mahmood Alvi	Postgraduate	240	–	12/1-K, Baluchistan Wala, District Okara
7.	Jamia Najmul Huda	Abu Bakar Siddique	Postgraduate	500	–	Jama Masjid Ahl-e Hadith, Ahata Thanedar, Lahore
8.	Jamia Tatheerul Islam	Qazi Ahsanul Haq	Postgraduate	300	–	240 GB Tehsil, Jaranwala
9.	Darul Hadith, Jamia Kamaliya	Maulana Mohammad Yusuf	Postgraduate	600	9 lakhs	Rajuwal, Okara

Gateway to Terrorism

Sr. No.	Madrasa	Principal/ Headmaster	Class	No. of Students	Annual Expenses (Rupees)	Address
10.	Madrasa Abdul Aziz Ahl-e Hadith	Abdul Aziz	Postgraduate	300	—	Pind Pernawan Bhai Pheeru, District Qasoor
11.	Darul Hadith Jamia Moaviya	Mohammad Idris Hashmi	Postgraduate	250	4 lakhs	Rahim Town, Firozwala, Lahore
12.	Jamia Islamia		PhD	700	3 lakhs	Gujranwala
13.	Madrasa Nasirul Islam	Hafiz Abdur Rahim	Postgraduate	400	3 lakhs	Tehsil Nankana, District Shekhupura
14.	Jamia Islamia	Maulana Abdullah Gurdaspuri	Postgraduate	400	3 lakhs	Mohalla Syed Jalal Pakpatan
15.	Jamia Farooqul Islamia		Postgraduate	500	—	Al Farooq Road, Rahim Yar Khan
16.	Madrasa Mahmoodiya		Fifth level	400	—	Mahmood Kot City, Muzaffargarh
17.	Madrasa Talimul Islam	Hafiz Mohammad Yaqoob	Postgraduate	300	—	Rati Pindi, District Qasoor
18.	Madrasa Rahmaniya	Haji Sabir Ali	Postgraduate	190	9 lakhs	Near I G Office, Shekhupura
19.	Jamia Rahmaniya	Hafiz Mohammad Abdullah	Postgraduate	150	—	Sargodha Road, Shekhupura
20.	Jamia Aqsa	Maulana Mohammad Hussain	Postgraduate	131	—	Sargodha Road, Shekhupura

654

Sr. No.	Madrasa	Principal/ Headmaster	Class	No. of Students	Annual Expenses (Rupees)	Address
21.	Jamia Ahl-e Hadith	Mohammad Yaqoob	PhD	165	10 lakhs	Main Road, Farooqabad, District Shekhupura
22.	Madrasa Jamia Rahmaniya	Abdur Razzaq	Postgraduate	100	10 lakhs	Lorry Adda, Faruqabad, District Shekhupura
23.	Jamia Islamia	Qari Shafiqur Rahman	Postgraduate	85	3 lakhs	Jandiyala, Narang, District Shekhupura
24.	Madrasa Imaratul Quran	Maulana Mohammad Saleem	Third Level	105		Mecca Colony, Warbarton, District Shekhupura
25.	Darul Islam Salafiya	Maulana Khaliq	Postgraduate	67		Near Police Station, Khadiyan, Qasoor
26.	Jamia Umar	Maulana Mohammad Akram	Postgraduate	85	6 lakhs	Kachcha Pacca, Khadiyan, District Qasoor
27.	Madrasa Darul Uloom	Hafiz Mansha Ahmad	Third Level	75	2 lakh	Dhoulan, Khadiyan, District Qasoor
28.	Madrasa Ziaul Quran	Haji Khushi Mohammad	Fifth Level	83	3 lakh	Clarkabad, Kot Radha Kishan
29.	Madrasa Ziaul Quran	Haji Abdul Waheed	Fifth Level	69		Raja Jung, District Qasoor
30.	Madrasa Qasimul Uloom	Hafiz Mohammad Yaqoob	Fifth Level	102		Kot Radha Kishan
31.	Jamia Mohammadiya	Prof. Abdul Hakim	Postgraduate	115	12 lakhs	Kot Radha Kishan

Gateway to Terrorism

Sr. No.	Madrasa	Principal/ Headmaster	Class	No. of Students	Annual Expenses (Rupees)	Address
32.	Madrasa Tajyeedul Quran	Maulana Riyazul Haq	Fifth Level	115	3 lakhs	Usmanwala, Khadiyan, District Qasoor
33.	Jamia Bidaal	Maulana Mohammad Akhtar	Postgraduate	82		Sulaimanpura, Khadiyan, Qasoor
34.	Madrasa Darul Khuda	Hafiz Muneer Ahmad	Third Level	112		Mouza Piyal Kalan, Patoki
35.	Darul Uloom Ahl-e Hadith	Hafiz Abdul Mushtaq	Postgraduate	102	5 lakhs	Mouza Kannoowala, Khanda Mangoowala, Qasoor
36.	Madrasa Mubarak Ahl-e Hadith	Mohammad Haroon	Fifth Level	98		Hotel Bazar, Patoki
37.	Jamia Mohammadiya Shadman	Sabir Ahmad Tahir	Postgraduate	89	4 lakhs	Mouza Shadman Colony, Patoki
38.	Madrasa Talimul Quran	Qari Mohammad Sadiq	Fifth Level	80	3 lakhs	Hospital Road, Kanganpur, Qasoor
39.	Madrasa Ibrahimiya Rahmaniya	Mohammad Ibrahim Khadim	Seventh Level	113	–	Mandi Kanganpur, Qasoor
40.	Madrasa Shamsul Ghani	Haji Abdul Nawab	Seventh Level	116		Mandi Kanganpur, Qasoor
41.	Madrasa Ziaul Quran	Hafiz Mohammad Ashraf	Seventh Level	97	–	Sharnkot, Kanganpur, Qasoor
42.	Madrasa Abu Bakar	Qari Mohammad Akbar	Postgraduate	89	–	Chooniyan, Qasoor

Sr. No.	Madrasa	Principal/ Headmaster	Class	No. of Students	Annual Expenses (Rupees)	Address
43.	Madrasa Talimul Quran	Qari Mohammad Siddique	Postgraduate	100	–	Tauhidabad, Chooniyan
44.	Madrasa Abu Harisa Islamia	Qari Rafiuddin	Postgraduate	95	–	Mustafabad, Qasoor
45.	Idara Islah Akbar	Hafiz Mohammad Yahya	Postgraduate	64	–	Sarai Fasil, Qasoor
46.	Madrasa Darul Uloom	Mufti Abdul Khaliq Shamghi	–	100	2 lakh	Main Bazar, Faizabad, Lahore
47.	Madrasa Iblagh Tauhid	Dr Abdul Ghafoor Choudhury	–	125	3 lakhs	Near Shad Bagh, Lahore
48.	Jamia Abi Bakar	Maulana Mahmood Ahmad Hasan	Postgraduate	700	9 lakhs	Karachi
49.	Darul Uloom Mohammadiya	Abdul Qayyum	Third Level	500	9 lakhs	Railway Loco Workshops, Lahore
50.	Mahad Ashriya Al-Zaa		Postgraduate	350	12 lakhs	Kot Addo
51.	Jamia Mohammadiya	Abdus Salam Phatvi	Postgraduate	600	25 lakhs	Gujranwala
52.	Madrasa Riyazul Quran Wa Ahl-e Hadith		Postgraduate	350	–	Mujahidabad, Mughalpura, Lahore
53.	Jamia Uloom Asariya	Maulana Mohammad Madni	Postgraduate	700	25 lakhs	Jhelum

Gateway to Terrorism

Sr. No.	Madrasa	Principal/Headmaster	Class	No. of Students	Annual Expenses (Rupees)	Address
54.	Jamia Talimul Islam	Abdul Qadir Randvi	Postgraduate	350	–	Mamoon Kkanjan, District Faisalabad
55.	Markaz Al-Darasat Islamia	Hafiz Abdus Sattarul Madad	Postgraduate	400	10 lakhs	Sultan Colony, Mian Chunno
56.	Markazut Tauhid Ahl-e Hadith	Qari Abdur Rahim Kalim	Postgraduate	450	7 lakhs	Chowk Chourhatta, Dera Ghazi Khan
57.	Jamia Salafiya Dawatul Haq	Ali Mohammad Abu Turab	Postgraduate	700	20 lakhs	Muslimabad, Airport Road, Quetta, Baluchistan
58.	Jamia Mohammadiya, Muzaffarabad	Maulana Mohammad Yunus Asri	Graduate	200	20 lakhs	Upper Chattar, Muzaffarabad, Azad Kashmir
59.	Jamia Mohammadiya Ahl-e Hadith, Jampur	Mohammad Ismail Majid	Postgraduate	350	–	Jampur, District Rajanpur
60.	Jamia Mohammadiya Ahl-e Hadith		Postgraduate	400	–	Fort Munro, Dera Ghazi Khan
61.	Jamia Al-Darsat Al-Salafiya		Graduate	500	–	Saidoo Sharif Sawat, Frontier Province
62.	Jamia Mohammadiya Ahl-e Hadith, Khanpur		Postgraduate	450	–	Khanpur, District Rahim Yar Khan
63.	Jamia Salafiya	Maulana Yasin Zafar	Postgraduate	800	30 lakhs	Faisalabad

Sr. No.	Madrasa	Principal/ Headmaster	Class	No. of Students	Annual Expenses (Rupees)	Address
64.	Jamia Darul Hadith Mohammadiya Qudsiya		Postgraduate	200	–	Kot Radha Kishan, District Qasoor
65.	Jamia Ahl-e Hadith, Lahore	Hafiz Abdul Ghaffar	Graduate	350	16	Chowk Dalgiran, Lahore
66.	Darul Hadith Jamia Moaviya	Shaikh Mohammad Yahya	Postgraduate	300	6 lakhs	66, Ravi Road, Lahore
67.	Jamia Al-Dawat Al-Islamia		Postgraduate	700	6 lakhs	Markaz Tayyaba Muridke, Shaikhupura
68.	Almohtadul Ali Al-Dawa Al-Islamia	Maulana Abdullah Salafi	Postgraduate	300	–	Markaz Tabook Shujaabad Road, Lar, Multan
69.	Almohtadul Ali Al-Dawa Al-Islamia		Postgraduate	250	–	Markaz Mir Chowk, Araian Model Kharim, Multan Road, Patoki, District Qasoor
70.	Almohtadul Ali Al-Dawa Al-Islamia		Postgraduate	300	–	Markaz Husnain Railway Go-down Road, Haveli Lakha, District Okara
71.	Almohtadul Ali Al-Dawa Al-Islamia		Postgraduate	250	–	Markaz Ummul Qura, Mohalla Old Orphanage, Junoobi Qabristan, Mianwali
72.	Almohtadul Ali Al-Dawa Al-Islamia		Postgraduate	215	–	Markaz Khaibar Thatha Tehsil Duska, Sialkot

Gateway to Terrorism

Sr. No.	Madrasa	Principal/ Headmaster	Class	No. of Students	Annual Expenses (Rupees)	Address
73.	Almohtadul Ali Al-Dawa Al-Islamia		Postgraduate	350	–	Masjidul Qura Kohat (Border)
74.	Almohtadul Ali Al-Dawa Al-Islamia		Postgraduate	400	–	Markaz Aqsa, Jama Masjid Taqwa, New Zarghoon Road, Quetta
75.	Almohtadul Ali Al-Dawa Al-Islamia		Postgraduate	250	–	Markazul Quddus Turbat, Baluchistan
76.	Kulliyatul Banat	Shaikh Abdul Karim	Postgraduate	500	10 lakhs	Dera Ghazi Khan
77.	Kulliyat Darul Quran O Hadith	Mohammad Anas Madani	Graduate	500	7 lakhs	433, Jinnah Colony, Faisalabad

Jihadi Madrasas of Barelvi Persuasion

There are 5,000 madrasas of Barelvi persuasion in Pakistan. Of them, only 400 have facilities up to the postgraduate level. Very few madrasas extend practical help to jihadi activities, although many madrasas are known for fomenting sectarian controversies and violence.

There are twelve Barelvi jihadi organisations. But the number of madrasas in Pakistan and Azad Kashmir extending help to them is only twenty-three. Some important madrasas among them are discussed here:

Darul Uloom Jamia Naimia, Garhi Shaho, Lahore
Jamia Naimia, Lahore, is a known institute of Barelvi persuasion. This madrasa was founded by Maulana Mufti Muhammad Husain in 1952. After his death in 1988, Maulana Sarfaraz Naimi has become the principal. It conducts courses of Tanzeemul Madaris up to the postgraduate level. It also imparts general education up to BA. There is also a computer centre in the madrasa. There are about 600 students in the madrasa. It has four branches in Lahore:

1. Jamia Umm Ashraf Jamal, Ferozepur Road. Secretary: Maulana Haji Imdadullah Naimi
2. Jamia Khalil Akbar. Secretary: Maulana Muhammad Anwar Qadri
3. Jamia Usmania, Band Road. Secretary: Maulana Muhammad Arif
4. Darul Uloom Sirajia Naimia, Mughalpura

This madrasa is the biggest centre of Barelvi political, sectarian, and jihadi activities in Pakistan. Barelvi jihadi organisations are accorded good welcome and hospitality here, particularly Lashkar-e Islam, Sunni Jihad Council, and Lashkar Ababeel.

More than 1,000 alumni of this madrasa have passed out so far having acquired the final degree, whereas students who passed out from lower classes or dropped out number more than 10,000.

Jamia Nizamia Rizwia, Lahore, Shekhupura

This madrasa, spread over a three-*kanal* plot houses the central offices of Tanzeemul Madaris, the educational board of Barelvi madrasas. The principal of the madrasa is Mufti Abdul Qayoom Hazarwi. It has one of its big branches in Shekhupura on a sprawling campus. The total number of students, male and female, in both the madrasas is 1,500, including 1,200 boarders. Foreign students number fifty. The teaching staff is fifty. The annual outlay of both the madrasas is seven lakh rupees. This madrasa is also affiliated to Jamia Al-Azhar, Cairo, and students from here go to Al-Azhar for higher studies. The madrasa has an important department of publication that publishes books pertaining to the sect, as also books on comparative study of different sects.

This madrasa also receives aid from the government. It provides material and human resources to the Barelvi jihadi organisations. Several students have acquired jihadi training through Sunni Jihad Council and Al-Barq and gone to Occupied Kashmir.

Hizbul Ahnaf, Lahore

Hizbul Ahnaf in Ganj Bakhsh Road is a very old Barelvi institution. Its founder was Abu Muhammad

Syed Didar Ali Shah. Currently, its principal is Maulana Masood Ahmad Rizvi. Many important maulanas of Barelvi persuasion were either alumni of this institution or associated with it. However, the educational opportunities here have shrunk now. Only about two-dozen students are there. The huge building has been turned into many shops that have been rented out, or the rooms have been rented out either for residential or commercial purposes. The students here said that the management is more interested in earning money than imparting education. Despite this, it is a centre of jihadi and sectarian activities, and several rooms have been occupied by leaders of different organisations who seem to be busy either fighting among themselves or occupying one another's rooms.

Darul Uloom Muhammadia Ghausia, Bhera Sharif, Sargodha

Darul Uloom Muhammadia Ghausia, Bhera Sharif, Sargodha, is an important madrasa of the Barelvi sect where Dars-e Nizami is imparted according to the courses current in Jamia Al-Azhar, Cairo. It has also facilities for general education in sciences, including computers.

This madrasa was founded in 1957 by Pir Karamshah Azhari, and he brought it in line with modern madrasas. Jamia Al-Azhar, Cairo, has accorded it the status of a university. There are several departments working here. Besides Darul Iftah, its other important department is the department of publications that prints dozens of books every year. It runs its own course and is affiliated to an educational board that has twenty-two madrasas from Pakistan, Azad Kashmir, and foreign countries under it.

The madrasa is equipped with modern facilities. There are 1,500 boarders here, and seventy teachers. The students are not allowed to take part in sectarian activities, though several sectarian groups are active here. Organisations like Lashkar Ababeel, Sunni Jihad Council, and Harkat-e Inqilab Islami are popular among students, though practically very few students are associated with them.

Jamia Anwarul Uloom, Multan

This madrasa was founded by Maulana Ahmad Said Kazmi in 1944. In 1994, it shifted to its new building in T Block, New Multan. Currently, its principal is Professor Syed Mazhar Said Kazmi who is the patron of Jamat Ahl-e Sunnat and an important leader of Jamiat Ulema Pakistan. Four of its big branches are working in Kachahri Road, Husn Parwana Colony, Idgah, and Shadab Colony of Multan. Tanzeemul Madaris, the educational board of Barelvi madrasas, was founded here, and its central office was located here for a number of years. Besides having facilities for Dars-e Nizami in all stages, it has also facilities for general education up to BA. The total number of students in this madrasa is 2,500, of whom 2,000 are boarders. There are fifty teachers here.

This madrasa is a very important centre of Jamat Ahl-e Sunnat and Jamiat Ulema Pakistan. It hosted the Sunni Conference in Multan in 1998. It extends help to all Barelvi jihadi organisations, by providing human and material resources. However, students are not allowed to take part in practical jihad.

Jamia Khairul Ma'd, Multan
This madrasa, located in Kohna, Qasim Bagh, was founded by Maulana Hamid Ali Khan. It is an important educational institution of Barelvi sect in Pakistan. Eleven of its branches are working in Multan. It has facilities for instructions up to the postgraduate level. In the central madrasa, the total number of students is 300, of whom 250 are boarders. The current principal is Maulana Muhammad Mian Naqshbandi. Here students are given a course on comparative study of different religious ways. Students are allowed to take part in jihad. Students from this madrasa took part in the Afghan war. The Barelvi jihadi organisations are allowed to offer discourses to students here and raise funds.

Jamia Qadiriya Alamiya, Nek Abad, Gujrat
The chief secretary of this madrasa is Sahibzada Pir Afzal Qadri. He is the convener of Alami Tanzeem Ahl-e Sunnat and the patron of the Barelvi jihadi organisation, Lashkar Ahl-e Sunnat. It is for this reason that this madrasa is not only a centre of jihadi activities but also a centre for the political activities of Alami Tanzeem Ahl-e Sunnat.

This madrasa is affiliated to Tanzeemul Madaris. It has facilities for instructions up to the postgraduate level. The syllabus here incorporates books related to Deobandi, Ahl-e Hadith, and Shia ways of belief. This part of the syllabus is titled, 'Study of Contemporary False Beliefs'. The famous Barelvi scholar, Mufti Muhammad Ashraf Qadri is associated with this madrasa. Apart from Dars-e Nizami, students are also prepared privately for exams from FA to BA. The total number of students is 550, of whom 440 are boarders. There are twenty-five teachers. The annual outlay is seventeen lakh rupees.

Jamia Muhammadi Sharif, Jhang
Jamia Muhammadi Sharif, Jhang, was established by Maulana Muhammad Zakir in 1921. It has a high school and an Intermediate College in the campus also. Its current principal is Maulana Muhammad Rahmatullah. There are 500 students here of whom 300 are boarders. The annual outlay is ten lakh rupees. It does not receive any grant from the government.

Sectarian activities are not allowed in the madrasa, although a comparative study of different sects is a part of the syllabus. It is a centre for activities of the two Barelvi organisations, Sheeran-e Islam and Tanzeemul Arifin.

Darul Uloom Amjadiya, Karachi
This madrasa of Barelvi persuasion has Mufti Vaqaruddin as the principal and Maulana Syed Shah Turabul Haq Qadri as the vice principal. The latter is the secretary of Jamat Ahl-e Sunnat in Sindh and an important leader of Jamiat Ulema Pakistan. It has 500 students, including foreign students. It has facilities for instructions in Dars-e Nizami at all stages, and general education up to BA. It is a centre of Barelvi sectarian organisations in Karachi. Dozens of students of the madrasa are associated with Sunni Tahreek. Among the jihadi organisations, Lashkar-e Islam is the favourite. Several students of the madrasa have acquired jihadi training from the platform of Lashkar-e Islam.

Darul Uloom Qamrul Islam Sulaimania, Karachi
This madrasa, located in Punjab Colony, Karachi, was

founded in 1964 by Peer Syed Shah Manzoor Hamdani. The madrasa follows the course laid down by Darul Uloom Mahmudiya Ghousiya Baseera. It was established with help from the government of United Arab Emirates. It has two branches: Madrasa Ziaul Quran, Azam Basti, and Darul Uloom Usmania, Clifton. It has facilities up to the postgraduate level in Dars-e Nizami, and general education up to BA. There are 700 students here, and according to the policy of the government, no foreigner is admitted. The current principal is Syed Azmat Ali Shah Hamdani.

This madrasa is an important centre for Barelvi jihadi and sectarian organisations. Tahreek Jihad and Lashkar-e Islam are popular with the students here.

Darul Uloom Muhammadiya Ghousiya Gulzar-e Madina, Hasan Abdal

This madrasa, spread over a three-*kanal* plot, was established in 1980. It is affiliated to Darul Uloom Muhammadiya Ghousiya Baseera and follows the course devised by it. Maulana Hafizur Rahman is the principal here. There are 130 students here, and the annual outlay is two lakh rupees. This madrasa is a centre for the activities of Lashkar-e Islam.

Darul Uloom Gulzar Habeeb, Mirpur

This extremely important Barelvi madrasa in Azad Kashmir was established in 1986. It is affiliated to Darul Uloom Muhammadiya Ghousiya Baseera and follows the course devised by it. It has facilities for classes in Commerce and Computers also. There are about 200 students here, and the annual outlay is three lakh rupees. The principal of the madrasa is Allama

Hafizur Rahman Ghazali who is also the patron of Tahreek Jihad in Meerpur. Besides Tahreek Jihad, it also allows the mujahideen of Lashkar-e Islam to stay here and train the students.